Munich

Jeremy Gray

D0367744

LONELY PLANET PUBLICATIONS
Melbourne • Oakland • London • Paris

Munich
1st edition – April 2000

Published by
Lonely Planet Publications Pty Ltd A.C.N. 005 607 983
192 Burwood Rd, Hawthorn, Victoria 3122, Australia

Lonely Planet Offices
Australia PO Box 617, Hawthorn, Victoria 3122
USA 150 Linden St, Oakland, CA 94607
UK 10a Spring Place, London NW5 3BH
France 1 rue du Dahomey, 75011 Paris

Photographs
Many of the images in this guide are available for licensing from
Lonely Planet Images.
email: lpi@lonelyplanet.com.au

Front cover photograph
Amusement ride, Oktoberfest (David Peevers)

ISBN 1 86450 055 7

text & maps © Lonely Planet 2000
photos © photographers as indicated 2000

Printed by The Bookmaker Pty Ltd
Printed in China

Although the authors
and Lonely Planet try
to make the informa-
tion as accurate as
possible, we accept
no responsibility for
any loss, injury or
inconvenience sus-
tained by anyone
using this book.

Contents – Text

Contents – Maps

MAP LEGEND   **back page**

The Author

Jeremy Gray

A Louisiana native, Jeremy studied German literature in the wilds of Texas before moving to Mainz, Germany to take up a scholarship in 1984. He stayed to teach English, translate and (with his usual single-mindedness) file plumbing orders for the US Air Force. Later he took a master's degree in international relations at Canterbury and became a journalist in bustling Woking, Surrey.

Much of the 1990s were spent in scenic Frankfurt, Germany, alternating stints at wire services, newspapers and television. He upped stakes in 1998 to freelance for the Financial Times in the Netherlands and, to give his life a non-financial balance, for Lonely Planet.

Jeremy lives in Amsterdam with Petra, his graphic-designer wife.

FROM THE AUTHOR

A heartfelt *Vielen Dank* to the generous staff members of the Munich Tourist Office – especially Vera Golücke, Hedda Manhard and Stefan Böttcher – for helping me to unlock Munich's wild and wonderful secrets.

I'm also indebted to Ann Elbing of EurAide, for digging up timetable details and co-sampling mounds of restaurant food, and to Maxine Ryder of Munich Walks, for her sparkling anecdotes and boundless enthusiasm.

LP authors Andrea Schulte-Peevers and Ryan ver Berkmoes earn kudos for moral support. Editors Chris Wyness and Kalya Ryan, designers Michelle Lewis, Lisa Borg and Joelene Kowalski were among those back in Melbourne who showed unfathomable patience in the final stages of the project.

The greatest thanks is due my wife, Petra Riemer, who deserves a medal for the long weeks while I was either away or chained to my desk writing.

This Book

From the Publisher

This 1st edition of *Munich* was edited in Lonely Planet's Melbourne office by Kalya Ryan. Editing and proofing assistance was provided by Hilary Ericksen, Joanne Newell and Susannah Farfor. Mapping and design were coordinated by Joelene Kowalski, who was assisted by Mark Germanchis, Jacqui Saunders and Brett Moore. Thanks go to Jocelyn Harewood for the index, Quentin Frayne for the Language chapter, Jamieson Ross who designed the cover, Mick Weldon who provided the illustrations, and Tim Uden for his Quark expertise. Photographs were provided by Lonely Planet Images, with special thanks to Fiona Croyden.

Our thanks also go to the Munich Transport Authority (MVV) for permission to use their material.

Foreword

ABOUT LONELY PLANET GUIDEBOOKS

The story begins with a classic travel adventure: Tony and Maureen Wheeler's 1972 journey across Europe and Asia to Australia. Useful information about the overland trail did not exist at that time, so Tony and Maureen published the first Lonely Planet guidebook to meet a growing need.

From a kitchen table, then from a tiny office in Melbourne (Australia), Lonely Planet has become the largest independent travel publisher in the world, an international company with offices in Melbourne, Oakland (USA), London (UK) and Paris (France).

Today Lonely Planet guidebooks cover the globe. There is an ever-growing list of books and there's information in a variety of forms and media. Some things haven't changed. The main aim is still to help make it possible for adventurous travellers to get out there – to explore and better understand the world.

At Lonely Planet we believe travellers can make a positive contribution to the countries they visit – if they respect their host communities and spend their money wisely. Since 1986 a percentage of the income from each book has been donated to aid projects and human rights campaigns.

Updates Lonely Planet thoroughly updates each guidebook as often as possible. This usually means there are around two years between editions, although for more unusual or more stable destinations the gap can be longer. Check the imprint page (following the colour map at the beginning of the book) for publication dates.

Between editions up-to-date information is available in two free newsletters – the paper *Planet Talk* and email *Comet* (to subscribe, contact any Lonely Planet office) – and on our Web site at www.lonelyplanet.com. The *Upgrades* section of the Web site covers a number of important and volatile destinations and is regularly updated by Lonely Planet authors. *Scoop* covers news and current affairs relevant to travellers. And, lastly, the *Thorn Tree* bulletin board and *Postcards* section of the site carry unverified, but fascinating, reports from travellers.

Correspondence The process of creating new editions begins with the letters, postcards and emails received from travellers. This correspondence often includes suggestions, criticisms and comments about the current editions. Interesting excerpts are immediately passed on via newsletters and the Web site, and everything goes to our authors to be verified when they're researching on the road. We're keen to get more feedback from organisations or individuals who represent communities visited by travellers.

Lonely Planet gathers information for everyone who's curious about the planet – and especially for those who explore it first-hand. Through guidebooks, phrasebooks, activity guides, maps, literature, newsletters, image library, TV series and Web site we act as an information exchange for a worldwide community of travellers.

Research Authors aim to gather sufficient practical information to enable travellers to make informed choices and to make the mechanics of a journey run smoothly. They also research historical and cultural background to help enrich the travel experience and allow travellers to understand and respond appropriately to cultural and environmental issues.

Authors don't stay in every hotel because that would mean spending a couple of months in each medium-sized city and, no, they don't eat at every restaurant because that would mean stretching belts beyond capacity. They do visit hotels and restaurants to check standards and prices, but feedback based on readers' direct experiences can be very helpful.

Many of our authors work undercover, others aren't so secretive. None of them accept freebies in exchange for positive write-ups. And none of our guidebooks contain any advertising.

Production Authors submit their raw manuscripts and maps to offices in Australia, USA, UK or France. Editors and cartographers – all experienced travellers themselves – then begin the process of assembling the pieces. When the book finally hits the shops, some things are already out of date, we start getting feedback from readers and the process begins again …

WARNING & REQUEST

Things change – prices go up, schedules change, good places go bad and bad places go bankrupt – nothing stays the same. So, if you find things better or worse, recently opened or long since closed, please tell us and help make the next edition even more accurate and useful. We genuinely value all the feedback we receive. Julie Young coordinates a well travelled team that reads and acknowledges every letter, postcard and email and ensures that every morsel of information finds its way to the appropriate authors, editors and cartographers for verification.

Everyone who writes to us will find their name in the next edition of the appropriate guidebook. They will also receive the latest issue of *Planet Talk*, our quarterly printed newsletter, or *Comet*, our monthly email newsletter. Subscriptions to both newsletters are free. The very best contributions will be rewarded with a free guidebook.

Excerpts from your correspondence may appear in new editions of Lonely Planet guidebooks, the Lonely Planet Web site, *Planet Talk* or *Comet*, so please let us know if you *don't* want your letter published or your name acknowledged.

Send all correspondence to the Lonely Planet office closest to you:

Australia: PO Box 617, Hawthorn, Victoria 3122
USA: 150 Linden St, Oakland, CA 94607
UK: 10A Spring Place, London NW5 3BH
France: 1 rue du Dahomey, 75011 Paris

Or email us at: talk2us@lonelyplanet.com.au

For news, views and updates see our Web site: www.lonelyplanet.com

HOW TO USE A LONELY PLANET GUIDEBOOK

The best way to use a Lonely Planet guidebook is any way you choose. At Lonely Planet we believe the most memorable travel experiences are often those that are unexpected, and the finest discoveries are those you make yourself. Guidebooks are not intended to be used as if they provide a detailed set of infallible instructions!

Contents All Lonely Planet guidebooks follow roughly the same format. The Facts about the Destination chapters or sections give background information ranging from history to weather. Facts for the Visitor gives practical information on issues like visas and health. Getting There & Away gives a brief starting point for researching travel to and from the destination. Getting Around gives an overview of the transport options when you arrive.

The peculiar demands of each destination determine how subsequent chapters are broken up, but some things remain constant. We always start with background, then proceed to sights, places to stay, places to eat, entertainment, getting there and away, and getting around information – in that order.

Heading Hierarchy Lonely Planet headings are used in a strict hierarchical structure that can be visualised as a set of Russian dolls. Each heading (and its following text) is encompassed by any preceding heading that is higher on the hierarchical ladder.

Entry Points We do not assume guidebooks will be read from beginning to end, but that people will dip into them. The traditional entry points are the list of contents and the index. In addition, however, some books have a complete list of maps and an index map illustrating map coverage.

There may also be a colour map that shows highlights. These highlights are dealt with in greater detail in the Facts for the Visitor chapter, along with planning questions and suggested itineraries. Each chapter covering a geographical region usually begins with a locator map and another list of highlights. Once you find something of interest in a list of highlights, turn to the index.

Maps Maps play a crucial role in Lonely Planet guidebooks and include a huge amount of information. A legend is printed on the back page. We seek to have complete consistency between maps and text, and to have every important place in the text captured on a map. Map key numbers usually start in the top left corner.

Although inclusion in a guidebook usually implies a recommendation we cannot list every good place. Exclusion does not necessarily imply criticism. In fact there are a number of reasons why we might exclude a place – sometimes it is simply inappropriate to encourage an influx of travellers.

Introduction

Is Munich really 'Germany's Secret Capital', as the marketing gurus would have us believe? Or is 'Village of Millions' more accurate?

Both hats fit, but it's a riddle as to how. Few visitors leave Munich without wondering how the fashion queens and *Marktfrauen*, the BMWs and horse-drawn coaches, the hearty sausages and *haute cuisine* could possibly be cast together in this south German parody. In one scene it's an infuriating nest of *petit bourgeois* and small-minded bureaucrats; in the next, the stage is filled with high-minded sophisticates wearing lots of black and designer glasses.

But sophistication didn't come early to Munich, which spent centuries in the shadow of Regensburg, Bamberg and other religious centres. Although capital of Bavaria since 1503, this salt-trading town only achieved real prominence under Ludwig I in the 19th century. Napoleon elevated Bavaria to a kingdom, but the monarchy lasted only a century (not counting the dukedoms under the Holy Roman Empire). Still, 'Müncheners' regard this period as their Golden Age, it was a time in which the arts and sciences blossomed as never before – and really never since. Munich found its bohemian 'alter ego' in Schwabing, the Altstadt became a shrine to architecture and the royal family's obsession with gadgetry left its mark on the industrial revolution.

In a millennium packed with turbulent times, the past century was particularly rough on Munich. WWI practically starved its inhabitants to death, and Hitler turned the city into a stage set for Nazi propaganda. Seeds of war were sown with the infamous Munich Agreement, and WWII brought unimaginable destruction and more than 30,000 deaths.

Few expected Munich's post-war recovery to be as swift and decisive as it was during the *Wirtschaftswunder* (Economic Miracle); the magic seemed to continue during the 1950s and 1960s, which brought rapid expansion.

The division of Europe during the Cold War was a mixed blessing for Munich. Major trade routes shifted west to Bavaria, but the city was marginalised as a tourist destination. Only after reunification did it become the second-most favourite German destination, after Berlin. The proximity to gems that were once beyond the reach of western visitors (such as Prague or Budapest), as well as an efficient transport network make Munich a good launch point into Eastern Europe.

Some of Europe's biggest companies are attracted to Munich by its lovely environs (as well as by hefty tax breaks). Munich is the country's most prosperous city in per-capita terms, but the social costs have been high. Steep rents mean traditionally lower-paid jobs in nursing or policework are poorly filled. It's a problem that city elders seek to solve with stop-gap measures, as Germany's social system remains badly in need of reform.

Today's Munich remains a city of superlatives. In Germany it's outranked only by Berlin in its variety of museums, theatres and cultural events (although the Bavarians reign supreme in film-making). Its sprawling English Garden is Europe's largest municipal park, and Munich's idyllic location is virtually unparalleled in Germany: windsurfers scud over the lovely lakes to the south, and the Alpine pistes beyond attract legions of skiers. Little wonder that national polls regularly pick Munich as the most popular place to live in Germany.

Whether you see Munich during the vibrant, tourist-packed summer, the madness of Oktoberfest or the calm, cold stillness of a February afternoon, the city offers the chance to sample the values and attitudes that so dominate the exported image of Germany – with the odd unique ingredient thrown in.

Facts about Munich

HISTORY
Early Settlements

Munich's origins are veiled in mystery. The most solid evidence of a settlement dates back to the 5th century, when the Romans fled the area and a tribe known as the *Baiuvarii* (Bavarians) made it their home. However, recent excavations under Marienplatz and St Peter's Church uncovered remains of a village and stone church that date to a much earlier period; there are also traces of a Roman army post in Gauting, a suburb of Munich, from around 17 AD.

The city's name is unequivocally Catholic: it derives from *Ze den Munichen* or 'with the monks'. These monks were 8th century Benedictines, either from a monastery on Tegernsee (Lake Tegern) or from Schäftlarn, a community near present-day Starnberg. This period spawned place names with the ending 'ing' which still exist today (eg Schwabing, Sendling or Pasing), and the villages of Haidhausen, Bogenhausen and Laim, which were later absorbed into Munich. After that, there's a gap of nearly four centuries in local records.

The history of Munich as a town begins with one of the seven deadly sins – envy. In 1156, Frederick Barbarossa, ruler of the Holy Roman Empire, gave the Duchy of Bavaria to his cousin, the Guelph duke, Henry the Lion (Heinrich der Löwe). The duke was an ambitious sort, and coveted the fortune that the powerful Bishop of Freising was making from the Isar toll bridge, located a few miles upstream from Munich. So Henry had his men destroy the bridge and built his own crossing to the south, near *Ze den Munichen*.

As Duke of Saxony, Henry had already founded several towns in northern Germany, so he knew what it took to make a settlement stand up. He bestowed on Munich the rights to mint money and to hold markets. The duped Freising bishop appealed to Emperor Barbarossa, who hammered out a compromise at the Imperial Diet of 1158: Henry could keep his bridge, but had to pay one-third

of his tolls to the bishop. The duke's hold over the town remained tenuous, however, and the Freising bishop continued to meddle in Munich's affairs. Three decades later Barbarossa finally handed the town over to Count Otto von Wittelsbach, whose family would rule Bavaria for nearly 800 years.

The Imperial City

Munich became a ducal residence in 1255. The first Wittelsbach who installed himself in Munich was Ludwig the Bavarian (also known as 'Ludwig the Stern', or Ludwig IV) who was elected king by the German princes in 1314. He had a royal residence built in the north-east corner of the city, which later came to be called the Alter Hof (Old Court). He didn't reign in peace for long.

Ludwig's arch-enemy and pretender to the Imperial crown, the Habsburg Frederick the Handsome, laid siege to Munich in 1319. Against superior odds, the Wittelsbach armies managed to defeat Frederick at the battle of Mühldorf and even to take him prisoner. The pope (who was exiled in Avignon at the time) sided with the Habsburgs and excommunicated Ludwig. The Bavarian hung onto his throne, however, and became the last German emperor to be crowned in Rome (1328).

To reward Munich for its loyalty, Ludwig brought back with him from Rome a delightful gift: the upper arm of St Anthony, a relic which can still be viewed in the Monastery Church (Klosterkirche) St Anne in Lehel. Its citizens were more grateful for the salt-trading monopoly which Ludwig granted to the city in 1322.

Munich's infrastructure changed dramatically under Ludwig IV, who rebuilt areas destroyed by the Great Fire of 1328 and erected many of the old fortifications that you still see today. Ludwig's Alter Hof later became the inner courtyard of the Neues Rathaus (New Town Hall). The square out front, Marienplatz, held a special place in Ludwig's heart and he forbade any alterations;

while that decree no longer holds, the original dimensions remain.

Over the next 200 years, Munich grew fat from the salt trade and became the trading centre of Upper Bavaria (which against intuitive thinking, is actually southern Bavaria). By this time the Wittelsbach family had wrested the Bavarian crown from Frederick Barbarossa; they managed to retain control over Munich (and most of Bavaria) until the 20th century. It became Germany's longest-ruling royal dynasty, and to this day evokes feelings of nostalgic pride among Bavarians.

Ludwig's reign came to an abrupt end in 1347, when he died on a royal bear hunt. Death saved him from further disgrace: by this time the bohemian king had formed a pact with France and the Lombardy princedom against Bavaria, and Ludwig's expansionist policies had made even the pope his enemy. A year after Ludwig's death, Charles IV of Luxembourg succeeded in stealing the imperial crown from the heavily-guarded Alter Hof. From 1355 onwards, Charles' home town of Prague became the capital of the Holy Roman Empire, and for the next 400 years, the German crown became property of the king of Bohemia.

Plague & Social Turmoil

Dozens of outbreaks of the plague occurred in 1349 and continued for the next 150 years, despite frantic efforts to cordon off the city. Reinforcements were constructed and sewage and sanitation improved, but the city's population was ravaged. Huge pilgrimages were organised to holy places such as Andechs, Freising or Ebersberg.

Meanwhile, a feud between the people and the Wittelsbachs broke out. The royal family had already been weakened by internal disputes after the death of Ludwig IV, whose descendants divided up Bavaria and declared war on one another. In the late 14th century, Munich's 'businessmen' (mainly artisans and small merchants) came to despise the cronyism that had developed between the wealthy patrician families and the dukes. A leading patrician and Wittelsbach spokesman, Hans Impler, was beheaded by the masses on Marienplatz in 1385, and most of the patrician families were forced to flee in 1397. They returned five years later, when the citizens were granted a limited say in political life.

It was during this tumultuous period that some of Munich's greatest buildings were erected. In 1400, the Wittelsbachs constructed a fortress on the site of today's Residenz (more to protect itself from the civilian populace than from marauding armies). The Ratsturm (Town Hall Tower) was built in 1382, and the Altes Rathaus (Old Town Hall), of which only a sorry rump survived WWII, was finished in 1470. The Frauenkirche was built during this time also (see Architecture, later in this chapter).

By 1505, the city had 13,500 residents and had become the capital of the Duchy of Bavaria. As its wealth grew, Duke Albrecht IV the Wise had the first Bavarian gold ducats minted.

In 1517, as the plague passed, the *Schäffler* (coopers) began a ritualistic dance, which they vowed to perform every seven years as long as the city was spared further outbreaks. Now the tradition can be

Early Anti-Semitism in Munich

During the Middle Ages a tiny Jewish community prospered in Munich but, as elsewhere in Europe, they were persecuted for reasons of envy and religious prejudice. Jews, unlike Christians, were allowed to lend money at interest and many Christians became indebted to them. Jews were blamed for the plague, fires and natural disasters; in 1285, as many as 180 Jews were burned alive inside their synagogue (behind today's site of the Altes Rathaus) for the alleged ritual murder of a child. Jews were banished altogether from Munich in 1442, and didn't return to the city in large numbers until the 19th century.

witnessed more regularly: the *Schäfflertanz* is re-enacted daily by the charming figures on the city's *Glockenspiel* on Marienplatz.

Reformation & Renaissance

Albrecht's successor, Duke Wilhelm IV (1508–1550), was a conservative reactionist. After initial sympathies to Martin Luther's Reformation, Wilhelm feared that the new faith would undermine his authority and he began to clamp down.

In 1522 a baker's apprentice was beheaded on Marienplatz after professing himself a Protestant, and other followers were imprisoned, exiled, or executed. Many Protestants fled Munich or at least attended church services in Lutheran Augsburg; in response, the duke had the roads monitored for 'heretics'.

The Reformation was ultimately a flop in Bavaria. In 1583, Duke Wilhelm V declared that only the Catholic faith was permitted, and Munich became the centre of the Counter-Reformation – Germany's Rome. The ascendance to the throne of the easygoing Maximilian I as duke in 1597 failed to stem the religious tide. By the outbreak of the Thirty Years' War in 1618, local residents were resolutely Catholic.

The Counter-Reformation marked the beginning of the Renaissance in Munich. Wilhelm IV created the first Hofgarten (Court Garden) with an art gallery. The next duke, Albrecht V, had an art gallery and an Antiquarium (Antiques Hall) built in the Residenz, which rank among the finest interiors of the German Renaissance. He also laid the foundations of the wonderful Bayerischer Staatsbibliothek (Bavarian State Library), today one of the world's largest libraries. In 1583, under Duke Wilhelm V, building began on the largest Renaissance-style church north of the Alps; Michaelskirche (St Michael's Church) was completed over 14 years later at enormous expense, so much so that the Bavarian treasury was almost bankrupted.

Thirty Years' War & After

Maximilian I's greatest triumph was to pay off his predecessor's debts, within 12 years he had brought the state's accounts well into the black. On the battlefield he also chalked up a string of victories, earning him the rank of elector in 1623. Despite Maximilian's best efforts, however, Munich surrendered to Swedish King Gustav Adolphus without a fight in 1632.

Munich was forced to buy its freedom for 450,000 guilders (which included a guarantee that Adolphus wouldn't pulverise the city). The Mariensäule (St Mary's Column, 1638), on Marienplatz, is a token of Maximilian's gratitude to God for sparing his people from both the plague and the Swedes. Ironically, the war united the seriously divided Wittelsbach family, who from 1643 onwards elected the mayor of Munich.

After the Thirty Years' War, Munich and Bavaria were a financial shambles. Things didn't improve much under Maximilian's successor, Elector Ferdinand Maria (1651–79), a *bon-vivant* who modelled the Bavarian court on its French counterpart. Lavish parties were thrown on palatial barges at Starnberg and on the Nymphenburg canal, and operas and ballets became fixed events at the Residenz. The Theatinerkirche and Nymphenburg Palace, creations of Italian architects, were other preferred venues for court festivities. Italian products and styles were all the rage, and it was in this period that Munich established its far-fetched reputation as 'Italy's northernmost city'.

Spanish War of Succession

Elector Max Emanuel took over in 1679 and ruled till 1726. He carried on the high lifestyle of his predecessors, which led to the construction of the baroque Schloss Schleissheim (see the Excursions chapter). A dabbler in foreign intrigues, Max's five-year support of the Austrian war against the Turks cost more than 30,000 Bavarians their lives.

In gratitude for Max's support, the Habsburg emperor rewarded the Bavarian ruler with the hand of his daughter, the Polish princess Therese Kunigunde. Their son was the chosen heir to the Spanish throne, but died at the age of six. A protracted and bloody dispute over the successor began, which came to be known as the Spanish War of Succession (1704–14). What began as a lofty religious war provided an excuse for unalloyed greed and imperialism.

Bavaria sided with France against England and Austria, and Austrian troops occupied Bavaria from 1705 till 1714. A terrible massacre occurred in the first year of occupation when Bavarian peasants rose up against the Habsburg army at Sendlingen (now a southern suburb of Munich). As if the odds weren't already bad enough, the peasants (armed only with scythes and other farm tools) were betrayed before they could attack, and obliterated by Austrian soldiers. You can view paintings of the hopeless battle in Sendlingen Church today.

Bavaria was finally liberated from the Austrians with help of the French, but the land was left drained morally and economically. Bavaria became a political football again in 1742, when Prussia managed to have its puppet Prince Karl (Charles) Albrecht crowned king of Germany in Frankfurt. There were more lavish parties and building projects, yet his reign also brought some useful modern improvements (including Munich's first streetlamps in 1731). Austrian Empress Maria Theresia distrusted his ambitions and sent troops yet again into Bavaria. They were finally repelled upon Karl's death in 1745.

Early Liberalism
Max III Joseph (1745–77) became Elector of Bavaria after the death of Karl Albrecht, and his first task was to retrieve the state from under a mountain of debt. One of Max's key decrees allowed businesses to be set up outside the traditional trade guilds, with the aim of boosting tax revenue through economic growth. It didn't work: like many state-run enterprises today, these cloth-making, tapestry and cotton manufacturing factories ran at a loss. The Staatliche Porzellan-Manufaktur (Nymphenburg State Porcelain Factory) was founded in 1758 and, thankfully, turned a profit, as it still does today (see the Shopping chapter).

The Enlightenment came late to Munich. The first, rather amateurish newspaper was

published in 1702, followed by more mainstream publications in 1750. National laws were reformed in 1751 – but somehow failed to outlaw torture. The Bavarian Academy of Sciences, which had leanings away from Catholicism, was founded in 1759. Max himself reformed the school system in 1771, making education compulsory for all children up to the age of 16.

If Max III Joseph was an enlightened absolutist, his successor, Karl Theodor, could be called a conservative throwback. A 'foreign' Wittelsbach drafted in from Mannheim after Max's death, Karl had little feel for Munich society and was exceedingly unpopular. (Karlsplatz in the city centre was named after the ruler, but Müncheners stubbornly call it 'Stachus' after the one-time owner of a nearby beer garden.)

One of Karl's worst ideas was to swap Bavaria in exchange for the Austrian Netherlands, a plan that was thwarted by the French revolution and the intervention of King Frederick II (who unlike most Prussians, was a hit in Bavaria). Karl Theodor also introduced strict censorship and outlawed the Order of the Illuminati, an intellectual circle whose members included literary giant Johann Wolfgang von Goethe. When Karl died in 1799, the pubs filled with throngs of his jubilant subjects who partied for days.

The Kingdom of Bavaria
Bavaria had steered clear of political ties for half a century, so the rumblings of the French Revolution, in 1789, were hardly heard in Munich. It came as a complete shock when, in June 1800, French soldiers laid siege to Munich, forcing Bavarian elector Max IV Joseph (1799–1825) to flee to his countryside villa with his family. After a few months in hiding, Max took the easy way out and allied Bavaria with France against Austria. This spelled a formal end to the Holy Roman Empire of the German Nation, which had lasted for almost 1000 years.

In October 1805, Napoleon made a theatrical entry into Munich to the sound of church bells and cannon salutes. His royal coach made its way through the Karlstor, down the broad avenue that is today's pedestrian zone, and stopped at the Residenz, where the diminutive dictator emerged to cheering crowds. An odd way to treat an occupying army, perhaps, but Napoleon *had* elevated Bavaria to the rank of kingdom, doubled its size and tripled its population overnight. Bavaria was given Swabia and Franconia in return for the loss of the Palatinate, which France itself took over. Elector Max Joseph was crowned the first King of Bavaria, and the people rejoiced.

The French influence on Bavaria's modern institutions is still apparent today, for instance, the state's property and civil statutes bear hallmarks of Napoleonic law. Other reforms included the dissolution of the monasteries, nationalisation of church property and even the removal of the monk from the city's coat of arms in 1808 (it reappeared in 1835). The French constitution had followers in Bavaria, and in 1818 it became the first Germanic state to draft its own bill of rights.

The alliance with France finally fell apart in 1813 when Napoleon's empire started to unravel. Always the opportunist, Bavaria promptly re-aligned with Austria and Prussia.

The first half of the 19th century saw dramatic changes to Munich's layout. The old city wall was almost entirely razed (the last surviving section can be seen in Jungfernturmstrasse), and a broad, leafy avenue replaced the moat on the western edge of town – today's Sonnenstrasse.

Ludwig I & the Revolution of 1848

The runaway expansion continued under Max's son, Ludwig I (1825–48), who was determined to transform his capital into a cultural and artistic centre. In 1826, the growing importance of Munich as an intellectual centre prompted him to move the university from Landshut to the capital. He staffed it with respected teachers including philosopher Friedrich von Schelling, architect Friedrich von Gärtner and historian Joseph Görres. The king was also a fanatic for new technology, and promoted the development of the first German railway line (which reached Munich in 1840).

The bang-up party after Ludwig's wedding came to be celebrated every year as Oktoberfest (see that special section in the Entertainment chapter). However, the king committed an unpardonable sin in 1844 by raising the Oktoberfest beer price by a whole pfennig; many locals never forgave him.

Ludwig's reign was marked by reactionary ideas. His initial emphasis on Bavaria's constitution gave way to the leanings of an absolutist monarch. An arch-Catholic, the king backed the restoration of monasteries in Bavaria during the 1830s. In 1832, press censorship was introduced, and two years later Ludwig authorised arrests of students, journalists and university professors whom he judged to be dangerously liberal. Bavaria was turning restrictive, even as French and American democratic ideas were catching on elsewhere.

The biggest threat to Ludwig, however, turned out to be his own weakness for beautiful women. The king commissioned portraits of stunning females from all walks of life, and had them hung in a special Schönheitengalerie (Gallery of Beauties) in Schloss Nymphenburg (see the Things to See & Do chapter). Details of the king's many flings were kept out of the public eye, with one notable exception: his infatuation with dancer Lola Montez, which triggered his downfall (see boxed text 'Lola Montez, Femme Fatale').

The Lola Montez affair coincided with the democratic revolutions which swept Europe in 1848. In March of that year, 10,000 Müncheners (or nearly 10% of the town population) signed a petition demanding freedom of the press, and a rabble of them stormed the royal arsenal. On March 22, the 60-year-old Ludwig finally stepped down in favour of his son, Maximilian II, but only on the condition that his grand building plans would be realised. Munich provided many architects with a lot of work for the rest of the century.

Industrial Revolution

With Max II on the throne, Bavaria enjoyed a period of liberalist expansion and relative tranquillity. Like his father, Max was a

Lola Montez, Femme Fatale

A whip-toting dominatrix and seductress of royalty, Lola Montez (1818–61) showed the prim Victorians what sex scandals were all about. Born as Eliza Gilbert in Limerick, Ireland, to a young British army officer and a 13-year-old Creole chorus girl, Lola claimed to be the illegitimate daughter of poet Lord Byron (or depending on her mood, of a matador). When her father died of cholera in India, her mother remarried and shipped the seven-year-old Eliza home to Scotland, where she occasionally ran stark naked through the streets (to the dismay of her stepfather's piously Presbyterian parents). She finished school in Paris and after an unsuccessful stab at acting, reinvented herself as the Spanish dancer, Lola Montez.

She couldn't dance either and, after gigging around Europe for several years, danced just as badly as before. But her beauty fascinated men, who fell at her feet – sometimes under the lash of her ever-present riding crop. One time she fired his pistol at a lover who'd performed poorly, but he managed to escape with his trousers about his knees.

Those succumbing to her charms included the Czar of Russia, who paid her 1000 rubles for a 'private audience', novelist Alexandre Dumas and composer Franz Liszt, with whom she had a sizzling affair in Dresden. Eventually Liszt tired of Lola's incendiary temper, locked his sleeping mistress in their hotel room, and fled – leaving a deposit for the furniture Lola would demolish when she awoke.

When fired by a Munich theatre manager, Lola took her appeal to the court of Ludwig I himself. As the tale goes, Ludwig asked casually whether her lovely figure was a work of nature or art. The direct gal she was, Lola seized a pair of scissors and slit open the front of her dress, leaving the ageing monarch to judge for himself. Predictably, she was rehired (and the manager sacked).

The king fell head over heels for Lola, giving her a huge allowance, a lavish palace and even the doubtful title of Countess of Landsfeld. Her ladyship virtually began running the country, too, and when Munich students rioted during the 1848 revolution, Lola had Ludwig shut down the university. This was too much for the townsfolk, who joined the students in revolt. Ludwig was forced to abdicate and Lola, after a brief stay in quarters near today's Grosshesselohe beer garden, was chased out of town.

Lola can-canned her way around the world; her increasingly lurid show was very popular with Californian gold miners. Next came a book of 'beauty secrets' and a lecture tour (sample topic: 'Heroines of History and Strong-Minded Women'). She shed her Spanish identity, but in doing so Lola – who had long publicly denied any link to her alter ego, Eliza – became a schizophrenic wreck. She spent her final two years as a pauper in New York, shuffling through the streets muttering to herself, before dying of pneumonia and a stroke at age 43.

MICK WELDON

staunch supporter of the arts and sciences, but given his bookish nature he'd have preferred teaching to running the country.

Max's projects included extending the railway line and having a main train station built (a modern hall with a steel framework) by Frederick Bürcklein, as well as a railway bridge over the Isar. The king also commissioned a crystal palace (a replica of London's) in the Old Botanical Garden for the Industrial Exhibition of 1854. (The building was destroyed by fire in 1931.)

The industrial era triggered rapid growth in the city, and suburbs sprang up willy-nilly around the old core, with precious little planning. The first suburbs, all to the east of the city, were incorporated into Munich in 1854: Haidhausen, Au and Giesing. The communities on the east bank of the Isar which weren't absorbed became the neighbourhoods of the sick, the unemployed, prostitutes and other social outcasts. You'd never guess it today but in the 1850s, these areas became Munich's first slums.

Kooky King Ludwig

Ludwig II took the reins after his father's death in 1864. The new king took little interest in building in Munich, especially after the city prevented him from financing an opera house for Richard Wagner. (The composer had made himself unpopular with Müncheners, describing them as 'devoid of artistic sense'.) As a result, in 1865 Ludwig saw himself forced to exile Wagner from the city where his operas, including *Tristan und Isolde* (1865), *Die Meistersinger von Nürnberg* (1867) and *Die Walküre* (1870), made their debut.

Ludwig channelled his fortune into projects that were seen by other members of the royal family as, to put it mildly, nutty – particularly the castles Neuschwanstein, Linderhof and Herrenchiemsee (see the Excursions chapter). The king's bizarre shyness, dreamy nature and predilection towards ever more grandiose projects earned him the moniker of 'Loony Ludwig'. Ironically, the very castles that bankrupted the government and royal house are today's biggest money-spinners for the Bavarian tourism industry.

Ludwig had little interest in politics, and his naivety led him to side with Austria and France against a more powerful Prussia in the Franco-Prussian war of 1866. The conflict lasted just a few months; Bavaria became a vassal state of Prussia, and was finally absorbed into the new German Reich in 1871. Only the post office and the railway retained the label 'Royal Bavarian'. Ludwig was humiliated, but Bismarck (Prussia's famous 'Iron Chancellor') approved a large annual allowance for Ludwig, who pursued his castle-building with a vengeance.

Declared mentally unfit in a dubious psychological exam in 1886, Ludwig was arrested. Soon afterward, he and his doctor were found drowned in highly mysterious circumstances in Lake Starnberg. His brother Otto, a certified nut case, was unable to take the throne, so his regent Prince Luitpold – then already 65 years of age – took charge and began yet another expansion of the city.

'Good Old Days'

Under the relaxed hand of Luitpold, the third son of Ludwig I, Munich enjoyed a golden age of sorts. Despite the irregular circumstances of his rise to power, Prince-Regent Luitpold became one of Bavaria's most popular rulers. His motto 'the people's will is the highest law' revealed a refreshing lack of absolutist ambition.

Between 1886 and Luitpold's death in 1912, Munich's population more than doubled to almost 600,000, making it Germany's third-largest city (after Berlin and Hamburg). Munich gradually assumed the character of a modern metropolis; by 1893, it had the best electrical lighting of any city in Europe.

The artistic scene flourished as never before. Painters such as Wassily Kandinsky, Franz Marc, Paul Klee, and Max Liebermann congregated in Munich, and the portraitist Franz von Lenbach founded the *Künstlergesellschaft* (Artists' Society) in 1873. Other famous names included composer Richard Strauss and writers Henrik Ibsen and Thomas Mann. In contrast to earlier periods, most of these creative spirits came from the Munich area; from about 1890 until the beginning of WWI, the bohemian district of Schwabing was the focal point of artistic life. Even would-be revolutionary Lenin lived here under a pseudonym while editing an underground paper.

The first signs of social unrest emerged shortly before WWI – protests by the unemployed, speeches by social activists such as Rosa Luxemburg, and chronic overcrowding in the slums. WWI broke out before anything like a revolution could occur.

Munich's Ill-Fated Republic

Bavaria's last king, Ludwig III (1913–18) ascended the throne on the eve of the Great War. Munich was spared collateral damage – just three bombs fell in the first and only air raid in 1916, and these pretty much missed their targets – but the city was soon gripped by hunger and unemployment. Moreover, what began as a patriotic diversion led to the death of 13,000 Müncheners on the battlefield; the city was gripped by appalling conditions of hunger, poverty and unemployment.

In November 1918, more than 100,000 people gathered on the Theresienwiese to protest for peace. Erhard Auer of the Social Democratic Party (SPD) and Kurt Eisner of the German Independent Socialist Party (USPD) held fiery orations, calling for revolution and a democratic constitution. Under Eisner's direction, the masses marched through town, won over what was left of the army and proclaimed a republic. The monarchy capitulated without a fight, and Ludwig III fled the Residenz with his family in the middle of the night. Five days later the king was tracked down in the north Bavarian town of Bamberg, where Eisner's officials forced him to sign his abdication.

The factions behind Eisner were badly divided, and what began as a peaceful revolution deteriorated into violence. Left and right-wing Social Democrats, anarchists and communists quarrelled over the shape of the new government. In early 1919 several people died in street battles. The new prime minister also failed to win over the common people to his cause: farmers refused to provide Munich with food, and state elections two months after the revolution produced a crushing defeat for the USPD.

In February 1919, Eisner decided to yield to growing demands from all parties for him to step down. He would never get the chance. On the way to parliament to announce his resignation, Eisner was shot dead near Promenadeplatz by a young Bavarian aristocrat, Count von Arco-Valley. A brass plaque commemorates the assassination (see the Things to See & Do chapter).

Dramatic events followed. In March 1919, the parties' central council elected Social Democrat Johannes Hoffmann as prime minister, but it soon became clear that his democratic ideas weren't radical enough to please the workers. A few weeks later, writers Gustav Landauer, Erich Mühsam and Ernst Toller proclaimed a *Räterepublik* (republic of councils) along Russian lines, and Hoffmann and his officials fled to Bamberg.

The Räterepublik was too fragmented to last, however. The Communists seized power in April 1919, themselves to be overthrown only a few weeks later by the German Army and the Volunteer Corps, who were both loyal to Hoffmann. Council leaders were imprisoned or executed, and Hoffman was reinstalled – but he didn't stay in power long.

The 1920s

In the early 1920s Munich remained a political tinder-box. In March of that year, the Hoffmann government was replaced by the reactionary regime of Gustav von Kahr. Many right-wing splinter groups set up their headquarters in Munich, meeting in beer halls and pubs. Among them was the *Thulegesellschaft*, an anti-Semitic association that gathered in the back rooms of the Hotel Vier Jahreszeiten. A related organisation, the German Workers' Party DAP, was founded in 1919 by toolmaker Anton Drexler and met in the Hofbräuhaus. The party was renamed the National Socialist Workers' Party (NSDAP) in October 1919, by which time its members included a failed Austrian artist – Adolf Hitler (see boxed text 'Hitler & the Beer-Hall Putsch').

Hitler & the Beer-Hall Putsch

"Munich is the city closest to my heart. Here, as a young man, as a soldier and as a politician I made my start." – Adolf Hitler

Political turmoil, hyperinflation and anti-Semitism created fertile ground for the Nazi movement in the 1920s. A native Austrian, Adolf Hitler quit school after the death of his father in 1903 and dedicated himself to painting (mostly maniacal watercolour) and a self-conceived philosophy based on anti-Semitism, knights and Germanic folklore. After he'd failed the entrance exam to the Vienna arts academy, Hitler moved to Munich in 1913 and enlisted in the German army during WWI. A gas attack left Corporal Hitler temporarily blind, giving him time to brood over scapegoats for Germany's humiliating defeat.

By 1921, Hitler managed to unite the militant right-wing parties in his Schutzarmee (SA), and waited until the time was ripe for a coup. On 8 November 1923, he and about 600 SA troops stormed Munich's Bürgerbräukeller, proclaimed a 'National Socialist revolution' and wheeled in a machine gun to show they meant business. The mayor of Munich and other officials of the Bavarian provincial government were kidnapped and taken to forests east of town, and the daring move seemed successful.

The next day, Hitler, SA General Erich Ludendorff and armed comrades marched victoriously through Munich to the Feldherrnhalle – where they were stopped by Bavarian police. Shots were fired, and when it was all over 19 Nazis and several policemen lay dead or dying. Hitler fled, but was apprehended several days later and sentenced to five years' prison in Landsberg, west of Munich. Here he began work on his turgid nationalist work, *Mein Kampf* (My Struggle), dictated in extended rantings to his secretary Rudolf Hess. Incredibly Hitler was released just a year later, in 1924, on grounds of 'good behaviour'.

Hitler then set about rebuilding the party, having sworn to authorities that he would thereafter only pursue legal means of change. The budding dictator spent the next several years consolidating power and raising money, with great success.

Economic collapse was made worse by Germany's crushing repayments to the victorious WWI powers under the Treaty of Versailles, and inflation spiralled higher. By early 1924, a wheelbarrow full of Reichsmarks was needed to buy a single loaf of bread. This and another burst of hyperinflation at the end of WWII left Germans with a deep respect for stable money; on the eve of its disappearance, the Deutschmark remains one of the world's strongest currencies.

Germany's monetary system was reformed in late 1924 and bit by bit, the economy began to stabilise. In the five years before the stock market crash of 1929, Munich enjoyed a spurt of rapid growth. The science and technology halls of the Deutsches Museum (German Museum) were opened in May 1925, an event reported live by the Bayerischer Rundfunk (Bavarian Broadcasting Corporation), which was set up the previous year. Munich's first airport was opened on the Oberwiesenfeld, site of today's Olympiapark. Housing estates were built in Neuhausen and Ramersdorf, and new suburbs emerged on the outskirts of Munich, including Daglfing, Perlach and Freimann.

There were few signs of the 'Roaring Twenties' in Munich, which sank into a cultural stupor. Experimental or racy works were banned, and artists and musicians left town in droves for Berlin (including Bertold Brecht and Carl Zuckmayer). Thomas Mann, one of the few leading writers who remained in Munich until 1933, condemned the city, in a 1926 speech, as 'notorious', 'anti-Semitic' and a 'stronghold of reaction'.

Capital of the Nazi Movement

Hitler took power of Germany in January 1933, and Munich's most disgraceful period of history began. The National Socialists won a clear majority in local elections in March, and replaced the city council with a Nazi apparatus. Just a few weeks later, Hitler's chief henchman Heinrich Himmler established the first concentration camp in Dachau, north of Munich (see the Excursions chapter). As the site of Hitler's first political efforts, Munich was declared 'Capital of the Movement' in 1935.

Königsplatz was paved over with granite slabs for military parades (the stones were removed and grass put down in 1988). The music academy in Prinzregentenstrasse was remodelled into the Deutsches Haus der Kunst (German House of Art), which opened with an exhibit of what the Nazis considered to be 'degenerate art' in 1937. It was here that Hitler and the British prime minister, Neville Chamberlain, signed the Munich Agreement ceding Czechoslovakia to Germany in 1938. Many buildings in 'Reich Style' appeared in the Arcisstrasse, not far from the NSDAP party headquarters ('The Brown House') on the corner of Briennerstrasse and Arcisstrasse.

The square in front of the Feldherrnhalle – site of Hitler's failed putsch attempt – was declared a Nazi shrine, and all passers-by were required to raise their hands in the Hitler salute. Those less than loyal to the Nazi cause took the nearby Viscardigasse, which became known as Drückebergergassl (Dodger's Alley).

As was the case throughout Germany, a reign of terror against the Jews began in Munich in 1938 with the *Reichskristallnacht* (Night of Broken Glass). Jewish businesses were destroyed and the synagogue in the Herzog-Rudolf-Strasse was burned to the ground. Many Jews were interned in camps in Milbertshofen and Berg am Laim before being sent to Dachau, and few would ever return.

WWII & Reconstruction

Germany invaded Poland on 1 September 1939, and the bloody nightmare known as World War II began. Hitler had eliminated most opponents in the so-called Röhm-Putsch of the SA in 1934, leaving only isolated pockets of resistance to the Third Reich. In November 1939, Hitler narrowly escaped assassination in the Bürgerbräukeller (on the site of today's Forum hotel) when a bomb made by Swiss craftsman Jakob Elser killed seven people. (Against his normal habits, Hitler had left the meeting early.)

Few people in Munich dared to speak out against the Nazis; one of the few exceptions was the White Rose, a resistance group led by Munich university students Hans and Sophie Scholl (see boxed text 'The White Rose'). Jesuit father Alfred Delp was hanged for his suspected involvement in the July 1944 attempt on Hitler's life, and another priest and underground activist, Rupert Mayer, suffered many years in Dachau concentration camp. He died shortly after the war and was beatified (see the boxed text 'Father Mayer's Anti-Nazi Crusade' in the Things to See & Do chapter).

Munich was damaged beyond recognition by Allied bombing during WWII. The first big Allied air raid took place in 1942, and a year later bombs destroyed a large number of historical buildings, including the opera house, the Old Courtyard and the state library, together with 500,000 books. Broken and paranoid, Hitler declared 'total war' and 15-year-olds were drafted to defend Munich in a senseless last-ditch battle. By the end of the war, over 22,000 Munich soldiers had fallen and more than 6,000 citizens had perished in air raids; nearly half the city's buildings lay in ashes.

On 30 April 1945 the city was occupied by US forces. The military government reinstated Karl Scharnagl, Munich mayor before the Third Reich, to his former office. His deputy, Thomas Wimmer, called for a large-scale clean-up of the wartime debris, an action which became known as 'Rama Dama'. Repairs to Munich's shattered infrastructure began, and there emerged the first institutions of a democratic Germany (modelled heavily along American lines). The first edition of the *Süddeutsche Zeitung* appeared in 1945. Free

The White Rose

Public protests against the Nazis were rare during the Third Reich. One of the few groups to rebel openly was the ill-fated *Weisse Rose*, led by Munich University students Hans and Sophie Scholl.

Robert Scholl had warned his children against the Nazis, but Hans joined the Hitler Youth and his older sister, Inge, became a group leader of its female counterpart, the Bund Deutsche Mädels. Hans soon became disillusioned with the Nazis and attempted to build his own, liberal group within the Hitler Youth. This triggered a Gestapo raid on the Scholl home in Ulm in 1937, and from then on the family were marked as enemies of the state.

In 1942, Hans and his younger sister, Sophie, linked up with like-minded students in Munich and formed the 'White Rose', an underground movement which encouraged Germans to resist Hitler. At first they acted cautiously, creeping through the streets of Munich at night and smearing slogans such as 'Freedom!' or 'Down With Hitler!' on walls. Later they printed and distributed anti-Nazi leaflets, leaving them in telephone call boxes and sending them to other German cities.

In February 1943, Hans and Sophie took a suitcase of leaflets to the university and placed stacks outside each lecture hall. Then, from a top landing, Sophie dumped the remaining brochures into an inner courtyard. A janitor saw them, and Hans and Sophie were arrested and charged with treason along with their best friend, Christoph Probst. After a four-hour trial, the trio was condemned to death for 'civil disobedience' and beheaded the same afternoon.

After WWII, Inge set up an adult education centre in Ulm (Baden-Württemberg) to help ensure that the Nazi horrors should never happen again. In 1953, she and her husband Otl opened a design college, but Inge devoted most of her time to preserving the memory of the 'White Rose'.

elections held in 1946 were won by the newly-formed conservative party, the Christian Socialist Union (CSU) which has run Bavaria ever since.

The 'Economic Miracle'

Munich's post-war recovery was swift. When the Federal Republic of Germany was founded in 1949, the city had nearly 800,000 inhabitants, up from 470,000 at the end of the war. By the early 1950s local unemployment had dropped to 9%. Slowly but surely, the city's historic core was restored at enormous expense, and new but unexciting suburbs were laid out in Arabellapark, Neuperlach and other outlying areas. Companies such as Siemens, BMW, and truckmaker MAN set up their headquarters in town; Munich also became Germany's largest publishing centre, a fashion hub and home to a renowned film industry. The population exceeded one million in 1957, just in time for the city's 800th anniversary the next year.

The 1960s saw some of Munich's worst architectural sins as planners threw up unsightly concrete blocks and sought to make the city more accessible by car. The broad Altstadtring was built through the old-world facades of Maximilianstrasse; farther out, another traffic artery called the Mittlerer Ring (Middle Ring) only brought more congestion to the city. The idea of creating car-free areas in the inner city won backers, however, and an underground network (U-Bahn) and pedestrian zone were completed in time for the 1972 Olympic Games. The competition was meant to be a showpiece for the new Munich, but ended in tragedy (see boxed text 'Munich's Olympic Tragedy').

Today Munich wears a rich, self-assured reputation as, according to national opinion polls, the most popular place to live in

Germany. Its large student population gives the city a young feel and – despite the exodus of artists earlier this century – it has a vibrant theatre and arts scene. Yet its cultural sophistication is tempered by conservative traditions. Müncheners will be the first to admit that their 'metropolis' is nothing more than a big village.

GEOGRAPHY

Munich is relatively flat, located on the Swabian-Bavarian Plateau at an average 530m above sea level. East to west, it measures 26.4km at its broadest point, while the north-south extent is no more than 20.9km, amounting to a total surface area of just over 310 sq km. Of that, 44% is urban and 16% consists of streets and highways; the remainder is made up of recreational and agricultural areas.

The city is bisected by the chilly Isar River, which runs down from the Alps and flows south to north-east through the city centre (and just east of the Altstadt). Measured at the Frauenkirche, the geographical centre of Munich, the city lies at 48° 8' 23" latitude north and 11° 34' 28" longitude east, putting it on a par with Oslo to the north and Vienna to the east. Munich also lies broadly on the Paris-Vienna and Rome-Hamburg highway networks.

CLIMATE

Munich has a relatively cool, wet climate. Most noticeable is the *Föhn*, a warm, dry, static-charged wind that comes down off

Munich's Olympic Tragedy

Munich's bid for the 1972 Olympic Games came after official recognition of the GDR by the UN in 1965. The philosophy behind the move was that, through the Olympics, West Germany would put itself forward as a rebuilt nation, a model of international cooperation and the proud father of Munich, which had undeniably become a world-class city.

The Games got off to an auspicious start: these were the heady days of the Cold War, and much of the action was dominated by contests between east and west. The main attractions included the contest between the US and Soviet basketball teams and the brilliant individual performances by US swimmer Mark Spitz (who won a record seven gold medals) and Soviet gymnast Olga Korbut.

However, on Wednesday, 6 September, the Israeli athletes' dormitory in the Olympic Village was raided by Palestinian terrorists from the Black September movement. Nine athletes and coaches were kidnapped and two were killed immediately.

Black September demanded the release of prisoners from Israeli jails and threatened to kill the hostages if their demands weren't met immediately. German authorities frantically negotiated for the release of the athletes.

The Germans offered money – to no avail. They even offered a swap of the Israelis for 'substitute' hostages, including federal interior minister Hans-Dietrich Genscher, the former Munich mayor Han-Jochen Vogel and Bavarian interior minister Otto Merk, but this move was also rejected.

After hours of failed negotiations, and with every indication that the terrorists were about to start killing the hostages, the Germans decided to take military action. They arranged for three helicopters to fly the terrorists and hostages to a military airfield at Fürstenfeldbruck, west of Munich, where they were promised a plane that would fly them all to Cairo.

When the choppers arrived at Fürstenfeldbruck, police sharpshooters opened fire on the terrorists, who immediately began shooting hostages. One terrorist detonated a hand grenade inside a helicopter. The remaining nine Israelis, as well as four of the terrorists and a Munich police officer, were killed in the shootout.

euro currency converter DM1 = €.51

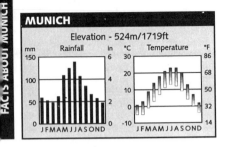

MUNICH

Elevation - 524m/1719ft

Rainfall

Temperature

J F M A M J J A S O N D

the Alps. It brings both exquisite views of the mountains and an area of dense pressure that hovers over the city. Asthmatics, rheumatics and hypochondriacs complain of headaches; Müncheners generally say it makes them cranky and lethargic.

Alternating maritime and continental weather masses make for changeable weather conditions, and there can be strong fluctuations within the seasons. Low-pressure zones from the Mediterranean cross the Alps with large amounts of precipitation, and on average it rains about every other day. On the other hand, broad air masses from the east can bring dry, hot spells in summer and lengthy cold periods in winter. Generally speaking, it can rain at any time so be prepared. Inversions of hot and cold air can help to cause smog, and summer has the highest ozone levels.

The hottest months are June, July and August, and there are nearly 50 days when it's 25 degrees or warmer every year. Winter's at its coldest and snowiest in January, February and early March, and the mercury dips below freezing on more than 70 days on average. Agreeably warm, sunny days can be experienced in spring from mid-April to June, and in autumn during September and October.

ENVIRONMENT

Munich has mostly 'clean' industries but that doesn't mean it has no environmental problems. Its nearly 800,000 registered vehicles are the worst offenders, and the arteries through and around the Altstadt can get awfully thick with vehicle fumes. There's a number of smog-warning displays set up throughout the city (such as the one in the U-Bahn station at Karlsplatz), which are activated when the levels begin to rise. Despite a large, efficient S-Bahn, U-Bahn and bus network, the city's efforts to pry commuters away from their cars have met with limited success. Germany remains a car-loving society, and even stiff fuel taxes (over 70% of the petrol price is tax) haven't proved to be a deterrent.

As most anywhere in Germany, tap water in Munich is regarded as clean and safe to drink. The rivers and streams are a different matter, though, and the Bavarian health ministry doesn't recommend swimming in the Isar due to high levels of noxious bacteria (e-coli and other nasty devils). Many Müncheners do anyway, but you're better advised to take a dip in one of the city swimming pools or swim-approved lakes outside the city.

Germany has tightened its rubbish laws in recent years, and most Müncheners sort their home waste to some degree. Municipal services have pick-ups for biodegradables, plastics and packaging, and paper. You'll also see compartmentalised rubbish bins in some public places (eg the airport and train stations), as well as bottle and battery banks. The average German is so diligent in sorting their waste that the recycling firms began to creak under the strain; it's only recently that the government has instead begun to promote waste *avoidance*. Reusable packaging (such as for shampoos and detergents) has caught on to a certain extent, but the line's drawn when it comes to beer: in 1991, a Bavarian referendum rejected a proposal to outlaw throw-away cans (although two-thirds of Müncheners voted in favour).

FLORA & FAUNA

Royal designers flattered Munich with a wealth of green areas: parks, gardens, woods and rivers make up 44-sq-km of its space. That amounts to just 14% of the city's surface area, but big chunks of that are locked in vast expanses such as the English Garden, Schloss Nymphenburg, the Olympiapark and the Hellabrunn Zoo.

Many neighbourhoods also have their own green areas, and the southern edge of the city is encircled by a swathe of wilder, less visited forest and parkland.

The chestnut is something of a national tree in Bavaria, as its broad leaves provide useful shade to beer-drinkers and helps keep the underground cellars cool. You'll also find that maples, oaks, and plane trees are quite common, and landscape gardeners have had a ball with exotic imports such as the delicate Japanese maple.

Munich's rapid growth this century has driven most of its indigenous animal life outside the city limits. Animal-lovers can seek solace at Hellabrunn Zoo, which has 4000 species from around the world (see the Things to See & Do chapter).

GOVERNMENT & POLITICS

Once home to a short-lived and wobbly Soviet-style republic, Munich is now a bastion of political stability. Candidates of the Bavarian conservative party, the Christian Social Union (CSU), may have emerged as winners in every parliamentary election since WWII, but when it comes to choosing Munich's mayor or city council, the left-of-centre Social Democratic Party (SPD) has always been a step ahead. The council consists of representatives from 25 Munich districts and meets in the Neues Rathaus.

Thanks to a direct mandate, SPD mayors have had a great degree of freedom despite a typically narrow majority on the city council. Sometimes a coalition with the CSU becomes necessary to pass legislation, and that's when proceedings get really lively.

Munich is also the seat of the Bavarian government, which meets in the *Landtag* (state parliament) in the grand hilltop Maximilineum above the Isar's eastern bank. The glassy *Staatskanzlei* (state chancellery), commissioned by now-deceased CSU party boss Franz-Josef Strauss, is at the east end of the Hofgarten. There are ministries scattered around town, including the *Innenministerium* and *Finanzministerium* (interior and finance ministries) in attractive old buildings on Odeonsplatz.

As a *Freistaat* (free state), Bavaria also had a state senate which met in the Maximilineum through the end of 1999. The Bavarian people voted in a 1998 referendum to abolish the body, which had become increasingly superfluous.

ECONOMY

Munich has weathered 1990s economic sluggishness better than other German cities. One reason for this is that the city government is the biggest customer: Munich invests more in itself per capita than any other German city. In the four years through 2003, Munich plans to spend DM6 billion on projects including infrastructure, new residential housing and transport.

Apart from being the Bavarian capital, Munich is an important centre of manufacturing and financial services. Above all, the city is wealthy: average per capita income is over DM80,000, the highest of any large German city. Unemployment in the Munich region in late 1999 was around 5%, about half the national figure.

Munich can claim plenty of economic superlatives. Some of Germany's biggest companies are based here, including electronics and computing giant Siemens, turbine maker MTU and vehicle producers BMW and MAN. Manufacturing accounts for about half the region's business, which amounts to over DM330 billion. More than 100 banks and 20 insurers are located here (including Europe's largest insurer, Allianz). Many foreign firms, such as Motorola, Digital Equipment, IBM and Intel, have their German or European headquarters or at least large offices in the region.

The media industry is another mainstay: about 115,000 people (10% of the working population) are employed in television, radio and other communication services. Munich developed the film industry in leaps and bounds during the 1970s and 1980s, and today more productions are shot here than in Hamburg, Berlin or Cologne. A further 7% of employees work in the tourism industry, helping to serve some 3.4 billion people who visited the Bavarian capital in 1998.

euro currency converter DM1 = €.51

Among other factoids, Munich is also Germany's leading centre of new technologies. To the east of town are many start-up companies protected from harsh market forces in so-called 'incubators'; many receive generous government subsidies.

Munich is also Germany's single biggest publishing centre, with more publishing houses and bookshops than anywhere else in the country. Paperback publisher DTV and national book retailer Hugendubel are but two examples.

POPULATION & PEOPLE

With 1.3 million city inhabitants and about 2.3 million in its greater environs, Munich is Germany's third-largest city (after Berlin and Hamburg). It's a cosmopolitan place in terms of population structure – about 20% are foreign citizens. Another little interesting item to note is that there are about 40,000 more women than men (are you singles listening?).

Thanks to its large student population, Munich is a relatively young city. Nearly half of its residents are between the ages of 18 and 45. The death rate has been slightly higher than births in recent years, but the population has grown slightly due mainly to newcomers from the former east Germany and from Eastern European countries.

EDUCATION

Munich has a highly educated population, thanks to one of the world's most thorough education systems. There are private and religious schools, but the overwhelming majority of students attend government schools.

After kindergarten, children then attend a *Grundschule* (basic school), usually from the ages six to 10. After a two-year orientation phase, they enter one of five different types of school: a *Hauptschule* (main school), a *Realschule* (practical school), a combined *Hauptschule-Realschule*, a *Gesamtschule* (comprehensive school), or a *Gymnasium* (senior secondary school). Only at the last institution can students take the *Abitur* – the university entrance qualification. Most students take it at age 19.

Munich is home to about 100,000 university students. Three-quarters of them attend the Ludwig-Maximilians-Universität München (☎ 218 00), at Geschwister-Scholl-Platz 1. The top three faculties are medicine, economics and law. Most of the rest go to the Technische Universität München (☎ 289 01), Arcisstrasse 21, which offers degrees in mathematics, physics, chemistry, biology and earth sciences.

Students study for a *Diplom* (diploma) or *Staatsexamen* (state examination), *Magister* (master of arts), or *Doktortitel* (doctorate). The minimum study period is eight to nine semesters, or about 4½ years, but the usual length of stay is seven years.

ARTS
Painting & Sculpture

Munich is paradise for any museum lover. Some of the best museums to visit for a good overview of German painting and sculpture are the Alte and Neue Pinakothek, the Modern Art Gallery in the Haus Der Kunst, and the Lenbachhaus.

Early Works The art forms common elsewhere in Germany during the early Middle Ages hardly left their mark on Munich. In other larger, older and richer Bavarian cities such as Augsburg and Regensburg, the two dominant art forms of the Carolingian period – the church frescoes and manuscript illumination – were well represented, even if few have survived until today. In its infancy, Munich was a tiny salt-trading town that earned little attention from its new masters, the Wittelsbach family.

Portraiture and panel painting appeared in Germany around 1300. A number of such works were commissioned by the Wittelsbachs, but most are believed to have been lost or destroyed. Late panel works that did survive include those by Polish artist Jan Polack, who is regarded as Munich's most important late-Gothic painter. He produced two altars in Peterskirche (St Peter's Church) in 1492 as well as the altar in the Schloss Blutenburg chapel (1491). Another beautiful example of panel painting, by Tyrolean artist Michael Pacher, is the

Kirchenväteraltar (1483) which can be viewed in Alte Pinakothek.

The first Munich-based carver of historical note was Erasmus Grasser, who produced Munich's coat of arms in 1477. The emblem and his late Gothic wooden Morris dancers are on display in the Stadtmuseum (City Museum). In 1500, Grasser was commissioned to decorate the choir stalls of the newly-built Frauenkirche. The style of Munich's visual arts remained decidedly Gothic for a long, long time after the Renaissance had taken hold elsewhere in Europe.

Renaissance The arts continued to slumber in Munich until the 16th century, when Duke Wilhelm IV had the first sections of the Residenz built. Between 1528 and 1540, he also had a double cycle of pictures painted for the palace; these are acknowledged as some of the earliest surviving German Renaissance paintings, depicting famous heroes of classical and Christian antiquity. The most important of these, *The Battle of Alexander the Great* (1529), is impressive for its field of ant-like soldiers and sweeping cosmos; it hangs today in the Alte Pinakothek.

In Germany, the Renaissance is synonymous with one great figure, Albrecht Dürer (1471–1528), who was born in Nuremberg. His influence was so great that the period is often referred to as the *Dürerzeit* (Age of Dürer). He was the first German to grapple seriously with the theory and practice of Italian Renaissance art. Closely tied to a Gothic tradition in early years, his woodcuts often had apocalyptic elements. His drawings of nature and animals were exact in their detail, and he left a surviving legacy of about 70 paintings, 350 woodcuts and 900 drawings. Some of his work also hangs in the Alte Pinakothek, including the delicate and moving *Four Apostles* (1526).

Baroque & Rococo Whatever artistic spirit had developed under Wilhelm was crushed by the Thirty Years' War, and it wasn't until the mid-17th century that the court began to commission artworks again in a big way. A novelty of the 17th and 18th centuries was an elaborate integration of painting, sculpture and architecture to form a *Gesamtkunstwerk* (total artwork), and Munich's churches are full of it.

The two most influential artists of the era were the brothers Egid Asam (1692–1750) and Cosmas Asam (1686–1739), whose works include lavish and flowing baroque sculptures in the St Anne Church in Lehel (1738), frescoes in Schloss Schleissheim (1720–21) and, of course, fantastic ceiling frescoes in Munich's Asamkirche (1738). The work of Cosmas Asam is famous for tricky optical illusions, for which Ingolstadt's town church is also famous.

Many of Germany's palace frescoes of the time were done by Italians. Johann Baptist Zimmermann (1680–1758) was an important southern German fresco painter who worked in pastels typical of the rococo style. Scores of Zimmermann's stucco decorations and frescoes can be seen, mostly in reconstructed form, in the Residenz, St Peter's Church, the Amalienburg at Schloss Nymphenburg and in Schloss Nymphenburg itself. In the old St Michael Church in Berg am Laim, a suburb in the south-east of Munich, the interior is a joint venture of Zimmermann and Johann Baptist Straub (1704–1784). Some art historians regard Straub as the 'father' of Munich rococo.

In the mid-18th century, porcelain came into vogue as an artistic genre. The Staatliche Porzellan-Manufaktur (Nymphenburg State Porcelain Factory) was founded in 1758, and its high quality (if dated) products can still be purchased today.

19th Century The 19th century saw a proliferation of styles which, in some ways, reflected the socio-political undercurrents throughout Europe at this time. New political and economic ideas coming to Germany from England resonated with the increasingly educated middle classes. These new attitudes brought a formal shift to line and body, with an emphasis on Roman or Greek mythology and the human form.

The German works from this period are influenced strongly by the writings of August Wilhelm Schlegel, and its most famous advocate was the Caspar David Friedrich, a north German. Friedrich's images of nature infused with melancholy contrast sharply with 'Biedermeier' realism, a style popular among Munich artists at the time. 'Biedermeier' realism was embodied by such late works by Wilhelm von Kobell as *Landscape with the Tegernsee* (1833).

Under the generous sponsorship of Bavaria's King Ludwig I, Munich developed into an important artistic centre. Countless artists enjoyed the king's patronage, which was guided by enthusiasm for Italian and Greek art forms. (Karl Rottmann, for example, created landscapes based on both countries, apparently to flatter the monarch.) However, the leading portrait painter of Ludwig's reign was Joseph Karl Stieler, whose *Portrait of Goethe* (1828) shows the poet clutching a piece of paper with – guess what? – lines of homage to Goethe by Ludwig I.

The Munich Secession In both Munich and Berlin, in the late-19th century, there emerged groups of artists intent on shaking up the art establishment. At the heart of Munich's movement was Franz von Stuck (1863–1928), a quirky Expressionist whose sensual work *The Sin* triggered a split of the artistic establishment in 1893. The *Sezessionisten* (secessionists) preferred scenes from daily life to historical and religious themes, thereby rejecting what they saw as reactionary attitudes towards the arts. Stuck's odd mixture of *Jugendstil* (Art Deco), wit and dark melancholy was widely copied in interior furnishings of the day.

The toughest opponent of Secessionism was Franz von Lenbach (1836–1904), a legendary portrait artist of the *Gründerzeit* (the period of Germany's industrial expansion after 1871). Lenbach was head of Munich's *Künstlergesellschaft* (Artist's Society), whose ranks included Romantic painters as well as figures representing the 'establishment' (Prince Otto von Bismarck, who frequently sat for Lenbach, was a prominent patron). A power struggle ensued, and some Secessionist painters moved (or were practically expelled) to nearby Dachau to work. But a Secessionist movement had already taken

hold in Berlin, backed by Max Liebermann (1847–1935), Franz von Stuck and other experimentalists, and by the end of the decade von Lenbach's group had waned in influence.

Other important turn-of-the-century artists in Munich included a group called *Der Blaue Reiter* (Blue Rider), which was based around the key figures of Wassily Kandinsky (1866–1944), Gabriele Münter (1877–1962), Paul Klee (1879–1940) and Franz Marc (1880–1916). Like Die Brücke, an organisation of Expressionist artists founded in 1905, the movement tried to find a purer, freer spirit through colour and movement; many of its great names attended the Akademie der Bildenden Künste (Academy of Visual Arts) on Munich's Akademiestrasse.

Kandinsky's 1909 *Eisenbahn bei Murnau* (Railway at Murnau) shows a train passing through an evocatively colourful landscape. It is in Munich's Städtische Gallerie im Lenbachhaus (Municipal Gallery in the Lenbachhaus), where many of the movement's works are housed. The Russian-born Kandinsky wrote much about expressionist theory, comparing the creation of form to the creation of life. Many of the Blue Rider artists didn't survive WWI after volunteering for German military service.

Neue Sachlichkeit 'New Objectivity' describes a loose movement in the early 20th century that reached its zenith with *Bauhaus*. Architecture formed the basis of *Bauhaus*, but ideas spilled over into painting with the publication of the movement's ninth book by Kandinsky, who had moved on from expressionism.

Kandinsky's work *Punkt und Linie zu Fläche: Beitrag zur Analyse der Malerischen Elemente* (Point and Line to Surface: Contribution to the Analysis of Elements of Painting) was a landmark in Bauhaus art theory. As well as Kandinsky and Klee, the movement included the sculptor Gerhard Marcks (1889–1981).

With war approaching, art became increasingly bleak, often taking the themes of silence and death. Many artists suffered the fate of being classified 'degenerate' or were forced to resign their positions and go into exile. Others were murdered or went into 'internal exile'.

Nazi Art Hitler was no great fan of 20th century painting unless he had done it himself. In 1937, the Nazis organised an exhibition of *Entartete Kunst* (Degenerate Art) in Munich's Deutsches Haus der Kunst (German House of Art), now simply called Haus der Kunst. Leading works of the day were displayed, but most were banned after the exhibition; most of the artists had already left Germany anyway.

Post-1945 After WWII, Munich's artistic scene was fragmented and the momentum for true revival came from elsewhere. Respected figures such as Kandinsky, Karl Schmidt-Rottluf (1884–1976) and Emil Nolde (1867–1956) returned to Germany to pull the decimated cultural scene back onto its feet. Willi Baumeister and Ernst Nay are considered two of Germany's best post-war abstract expressionists. Nay tried to capture rhythm in his work, often using erotic motifs and mythology.

The Düsseldorf-based *Gruppe Zero* (Group Zero) plugged into the Bauhaus legacy. Otto Piene (1928) and Heinz Mack (1931) were two key members who used light and space cleverly in endeavours to create a harmonious whole. Mack's sculpture is predominantly of metal, whereas Piene has used projection techniques to create his so-called 'light ballets'. More recently, Anselm Kiefer (1945) has gone for size in his 32-tonne work *Zweistromland* (Mesopotamia), which consists of 200 lead books arranged on shelves.

The *Neue Wilde* (New Wild Ones) movement of the late 1970s and early 1980s brought together new-wave music and the visual arts, with Cologne, Berlin and Hamburg as its main centres. Markus Lüpertz (1941) is one survivor from the scene still active today.

Cinema

The Bavarians played an important role in the early development of German film.

Comedian Karl Valentin set up his own makeshift studio near the Hofbräuhaus in 1912, and produced the first of 50 films made during his lifetime. Although Berlin was Germany's undisputed film capital in the 1920s, talent and money flowed into Munich as well, thanks to the excellent technical facilities at the Bavarian Film Studios, founded in 1919. Its first production was *Der Ochsenkrieg* (The Oxen War), a sentimental drama based on a novel by Ludwig Ganghofer.

Most directors from this period have been forgotten today, with the exception of a then unknown, young English director. Unable to raise funds for his projects in London, Alfred Hitchcock came to Munich in 1925, and quickly found local backers for his first film *The Pleasure Garden*; a year later *The Mountain Eagle* also hit the big screen. But the early promise wasn't born out; Munich's artistic scene dulled at the end of the decade and many of its leading lights left for Berlin. In the 1930s, the studios (located in the southern Munich suburb of Geiselgasteig) were pressed into service for Third Reich propaganda. Its buildings were severely damaged during WWII.

Munich benefited from the isolation of the big Berlin studios during the Cold War. Refurbished in the late 1950s, Bavaria became a laboratory studio for young German writer-directors on slim budgets. It wasn't long, however, before Munich began to lure big-name international directors and actors. Richard Fleischer's sweepingly photographed epic *The Vikings* (1958) was shot here with a star-studded cast including Kirk Douglas and Tony Curtis. Billy Wilder finished his comedy epic *One, Two, Three* in Munich when the 1963 division of Berlin fouled up on-location shooting. Dirk Bogarde, Gregory Peck, Burt Lancaster, Liz Taylor and Richard Burton were other household names committed to celluloid here. Sci-fi fans will fondly remember the low-budget TV series *The Adventures of Space Patrol Orion*, Germany's answer to *Star Trek*, which emerged at the Geiselgasteig.

During the 1970s, the 'New German Cinema' emerged under the leadership of

Rainer Werner Fassbinder, Werner Herzog, Wim Wenders and Volker Schlöndorff, who all produced a number of acclaimed films and TV series in Munich. As a result, the city became known (within Germany at any rate) as 'Hollywood on the Isar'. Bob Fosse made his first appearance here with the Oscar-winning *Cabaret* (1972), and Monty Python also worked in Munich.

But the real breakthrough onto the international film scene came with Wolfgang Petersen's *Das Boot*, the epic submarine drama set during WWII. It was one of the most elaborate and expensive German productions ever, and much of the set has been preserved at Bavaria. Petersen's success led to other international hits such as *The Never-Ending Story* (1984), *Enemy Mine* (1985), and *Stalingrad* (1993). Many made-for-TV films and popular German soaps such as *Marienhof* and *Berliner Strasse* are also produced at the Geiselgasteig.

Music

Munich has made relatively few original contributions to music history and for centuries was largely eclipsed by Vienna, Leipzig and other European cities. But because Germany has produced some of the world's greatest composers, an overview of Munich culture wouldn't be complete without them.

Early Forms The Church was the focal point of early German music. The *Lied* (song) describes a variety of popular styles sung as marching tunes or to celebrate victory or work. These later divided into *Volkslieder* (folk songs) and *Kunstlieder* (artistic songs). Among the latter were religious songs, such as the *Marienlied*, which had a mixture of German and Latin lyrics.

From 1100–1300, the *Hof* was the focus of music. *Minnesang*, as the new style was called, had Moorish origins and was imported from southern France. These love ballads praised the women of the court, and were often performed by knights. The most famous minstrel of the time was Walther von der Vogelweide (c. 1170–1230), whose work has been re-recorded by modern artists.

Around the 15th century the troubadour tradition was adopted by a class of burghers who earned a living from music and were often tradesmen on the side. They established schools and guilds, and created strict musical forms. Their model was the tradesmen's guild, with *Altmeister* and *Jungmeister* (old and young masters). To become a *Meistersinger*, a performer had to pass a test and bring something new to melody and lyric. One famous Meistersinger, Hans Sachs (1494–1576), was the subject of a Richard Wagner opera, *Die Meistersinger von Nürnberg*, in the 19th century.

Renaissance & Baroque The Lied remained an important secular form in the 15th and 16th centuries, with Ludwig Senfl (1486–1546) one of the most important composers.

The most significant development took place in the Church when Martin Luther (1483–1546) created the tradition of Protestant hymns. He collaborated with Johann Walther (1496–1570) to publish the first book of hymns sung in German. He also translated Latin hymns and, an amateur musician himself, wrote a dozen of his own, some set to the melodies of Volkslieder.

Johann Sebastian Bach (1637–1707) and Georg Friedrich Händel (1685–1759) are two German composers synonymous with the baroque period.

Bach's legacy includes his *Brandenburg Concerts*, passions, cantata and oratorios. Händel's music was greatly influenced by his Italian travels. He wrote operas, instrumental works and oratorios such as his *Messiah*. From 1714 he lived and worked almost exclusively in London. Halle and Göttingen both celebrate his works with annual festivals.

Wiener Klassik The late-18th century saw a shift to Vienna. Austria lured talented composers from the 18th century onward, and their style became known as Wiener Klassik (Viennese Classical). Oddly, none of the three great names associated with the movement came from Vienna. Both Joseph Haydn (1732–1809) and Wolfgang Amadeus Mozart

(1756–91) were Austrian (but not Viennese), and therefore not really German in today's sense. Nevertheless, their influence on German music is immeasurable. Mozart, incidentally, made his operatic debut with *Idomeneo* at the Munich Opera House.

Ludwig van Beethoven (1770–1827), the third great name, was born in Bonn and went to Vienna, where he was taught by Haydn and Salieri. His work reflects the Enlightenment, and he intended to dedicate his third symphony, *Eroica*, to Napoleon until he saw a betrayal of democratic ideals in Napoleon accepting the imperial crown. Beethoven's compositions became more abstract with the onset of deafness. By 1819 he had lost all hearing. Four years later, inspired by a Schiller ode, he composed his monumental ninth symphony, which included a choral finale.

Romantic Romantic composers of the 19th century continued the tradition of musical independence (ie living from their work), which was established in Beethoven's time. This fitted in well with the ideology of the free, if sometimes hungry, artist.

Felix Mendelssohn-Bartholdy (1809–47) from Hamburg gave his first concert recital when nine years old and at 17 composed his first overture, based on Shakespeare's *A Midsummer Night's Dream*. He later dug up works by JS Bach and gave the latter the fame he enjoys today. Carl Maria von Weber (1786–1826) set the Romantic tone early with idealisations of Germanic myths.

The most influential composer of the 19th century was Richard Wagner (1813–83), an occasional Munich resident who balanced all the components of operatic form to produce the *Gesamtkunstwerk* (complete work of art). He was strongly influenced by Weber, Beethoven and Mozart. He once described his *Die Meistersinger von Nürnberg*, (which like most of his major works, premiered in Munich) as perfect. *Der Fliegende Holländer* (The Flying Dutchman) is another of Wagner's famous operas still popular today. His choice of mythological themes also made him popular with Nazis. However, Friedrich Nietzsche, another Nazi

favourite, fell out with him metaphysically and condemned his works.

Johannes Brahms' (1833–97) fine symphonies, chamber and piano works and Lieder were important landmarks. Robert Schumann (1810–56) began his career as a pianist, turning to composition after suffering paralysis of the fingers. In 1840 he married Clara Wieck (1819–96), a gifted pianist in her own right who had begun concert tours at age 13. In 1843 Schumann opened a music school at Leipzig in collaboration with Mendelssohn-Bartholdy.

The Hungarian-born Franz Liszt (1811–86) was at the centre of a group of composers in Weimar from 1844 to 1860. Wagner married his daughter. Richard Strauss (1864–1949) worked in the late-Romantic tradition of Wagner, only to delve into a style reminiscent of Mozart at the end of his career.

20th Century Arnold Schönberg (1874–1951) was born in Vienna and died in Los Angeles. Between that, however, he lived in Berlin (in the 1920s) and exerted an enormous influence on Germany's classical music. He is arguably the inventor of a new tonal relationship.

Hanns Eisler (1898–1962) was a pupil of Schönberg's who went into exile in 1933 and returned to teach in East Berlin in 1950. Eisler wrote classical music, pop songs, film music, scores for one-time Munich resident Bertolt Brecht and, his most notorious work, the East German national anthem. Paul Dessau (1894–1979) also collaborated with Brecht and composed in a broad range of styles. Paul Hindemith (1895–1963) emerged as a talented composer before WWII. Banned by the Nazis, he emigrated to the USA in 1938 and only returned for tours and brief visits after the war. His early works had baroque leanings; his late orchestral compositions, mostly completed in America, confirm his status as one of Germany's best modern composers.

Contemporary German rock began to roll in 1969, when Amon Düul released its first album – a psychedelic work with long instrumental breaks. Can, a Cologne-based experimental group, earned a name with their *Monster Movie* album. Better known internationally is Tangerine Dream, which gained recognition with its 1974 *Phaedra* album, and went on to record with Virgin.

Old hands will remember Kraftwerk's *Autobahn* album, which hit the turntables worldwide in the early 1970s. This band, one of the first to recognise the potential of computer-assisted music, is hailed as the 'mother of techno'.

Rolf Kaiser was an important producer in the 1970s who did much to promote German music, but British and American bands usually thrived at the expense of local talent. The advent of punk initially left the industry gaping at its guitars. A local movement – *neue deutsche Welle* (German new wave) – soon took shape with German lyrics.

Nena's extremely tame *99 Luftballons* (released in Britain as *99 Red Balloons)* was a No 1 in the UK; in the USA, where the original German version was released, it was No 2. Spliff, Ideal and Palais Schaumberg were other bands that built up strong reputations.

Nina Hagen, born in East Berlin, was the foster child of the writer Wolf Biermann. After Biermann was stripped of East German citizenship, she followed him to West Germany and soon became a symbol of German punk. She worked with the British all-girl group The Slits and, as The Nina Hagen Band, struck gold with her first album. Her laconic Berlin style blended well enough with English-American punk for the *New Musical Express* to describe her as an epileptic Edith Piaf and a cross between Johnny Rotten, Maria Callas and Bette Midler.

German New Wave grew weary and lost momentum around the early 1980s, with few new bands to emerge. Nevertheless, Udo Lindenberg, who was involved in early bands, went solo with political engagement, and anarchists still have a soft spot beneath their leather for the old rocker. Generally, however, rock became more conservative, a lot of it indistinguishable from *Schlager* (see the following section).

Herbert Grönemeyer ('the German Springsteen') achieved success in 1984 with his *Bochum* album, which stayed in the charts for 79 weeks. His single *Männer* was another big hit. Grönemeyer's strained vocal style is not everyone's cup of tea, but his lyrics often have a nice irony. BAP is a renowned Cologne-based band which sings in the local *kölsch* dialect, which means most Germans can't understand them either. Cologne has a lively rock scene, and BAP is worth seeing if rock archaeology is your interest.

Fury in the Slaughterhouse is currently one of Germany's most important mainstream rock bands. Die Toten Hosen (literally 'the dead trousers', but based on an expression to say nothing much is going on) continue to serve up their orthodox punk, much of it in English, while The Scorpions continue to play their own brand of heavy metal, choosing to groom an international image at the expense of their German roots.

The rap group, Die Fantastischen Vier, which lent German rap popular tones in the early 1990s, have proved to be survivors on the scene. Other well known rap bands and performers to follow in their wake are Fischmob, Rödelheim Hartreim Project, Fettes Brot, 5-Sterne Deluxe, Eins/Zwo, Die Absoluten Beginner and Sabrina Setlur.

Schlager & Chanson Schlager is what Germans call your traditional nondescript pop song. Some have a country & western or folk flavour, others are influenced by French and Italian pop. You can hear it all over Germany, but especially in mountaintop restaurants, and as *Meyers*, one highbrow music encyclopaedia, points out: 'All attempts to raise the standard of Schlager have failed so far – even the last resort of parodying it. What was intended as a parody ended up a Schlager success.'

Cabaret Originally imported from Paris' Montmartre district in the late-19th century, Kabarett, the German form, has a strong political flavour and relies heavily on satire and the Lied.

While the form hardly made it to Munich, in Berlin in 1922 there were over 38 venues to help Germans forget about the troubled Weimar Republic. A few of these,

MICK WELDON

'Those were the days, my dear'

such as Schall und Rauch (Noise and Smoke), were political snakepits.

Many well known creative figures of the era worked in Kabarett – Bertolt Brecht, Erich Kästner and Kurt Tucholsky, just to mention a few. Tucholsky wrote lyrics for one famous performer, Gussy Holl (nicknamed 'the silver-blonde elegant witch'). Annemarie Hase, Trude Hesterberg and Rosa Valletti were three other Kabarett stars of the 1920s.

In 1933 the stakes were raised by Hitler's power takeover. Almost all political Kabarett was closed down, with performers and writers forced into exile. Others died in concentration camps.

Today, cabaret is alive and well on several Munich stages including the Münchner Lach- und Schiessgesellschaft (Munich 'Laughing and Shooting Company'), Theater im Fraunhofer, the Schlachthof (the Slaughterhouse) and at numerous smaller venues.

Literature

Apart from early religious and folk writings, Munich only really burst on to the literary scene in the late-19th century, after German unification in 1871. In parallel to the Secession of the painting world, these writers shunned the lofty Romanticism popular at the royal court in favour of a more realistic, often politically-engaged tone.

The hottest publication of the time was *Simplicissimus*, a satirical magazine with a symbol of a red bulldog. All the big Munich names contributed, including Thomas Mann, Rainer Maria Rilke, Hermann Hesse and Heinrich Mann. The editors cut it a bit close with the royal court, however, and two artists were arrested for a scurrilous caricature of Kaiser Wilhelm.

Ludwig Thoma (1867–1921), a lawyer from Dachau, was a leading satirist who wrote for *Simplicissimus*. His rather harmless parodies of Bavarian village life ruffled the feathers of his countrymen. You'll still find his works on the shelves of Munich bookshops today.

Thomas Mann (1875–1955) wasn't a Münchener per se but, in 40 years' living there wrote a pile of acclaimed works, one of which contained a great advertising jingle for the city (see boxed text 'Thomas Mann & the Nazis').

Karl Valentin (1882–1967) was a screenwriter, stage comedian and film maker whose works also graced the pages of *Simplicissimus*. His visual style was similar to Charlie Chaplin's, although the written jokes tended to be heavy going.

One of the few modern Bavarian writers known outside Germany was Oskar Maria Graf (1894–1967). His most famous novel, *We are Prisoners*, captures the sense of disillusionment (and confusion) felt by many towards the German authorities between the world wars. His books weren't banned by the Nazis in 1933, although Graf (always the wit) commented that they deserved to be.

Architecture

As is the case in most German cities, Munich's dazzling array of architectural styles is really just an illusion. As the vast majority of historic buildings were destroyed during WWII, what you see today is the product of painstaking reconstruction (sometimes with the aid of ancient royal blueprints).

Middle Ages The Gothic movement, which began in northern France around 1150, was slow to reach Germany. Gothic interiors usually had ribbed vaults, pointed arches and flying buttresses – which allowed height for larger windows.

Thomas Mann & the Nazis

'Munich shone,' was how Thomas Mann opened his novella *Gladius Dei* in 1902. '... and on all squares and pavements, the unhurried, happy events of the beautiful, confident city rolled, rattled and hummed'.

Born in the Baltic town of Lübeck in 1875, Mann moved to Munich in 1893 and promptly fell in love with the city, writing volumes of work (including his celebrated *'Death in Venice'*) there before his departure 40 years later. Like countless other artists, poets and bohemians, Mann lived in Schwabing, where he wrote profusely and contributed to the satirical periodical *Simplicissimus* in the 1890s. By the time he won the Nobel Prize for literature in 1929, Mann was lionised as a cultural icon and one of Munich's most sought-after public speakers.

Yet Mann's attitude towards his adopted home had soured. In 1926, he decried its 'Anti-Semitic Nationalism' and condemned Munich as 'notorious in Germany and beyond, as a stronghold of reaction and a seat of obduracy and intractability'.

In the spring of 1933, the Third Reich banned the books of hundreds of authors, and Mann wisely stayed in Switzerland after a lecture tour. His Bogenhausen villa (which was at No 10 in the street now called Thomas-Mann-Strasse) was confiscated, and Mann and his wife fled to the United States. For many Germans, the writer became their torchbearer in exile, publishing numerous articles and protests against the Hitler regime. It wasn't until 1949 that he returned for the last time to Munich, briefly, for a reception held in his honour.

Munich's late Gothic Frauenkirche, designed as a symbol of wealth and power by architect Jörg von Halspach, was erected between 1468 and 1488. The famous onion domes were added in 1524. Late Gothic (from about the 15th century) tended to have more elaborately patterned vaults, and hall churches (where the nave is the same height as the aisles) became more common.

Germany's most famous Gothic building is the massive Dom in Cologne (a UNESCO World Heritage building), which was begun in 1248 and not completed until 1880. The Ulm Münster is a good example of how high Gothic can go in Germany (161m, in this case). Freiburg's Münster and the Marienkirche in Lübeck are others. The Rathaus buildings in Bremen and Lübeck are both secular Gothic styles.

Renaissance The Renaissance had a slow birth in Germany, gaining importance only around the mid-16th century and overlapping with late Gothic. Its main centre was in southern Germany and around the trade routes of the Rhine, where there was much contact with Italy. Herms (usually stone heads of Hermes) placed on structural features, leafwork and sculptured human figures, used as columns and pillars, became popular.

Oddly, the Counter-Reformation ignited an architectural spark in Munich. Many influential buildings emerged, including the first Hofgarten, which Duke Wilhelm IV had built on the present-day Marstallplatz; the Münzhof (Mint), with its beautiful courtyard arcades; and the early sections of the Residenz. Restraint was not a familiar term in the Bavarian court: for instance, the lengthy construction of St Michael's Church (1583–99), a late Gothic hall church and the largest north of the Alps at the time, nearly emptied the state's coffers.

The 16th century brought colour and decorative facades to half-timbered houses in Munich, many of which have elaborately carved surfaces.

Baroque Loosely describing a period in German architecture from the early 17th century to the mid-18th century, baroque is linked to the period of absolutism following the Thirty Years' War, when feudal rulers asserted their importance through grand

Deutsches Museum

St Anne Monastery Church

Flugwerft Schleissheim

Unusual automobiles in the Deutsches Museum

Residenz interior

Glockenspiel on Marienplatz

Pub sign with Münchner Kindl

A Munich street performer strikes a pose.

Taurus o'clock at the Spielzeugmuseum

residences. Many took their inspiration from the Palace of Versailles. Structures tended to dominate their surroundings, with grand portals, wide staircases, and wings that created enclosed courtyards. Ornate and excessive, baroque buildings also incorporated sculpture and painting into their design.

During this period many Italian architects such as Agostino Barelli (1627–1687) and Enrico Zuccalli (1642–1724) worked in Germany. Barelli created Schloss Nymphenburg in Munich.

Some opulent Munich buildings originated in this period, including the Monastery Church St Anne in Lehel, the Asam Church in Sendlinger Strasse and another St Michael's Church in Berg am Laim. The Belgian Francois de Cuvilliés (1695–1768) designed the Grüne Galerie (Green Gallery) in the Residenz and the lovely rococo theatre which bears his name.

Munich townspeople were incensed by the stiff taxes that these buildings required; when the Residenz caught fire in 1674, they waited a full hour before responding to cries for help.

Neoclassicism In the late-18th century, baroque folly and exuberance were replaced by the strict geometry of neoclassicism. In Munich, Leo von Klenze and Friedrich von Gärtner were hired in the early 19th century to design Königsplatz, the Alte Pinakothek and Ludwigstrasse, as well as the Königsbau and Festsaalbau sections of the Residenz.

Another leading architect of the style was Karl Friedrich Schinkel. His Altes Museum, Neue Wache and Schauspielhaus, all in Berlin, are pure forms of neoclassicism. What Schinkel was to Berlin, von Klenze was to Munich.

In 1789, Munich Elector Karl Theodor commissioned an American, Benjamin Thompson (later made Count Rumford by the German royal court), and landscape gardener Friedrich von Sckell, to design Europe's first people's park, which became the English Garden. The Chinesischer Turm (Chinese Tower) was completed as a simple folly in 1790, long before it became a beerlover's mecca.

In 1808, King Max Joseph held Germany's first architectural contest to develop areas to the north and west of the city. Architects Ludwig von Sckell and Karl von Fischer won the commission, and with the help of Leo von Klenze (from 1816) they created the suburbs Maxvorstadt and Ludwig-Vorstadt.

Von Gärtner took over from von Klenze in 1827, and created landmarks such as the Staatsbibliothek (State Library) and the University. It was in this period that Ludwig I's court began to refer to Munich as the 'New Athens'.

Other buildings from this period are the neo-Gothic Maximilianeum (seat of the Bavarian parliament) and the Ethnology Museum. As the industrial revolution took hold, Munich's new brass foundries allowed Max II, the son of Ludwig I, to fulfil an old dream: the Bavaria statue, which was poured in hulking sections by artist Ferdinand von Miller. It was erected with great fanfare on the Theresienwiese in 1850, in time (of course) for Oktoberfest.

Revivalism The late-19th century brought a wave of derivative architecture based on old styles. On one hand, the use of steel allowed greater spans and large glass surfaces (exemplified by your average German Hauptbahnhof), which was taken up by the Art Nouveau movement in the early 20th century.

This development was preceded by the emergence of a graceful, intricate and at times irreverent style influenced by Englishman William Morris' flowing designs. In Germany this was called Jugendstil, and in Munich some lovely examples of this style can be found in Schwabing, Neuhausen, and Bogenhausen, among other districts.

A spate of new avenues and buildings appeared in Munich before the turn of the century, including the Prinzregentenstrasse and the Prince Regent Theatre, the Palace of Justice, the Bavarian National Museum, the German Museum as well as the Friedensengel (Angel of Peace) monument. Most of these works were supervised by master architects Gabriel von Seidl and August von Thiersch. The crowning glory of Marienplatz, the neogothic Neues Rathaus, was only completed in 1908 (although the layers of grime make it look much older).

Bauhaus Although it's hard to spot its traces in Munich today, the Bauhaus movement has been one of the 20th century's most influential styles. It began in 1919 with the founding by Walter Gropius of the Staatliches Bauhaus, a modern art and design institute in Weimar. The institute was later moved to Dessau and then to Berlin, before being closed by the Nazis in 1933. Gropius' aim, which he set out in his *Bauhaus Manifest*, was to bring together architects, painters, furniture designers and sculptors to create a unity of the arts. Detractors claim that it was often functional and impersonal, relying too heavily, for their liking, on cubist and constructivist forms. The institute's building in Dessau is typical of the style, but you can find the influence of Bauhaus everywhere in modern design. Wassily Kandinsky and Paul Klee, both painters of *Der Blaue Reiter* (the Blue Rider) group in Munich, taught at the institute before going into exile.

Post-1945 Nazi architecture, like Nazism itself, revelled in pomposity. Hitler's architect and political crony, Albert Speer, received the order to create works that would befit the Thousand Year Reich. Unfortunately for Speer, classicism had two 'neo' prefixes by the time he got his hands on it, which perhaps explains why Nazi monumentality often seemed absurd.

After Hitler, it took German architects a few years to plug back into the world scene. Postwar reconstruction demanded cheap buildings that could be erected quickly. Hubert Petschnigg's Thyssenhaus in Düsseldorf is considered one of the best works of the 1960s. The interior of Hans Scharoun's Philharmonie (1963) in Berlin hints at a terraced vineyard.

In Munich, Günther Behnisch and Frei Otto's Olympisches Stadion, built for the 1972 Olympic Games, is tent-like and one of Germany's best postwar constructions. Frei Otto had achieved fame a few years

earlier with his German pavilion at the 1967 Montreal World Expo.

SOCIETY & CONDUCT

In Munich, designer fashion co-exists with *Lederhosen* so you needn't dress up for dinner (unless you go to one of the top-end restaurants). Depending on the venue, slightly smarter clothing is recommended for a night at the theatre or the opera, but you might get by with jeans and a nice shirt or blouse. Many nightclubs have a dress code, but it's not always easy to figure it out – some bouncers simply have orders to let in a cross-section of characters, at other places beautiful people in black seem to have the best chances.

Müncheners are generally pretty helpful towards visitors. Many people speak English and may even volunteer directions or help you get to your destination if you're lost. At the same time, you may experience the odd gruff encounter to remind you that you're in a big city with large numbers of tourists. This can also happen if your clothing, skin colour or accent (if you speak German) is construed as 'foreign'. Note that this can easily also happen to *Zuogereisten* – basically, anyone who wasn't born and bred in the Munich region.

When invited to dinner you'd be advised to bring a little something – perhaps wine, flowers or a box of chocolates. If the host clearly went to a lot of trouble, it's a nice gesture to ring the next day or to write a little thankyou note. You may have to feel your way along for what works in conversation: the more 'intellectual' Müncheners will talk about anything, and everything, while some of the locals may not be able to see beyond the city limits. It *is* okay to mention the war, if done with tact and reverence; what will cause offence is a 'victor' mentality, which is perceived as righteous and gloating, or the notion that fascist ideas are intrinsically German.

At the start of a meal it is customary to declare 'Guten Appetit' (the closest equivalent in Anglo-Saxon countries is the French 'Bon Appetit') with a look around at your tablemates. Saying nothing before you dig in is considered bad manners. Before clinking glasses, the most common toast is 'prost' or 'prosit' (cheers).

Shaking hands is common among both men and women, as is a hug or a kiss on the cheek among young people (two to three times, on alternating cheeks). When making a phone call, give your name at the start (eg 'Smith, Grüss Gott'). This is especially important when booking a room by telephone. Germans consider it impolite or simply get annoyed when no name is given. If you don't want to give your name (when dealing with bureaucracy, for instance), just make one up.

It's important to use the formal 'Sie' form of address; some colleagues who've known each other for years never change to the informal 'du'. In bars or discos, the informal is heard more often but don't even consider saying 'du' to a shop assistant or to waiters unless you want bad service. The same applies to 'Ober', a term for head waiter which went out of fashion decades ago.

Academic titles are *very* important. If someone introduces him or herself as Dr Schnauzbart, then you should address that person as 'Doktor' or even 'Herr/Frau Doktor Schnauzbart'. If you have a title yourself, you may like to use it as well; it can be useful in situations where you want the extra respect.

In conversation, Germans like to look each other squarely in the eye. If you need to assert yourself, look back but keep an even tone of voice. Bureaucrats, shop owners, taxi drivers etc generally don't react well to excited protests (which doesn't mean you shouldn't stand your ground).

On the whole, Germans are not prudish. Nude bathing and mixed saunas are commonplace (many women, however, prefer single-sex saunas). Nude bathing areas are marked FKK, or form spontaneously in certain areas on beaches or the shores of lakes.

RELIGION

Given its monastic origins, it's no surprise that Munich is staunchly Catholic. The Reformation didn't make great inroads in Bavaria, and at the last census some 67% of the state's residents were registered as Roman Catholic and 24% Protestant. In cosmopolitan Munich the relation is 46% to 17%, with Muslims accounting for much of the remainder. There are less than 3000 Jews registered at Munich synagogues (that's up from 200 at the end of WWI).

Although church and state are separate, most Bavarians pay the 5% national 'church tax' which goes towards supporting church charities. Payment isn't obligatory, but you must formally leave the church if you don't want to pay. Once considered a social taboo, more and more people have left the church in recent years to cut their tax bill. Agnosticism and atheism, however, are usually the more pressing reasons.

LANGUAGE

German belongs to the Indo-European language group and is spoken by over 100 million people throughout the world, including Austria and parts of Switzerland. There are also ethnic German communities in neighbouring Eastern European countries such as Poland and the Czech Republic, although expulsion after 1945 reduced their numbers dramatically.

High German is the official and proper form of the language throughout the country, though most people also speak a local or regional dialect. The same is true of Munich, though only a small number of native Müncheners speak pure Bavarian.

It was the reformer Martin Luther who laid the groundwork for a unified written German language through his translation of the New Testament from the Greek in 1521–22. Until that time, nearly every German state had its own dialect, which was not necessarily understood elsewhere.

The advancement and establishment of German as an official language was the mission of language societies in the 17th century. In the 19th century Jacob Grimm, the founder of German philology, co-wrote the first German grammar book with his brother Wilhelm.

Regional dialects still thrive throughout Germany, especially in Cologne, rural Bavaria, Swabia and parts of Saxony. The

Bavarian for Beginners

Even those who've already mastered High German (native Germans included) can find *bayrisch* – the Bavarian dialect – nothing short of impenetrable. Twisted vowels, dropped endings, and a tendency to project from the gullet are but a few of the barriers to communication with the Lederhosen-and-Dirndl crowd. Not that it makes much sense to actually learn Bavarian: Müncheners don't take kindly to outsiders even trying, as it sounds all too often like parody. Nonetheless, it's useful to know a few basic words and phrases (High German and English translations are provided).

Grüss Gott! = Guten Tag! = Hello/G'day!
Isch mog gern a Bia = Ich möchte gerne ein Bier = I'd like a beer!
Schmeggst? = Schmeckt es? = Does it taste good?
Woa isscht de Toiletta? = Wo ist die Toilette = Where is the toilet?
Auf da Wiesn hods heidzudog nur no a Gwurl = Auf dem Wiesen war es heute ein einziges
   Gedränge = Oktoberfest was really jam-packed today.
Pfüad di = Auf Wiedersehen = Goodbye.

Sorb minority in eastern Germany has its own language. In northern Germany it's common to hear Plattdeutsch (Low German) spoken. Both High and Low German are distant relatives of English, and the fact that many German words survive in the English vocabulary today makes things easier for native English speakers.

For useful phrases in German, see the Language chapter.

Facts for the Visitor

WHEN TO GO

Munich's moods change with the seasons, and they all have something to offer. The biggest tourist rush naturally occurs between May and September, when the weather's the most reliable, leaving plenty of leeway for an intimate stay the rest of the year (except during the Christmas holidays and ski season). The shoulder seasons attract fewer tourists and if you're lucky, the weather can be wonderful. April and May are the flowering months, when Munich's many gardens and green areas are transformed. Early autumn can be unseasonably mild and sunny; Indian summers that last for weeks are not uncommon.

From November to March, however, Munich can be quite cold and miserable and the number of visitors plummets. In December and January, count on the sun going down around 4 pm (it gets dark earlier if it's overcast), and there are days when it seems like the sun never really comes up.

If you're keen on winter sports, note that there are a slew of ski resorts, slopes and cross-country trails in the nearby Bavarian Alps begin operating in (usually late) November and move into full swing after the New Year, closing down again when the snows begin to melt in March.

The Climate section and the Climate Charts in the preceding Facts about Munich chapter explain what to expect and when to expect it.

ORIENTATION

Munich is the capital of Bavaria, located on a vast plain in the south-eastern part of the state. A city of 1.3 million, Munich and its surrounding area is a separate region in itself. The Isar River wends its way down from the Alps some 60km to the south and up through Munich's core, just east of the Altstadt.

The Hauptbahnhof is less than 1km west of the Altstadt, the historic old centre of town. The Isar River flows through the eastern part of the city from south to north.

Munich is officially divided into numerous districts; formerly separate villages, they have been absorbed into the greater metropolitan area.

Hauptbahnhof On the north side of the Hauptbahnhof are mainly hotels; to the south and east is Munich's own 'silicon valley' with dozens of shops selling everything the computer geek could possibly want; to the south is Ludwigs-Vorstadt, a half-seedy, half-lively area that's packed with Turkish shops, restaurants, cafes and relatively inexpensive (if grotty) pensions and hotels.

Altstadt The Altstadt is the city centre. It's difficult to get lost in sight of the onion-domed towers of the Frauenkirche, which is a stone's throw from Marienplatz, the heart of the Altstadt. Pedestrianised Kaufingerstrasse runs west from Marienplatz to Karlsplatz (also known as Stachus) at the western boundary of the Altstadt. On its eastern side lies Lehel, a pretty residential district somewhat removed from the tourist rabble, with a few nice restaurants and pubs.

The city's historical centre is encircled by ring-roads in the position of the former city fortifications: Sonnenstrasse to the west, Oskar-Von-Miller-Ring and Von-der-Tann-Strasse to the north, Franz-Josef-Strauss-Ring, Karl-Scharnagl-Ring and Thomas-Wimmer-Ring – one road with three named sections – at the east, and Blumenstrasse and Frauenstrasse to the south.

North of Marienplatz is the Residenz (the former royal palace), with the National Theatre and Residenz Theatre. Just north of the Residenz is Odeonsplatz, home to the spectacular Theatinerkirche St Kajetan. East of Marienplatz is the Platzl quarter, with pubs and restaurants, and Maximilianstrasse, a fashionable street that's fun for strolling and window-shopping.

Just south of the centre on Museumsinsel, an island in the Isar, is the Deutsches Museum and the Forum Der Technik.

Westend Once a slum area, Westend, south-west of the Hauptbahnhof, now bristles with renovated houses, hip cafes, wine bars and some nicer hotels. It's also just west of the Theresienwiese, the sprawling meadow where Oktoberfest is held.

Schwabing The centre of the city's university and student life, Schwabing, north of Marienplatz, is bursting with energy.

The main stretch of chic cafes is along Leopoldstrasse, just west of the English Garden (Englischer Garten), but west Schwabing, south and west of the university, is more down-to-earth, with bookshops, cafes and reasonably-priced restaurants.

Eastern Munich North-east of the Altstadt but on the west side of the Isar, the English Garden sprawls northward. About 5km long and 1.5km wide, it's Europe's largest city park, stretching from the Prinzregentenstrasse (laid out by Prince Luitpold in the late 19th century) to the city's northern boundary. On the east side of the Isar, near the Ostbahnhof (East Train Station) is an enormous nightlife attraction, the Kunstpark Ost, a complex containing discos, restaurants, bars and cinemas.

Neuhausen North-west of the Hauptbahnhof is cosmopolitan Neuhausen, a more residential area that's home to the city's most popular hostel. The neighbourhood's hub, Rotkreuzplatz, is the terminus for the U1.

Western Munich Walking along Nymphenburger Strasse north-west from Rotkreuzplatz in Neuhausen brings you to Schloss Nymphenburg, the royal family's former summer residence, and its lovely gardens.

Northern Munich The main attraction north of the city is Olympiapark, site of the 1972 Olympic Games. The park today hosts a wide range of attractions, including major sporting events and the Tollwood Festival (see Public Holidays & Special Events later in this chapter). The BMW Museum is just north of the park.

MAPS
The tourist office produces a passable map of Munich. For the larger view, the auto association, Allgemeiner Deutscher Automobil Club (ADAC), Sendlinger-Tor-Platz 9, produces excellent road maps. More detailed maps can be obtained at most bookshops. Among the best city maps are those made by Falkplan, with a patented folding system, though some people prefer the one-sheet maps published by Hallwag or RV Verlag's EuroCity maps.

RESPONSIBLE TOURISM
Müncheners are big on recycling. There are services for the pick up of biodegradables, plastics and packaging, and paper. On the streets and in some public places (eg the airport and train stations) you will see compartmentalised rubbish bins and bottle and battery banks. In fact, Müncheners (and Germans in general) have become so efficient in sorting their rubbish that the recycling services are known to creak under the strain.

TOURIST OFFICES
Tourism in Munich runs like the train system – very efficiently. The legions of visitors, however, mean that queues can be long and staff are sometimes curt.

Local Tourist Offices
The central city tourist office is in the Neues Rathaus at Marienplatz (Map 7a, ☎ 23 33 02 72/73, fax 23 33 02 33, email tourismus@ muenchen.btl.de). It's open from 10 am to 8 pm weekdays (Saturday to 4 pm).

The city tourist office (Map 7a, ☎ 23 33 02 57/58, fax 23 33 02 33), at the eastern end of the Hauptbahnhof, is open from 9 am to 8 pm Monday to Saturday, from 10 am to 6 pm Sunday.

EurAide (Map 7a, ☎ 59 38 89), near platform No 11 at the Hauptbahnhof, is usually the best place to head for when you get into town. The office makes reservations, sells tickets for DB (Deutsche Bahn) trains and Munich public transportation. It also finds rooms for a small fee (see the Places to Stay chapter). Opening hours are from 7.45 am to noon and 1 to 6 pm daily, April to the end of Oktoberfest (early October) and from 9.30 am to noon and 1 to 4 pm weekdays, as well as Saturday morning, from October to June.

EurAide's free newsletter, *The Inside Track*, is packed with practical information about the city and it's surroundings, and gives discounts on money-changing (see the Money section later in this chapter). You can pick it up from a rack outside the door.

The room-finding service at the tourist office is free. You can book by calling with a credit card number (☎ 233 03 00), dropping by in person or by writing to Fremdenverkehrsamt München, 80313 Munich. There's no genuine tourist office in the airport, but the information desk in the main hall will field simple inquiries (such as for maps of the city or the underground rail network).

The Jugendinformationszentrum (Youth Information Centre, ☎ 51 41 06 60), a couple of blocks south of the Hauptbahnhof at the corner of Paul-Heyse-Strasse and Landwehrstrasse, is open from noon to 6 pm Monday to Friday (until 8 pm on Thursday). It has a wide range of printed information for young visitors to Munich and Germany.

The excellent *Infopool* (DM1), a young people's guide to Munich, is available from all of the tourist offices listed here.

Tourist Offices Abroad

The German National Tourist Office is a central, government-run agency which disseminates a wealth of free information about Germany. Phone, fax or email, and staff will send you pamphlets and maps of Munich and, of course, just about anywhere else in Germany.

The head office in Germany is at Beethovenstrasse 69, 60325 Frankfurt-am-Main (☎ 69 97 46 40, fax 75 19 03, email 113775.2520@compuserve.com). Its comprehensive Web site (also in English) is at www.germany-tourism.de. Branches and representative offices abroad include:

Australia
 (☎ 02-9267 8148, fax 9267 9035),
 PO Box A980, Sydney South, NSW 2135

Austria
 (☎ 01-513 27 92, fax 513 27 92 22, email 106167.3214@compuserve.com),
 Schubertring 12, 1010 Vienna
Canada
 (☎ 416-968 1570, fax 968 1986, email germanto@idirect.com),
 175 Bloor St East, North Tower, Suite 604, Toronto, Ont M4W 3R8
France
 (☎ 01 40 20 01 88, fax 40 20 17 00, email gnto_par@compuserve.com),
 9 Blvd de la Madeleine, 75001 Paris
Japan
 (☎ 03-3586 5046, fax 3586 5079, email dzt_tokyo@compuserve.com),
 7-5-56 Akasaka, Minato-ku, Tokyo 107-0052
Netherlands
 (☎ 020-697 8066, fax 691 2972, email duitsland@compuserve.com),
 Hoogoorddreef 76, 1101 BG Amsterdam ZO
Russia
 (☎ 095-975 3001, fax 975 2383),
 c/o Lufthansa German Airlines, Hotel Olympic Penta, Olimpiski prospekt 18/1, 129 110 Moscow
South Africa
 (☎ 011-643 1615, fax 484 2750),
 c/o Lufthansa German Airlines, 22 Girton Rd, Parktown, PO Box 10883, Johannesburg 2000
Switzerland
 (☎ 01-213 22 00, fax 212 0175, email gnto_zrh@compuserve.com),
 Talstrasse 62, 8001 Zürich
UK
 (☎ 020-7317 0908, fax 495 6129, email 106167.3216@compuserve.com),
 PO Box 2695, London W1A 3TN
USA
 (☎ 212-661 7200, fax 661 7174),
 Chanin Building, 122 East 42nd St, 52nd Floor, New York, NY 10168-0072
 (☎ 312-644 0723, fax 644 0724),
 401 North Michigan Ave, Suite 2525, Chicago, IL 60611

There are also offices or representatives in Brussels, Budapest, Copenhagen, Helsinki, Hong Kong, Madrid, Mexico City, Milan, Oslo, Prague, São Paulo, Seoul, Stockholm, Tel Aviv and Warsaw.

DOCUMENTS
Visas
Citizens of Australia, Canada, Israel, Japan, New Zealand, Singapore and the USA require

FACTS FOR THE VISITOR

only a valid passport (no visa) to enter Germany for stays of up to three months. European Union (EU) nationals and those from certain other European countries, including Switzerland and Poland, can enter on either a passport or their official identity card.

Nationals from most other countries need a so-called Schengen Visa, named after the Schengen Agreement that abolished passport controls between the Netherlands, Belgium, Austria, Luxembourg, Germany, France, Italy, Greece, Spain and Portugal. A visa for any of these countries should, in theory, be valid throughout the area, but it pays to double-check with the embassy or consulate of each country you intend to visit (the French in particular may prove to be difficult). Residency status in any of the Schengen countries (those listed above) negates the need for a visa, regardless of your nationality.

Three-month tourist visas are issued by all German embassies or consulates. They can often take a while to be processed, so make sure you leave enough time before your departure to apply. You will need a valid passport and sufficient funds to finance your stay. Fees will vary depending on the country.

Driving Licence

If you don't hold a European driving licence and plan to drive in Germany, obtain an International Driving Permit (IDP) from your local automobile association before you leave – you'll need a passport photo and a valid driving licence. IDPs are usually inexpensive and valid for one year. You're not required by law to carry an IDP when driving in Germany, but having one helps Germans make sense of your unfamiliar local licence (make sure you take that with you, too) and can make life much simpler, especially when hiring cars and motorcycles.

Useful Cards

You must be a member of a Hostelling International-affiliated organisation in order to stay at hostels run by the Deutsches Jugendherbergswerk (DJH). Non-Germans who don't have a HI card may obtain a so-called International Guest Card (IGC) at any hostel. It costs DM30 and is valid for one year. If you don't want it, DM6 per night will be added to your regular hostel rate; you'll be given a pass which is stamped once for each night and after six nights you automatically get the IGC. If

Travel Insurance

No matter how you're travelling to Germany, be sure to take out travel insurance. Depending on the scope of your coverage, this will protect you against sudden medical or legal expenses, luggage theft or loss, personal liability and the cancellation of, or delays in, your travel arrangements. Before you take out any insurance, be certain that you understand all the ramifications and what to do in case you need to file a claim. Also check your medical policy at home, since some already provide coverage worldwide, in which case you only need to protect yourself against other problems (also see Health later in this chapter).

Buy travel insurance as early as possible. If you buy it the week before you leave you may find, for example, that you are not covered for delays to your trip caused by strikes or industrial action. Some policies also cover ticket loss, so be sure to keep a photocopy of your ticket in a separate place. It's also a good idea to make a copy of your policy, in case the original is lost.

Paying for your airline ticket with a credit card often provides limited travel accident insurance, and you may be able to reclaim the payment if the operator doesn't deliver. In the UK, for instance, institutions issuing credit cards are required by law to reimburse consumers if a company goes into liquidation and the amount in contention is more than £100. Ask your credit card company what it's prepared to cover.

you're German or you have residency status in Germany, you are able to purchase the DJH/HI cards at the hostel (DM21/DM34 for juniors/seniors) when checking in. Independent hostels, usually called 'non-DJH hostel' in this guide, don't require a card, but in some cases you will be charged less if you have one.

The International Student Identity Card (ISIC), a plastic ID-style card with your photograph, provides discounts on many forms of transport (including airlines and local public transport), cheap or free admission to museums and sights, and cheap meals in some university cafeterias. If you're aged under 26 but not a student, you can apply for a GO25 card issued by the Federation of International Youth Travel Organisations (FIYTO) or the Euro 26 card, which go under different names in various countries. Both give much the same discounts and benefits as an ISIC.

All these cards are issued by student unions, hostelling organisations or youth-oriented travel agencies. They do not automatically entitle you to discounts, and some companies and institutions refuse to recognise them altogether, but you won't find out until you flash the card.

Seniors' Cards Museums and other attractions, public swimming pools, spas and some forms of transport such as DB may offer discounts to retired people, old-age pensioners and those over 60 (slightly younger for women). Make sure you bring proof of age in case that helpful *Herr* or friendly *Frau* in Munich – polite to a fault – is not going to believe you're a day over 39.

For a small fee, European nationals aged over 60 can get a Rail Europe Senior Card as an add-on to their national rail senior pass. It entitles the holder to reduced European fares; the savings vary according to the route.

Photocopies
The hassles brought on by losing your passport can be considerably reduced if you have a record of its number and issue date, or even better, photocopies of the relevant data pages. A photocopy of your birth certificate can also be useful.

Also add the serial numbers of your travellers cheques (cross them off as you cash them) and photocopies of your credit cards, airline ticket and other travel documents. Keep all this emergency material separate from your passport, cheques and cash, and leave extra copies with someone you can rely on back home. Add some emergency money, US$100 in cash, say, to this separate stash. If you do lose your passport, notify the police immediately to get a statement, and contact your nearest consulate.

EMBASSIES & CONSULATES
Your Own Embassy
As a tourist, it's important to realise what your own embassy – the embassy of the country of which you are a citizen – can and can't do.

Generally speaking, it won't be much help in emergencies if the trouble you're in is remotely your own fault. Remember that you are bound by the laws of the country you're visiting. Your embassy will not be sympathetic if you end up in jail after committing a crime locally, even if such actions are legal in your own country.

In genuine emergencies you might get some assistance, but only if other channels have been exhausted. For example, if you need to get home urgently, a free ticket home is exceedingly unlikely – the embassy would expect you to have insurance. If you have all your money and documents stolen, it might assist in getting a new passport, but a loan for onward travel is out of the question.

Embassies used to keep letters for travellers or have a small reading room with home newspapers, but these days the mail holding service has been stopped and even newspapers tend to be out of date.

German Embassies Abroad
German embassies around the world include the following:

Australia
(π 02-6270 1911),
119 Empire Circuit, Yarralumla, ACT 2600

FACTS FOR THE VISITOR

Austria
(☎ 0222-711 54),
Metternichgasse 3, Vienna 3
Canada
(☎ 613-232 1101),
1 Waverley St, Ottawa, Ont K2P 0T8
France
(☎ 01 53 83 45 00),
13–15 Ave Franklin Roosevelt, 75008 Paris
Ireland
(☎ 01-269 3011),
31 Trimleston Ave, Booterstown, Dublin 4
Japan
(☎ 03-3473 0151),
5–10, 4-chome, Minami-Azabu, Minato-ki, Tokyo 106
Netherlands
(☎ 070-342 0600),
Groot Hertoginnelaan 18–20, 2517 EG The Hague
Russia
(☎ 095-956 1080),
Ul Mosfilmovskaya 56, 119285 Moscow
New Zealand
(☎ 04-473 6063),
90–92 Hobson St, Wellington
South Africa
(☎ 012-344 3854),
180 Blackwood St, Arcadia, Pretoria 0083
Switzerland
(☎ 031-359 4111),
Willadingweg 83, 3006 Bern
UK
(☎ 020-7824 1300),
23 Belgrave Square, London SW1X 8PZ
USA
(☎ 202-298 8140),
4645 Reservoir Rd NW, Washington, DC 20007-1998

Consulates in Munich

Excellent consular representation as well as a superb rail and bus network make Munich a popular place to begin a journey into Eastern Europe or Asia.

Most of the countries below have embassies in Berlin, but the queues at their consulates in Munich are generally shorter. The main ones include:

Austria
(☎ 99 81 50) Ismaninger Strasse 136
Belgium
(☎ 286 60 90) Brienner Strasse 14
Bulgaria
(☎ 15 50 26) Böcklinstrasse 1

Canada
(☎ 219 95 70) Tal 29
Czech Republic
(☎ 95 01 24/25/26) Siedlerstrasse 2, Unterföhring
Denmark
(☎ 545 85 40) Sendlinger-Tor-Platz 10
Finland
(☎ 91 07 22 57/58) Arabellastrasse 33
France
(☎ 419 41 10) Möhlstrasse 5
Greece
(☎ 49 20 61) Dingolfinger Strasse 6
India
(☎ 38 21 16 55/56) Petuelring 130
Indonesia
(☎ 29 46 09) Widenmayerstrasse 24
Ireland
(☎ 98 57 23) Mauerkircherstrasse 1a
Italy
(☎ 418 00 30) Möhlstrasse 3
Japan
(☎ 471 60 40) Prinzregentenplatz 10
Netherlands
(☎ 545 96 70) Nymphenburger Strasse 1
Norway
(☎ 22 41 70) Promenadeplatz 7
Poland
(☎ 418 60 80) Ismaninger Strasse 62a
Portugal
(☎ 29 16 31 25) Maximiliansplatz 15
Russia
(☎ 59 25 28) Seidlstrasse 28
Slovakia
(☎ 910 20 60) Vollmannstrasse 25d
Slovenia
(☎ 543 98 19) Lindwurmstrasse 14
Spain
(☎ 998 47 90) Oberföhringer Strasse 45
Sweden
(☎ 54 52 12 15) Josephspitalstrasse 15
Switzerland
(☎ 286 62 00) Brienner Strasse 14
Thailand
(☎ 168 97 88) Prinzenstrasse 13
Turkey
(☎ 178 03 10) Menzinger Strasse 3
UK
(☎ 21 10 90, also for Australian nationals during Oktoberfest) Bürkleinstrasse 10
USA
(☎ 288 80, ☎ 288 87 22 for US citizen services and passport issues) Königinstrasse 5

CUSTOMS

Articles that you take to Germany for your personal use may be imported free of duty and tax with some conditions. The usual allowances apply to duty-free goods purchased at the airport or on ferries: tobacco (200 cigarettes or 100 cigarillos or 50 cigars or 250g of loose tobacco), alcohol (1L of strong liquor or 2L of less than 22% alcohol by volume *plus* 2L of wine), coffee and tea (500g or 200g of extracts *and* 100g of tea or 40g tea extracts), perfume (50g of perfume or scent *and* 0.25L of eau de toilette) and other products up to a value of DM350.

Do not confuse these with duty-paid items (including alcohol and tobacco) bought at normal shops and supermarkets in another EU country and brought into Germany, where certain goods might be more expensive. Then the allowances are more than generous: 800 cigarettes, 200 cigars, or 1kg of loose tobacco; 10L of spirits (more than 22% alcohol by volume), 20L of fortified wine or aperitif, 90L of wine or 110L of beer; petrol reserves of up to 10L.

Tobacco products and alcohol may only be brought in by people aged 17 and over; the importation of duty-free coffee, oddly, is barred to those under 15. There are no currency import restrictions.

Note that duty-free shopping within the EU was abolished in mid-1999. This means that you can still enter a EU country, like Germany, from, say, the USA or Australia, but you can't buy duty-free goods in, say, France and go to the UK.

MONEY
Currency

The Deutschmark (DM), usually just called the Mark or D-Mark (pronounced 'daymark'), consists of 100 Pfennigs. Coins include one, two, five, 10 and 50 Pfennigs, as well as DM1, DM2 and DM5. There are banknotes of DM5, DM10, DM20, DM50, DM100, DM200, DM500 and DM1000 (though, if you're lucky enough to have one or both of the last two, you may have trouble changing them). Beware of confusing the old DM5 and new DM20 banknotes, which are the same colour and have similar designs, although the DM20 note is larger. And watch out for counterfeit banknotes made on colour photocopy machines!

Exchange Rates

Exchange rates at the time of writing were as follows:

country	unit		DM
Australia	A$1	=	DM1.23
Austria	AS1	=	DM0.14
Canada	C$1	=	DM1.31
Denmark	Dkr1	=	DM0.26
France	1FF	=	DM0.30
Japan	¥100	=	DM0.02
Netherlands	fl	=	DM0.89
New Zealand	NZ$1	=	DM0.99
South Africa	R1	=	DM0.31
Switzerland	Sfr	=	DM1.22
UK	UK£1	=	DM3.11
USA	US$1	=	DM1.94

Exchanging Money

The easiest places to change money are banks or foreign-exchange counters at the airport and train stations. Post offices often have money-changing facilities as well, and rates for cash – though not for travellers cheques – tend to be better than at banks. Commissions here are DM2 for cash transactions if the exchanged amount is under DM200, and no fee if it's higher. Travellers cheques cost a flat DM6 each.

At banks and exchange offices, the charge usually comes to between DM5 and DM10 per transaction. Some banks have currency exchange machines outside the main entrance but they don't give very good rates. The branches of the main German banks, such as Hypovereinsbank on the corner of Schillerstrasse in front of the Hauptbahnhof, have ATMs that accept major credit cards.

Reisebank has two branches at the Hauptbahnhof; it's useful to note that presenting a copy of EurAide's newsletter *The Inside Track* will get you a 50% reduction on commissions at those branches (see Local Tourist Offices earlier in this section). There are also branches of Deutsche Bank, Hypovereinsbank and Sparkasse on Marienplatz (the Deutsche Bank has a currency-exchange machine outside).

Deutsche Bank and Citibank both have offices on Rotkreuzplatz, close to the hostel

(Jugendherberge München). The Postbank, which offers very good exchange rates, is in the post office opposite the Hauptbahnhof at Bahnhofplatz 1.

Cash Nothing beats cash for convenience or risk. If you lose it, it's gone forever and very few travel insurers will come to your rescue. Those that will, limit the amount to about US$300.

It's still a good idea, though, to bring some local currency in cash, if only to tide you over until you get to an exchange facility or find an automatic teller machine (ATM). The equivalent of, say, US$100 should usually be enough. Remember that banks and exchange offices always accept paper money but very rarely coins in foreign currencies.

Travellers Cheques & Eurocheques The main idea of carrying travellers cheques rather than cash is the protection they offer from theft, though their popularity is waning as more travellers – including those on tight budgets – deposit their money in their bank at home and withdraw it as they go along through ATMs.

Travellers cheques are *not* commonly used to pay for store-bought goods, at restaurants or hotels, especially if they are not issued in Deutschmarks. Cheques issued in any other currency must be exchanged into local currency at a bank, exchange office or post office (bring your passport). Most commonly recognised are American Express and Thomas Cook cheques, and neither company charges commission for exchanges at their own offices. Both also have efficient replacement policies. You'll find American Express (Map 7a, ☎ 29 09 01 45) at Promenadeplatz 6 and Thomas Cook (☎ 383 88 30) at Kaiserstrasse 45.

Another method of payment is the Eurocheque, a guaranteed bank cheque. To obtain Eurocheques, you need a European bank account and a cheque-cashing card, the so-called EC-Card, which doubles as an ATM card. Depending on the bank, it takes at least two weeks after applying for the bank to issue the card and the cheques. Eurocheques cover a maximum of DM400.

Until now, they have been widely accepted in Germany, but their popularity is decreasing because of the high commission (DM4 to DM6 per cheque) charged by banks.

ATMs Automatic teller machines are ubiquitous in Munich; occasionally you may have to swipe your card through a slot to gain entry to a secure area. Most machines take Visa and MasterCard, and if your bank at home is part of the Cirrus, Plus or Maestro systems, you'll be able to use your ATM card to withdraw money right out of your home account. Check the fees and availability of services with your bank before you leave. Always keep the number handy of where to report lost or stolen cards.

International Transfers Money sent by wire transfer from your bank to a bank in Munich should reach you within a week. Note that some banks charge an exorbitant amount just for receiving the money (fees of up to DM50 are common), unless you have an account with them. Opening an account, however, may well be impractical or even impossible to do.

For emergencies, Western Union or MoneyGram offer ready and fast international cash transfers through agent banks such as

Credit Cards

All the major international cards (eg MasterCard, Visa and American Express) are recognised but still not widely accepted, except at major hotels, petrol stations and large shops and department stores. It's best *not* to assume that you'll be able to pay for your meal, room or purchase with a credit card. Some stores may require a minimum purchase, others may refuse to accept a credit card even if the credit card companies' logos are displayed in the window.

Nevertheless, it can't hurt to take your card along, if only for emergencies or for renting a car. Check with your credit card issuer about fees and interest rates for cash withdrawals through ATMs.

Postbank or Reisebank. Cash sent becomes available as soon as the order has been entered into the computer system, ie instantly. Commissions are paid by the person making the transfer; the amount varies from country to country. Count on about US$40 for amounts up to US$300 and US$70 for amounts over US$500 but under US$1000.

Costs

Naturally, it's easy to spend lots of money in Munich and a bit harder to spend little. The secret to spending less is to cut costs where you can, such as with accommodation and food. Hostels, private rooms and simple pensions all cost well under DM50 per person.

Preparing your own meal or getting food from an *Imbiss* (snack bar) can save you a bundle. If you're eating at a restaurant, avoid lots of drinks since even non-alcoholic beverages tend to be quite expensive.

Buying passes keeps public transport costs way down (see the Getting Around chapter). If you're a student, bring along your ID for heavy discounts (see Useful Cards earlier in this chapter). If you're very economical, you can expect to survive on DM60 to DM90 per day.

Tipping & Bargaining

At restaurants, the *Bedienung* (service charge) is always included in bills and tipping is not compulsory. If you're satisfied with the service, simply round up the amount by 5 to 10% (also see the Places to Eat chapter.) Rather than leaving your money on the table, tip as you're handing over the money by announcing the amount you want to pay. If your bill comes to DM57 and you want to give a DM3 tip, say '60, bitte'. If you have the exact amount, just say 'Stimmt so' (roughly, 'that's fine'). Taxi drivers, too, expect a small tip. In general, a tip of 10% is considered generous.

Bargaining almost never occurs in Germany, certainly not in shops or restaurants. At hotels, you can sometimes ask for a lower rate which you may get if business is slow. Haggling is commonplace, however, at flea markets and you should be able to

get at least 10 to 25% off the asking price as long as you appear confident. Prices at produce markets are usually not negotiable, though vendors may throw in an extra tomato or two towards the end of the day.

Discounts

Students, seniors, children and the unemployed are the groups that most commonly qualify for discounts. Expect to show ID or proof. At museums and major sights, you will get about 50% off the regular admission prices. There are also reduced rates for public transport, public pools, ice rinks and other facilities.

Taxes & Refunds

Most German goods and services include a value-added tax (VAT) called *Mehrwertsteuer* (or MwSt) of 16%. Non-EU residents leaving the EU can have this tax (minus processing fee) refunded for goods (not services) bought, which is definitely worth it for large purchases.

Check that the shop where you're buying from has the necessary Tax-Free Shopping Cheque forms. The shop will issue you a cheque for the amount of VAT to be refunded, which you can cash in at VAT Cash Refund offices when leaving the country. Before you can get your money, the Tax-Free Shopping Cheque, together with the invoices/receipts, must be stamped by German customs as you're leaving the country. You're not allowed to use the items purchased until you're outside of Germany.

If you're flying out of Germany, have the paperwork stamped at the airport *before* you check in for your flight (with the exception of Frankfurt airport, where you check in first and then proceed to customs with your luggage). Note that you will have to show the goods. Refunds are made directly at VAT Cash Refund desks at the airports. If you're travelling on to another EU country, you must go through the same procedure at the EU airport from which you're departing for your non-EU destination.

If you want to avoid the lines at the VAT Cash Refund office, you can mail the customs-stamped forms and receipts to

euro currency converter DM1 = €.51

them after you return home and ask that the refund be issued to your credit card or mailed as a cheque.

Some 17,000 shops, including Germany's biggest department stores, are affiliated with the Tax-Free Shopping Cheque service; they can be identified by a special label on their window reading 'Tax-Free for Tourists'. Printed information is available at affiliated shops, some tourist offices, major hotels, airports and harbours.

POST & COMMUNICATIONS

There are dozens of post offices in Munich, but most have restricted opening hours. The best you'll do is the main post office at Bahnhofplatz 1, in the spanking new building just opposite the Hauptbahnhof, with telephone and fax services. It's open from 7 am to 8 pm weekdays, from 8 am till 4 pm Saturday and 9 am to 3 pm Sunday.

Stamps are generally only sold at post offices, though there may be stamp machines outside the main entrance. Occasionally, souvenir and postcard shops in tourist resorts also carry stamps. Letters sent within Germany usually take only one day for delivery; those addressed to destinations within Europe or to North America take four to six days and to Australasia five to seven days. Most post offices also exchange currency and travellers cheques and are a good place to fall back on when the banks are closed (see Exchanging Money earlier in this section).

Postal Rates

Within Germany and the EU, normal-sized postcards cost DM1, a 20g letter is DM1.10 and a 50g letter is DM2.20. Postcards to North America and Australasia cost DM2, a 20g airmail letter is DM3 and a 50g airmail letter is DM4. If the postcard or letter is oversized, there is a significant surcharge, sometimes up to triple the base rate. German postal workers can be very finicky about this and are bound to measure any letter that looks even remotely like it might not be standard sized. A parcel up to 2kg within Germany costs DM6.90. Surface-mail parcels up to 2kg within Europe are

DM12 and to destinations elsewhere DM15. Fees for airmail parcels depend on weight and destination. For instance, a 2kg parcel sent somewhere within Europe is DM38, to the US it costs DM71 and to Australia DM91.

Sending & Receiving Mail

Mail can be sent *poste restante* to any post office (select one, then inquire about the exact address). German post offices will hold mail for only two weeks, so plan your drops carefully. Ask those sending you mail to clearly mark the letter or package *Postlagernd* and to write your name clearly, followed by the address of the post office (eg the main post office at Bahnhofplatz 1, 80074 Munich). Bring your passport or other photo ID when picking up mail. There is no fee for this service.

You can also have mail sent to the American Express office (☎ 29 09 01 45) at Promenadeplatz 6, 80333 Munich. In order to avoid a charge, you must present your Amex card or travellers cheques (otherwise it's DM2 per item). Make sure to include the words 'Client's Mail' somewhere on the envelope. American Express holds mail for 30 days but won't accept registered mail or parcels.

Telephone

Making phone calls in Germany is simple. You can make international phone calls from just about any post office, but it's cheaper and more convenient to go to a pay phone and use phonecards which allow you to make calls of any length to anywhere in the world. If you're calling abroad, look for a pay phone marked 'International.'

Most public phones in Germany only accept phonecards nowadays, which saves you carrying around a pocketful of change. Although it's a good idea to carry both a card and a few coins. Cards are sold at post offices and occasionally at tourist offices, news kiosks and public transport offices.

Phonecards are available for DM12 and for DM50. When using coins or the DM12 card, call units cost DM0.20; with the DM50 card it's DM0.19 per unit. If you can, refrain from calling from your hotel room, since you'll often be charged DM0.60 or even DM0.80 per unit. You can save considerably if the person you want to contact is willing to call you back. Just place a short call to relay your hotel and room number and tell whoever is calling you back to dial their international access code plus ☎ 4930 and that number. You can do the same thing from pay phones that also receive calls by passing on the number next to the notation *Standort* (location) somewhere in the box/booth.

Also note that calls made *to* cellular phones cost a lot more than those to a stationary number, though how much more depends on the service used by the cellular-phone owner. Numbers starting with ☎ 0130 are toll-free.

For directory assistance within Germany, dial ☎ 11833; for numbers abroad it's ☎ 11834. But it's expensive: charges for the first 30 seconds are DM0.96, then DM0.12 for every subsequent 3.8 seconds.

Telephone Rates Since the monopoly status enjoyed by Deutsche Telecom (DT) was lifted on 1 January 1998, a bewildering number of other long-distance providers have entered the market, driving prices down. (DT continues its grip on local calls.) In most cases, getting the low rates means dialling a five-digit access number before the number you're trying to reach. This only works from private lines and *not* from pay phones which are all owned by DT (so far).

Increasingly faced with competition, DT too has lowered rates, though these still do not apply to calls made from pay phones! This means that, for now, travellers will continue to depend on DT and their incredibly confusing rate plan divided into zones and time periods.

How long you can talk per phone unit depends on where and when you are calling. For example, a three-minute call from Munich to Berlin made at 3 pm on a weekday costs DM1.80; the same call after 9 pm costs DM0.96. If you're in Cologne and calling Düsseldorf, you pay DM0.72 at 3 pm and DM0.36 after 9 pm for three minutes.

International calls are also subject to zones and time periods. Reduced rates are available after 6 pm and before 8 am to EU countries and between 3 am and 2 pm to the USA and Canada. Calls to Australia and New Zealand cost the same all day. The length of time you can talk per unit is:

country	standard rates	reduced rates
USA/Canada	5 seconds	5.46 seconds
Australia/ New Zealand	3 seconds	3 seconds
EU countries	7.2 seconds	9 seconds

In other words, a three-minute call at standard rates to North America will cost you DM4.32, to the UK DM3 and to Australia DM7.20.

To ring abroad from Germany, dial ☎ 00 followed by the country and local area codes and number. The country code for Germany is ☎ 49.

A reverse-charge call (or *R-Gespräch)* from Germany is only possible to a limited number of countries. For phone calls through the German operator, dial ☎ 0010. To reach the operator direct in the USA dial ☎ 0130 followed by ☎ 0010 (AT&T), ☎ 0012 (MCI), ☎ 0013 (Sprint) and to Canada dial ☎ 0014. To Australia, dial ☎ 0130-80 06 61 for the Optus operator and ☎ 0130-80 00 61 for Telstra.

Fax & Telegraph

If you're staying at upmarket hotels, fax transmissions are generally not a problem. There's usually no fee for receiving faxes, though sending them can cost you a bundle, so it pays to check in advance. Most copy shops will also let you send faxes, as will some Internet cafes.

If you carry a laptop with a fax modem, you only pay for the cost of the telephone call (keep in mind that hotel phone rates are exorbitant). Cheaper, in most cases, is the use of public fax phones now in place at larger post offices. These operate with a phonecard from which the regular cost of the call, plus a DM2 service charge, is deducted if the connection

FACTS FOR THE VISITOR

succeeds. Occasionally you can also find public fax phones in train stations.

If you need to send a telegram, you can do so at post offices, from many hotels, or by calling ☎ 0180-512 12 10/11 (for telegrams sent within Germany) or ☎ 0800-330 11 33 (outside of Germany). Within Germany, up to 10 words cost DM29, up to 30 words are DM35. Up to 20 words within Europe cost DM40, outside of Europe it's DM50.

Email & Internet Access

In order to maintain your Internet links while in Munich, you can bring along your laptop PC and modem and dial your home country service provider (or even take out a local account).

Getting your modem to work with German phone lines can be quite frustrating. German phone plugs are unique and you're quite likely to need an adaptor to get online. It's best to pick one up in your home country, though they're also sold at electronics stores in Germany. There are usually no problems getting connected from a line in a private home. At some hotels, however, you'll find that the phone cable is wired right into the wall and/or the phone itself. Larger hotels sometimes have digital (ISDN) lines or complex internal phone systems that require you to make changes to your modem string in order to get an outside line.

If that doesn't work, try an Internet cafe where you can buy online time and have a drink. The cheapest, most practical place is the Cyberb@r on the 4th floor of the Hertie department store (Map 7a, ☎ 551 20) at Bahnhofplatz 7. It charges DM3 for 30 minutes, and they'll let you surf 15 minutes for DM1.50 if you ask. The Cyberb@r in the top storey of Karstadt am Dom department store (☎ 260 02 30), Neuhauser Strasse 21, charges the same rates.

The Internet Café (☎ 260 78 15), Altheimer Eck 12, near Marienplatz, has a dozen-odd cyberterminals of varying quality. You can send email and surf free with any food purchase, but both the chow and the service are mediocre. There's a branch (☎ 129

11 20) at Nymphenburger Strasse 145, just east of Rotkreuzplatz near the hostel.

On the south side of the Hauptbahnhof, the pretentious and crowded Times Square Online Bistro (Map 7a, ☎ 550 88 00), is open from 6 am to 1 am daily. The telecom links are ultra-quick, and it's one of the few places in Munich where you can transfer files to/from floppy disk, but it's expensive: DM9 per half-hour.

INTERNET RESOURCES

The World Wide Web is a rich resource for travellers. You can research your trip, hunt down bargain air fares, book hotels, check on weather conditions or chat with locals and other travellers about the best places to visit (or avoid!).

One place to start your Web explorations is the Lonely Planet Web site (www.lonely planet.com). Here you'll find succinct summaries on travelling to most places on earth, postcards from other travellers and the Thorn Tree bulletin board, where you can ask questions before you go, or dispense advice when you get back. You can also find travel news and updates to many of our most popular guidebooks, and the sub-WWWay section links you to the most useful travel resources elsewhere on the Web.

There's a huge number of Web sites dedicated to Munich history, culture, travel, education and institutions. The more useful ones include:

www.muenchen-tourist.de
> The home page of Munich's tourist office, with a wealth of information on sights, culture, accommodation, seasonal events, museum links, etc. In English and German.

www.munich-online.de
> Sleek, comprehensive site set up like a magazine, and run by a private Munich PR agency. Includes current listings of films, cultural events, travel, etc. In German only.

www.goon.de
> Similar to munich-online but from the Springer publishing house.

www.muenchenticket.de
> City-run site with all the latest concert listings and topical articles.

www.sueddeutschezeitung.de
> Daily national news coverage, strong on Munich

Can someone tie my shoelaces?

Soaking up the sun on Marienplatz

Street musician on Kaufingerstrasse

Browsing in bookshops on Rindermarkt

Brake at the Chinese Tower beer garden

Grotto courtyard at Residenz

Olympia Park

Schloss Blutenburg: once the summer residence of the Wittelsbach dynasty

Surf's up in the English Garden

Bavaria Statue

and Bavaria. Read tomorrow's paper the night before. In German only.

www.abendzeitung.de
Same thing as the Süddeutsche's page, except that it appears in the morning for this popular local broadsheet. In German only.

www.uni-muenchen.de
Site maintained by the Ludwig-Maximilian-Universität, with lots of info and links. In German only.

www.bayern.de/BayernInfo/welcomeE.html
The Bavarian government's official site, with background of politics, economy, culture, tourism etc. Strong on statistics. In English.

bahn.hafas.de
The German Railways' timetables page. Useful for arranging train travel to/from Munich. In English and German.

BOOKS
Lonely Planet

Lonely Planet's *Germany* guide is an excellent source for those planning to tour the country extensively. It contains up-to-date information on all popular mainstream travel spots, as well as fascinating off-the-beaten track destinations. For those spending more time in Germany, LP's city guide to *Berlin*, should come in handy. Lonely Planet's *Western Europe*, *Central Europe* and *Europe on a shoestring* all include a big and comprehensive Germany chapter for those on a grand European tour. Lonely Planet also publishes a useful *German phrasebook*. All books are available at good bookstores or may be ordered from the Lonely Planet Web site at www.lonely planet.com.

Guidebooks

General English-language travel guides to Munich are thin on the ground.

If you're planning an extensive stay in Munich, you might invest in *Munich in Your Pocket* by Dee Pattee, a thoughtful little volume packed with tips on dealing with bureaucracy to children's amusements to visiting an estate agent.

One quirky little title is *Munich Up Close* by Christopher Middleton, which zooms into individual neighbourhoods with the aid of dozens of isometric maps with short but interesting text descriptions. It's out of print but still available via some Internet book shops.

And of course, there's Larry Hawthorne's specialised *The Beer Drinker's Guide to Munich* with detailed descriptions of nearly 50 beer gardens in Munich and environs.

Those able to read German will find a big choice of guidebooks on Munich. Cultural guidebooks are very popular, and any German speaker with a special interest in architecture and the arts should pick up a copy of *Knaurs Kulturführer München*, published by Ddroemer Knaur Verlag. A drier, but much more comprehensive overview is provided by Dumont's *Kunstreiseführer Oberbayern*.

The Falk Verlag, best known for its excellent maps, also publishes a series of magazine-sized guidebooks that are most useful for getting a pictorial overview of Munich (DM14.80). In the same vein are the *Bildatlas* published by HB Verlag (DM14.80) and the classy special-edition magazines by *Geo* (DM8.50).

History & Politics

Seminal overviews of Munich history and politics in English are virtually non-existent. Most authors focus on crucial, relatively short periods in the city's history (the Third Reich, naturally, is a favourite) or examine Munich's role in a larger German context.

Among the former group, *Where Ghosts Walked: Munich's Road to the Third Reich* by David Clay Large gives a fascinating account of the motives and personalities behind the city's descent into Nazism. *Spheres of Influence* by Lloyd C Gardner attempts to trace the division of Europe to British appeasement under the 1938 Munich agreement, which traded Czechoslovakia's freedom for a brittle, short-lived period of peace. In a similar vein, *Reappraising the Munich Pact*, edited by Maya Latynski, is a collection of essays from noted historians, written more than 50 years after the event.

One of the few German resistance movements is chronicled in *The White Rose: Munich 1942–1943* by Ingo Scholl and

Dorothee Solle. Frau Scholl's children were Hans and Sophie Scholl, who were executed in 1943 for their underground activities against Hitler.

Among more general offerings, *The Origins of Modern Germany* by Geoffrey Barraclough is an excellent introduction to the complex history of the country. *A History of Modern Germany* by Hajo Holborn is a three-volume work that begins with the 15th century and traces developments up to the division in 1945. *The German Empire 1871–1918* by Hans-Ulrich Wehler is a translation of an authoritative German work on the period from Bismarck to the Weimar Republic. Another highly readable translation is *The History of Germany since 1789* by Golo Mann. *Germany 1866–1945* by Gordon Craig is also worthwhile as a general overview.

The Course of German History by AJP Taylor outlines developments since 1815. *Bismarck, the Man and the Statesman* by the same author is a revealing study of the Iron Chancellor placed in historical context. *The Wars of Frederick the Great* by Dennis Showalter focuses on 18th century Prussia.

Special Interest

If you enjoy a lofty, intellectual tone, Thomas Mann's carefully sculpted short stories and novellas set in Munich are a delight. *Gladius Dei* begins with the classic phrase 'Munich shone' (which the city has adopted on numerous occasions), while *Herr und Hund* is set in and around the English Garden.

Art students and professionals will love *The Munich Secession: Art and Artists in Turn of the Century Munich* by Mara Makele, which takes a fresh look at that split of avant-gardists and traditional painters in the Bavarian capital.

Karl Valentin by Michael Schulte is a portrayal of the ultimately tragic life of Munich's most famous comedian, with extensive photography.

There's more than sausages and sauerkraut in *German Baking Today* and *German Cooking Today*. Both by Dr Oetker, these volumes take a healthy approach to the delights of German cuisine and are filled with easy recipes and some fine colour illustrations. One very beautiful book on the subject of German food is *Germany: A Culinary Tour* by Wolfgang Reichert. Within you'll find remarkable photographs of each classic recipe while learning to fend with such delights as roast leg of wild boar.

The *Xenophobe's Guide to the Germans* by Stefan Zeidenitz and Ben Barkow is the irreverent work of two German Anglophiles. The wit might wear thin at times, but beneath this and the book's unashamed stereotyping are some worthwhile tips on Germans and codes of conduct in Germany. Be warned, though – not all Germans will appreciate the humour.

Bertold Brecht's life in 1920s Munich is included in volumes such as *The Brecht Memoir* by Eric Bentley, and *Brecht: A Choice of Evils* by Martin Esslin.

NEWSPAPERS & MAGAZINES
German

Munich's most widely read newspaper is the *Süddeutsche Zeitung*, which can be surprisingly liberal given the conservative fabric of Bavaria. By some measures it's more widely read than the respected, if somewhat dusty, *Frankfurter Allgemeine Zeitung*.

The only other 'serious' Munich paper is the *Münchner Merkur*, the mouthpiece of the Bavarian conservative party, the CSU, and therefore difficult to take seriously.

The *Abendzeitung* is an easy-to-digest complement to the *Süddeutsche Zeitung* which, despite the name, appears in the morning. It teeters on the edge of the gutter but somehow manages to stay respectable. Its main rival is the *tz*, a colourful, thinner broadsheet which aims lower in editorial terms, as does the Munich edition of Europe's largest-circulation paper – the *Bild-Zeitung*, which carries headlines of the 'My Husband was an Alien' ilk and lots of topless girls.

Der Spiegel and *Focus*, both popular weekly magazines, offer hard-hitting investigative journalism, a certain degree of government criticism, and other deep thoughts between covers often featuring scantily clad models. *Stern* used to be similar but has become more light-weight and trivial in its coverage. *Die Zeit* is a high-brow weekly newspaper that has been struggling for years.

English

English-language newspapers and magazines – mostly from the UK and the USA – are readily available in railway stations, bookstores and international newsagents, such as Sussman's in the Hauptbahnhof.

The *International Herald Tribune*, edited in Paris with wire stories from the *New York Times* and *Washington Post*, is the most commonly available English-language daily paper; it sells for DM3.50.

The biggies on offer from the UK include *The Guardian* (DM3.80), the *Financial Times* (DM4.30), *The London Times* (DM5), as well as tabloids like the *Daily Mail* and *The Sun*. From the USA, *USA Today* (DM3.50) has made huge inroads, and the *Wall Street Journal* (DM4.20) is also available.

As for magazines, *The Economist* (DM8) is on sale widely, as are the international editions of *Time* (DM6.80) and *Newsweek* (DM6.90). Practically the whole gamut of women's, car, lifestyle and speciality magazines is available as well. *Spotlight* (DM9) is a monthly English-language magazine for Germans who want to learn English, with good feature articles and travel pieces.

RADIO

Munich radio is modelled increasingly on US stations, with oodles of pop, rock, adult contemporary and oldies. Classical and opera offerings are at the lower end of the dial.

For quality English-language programs, the BBC World Service broadcasts on 604 MW and 90.2 FM; Britain's Radio 4 is on 198 LW. The uplifting sounds of Voice of America are beamed to Central Europe on 1197 AM, but it includes programs in other languages. Relax FM (92.4 on the band) plays light jazz and has a short CNN Radio News every hour on the half-hour.

One of the BBC's opposite numbers in Bavaria is Bayern 3, a quality station with lots of classical, opera and literature readings on 98.5 FM. Antenne Bayern is another large state-run station with very weird programming – Abba meets the Zillertaler Schürzenjäger.

Jazz fiends should check out Jazzwelle at 92.4 FM, which runs from 6 am to 4 pm Monday to Sunday. Radio Arabella is Munich's most popular radio station at 105.2 FM, playing lots of Schlager and schmaltzy German melodies.

TV

Several English-language channels can now be received in Germany. The quality of the reception, though, depends on the location, on whether the TV is hooked up to cable or to a satellite dish and on the quality of the television set. In theory, you can get BBC World, CNN, the Sky Channel and CNBC.

Germany has two national (public) channels, the ARD (Erstes Deutsches Fernsehen) and ZDF (Zweites Deutsches Fernsehen). In addition, there are the 'Dritten Programme', regional stations like the Cologne-based WDR (Westdeutscher Rundfunk) and last but not least, the Munich-based (Bayrischer Rundfunk). In Munich, you can also receive Austria's main public network ORF (Österreicher Rundfunk).

Generally, programming is comparatively high-brow with lots of political coverage, discussion forums and foreign films. Advertising is limited to two hours between 6 and 8 pm when it is shown in eight to 10-minute blocks roughly every half hour.

These channels can usually be easily received with a TV antenna; no cable connection or satellite dish are necessary.

Private television stations have proliferated in Germany in recent years. They offer the familiar array of sit-coms and soap operas (including many dubbed US shows), chat and game shows and, of course, feature films of all kinds. DSF and EuroSport are dedicated sports channels, and MTV and its German equivalent VIVA can also be received. Commercial breaks are frequent on these stations.

Overall, the content of private TV is very liberal. There are frequent 'documentaries' about bizarre sexual behaviour that come within a whisker of being all-out XXX. The late-night fare of Munich's own TV-München carries lots of those early 1970s 'sexual enlightenment' films, including that evergreen series Sexreport.

VIDEO SYSTEMS

German video and television operates on the PAL (Phase Alternative Line) system that is predominant in most of Europe and Australia. It is not compatible with the American and Japanese NTSC or French SECAM standards; pre-recorded video tapes bought in countries using those standards won't play in Germany and vice versa. Dual standard VCRs, which play back NTSC and PAL (but only record in PAL), are available in better electronics and duty-free shops; expect to pay somewhere around DM500 for a decent one. A standard VHS tape costs about DM6 to DM10, depending on the brand.

PHOTOGRAPHY & VIDEO
Film & Equipment

German photographic equipment is among the best in the world and all makes and types are readily available, as are those manufactured in other countries. Print film is sold at supermarkets and chemists, but for B&W and slide film you'll have to go to a photographic store.

Buy film for the purpose you intend to use it. For general purpose shooting – for either prints or slides – 100 ASA film is just about the most useful and versatile as it gives you good colour and enough speed to capture most situations on film. If you plan to shoot in dark areas or in brightly-lit night scenes without a tripod, switch to 400 ASA.

The best and most widely available films are made by Fuji, Kodak and Agfa. Fuji Velvia and Kodak Elite are easy to process and provide good slide images. Stay away from Kodachrome: it's difficult to process quickly and can give you lots of headaches if not handled properly. For print film you can't beat Kodak Gold, though Fuji and Agfa have just about perfected their films for print as well.

Film of any type is rather inexpensive in Germany, so there's no need to stock up at home. For a roll of 36-exposure standard print film, expect to pay around DM6. The cost for good slide film should run around DM10 to DM13. The per-roll cost drops sharply if you buy in packages of five or 10 rolls, so shop around. Occasionally, processing is included with the purchase of the film, which is a great deal if you have the time to wait. With slide film, unless you specify that you want the images framed (gerahmt), you will get them back unframed.

Chemists and supermarkets are cheap places to get your film processed, provided you don't need professional quality developing. Standard developing for print film is about DM4, plus DM0.40 for each 10 x 15cm print (allow about four days), and about DM0.60 per print for overnight ser-

---

Germany's Media Master

No single individual holds more sway – or attracts more criticism – in the German media world than Leo Kirch, Bavaria's answer to Rupert Murdoch. The son of a Würzburg wine grower, Kirch started out in 1956 by acquiring film rights from a little-known Italian director, Frederico Fellini. Over the next four decades, the publicity-shy Kirch built a media empire which today counts five private TV stations (including Pro7 and Sat1), a big publishing house (Axel Springer) and partners in Austria, Switzerland and Italy. He's also the biggest supplier of celluloid to the German-speaking world – too big to ignore, in fact, because many stations can't fill their slots without him (Kirch's archive, located in the Munich suburb of Unterföhring, contains a staggering two million reels with over 100,000 hours of programs).

So the next time you catch a Hollywood blockbuster dubbed into German – or are unable to watch a hot sporting event, because the broadcast rights were sold to a pay TV channel – you know who's responsible.

vice. Processing slide film costs about DM3.50 in these shops; if you want frames your total comes to about DM7. All prices quoted are for rolls of 36.

For professional developing, one good place is Sauter Photographic (☎ 551 50 40), at Sonnenstrasse 26, by the Sendlinger Tor, a full-service professional shop with reasonable film and development prices. It's open from 9.30 am to 7 pm weekdays, and from 9 am to 4 pm Saturday.

Another professional developer is Pfaffenbichler (☎ 47 20 91), Prinzregentenstrasse 78, whose work is fast and top-notch.

TIME

Clocks in Germany are set to Central European Time (GMT/UTC plus one hour), the same time zone as Madrid and Warsaw. Daylight-saving time comes into effect at 2 am on the last Sunday in March, when clocks are turned one hour forward. On the last Sunday in October they're turned back an hour. Without taking daylight-saving times into account, when it's noon in Munich, it's 11 am in London, 6 am in New York, 3 am in San Francisco, 8 pm in Tokyo and 9 pm in Sydney and 11 pm in Auckland. Official times (eg shop hours, train schedules, film screenings etc) are usually indicated by the 24-hour clock (eg 6.30 pm is 18.30).

ELECTRICITY

Electricity is 220V, 50 Hz AC. Plugs are the European type with two round pins. Your 220V appliances may be plugged into a German outlet with an adaptor, though their 110V cousins (eg from the USA) require a transformer. Some electric devices like laptops or shavers work on both 110V and 220V.

WEIGHTS & MEASURES

Germany uses the metric system – there's a conversion table at the back of this book. Like other Continental Europeans, Germans indicate decimals with commas and thousands with points (ie 10,000.00 is 10.000,00).

Clothing sizes – especially those for women's clothing – are quite different from those in North America (NA) and UK.

Airport Security

In general, airport x-ray technology isn't supposed to jeopardise lower-speed film (under 1600 ASA). Recently, however, new high-powered machines, designed to inspect *checked* luggage, have been installed at major airports around the world. These machines can conduct high-energy scans that may destroy unprocessed film.

Be sure to carry film and loaded cameras in your hand-luggage and ask the airport security people to inspect them manually. Pack all your film into a clear plastic bag that you can quickly whip out of your luggage. This saves time at inspection and minimises problems with security staff.

Women's size 8 in NA (size 10 in the UK) equals size 36 in Germany. Sizes then increase in increments of two, making German size 38 a NA 10 and a UK 12 and so on. Our advice: try everything on before buying. Look for the sign *Anprobe* to find the fitting room.

Shoes are another matter altogether. NA 5 (UK 3) is size 36 in Germany. It continues in increments of one, so that NA 6 (UK 4) equals size 37. Just to make things more complicated, men's sizes are different yet. A men's 41 equates to a NA 8 and a UK 7. A men's 42 would be a NA 9 and a UK 8, etc.

LAUNDRY

Laundrettes (*Wäschereien*) are normally open from 6 am to 9 or 10 pm. A load of washing costs DM6 to DM7, including soap powder; the dryer is DM1 per 10 minutes. In most laundrettes you select your machine and deposit the coin(s) in a central machine with numbers corresponding to the washers and dryers. The panel also distributes the soap powder so have ready one of the plastic cups strewn around the laundrette.

The best laundrette close to the centre is Der Wunderbare Waschsalon, Theresienstrasse 134, open 6 am to midnight every day. It's spotless, has cafe-style tables and OK coffee. A load of laundry costs DM6 with powder, and drying is DM1 for 12 minutes.

FACTS FOR THE VISITOR

Close to the Hauptbahnhof, but swarming with layabouts, is City-SB Waschcenter (☎ 601 40 03) at Paul-Heyse-Strasse 21, open from 7 am to 10 pm daily. Loads cost DM6 including powder, dryers are DM1 for 10 minutes, and the last wash must be in by 8 pm.

Close by in Westend, there's the nicer SB Waschsalon, at Schwanthalerstrasse, that's the cheapest in town (just DM5 per load). The Waschcenter Schnell + Sauber, near the main theatre at Klenzestrasse 18, charges DM6 per load and DM1 per 15 minutes in the dryer.

In Neuhausen, there's a 24-hour Waschsalon on the west side of Landshuter Strasse at No 77, on the corner of Volkartstrasse, about 10 minutes from the Jugendherberge München in Wendl-Dietrich-Strasse. There's a tanning salon downstairs, lest you leave sallow.

TOILETS

Finding a public lavatory isn't usually a problem in Germany, but you may have to pay anything from DM0.20 to DM1.50 for the convenience. Perhaps better are the public facilities in department stores. If there's an attendant, it's nice to tip DM0.50, at least if the toilet was clean. The standard of hygiene is usually pretty high.

In the Hauptbahnhof, you can try the gleaming McClean on the 1st lower level (Arnulfstrasse side), which also has showers for DM10. If you're feeling less picky, the toilets downstairs near the Deutsche Touring office are free (and here you'll know why).

Public toilets also exist in larger parks, pedestrian malls and shopping areas. Some are ultra-modern self-cleaning pay toilet pods (with wide automatic doorways for easy wheelchair access), and usually cost DM1. Instructions are in English, French and German.

HEALTH

Munich's medical facilities are excellent. The best number to dial for immediate medical help is the Kassenärztlicher Notfalldienst (☎ 55 14 71). For an ambulance ring ☎ 192 22. For walk-in treatment evenings and weekends, you can visit the Bereitschaftspraxis der Münchner Ärzte (Map 7a, ☎ 55 17 71), Elisenstrasse 3. It's in the Elisenhof, a modern shopping complex across from the Hauptbahnhof. Hours are from 7 pm to midnight Monday, Tuesday and Thursday, from 2 pm to midnight Wednesday and Friday, and from 8 am to midnight weekends and holidays.

Most pharmacies will have some English-speaking staff on hand, but there are several designated 'international' ones with English-speaking staff: at the airport (☎ 97 59 29 50); Bahnhof-Apotheke (☎ 69 41 19), Bahnhofplatz 2; and Ludwigs-Apotheke (☎ 260 30 21) at Neuhauser Strasse 11. To find an open pharmacy in an emergency, call ☎ 59 44 75.

First aid and emergency health care is free for EU citizens with an E111 form. Any other treatment can be very expensive, so make sure than you have travel insurance (see the boxed text 'Travel Insurance' earlier in this section). The US and UK consulates can provide lists of English-speaking doctors on request.

The most central hospital, with a casualty department, is the huge Klinikum Innenstadt der Ludwig-Maximilian-Universität (☎ 516 00), Ziemssenstrasse 1, just west of the Sendlinger Tor.

For an emergency dentist, call ☎ 516 00.

WOMEN TRAVELLERS

Women should not encounter particular difficulties or forms of harassment in Munich, though naturally it pays to use common sense.

Younger German women are quite outspoken and emancipated, but this hasn't yet translated into equality at the work place where they are often still kept out of senior positions. Sexual harassment at the work place is more commonplace here than in countries like the USA and Australia.

Many women juggle jobs and children, but there's an extensive network of public, church-run and private kindergartens to fall back on.

Munich women are just as likely to initiate contact with the opposite sex as men are. Getting hassled in the streets happens infrequently and is most likely to be encountered when walking past a bunch of construction guys on break. Wolf whistles and hollering are best ignored as any response will be interpreted as encouragement.

There are quite a few women's centres in Munich. The *Frauenhaus München* runs 24-hour hotlines at ☎ 35 48 30 and ☎ 64 51 69; consultation is available during the day at ☎ 354 83 11.

The *Frauentherapiezentrum München* (☎ 747 37 00), Güllstrasse 3, offers counselling and therapy free of charge. Hours are from 10 am to 1 pm, Monday to Thursday and from 3 to 5 pm, Tuesday and Thursday (walk-in or by appointment).

GAY & LESBIAN TRAVELLERS

Germans are generally fairly tolerant of homosexuality and Munich has an active, if not always highly visible, gay and lesbian scene. In fact, Munich hosts the annual Christopher Street Day festival in July, one of the country's biggest gay parades (see Public Holidays & Special Events later in this chapter).

Today, the sight of homosexual couples holding hands isn't uncommon and kissing in public is becoming more practised and accepted. However, some homosexuals have been among the victims of skinhead attacks in recent years, so be cautious in rough neighbourhoods (see also Dangers & Annoyances later in this chapter). Gays are known as *Schwule* (once a pejorative term, it's now worn with pride), while lesbians are *Lesben*.

Information for gay men and lesbians is available through *Schwules Kommunikations und Kulturzentrum*, dubbed 'the sub' (☎ 260 30 56), Müllerstrasse 43, open from 7 to 11 pm Sunday to Thursday and to 1 am on Friday and Saturday nights. It's a very cool gay community centre, with two floors (a bar downstairs and a library upstairs) that are home to extensive gay resources and support groups.

Lesbians can contact *LeTra/Lesben-Traum* (☎ 725 42 72), Dreimühlenstrasse 23, open from 10.30 am to 1 pm on Tuesday, from 2.30 to 5 pm on Wednesday and

7 to 10 pm on Thursday. It advises on general lesbian topics and organises 'coming out' groups.

The *Rosa Seiten* (Pink Pages, DM5) is the best guide to everything gay and lesbian in the city; order it by mail from 'the sub' (see earlier in this section) or take the U2 to Theresianstrasse, where Weissblauer Gay Shop (☎ 52 23 52) is just outside the station. It also has free copies of *Our Munich*, a monthly guide to gay and lesbian life.

DISABLED TRAVELLERS

Overall, Germany caters well for the needs of the disabled *(Behinderte)*, especially the wheelchair-bound. You'll find access ramps and/or lifts in many public buildings, including toilets, train stations, shopping centres museums, theatres and cinemas. Other disabilities, like blindness or deafness are less catered for, however, and the German organisations for disabled people continue to lobby for improvements.

All InterCity Express (ICE), InterCity/EuroCity (IC/EC), InterRegio (IR) trains, suburban (S-Bahn) and underground (U-Bahn) trains and ferry services have wheelchair access, but stepped entrances to trams and buses remain obstacles.

A helpful organisation in Munich is *CBF Club Behinderter und ihrer Freunde e.V. München*, which provides free, trained assistants for wheelchair users at concerts and other events. Call ☎ 356 88 08 between 6 and 8 pm from Tuesday to Thursday.

Organisations

There are a number of organisations and tour providers that specialise in the needs of disabled travellers.

Access-Able Travel Source
    Has an excellent Web site with many links (www.access-able.com). PO Box 1796, Wheat Ridge, CO 80034 (☎ 303-232 2979, fax 303-239 8486)
Mobility International
    Advises disabled travellers on mobility issues and runs an educational exchange program. In the USA: PO Box 10767, Eugene, OR 97440 (☎ 541-343 1284, fax 541-343 6812, email info@miusa.org). In the UK: 228 Borough High St, London SE1 1JX (☎ 020-7403 5688)

SATH
Society for the Advancement of Travel for the Handicapped, 347 Fifth Ave, Suite 610, New York, NY 10016 (☎ 212-447 7284, email sath travel@aol.com)

RADAR
Britain-based Royal Association for Disability and Rehabilitation publishes the helpful *Holidays & Travel Abroad: A Guide for Disabled People*. They're at 12 City Forum, 250 City Rd, London, EC1V 8AF (☎ 020-7250 3222)

Twin Peaks Press
A quarterly newsletter; also publishes directories and access guides. PO Box 129, Vancouver, WA 98666 (☎ 360-694 2462, 800-637 2256)

SENIOR TRAVELLERS

Senior citizens are entitled to discounts in Munich on things like public transport, museum admission fees etc, provided they show proof of their age. In some cases they might need a special pass. See Seniors' Cards in the Documents section, for more information.

Occasionally, discounts will not be posted, so simply ask *Gibt es Ermässigungen für Senioren?* (Are there reductions for senior citizens?)

If you're on a tight budget, bear in mind that there are a number of independent hostels in Munich that, unlike the DJH hostels in Bavaria, have no age limits. The *Mensas* (student cafeterias) are open to virtually anyone – IDs are almost never checked at Munich's universities. European residents over 60 are eligible for the Rail Europe Senior Card.

TRAVEL WITH CHILDREN

Successful travel with young children requires planning and effort. Don't try to overdo things; even for adults, packing too much into the time available can cause problems. And make sure the activities include the kids as well – balance a day at the Deutsches Museum with a visit to the Hellabrunn Zoo.

The Munich tourist office publishes a useful free booklet, *Hits for Kids* with a list of child-friendly museums, cinemas, theatres, shops, special events and more. *Travel with Children* by Lonely Planet co-founder Maureen Wheeler is another good and general source of information.

Children's discounts are widely available for everything from museum admissions to bus fares and hotel stays. The definition of a child varies – some places count anyone under 18 eligible for children's discounts while others only include children under six.

Most car-rental firms in Munich have children's safety seats for hire at a nominal cost, but it is essential that you book them in advance. The same goes for highchairs and cots (cribs); they're standard in most restaurants and hotels, but numbers are limited. The choice of baby food, infant formulas, soy and cow's milk, disposable nappies (diapers) and the like is great in German supermarkets, but the opening hours may be restricted. Run out of nappies on Saturday afternoon and you're facing a very long and messy weekend.

It's perfectly acceptable to bring your kids, even toddlers, along to casual restaurants (though you would raise eyebrows at upmarket ones, especially at dinnertime), cafes and daytime events.

LIBRARIES

The Bayerische Staatsbibliothek (Map 7, ☎ 28 63 80) at Ludwigstrasse 16, is one of Germany's biggest libraries, housing 7.2 million volumes and over 42,000 periodicals. Tourists can't get library cards easily, but you can browse the general reading hall with 62,000 freely-accessible volumes. It's open from 9 am to 7.30 pm weekdays, and from 9 am to 4.30 pm Saturday (closed Saturday in August and September).

Munich's Stadtbüchereien (city libraries) have branches throughout town where you will usually find some books in English. Branches include those at Rosenheimerstrasse 5 (☎ 48 09 83 13) in the Gasteig, at Schrenkstrasse 8 (☎ 50 71 09) in Westend, and at Hohenzollernstrasse 16 (☎ 336 01 3) in Schwabing.

University libraries include the Universitätsbibliothek (☎ 21 80 24 28), Geschwister-Scholl-Platz 1, and the Technical University Library (☎ 28 92 86 21), opposite the Alte Pinakothek, at Arcisstrasse 21.

The libraries at the British Council (Map 7a, ☎ 22 33 26), Bruderstrasse 7, and the Amerika Haus (Map 7, ☎ 55 25 37 20), Karolinenplatz 3, both specialise in books about culture, business and travel in those countries.

CULTURAL CENTRES

Cultural organisations abound; the *München im...* publication (see Listings in the Entertainment chapter) has the complete list. The city has active branches of Amerika Haus (☎ 55 25 37 20), Karolinenplatz 3; the British Council (☎ 22 33 26), Bruderstrasse 7; the Institut Français (☎ 286 62 80), Kaulbachstrasse 13; and the Goethe Institute (Map 7a, ☎ 551 90 30), Sonnenstrasse 25.

DANGERS & ANNOYANCES

Crime and staggering drunks leaving the beer halls and tents are major problems during Oktoberfest, especially at the southern end of the Hauptbahnhof. It's no joke: drunk people in a crowd, trying to get home, can get violent, and there are about 100 cases of assault every year. Leave early or stay very cautious, if not sober, yourself.

The *Föhn* (pronounced 'foon') is static-charged wind that brings both exquisite clear views to the Alps and an area of dense pressure that sits on the city. Müncheners claim that it makes them cranky – asthmatics, rheumatics and hypochondriacs gripe too.

Theft and other crimes against travellers are relatively rare, but be careful in the Hauptbahnhof, where pickpockets are often active. Don't allow anyone to help you put your luggage into a coin locker. Once they've closed the locker, they might switch keys and later come back to pick up your things.

At times, Africans, Asians and southern Europeans may encounter racial prejudice. In recent years, there has also been a number of attacks by radical skinheads on punks, homosexuals, vagrants and people they consider 'alternative' or 'left-wing'. The Ostbahnhof and the western suburb of Pasing appear to have been the centre of their activities. In 1999 the Munich police arrested an active and violent ring of skinheads, but caution remains the watchword.

Emergency telephone numbers are:

Police	☎ 110
Fire/Ambulance	☎ 112

LEGAL MATTERS

Munich police don't have a reputation for friendliness but they're well trained, fairly 'enlightened' and usually treat tourists with respect. Most members of the police force can speak some English.

In Germany, you must be able to prove your identity if asked by a police officer, which means you should always carry your passport or a national identity card. A driving licence with a photograph will usually suffice, though carrying a passport may save you a lot of trouble.

Drivers should carry a driving licence and obey road rules carefully. Penalties for drinking and driving are stiff. The highest permissible blood-alcohol level is 0.05% nationwide (some bars have coin-operated breathalysers if you're unsure of your condition). If you're caught over the limit, your licence will be confiscated and a court will decide within three days whether or not you get it back. The same applies if you're involved in an accident with a blood-alcohol level over 0.03%, regardless of whether or not the accident was your fault. You would have to be unfortunate to lose your driving licence for riding a bicycle while over the limit, but this is theoretically possible.

German political demonstrations occasionally take on a violent character when left-wing anarchists *(Autonomen)* are involved. Munich police are well equipped to deal with them (at times it seems they're too well equipped). It's not uncommon for officers to seal off side streets and ask passers-by to show ID, and needless to say it's not a good idea to provoke them.

BUSINESS HOURS

Official shop trading hours in Germany were liberalised a few years ago and stores can now open from 7 am until 8 pm on weekdays and until 4 pm on Saturday, plus a maximum of three hours on Sunday. Bakeries can also open for a couple of hours on

euro currency converter DM1 = €.51

FACTS FOR THE VISITOR

Sunday afternoon. Supermarkets and many other shops in the Hauptbahnhof may stay open until 9 or 10 pm daily.

Banking hours are generally from 8.30 am to 1 pm and from 2.30 to 4 pm Monday to Friday (many stay open till 6 pm on Thursday). Travel agencies and other offices are usually open from 9 am to 6 pm weekdays and till noon on Saturday. Government offices, on the other hand, close for the weekend as early as 1 pm on Friday. Museums (except for the Deutsches Museum, the BMW museum and a couple of others) are closed on Monday; opening hours vary greatly, although many art museums are open late one evening per week.

PUBLIC HOLIDAYS & SPECIAL EVENTS

Public holidays in Bavaria include: New Year's Day (1 January); Epiphany (6 January); Good Friday, Easter Sunday & Easter Monday; Labour Day (1 May); Ascension Day (40 days after Easter); Whit/Pentecost Sunday & Monday (May or June); Corpus Christi (10 days after Pentecost); Assumption Day (15 August); Day of German Unity (3 October); All Saints' Day (1 November) and Christmas and Boxing/St Stephen's Day (25 and 26 December).

There are many festivals, fairs and cultural events throughout the year in Munich. Highlights include the following:

January & February
Carnival *(Fasching)* – More than six weeks of partying reaches fever pitch on *Rosenmontag*, with heaps of raucous street parades and celebrations. There are about 4000 balls, stage shows and other well-lubricated events, and it all ends on Shrove Tuesday, when the market women on the Viktualienmarkt dance with any and everyone.
Munich Fashion Week – Hundreds of models strut their stuff on catwalks across the city. A good time to ask designer Karl Lagerfeld exactly why he left Germany.

March
Starkbierzeit – held in the 3rd and 4th week before Easter, the 'strong beer season' dates back to the old days when the monks drank and drank to make up for all that fasting. Only throat-warming varieties ending in '-ator' are consumed (Triumphator, Salvator, Maximator etc). Hardly anyone fasts these days, but the custom has stuck. The Löwenbräukeller (see the Places to Eat and Entertainment chapters) stages a backwoods weight-lifting event called *Steineheben*.

April & May
Frühlingsfest – a mini-Oktoberfest held over the last two weeks of April at the Theresienwiese, but with far fewer tourists. There's a big flea market on the first Saturday.
Auer Dult – Munich's famous traditional flea market cum amusement park, beginning on the last Saturday in April and lasting eight days. Genuine antiques and junk abound, you just have to sort out what's what. The event is repeated in July and October.
The Munich Biennale – a gala of contemporary music and theatre held every two years in the Gasteig and Muffathalle (the next ones are in 2000 and 2002). Call ☎ 48 09 80 for program details.

June
Tollwood Festival – a world culture festival, with music, food, clothes and merchandise from around the world, held from late June to early July at the Olympiapark. There are nightly world-music concerts, weather permitting. Admission is free, but the concerts cost about DM5 to DM35. Information at ☎ 383 85 00.
Corpus Christi – street processions in Munich and throughout Bavaria. Heaps of traditional costumes and costumed horses.
Munich Film Festival – held the last week of June, this is a scaled-down version of Berlin's renowned International Film Festival. Venues are at the Gasteig and various cinemas around town. Call ☎ 48 09 87 46 for information.

July
Tollwood Festival (see June)
Christopher Street Day – a three-day-long gay and lesbian bash, presided over by the mayor. It's one of Germany's biggest gay events (though not as big as Berlin's), and there are parties on Marienplatz and throughout town. Don't miss the high-heeled Pumps Race held at the corner of Holzstrasse and Holzplatz, in the Glockenbach district. Information at ☎ 38 38 73 27.
Opera Festival – held every July at the Bayerische Staatsoper (Bavarian State Opera), this extravaganza consists mainly of shows staged during the past year. It always concludes on 31 July

with *Die Meistersinger von Nürnberg*. Call ☎ 21 85 01 for information.

Jakobi Dult (see April)

Sommerfest (Summer Festival) in Olympiapark – two weeks of live bands (mostly Munich talent) and outdoor sport contests (eg mountain biking, rowing and climbing). It starts and ends with a bang-up fireworks display. Information at ☎ 30 67 24 14.

September

Oktoberfest – the biggest folk festival and collective drink-up on the planet. Next dates are 16 September to 3 October 2000 and 22 September to 7 October 2001. Spectacles include the traditional brewers' and costume parades on the first Saturday and Sunday (see the Oktoberfest special section for more details).

October

Oktoberfest (see September)

Herbst Dult (see April)

November

Six-Day Cycle Race – held in the Olympiahalle, with lots of entertainment, eating and drinking on the fringes. Information at ☎ 54 81 81 81.

Christkindlmarkt – starts the first Sunday in Advent and ends Christmas Eve. The biggest one is at Marienplatz, with stalls around a huge Christmas tree selling ornaments, handicrafts, religious art and *Glühwein* (mulled wine) to the strains of carols played by brass bands. Other districts hold their own, less touristy markets (notably Schwabing).

December

Christkindlmarkt (see November)

Winter Tollwood – a smaller, more intimate version of the June 'world culture' event, held on the former freight depot in the Arnulfstrasse (behind the Häckerbrücke). It's no Christmas market but does sell some neat gifts.

DOING BUSINESS

As the world's third-largest economy, Germany is naturally also Europe's most important address for doing business. As the country's southern corporate hub, Munich is popular with businesspeople for its excellent infrastructure, leisure options in the nearby Alps and (it must be said) the tax breaks to firms that set up in the region. In addition, a modern congress centre completed in 1998 puts Munich almost on par with other leading German convention cities such as Berlin, Cologne or Frankfurt.

Munich has a high concentration of English-speakers, which makes getting around – and getting down to business – that much easier. Before you arrive, contact the trade or commercial office of the German embassy in your country, which can provide valuable assistance. The German Ministry of Economics, for instance, publishes a thorough English-language manual entitled *Doing Business in Germany: A Contact List for US Firms*. Although pitched towards US business, the trade and development agencies throughout Germany listed here should prove useful to anyone. You can order a free copy by writing to the Bundesministerium für Wirtschaft, Scharnhorststrasse 36, 10115 Berlin (☎ 030-201 49, fax 20 14 70 10, email info@bmwi.bund.de).

Many of the big banks and accounting firms publish their own advisory booklets, which can usually be obtained free of charge. PriceWaterhouseCoopers puts out the *Global Telecoms & Tax Profiles* which includes a useful overview of the German tax system. You can order it from PWC's office at Olof-Palme-Strasse 35, 60439 Frankfurt (☎ 069-958 50, fax 9585 10 00). If you're focussing on financials, Commerzbank's booklet *The Banking System in Germany* provides a good summary and descriptions of the more obscure aspects of the German credit industry. Write to Commerzbank, Department of Analysis and Communication, Postfach 10 05 05, 60005 Frankfurt (☎ 069-13 62 28 18, fax 13 62 20 08).

Munich in Your Pocket is an informative basic primer on how to survive and make the most of your time in the city. It is filled with practicalities such as tips on tax assistance, insurance, housing, vital phone numbers and relocating in general. It's available from all the Munich bookshops with English-language sections.

Business Services

Regus Business Centres provide a full range of turn-key business services (such as office rental, secretarial services, conventional organisation and telecoms, including video conferencing). They have a reputation for being price-conscious, reliable and service-oriented. The most central of their three Munich offices is at Arnulfstrasse 27 (☎ 59 04 70, fax 59 04 72 00, email municharnu@aol.com). Their 26 branches are located throughout Europe and across the globe.

Otherwise there's lots of local competitors to choose from – look under 'Büroservice' in the Yellow Pages. One alternative is BLM Büro-Service (☎ 45 83 50, fax 448 88 96, email BLM.Bueroservice@t-online.de), Zeppelinstrasse 71–73 near the Deutsches Museum, with conference rooms starting at DM185 per day.

At Franz-Josef-Strauss airport there's a business service centre in the Office Building South Conference Centre (☎ 97 59 32 00, fax 97 59 32 06). Sited east of terminal D and reachable via the airport's shuttle buses, the centre has reasonably well-equipped meeting rooms but you'll pay for the comfort and convenient location.

Munich teems with copy shops, many of which cluster around the university. A good professional place is Topp Digital (☎ 542 14 50) at Gabelsbergerstrasse 73, just northwest of the Altstadt. Its services include digital prints (colour and B&W), scanning, binding, mailings and project consultation. It's opening hours are from 9 am to 6.30 pm weekdays and from 9 am to 1 pm Saturday. Take the U2 to Theresienstrasse and walk one block south on Augustenstrasse to Gabelsbergerstrasse.

A cheaper option for basic copies is the Kopierfabrik (☎ 39 12 01), Adalbertstrasse 34, just north of the university U-Bahn station. Hours are from 8 am to 7 pm weekdays. It has a professional-quality sibling on the east side of town near the trade fairgrounds, the Kopierfabrik am Moosfeld (☎ 42 72 06 00) at Stahlgruberring 11, which specialises in industrial copies and prints and opens from 8 am to 9 pm daily. Take the U2 to Moosfeld.

The luxury and business hotels of Munich offer the usual business services such as fax and Internet connections, though you'll pay through the nose for it. Reputable, all-round translation services include Kern (☎ 29 16 15 14, fax 29 65 95, email kern-muenchen@t-online.de) at Frauenstrasse 32. Overhead monitors, projectors and sound equipment are rented by CS Congress Service (☎ 670 02 80, fax 670 02 82 80, email mail@congress-service.de) at Hoferstrasse 1.

Exhibitions & Conferences

If you're planning a larger event in Munich, your first port of call should be the Fremdenverkehrsamt München (Munich Tourist Office, ☎ 23 33 02 72/73, fax 23 33 02 33, email tourismus@muenchen.btl.de) in the Neues Rathaus at Marienplatz. Staff will send you an 80-page trilingual booklet (in English, German and French) called *Congress in Munich*, which gives a detailed overview of available facilities and services. The tourist office's mailing address is Sendlinger Strasse 1, 80331 Munich.

Another option is to tap the Convention Bureau of the Munich Tourist Office (☎ 23 33 02 13, fax 23 33 02 51) for free information about organising conferences or meetings. The shiny new International Congress Centre Munich in the eastern suburb of Riem is the city's premier conference venue, with a seating capacity of 6500 and a maze of meeting rooms for 30 to 3000 people (☎ 94 92 30 10, fax 94 92 30 09). It's located at the new fairgrounds, the Messe München, Messegelände, 81823 München; you can also contact the sales manager, Astrid Grosse, at grosse@messe-muenchen.de.

WORK

Germany's level of unemployment is still a major problem (nearly 10% in late 1999). The chances of finding work in Munich as a foreigner remain dim. Nationals from EU countries don't need a work permit and basically enjoy the same rights as Germans. However, they *do* need an EU residency permit *(Aufenthaltserlaubnis)* from the local authorities.

Special conditions exist for citizens of so-called 'recognised third countries', including the USA, Canada, Australia, New

Zealand, Japan, Israel and Switzerland. Citizens of these countries who have a firm job offer may apply for the necessary permits, providing the job cannot be filled by a German or EU citizen.

The best places to look for work are local Arbeitsamt offices, which have an electronic data bank (SIS) on vacant positions throughout the country. National newspapers are also a good option, especially the *Süddeutsche Zeitung* and *Frankfurter Allgemeine Zeitung*.

It is also possible to find work teaching English at language schools, but you will still need work and residency permits, as well as valid health insurance. Many schools will ask you to work on a semi-freelance basis, which means you are entirely responsible for your own social security payments and health insurance. These secondary costs are high – health insurance for around DM250 per month is quite usual, though you might be able to get insurance from your home country that will cover you abroad.

You probably won't get rich teaching English, but it might help keep your head above water or prolong a trip. Work as an au pair is easy to find. *The Au Pair and Nanny's Guide to Working Abroad* (Vacation Work) by Susan Griffith & Sharon Legg will help. *Work Your Way Around the World*, also by Susan Griffith and published by Vacation Work, is another suggestion. There are numerous approved au pair agencies in Germany.

Getting There & Away

If you're coming from outside of Europe, flying is really the only sensible way to get to Germany. Even if you're already on the Continent, a flight may still be the swiftest and cheapest option, especially from far-flung places like Portugal, Greece or southern Italy. The train is the next best option, though cross-country buses are a viable (and cheaper) alternative. Bear in mind that seats fill up quickly and prices soar during the summer school holidays.

No matter which mode of travel you choose, be sure to take out travel insurance. This can protect you against the sudden shock of medical or legal expenses, luggage theft or loss, personal liability and cancellation or delays in your flight schedule. Before you sign a policy, review the ramifications and what to do when filing a claim. Your home medical policy may already provide coverage worldwide; if this is the case, then you only need to protect yourself against other problems.

Travel insurance is useful, but be sure to buy *early*. If you purchase it the week before your flight you may find, for example, that you're not covered for delays caused by strikes. Some policies also cover ticket loss, so keep a photocopy of your ticket in a separate place. And make a copy of your policy, in case the original is lost.

AIR

Touch down at Munich's sparkling Franz-Josef-Strauss airport (☎ 975 00), about 28km north of the city centre, is a pleasure. Completed in 1992, this showpiece of German engineering rises from this former marshland with a steely elegance. It's the country's second-busiest airport, handling more than 20 million passengers a year. A second terminal will be added by 2003.

The multi-level airport complex embraces a huge shopping centre, an underground car park and bus and commuter train (S-Bahn) stations. Check-in, departures and arrivals are on level 4, with sections A to F.

Passengers to/from Schengen countries (Germany, France, Belgium, Luxembourg, the Netherlands, Spain, Portugal Italy, Greece and Austria) aren't usually required to show passports.

On level 4 you'll also find a host of snack bars and restaurants, a hairdresser, a chapel and lost and found offices and airport information desks in each section. There's also a green Megatel unit outside each arrivals door with a credit-card-operated telephone, fax machine and Internet screen.

On level 3 there are several German banks with ATMs, a pharmacy, a post office, car rental outlets, an international press store and more than 40 other shops that are open from 6.30 am to 10 pm daily. Indexed floor plans of this consumer temple are posted at strategic points, and a full list of facilities is available on the airport's Web site (www.munich-airport.de).

Level 3 has an information desk, which fields simple tourist queries (such as requests for Munich maps), and also has a bevy of tour operators, travel agencies and last-minute bucket shops. If you have time to kill, wander through the central hall into the new Forum, an office-cum-shopping complex with a space-age roof (40m high) spanning a cafe-studded courtyard.

The S-Bahn station is directly beneath the airport. For information about getting to/from the airport, see the Getting Around chapter.

Departure Taxes

A departure tax of DM6 to DM8 as well as airport security fees are included in the price of an airline ticket purchased in Germany. You shouldn't have to pay any more fees at the airport.

A sampling of departure taxes from other countries to Germany include: USA – $12; UK – £10; Canada – C$55; Australia – A$30; New Zealand – NZ$20. In most instances, children under 12 are exempt or qualify for a reduction.

Give Us a Sign

As your plane made its final descent at Munich airport, you perhaps couldn't miss seeing a mysterious swirl on a field just west of the runway. A crop circle? A sewage plant for aesthetes? In fact, the rhythmically arranged pattern is an 'earth sign' entitled 'An Island in Time' (1994), by landscape artists Wilhelm Holderied and Karl Schlamminger. The original idea was to plough a fantastic creature, a 'marsh spirit' (this area was once swampland) but its creators opted instead for a giant 'biotope for time' (270m long, 170m wide and 3.4m high).

Its appearance varies radically with the seasons and weather: after a downpour, for instance, shallow lakes of rainwater collect in the gravel-and-concrete furrows to mirror the clouds above, while in the spring the contrast with the surrounding greenery turns it into a giant treble clef.

According to artist Holderied, the work 'is a place for patience, a site without a practical purpose'. Now *that's* something to think about in the departure lounge.

This doesn't cover an extra airport levy where it applies; for instance, on flights from US international airports to Germany you may end up paying US$60 or more in various taxes. There's no such charge if you depart by sea or land.

Airlines

Lufthansa, Germany's premier airline, has a predictably strong presence in Munich. Its international partners are SAS, United Airlines, Air Canada and Thai Airways; its subsidiary, Condor, does charter flights mainly to holiday destinations in southern Europe.

LTU International Airways is an independent charter airline with flights to cities around the world. Eurowings is a regional carrier that does primarily short hops from major European cities to regional and international airports in Germany. It's also a feeder airline for KLM, Northwest Airlines and Air France. One major domestic competitor for Lufthansa is Deutsche BA, a subsidiary of British Airways.

For some tickets, especially those to Asia or cheap flights to the USA, you need to reconfirm by telephone 24 to 48 hours before your flight.

Airlines in Munich serving its Franz-Josef-Strauss airport include the following (see also 'Fluggesellschaften' in the Yellow Pages):

Air France
 (☎ 0180-536 03 70) Theatinerstrasse 23

Air India
 (☎ 0130-82 29 99) Maximilianplatz 12a
American Airlines
 (☎ 0180-324 23 24 for reservations)
 Franz-Josef-Strauss airport
British Airways/Deutsche BA
 (☎ 0180-334 03 40) Promenadeplatz 10
Debonair
 (☎ 97 59 26 80) Franz-Josef-Strauss airport
Delta Air Lines
 (☎ 0180-333 78 80) Maximiliansplatz 17
El Al
 (☎ 210 69 20) Maximiliansplatz 15
Eurowings
 (☎ 97 59 23 53) Franz-Josef-Strauss airport
Finnair
 (☎ 0180-334 66 24) Oskar-von-Miller-Ring 36
Iberia
 (☎ 54 59 02 30) Schwanthalerstrasse 16
Japan Air Lines (JAL)
 (☎ 0180-222 87 00) Prielmayrstrasse 1
KLM Royal Dutch Airlines
 (☎ 0180-521 42 01 for reservations)
 Franz-Josef-Strauss airport
Korean Air
 (☎ 53 03 79) Schwanthalerstrasse 10
Lufthansa
 (☎ 54 55 99 for flight information, ☎ 97 52 13 13) Lenbachplatz 1
Qantas
 (☎ 0130-74 70 for reservations)
 Franz-Josef-Strauss airport
Sabena
 (☎ 55 58 45) Schillerstrasse 5
SAS Scandinavian Airlines
 (☎ 0180-323 40 23 for reservations)
Swissair
 (☎ 559 80 00) Arcostrasse 5

GETTING THERE & AWAY

Air Travel Glossary

Baggage Allowance This will be written on your ticket and usually includes one 20kg item to go in the hold, plus one item of hand luggage.

Bucket Shops These are unbonded travel agencies specialising in discounted airline tickets.

Bumped Just because you have a confirmed seat doesn't mean you're going to get on the plane (see Overbooking).

Cancellation Penalties If you have to cancel or change a discounted ticket, there are often heavy penalties involved; insurance can sometimes be taken out against these penalties. Some airlines impose penalties on regular tickets as well, particularly against 'no-show' passengers.

Check-In Airlines ask you to check in a certain time ahead of the flight departure (usually one to two hours on international flights). If you fail to check in on time and the flight is overbooked, the airline can cancel your booking and give your seat to somebody else.

Confirmation Having a ticket written out with the flight and date you want doesn't mean you have a seat until the agent has checked with the airline that your status is 'OK' or confirmed. Meanwhile you could just be 'on request'.

Courier Fares Businesses often need to send urgent documents or freight securely and quickly. Courier companies hire people to accompany the package through customs and, in return, offer a discount ticket which is sometimes a phenomenal bargain. In effect, what the companies do is ship their freight as your luggage on regular commercial flights. This is a legitimate operation, but there are two shortcomings – the short turnaround time of the ticket (usually not longer than a month) and the limitation on your luggage allowance. You may have to surrender all your allowance and take only carry-on luggage.

Full Fares Airlines traditionally offer 1st class (coded F), business class (coded J) and economy class (coded Y) tickets. These days there are so many promotional and discounted fares available that few passengers pay full economy fare.

ITX An ITX, or 'independent inclusive tour excursion', is often available on tickets to popular holiday destinations. Officially it's a package deal combined with hotel accommodation, but many agents will sell you one of these for the flight only and give you phoney hotel vouchers in the unlikely event that you're challenged at the airport.

Lost Tickets If you lose your airline ticket an airline will usually treat it like a travellers cheque and, after inquiries, issue you with another one. Legally, however, an airline is entitled to treat it like cash and if you lose it then it's gone forever. Take good care of your tickets.

MCO An MCO, or 'miscellaneous charge order', is a voucher that looks like an airline ticket but carries no destination or date. It can be exchanged through any International Association of Travel Agents (IATA) airline for a ticket on a specific flight. It's a useful alternative to an onward ticket in those countries that demand one, and is more flexible than an ordinary ticket if you're unsure of your route.

No-Shows No-shows are passengers who fail to show up for their flight. Full-fare passengers who fail to turn up are sometimes entitled to travel on a later flight. The rest are penalised (see Cancellation Penalties).

Air Travel Glossary

On Request This is an unconfirmed booking for a flight.

Onward Tickets An entry requirement for many countries is that you have a ticket out of the country. If you're unsure of your next move, the easiest solution is to buy the cheapest onward ticket to a neighbouring country or a ticket from a reliable airline which can later be refunded if you do not use it.

Open Jaw Tickets These are return tickets where you fly out to one place but return from another. If available, this can save you backtracking to your arrival point.

Overbooking Airlines hate to fly empty seats and since every flight has some passengers who fail to show up, airlines often book more passengers than they have seats. Usually excess passengers make up for the no-shows, but occasionally somebody gets 'bumped' onto the next available flight. Guess who it is most likely to be? The passengers who check in late.

Point-to-Point Tickets These are discount tickets that can be bought on some routes in return for passengers waiving their rights to a stopover.

Promotional Fares These are officially discounted fares, available from travel agencies or direct from the airline.

Reconfirmation If you don't reconfirm your flight at least 72 hours prior to departure, the airline may delete your name from the passenger list. Ring to find out if your airline requires reconfirmation.

Restrictions Discounted tickets often have various restrictions on them – such as needing to be paid for in advance and incurring a penalty to be altered. Others are restrictions on the minimum and maximum period you must be away, such as a minimum of 14 days or a maximum of one year.

Round-the-World Tickets RTW tickets give you a limited period (usually a year) in which to circumnavigate the globe. You can go anywhere the carrying airlines go, as long as you don't backtrack. The number of stopovers or total number of separate flights is decided before you set off and they usually cost a bit more than a basic return flight.

Stand-by This is a discounted ticket where you only fly if there is a seat free at the last moment. Stand-by fares are usually available only on domestic routes.

Transferred Tickets Airline tickets cannot be transferred from one person to another. Travellers sometimes try to sell the return half of their ticket, but officials can ask you to prove that you are the person named on the ticket. This is less likely to happen on domestic flights, but on an international flight tickets are compared with passports.

Travel Agencies Travel agencies vary widely and you should choose one that suits your needs. Some simply handle tours, while full-service agencies handle everything from tours and tickets to car rental and hotel bookings. If all you want is a ticket at the lowest possible price, then go to an agency specialising in discounted fares.

Travel Periods Ticket prices vary with the time of year. There is a low (off-peak) season and a high (peak) season, and often a low-shoulder season and a high-shoulder season as well. Usually the fare depends on your outward flight – if you depart in the high season and return in the low season, you pay the high-season fare.

Thai Airways
(☎ 29 16 01 28) Herrnstrasse 11
Turkish Airlines
(☎ 51 41 09 20 25)
Bahnhofplatz 1/cnr of Bayerstrasse
United Airlines
(☎ 54 56 05 00) Lenbachplatz 1

Airline offices at Franz-Josef-Strauss airport are on level 5, section D, of the passenger terminal.

Buying Tickets

Your plane ticket will probably be the single most expensive item in your budget, and buying it can be intimidating. It always pays to do some research on the current state of the market. Start early: some of the best deals are available months in advance, and some popular flights sell out quickly.

Note that high season in Germany is from mid-June through mid-September, as well as the week before and after Christmas. The best flight deals are found from November through March, which is perfect for alpine skiers.

Cheap tickets come in two distinct categories: official and unofficial. Official tickets have a variety of names including advance-purchase tickets, advance-purchase excursion (Apex) fares, super-Apex and simply budget fares. Unofficial discount tickets are released tickets by airlines through selected travel agents (though usually not sold by the airline offices themselves).

You may find that the cheapest flights are advertised by obscure agencies whose names haven't yet reached the telephone directory. If you're sceptical, opt for the safety of a better-known travel agent. Firms such as STA Travel (www.statravel.com) and Council Travel (www.counciltravel.com), both with offices worldwide, Travel CUTS (www.travelcuts.com) in Canada and Flight Centre (www.flight-centre.com) in Australia are not going to disappear overnight, leaving you clutching a receipt for a nonexistent ticket.

Once you have your ticket, make a photocopy, or at least write down the ticket and flight numbers and other relevant details, and keep the information separate from the ticket. If the ticket is lost or stolen, this will help you get a replacement.

Return (round-trip) tickets often work out *much* cheaper than two one-way fares. Be aware that immigration officials sometimes ask for a return or onward ticket, and if you can't show either, you'll have to provide proof of 'sufficient means of support' – ie a lot of money or, in some cases, valid credit cards.

Round-the-World Tickets Round-the-world (RTW) tickets often work out no more expensive (or even cheaper) than an ordinary return ticket. Official airline RTW tickets are usually put together by a combination of two or more airlines and permit you to fly anywhere you want on their route systems so long as you do not backtrack. Other restrictions are that you (usually) must book the first sector in advance (cancellation penalties then apply). There may be restrictions on how many stops you are permitted or how far you can travel. Usually the tickets are valid for 90 days up to a year from the date of the first outbound flight.

Prices start at about UK£800/US$1300/A$2000, depending on the season and length of validity. An alternative type of RTW ticket is one put together by a travel agent using a combination of discounted fares. These can be much cheaper than the official tickets but will often carry a lot of restrictions.

Travellers with Special Needs

If you have any special needs – you're vegetarian or require a special diet, are travelling in a wheelchair, taking the baby, are terrified of flying, or whatever – let the airline know as soon as possible so that they can make the necessary arrangements. Remind them when you reconfirm your booking (at least 72 hours before departure) and again when you check in at the airport. It may also be worth ringing around the airlines before you make your booking to find out how they can handle your particular needs.

Guide dogs for the blind will often have to travel in a pressurised baggage compartment with other animals, away from their owner, though smaller guide dogs may be admitted to the cabin. Guide dogs are not subject to quarantine if they have proof of having been vaccinated against rabies.

Deaf travellers can ask for airport and in-flight announcements to be written down for them.

Children aged under two travel for 10% of the full fare (or free on some airlines) as long as they don't occupy a seat. They don't get a baggage allowance in this case. 'Skycots', baby food and nappies (diapers) should be provided by the airline if requested in advance. Prams and strollers can often be taken as hand luggage. Children aged between two and 12 can usually occupy a seat for half to two-thirds of the full fare, and they get a standard baggage allowance.

Baggage
On most domestic and international flights you are limited to two checked bags, or three if you don't have carry-on luggage. There could be a charge if you bring more or if the size of the bags exceeds the airline's limit. It's best to check with the individual airline if you've any doubts. On some international flights the luggage allowance is based on weight.

If your luggage is delayed upon arrival (which is rare), some airlines give a cash advance to purchase necessities. If sporting equipment goes missing, the airline may pay for rentals. Should the luggage be lost, it's important to submit a claim. The airline doesn't have to pay the full amount of the claim, but they can estimate the value of your lost items. Be patient: it may take them anywhere from six weeks to three months to process the claim and pay you.

The USA
Flights to Germany from major cities in the USA abound and bargains are often available. Several airlines fly directly to Germany, most landing in Frankfurt, where you can catch a connecting flight to Munich. Lufthansa connects Frankfurt with Chicago, New York, Los Angeles and other major US cities.

American carriers serving Munich include American Airlines, Delta Air and United Airlines. In the off-season you can often pick up a return flight for US$400 or less. There are also direct flights to other German cities, including LTU's flights to Düsseldorf from Los Angeles, Phoenix and Daytona. Generally, though, flights to Frankfurt are the cheapest. One-way budget fares to Frankfurt in summer cost from about US$250 from New York, US$350 from Los Angeles and US$380 from Chicago (although you could easily do better than this).

The *New York Times*, *Los Angeles Times*, *Chicago Tribune*, *San Francisco Examiner* and many other major Sunday newspapers produce weekly travel sections in which you'll find lots of advertisements placed by travel agents.

Standard fares on commercial airlines are expensive and best avoided, especially since various types of discounts on scheduled flights are usually available. Besides advertised discount fares, options include charter flights, stand-by fares and courier flights.

The US-based *Travel Unlimited* newsletter (PO Box 1058, Allston, Massachusetts 02134) publishes details of the cheapest airfares and courier possibilities for destinations all over the world from the USA and other countries, including the UK. It's a treasure trove of information. A single monthly issue costs US$5 and a year's subscription is US$25 (US$35 abroad).

Charter Flights These are often cheaper than scheduled flights. Reliable travel agents specialising in charter flights, as well as budget travel for students, include STA Travel and Council Travel, both of which have offices in major US cities.

STA Travel
(☎ 212-865 2700) 2871 Broadway Ave, Columbia University, New York, NY 10025
(☎ 310-824 1574) 920 Westwood Blvd, Los Angeles, CA 90024
(☎ 415-391 8407) 51 Grant Ave, San Francisco, CA 94108
(☎ 312-786 9050) 429 South Dearborn St, Chicago, IL 60605

euro currency converter DM1 = €.51

GETTING THERE & AWAY

Council Travel
   (☎ 212-254 2525) 148 West 4th St, New York,
   NY 10012
   (☎ 212-822 2700) 205 East 42nd St, New
   York, NY 10017
   (☎ 310-208 3551) 10904 Lindbrook Drive,
   Los Angeles, CA 90024
   (☎ 415-421 3473) Ground floor, 530 Bush St,
   San Francisco, CA 94108
   (☎ 312-951 0585) 2nd floor, 1153 North Dearborn St, Chicago, IL 60610

Stand-by Fares These tickets are often sold at 60% of the standard price for one-way tickets. You will need to give a general idea of where and when you want to go. A few days before departure, you will be presented with a choice of two or three flights.

Airhitch, a telephone-based operation, some 30 years in the business, specialises in stand-by tickets. You can hook some unbeatable deals (eg New York-Frankfurt one-way from US$159). However, the flight selection can be limited (eg to the US west coast) and its customer service iffy, especially in their European offices where employees don't always speak English well. You'll find the Web site at www.airhitch .org. Their main US and European offices are listed below.

New York City
   (☎ 212-864 2000 or toll-free ☎ 800-326 2009)
Los Angeles
   (☎ 310 726 5000 or toll-free ☎ 800-397 1098)
San Francisco
   (☎ 415-834 9192 or toll-free ☎ 800-834 9192).
Paris
   (European head office, ☎ 33 1 47 00 16 30)
Berlin
   (☎ 49 30 440 86 87)
Amsterdam
   (☎ 31 20 620 32 20)

Air-Tech in New York (☎ 212-219 7000) is a smaller but arguably more professional outfit, providing stand-by fares from New York to Frankfurt and Düsseldorf from as little as US$169. Flights offered may not get you exactly where you want to go, but the savings are so huge that you might opt for an onward train or bus. Check out its Web site at www.airtech.com.

If you're feeling enterprising, Priceline in Connecticut (☎ 1-800-PRICELINE) offers an auction-based booking system for flights. It works like this: you say how much you want to pay for a return flight and provide the dates and your credit card number. If an airline's offer matches or undercuts your bid, Priceline automatically books the flight and charges your account. There are a couple of catches, bookings are non-refundable and you may end up flying at kooky times on kooky airlines. Its Web site is at www.priceline.com.

Courier Flights Travelling as a courier means that you accompany freight to its destination, usually only on the outgoing flight. All you do is carry an envelope with the freight papers with you on board and hand it to someone at your destination. The freight takes the place of your check-in luggage, so you will be restricted to carry-on luggage. You may have to be a US resident and present yourself in person before the company will take you on. Also keep in mind that only a relatively small number of these tickets are available.

Most courier flights depart from New York, and a New York-Frankfurt return may cost as little as US$100 in the low season. Generally, you are required to return within a specified period (sometimes within one or two weeks, but often up to one month). Good sources of information on courier flights are International Association of Air Travel Couriers (☎ 561-582 8320, fax 582 1581) and the Worldwide Courier Association (☎ 718-252 0555 or toll-free ☎ 800-780 4359), 1789 Flatbush, Brooklyn NY 11210. Check out their Web sites at www.courier.org and www.wallstech.com respectively.

Canada
Air Canada and Lufthansa offer flights to Frankfurt from Toronto, Vancouver and Montreal. Travel CUTS (☎ 888-838 2877) specialises in discount fares for students, and has offices in major cities. Also check the travel sections of the *Globe & Mail*, *Toronto Star* and the *Vancouver Sun* for

travel agents' ads. See the previous section for information on courier flights. The magazine *Great Expeditions* (PO Box 8000-411, Abbotsford, BC V2S 6H1) is a useful source as well.

Australia

Qantas flies from Melbourne and Sydney to Frankfurt via Singapore or Bangkok. STA Travel and Flight Centre are major dealers in cheap airfares, though your local travel agent may also offer some heavily discounted fares. Check the Saturday travel sections of the *Sydney Morning Herald* and Melbourne's *The Age* for ads for cheap fares to Europe. Don't be surprised if they happen to be 'sold out' when you contact the agents (who then offer you a more expensive fare) or if they turn out to be low-season fares on obscure airlines with lots of conditions attached.

Discounted return airfares on major airlines through reputable agents can be surprisingly cheap, with low-season fares around A$1300 and high-season fares up to A$2500. The following are addresses and contact numbers of agencies selling tickets at bargain prices.

STA Travel
(☎ 03-9663 7365) Level 4, Union Bldg, RMIT, Melbourne, Victoria 3000
(☎ 02-9411 6888) Shop 17, 3–9 Spring St, Chatswood, Sydney, NSW 2067
(☎ 08-9380 2302) 1st floor, New Guild Bldg, University of Western Australia, Crawley, Perth, WA 6009
Flight Centre
(☎ 03-9650 2899) 19 Bourke St, Melbourne, Victoria 3000
(☎ 02-9235 0166) Shop 5, State Bank Centre, 52 Martin Place, Sydney, NSW 2000
(☎ 08-9325 9222) Shop 25, Cinema City Arcade, Perth, WA 6000

New Zealand

STA Travel and Flight Centre are popular travel agents in New Zealand. The cheapest fares to Europe are routed through the USA, and a round-the-world ticket may be cheaper than a simple return fare. Air New Zealand has flights from Auckland to Frankfurt, with a stop-over in either Asia or Los Angeles.

Otherwise, you can fly to Melbourne or Sydney to pick up a connecting flight.

STA Travel
(☎ 09-307 0555) 2nd floor, Student Union Bldg, Princes St, Auckland University, Auckland
Flight Centre
(☎ 09-309 6171) Shop 3a, National Bank Towers, 205-225 Queen St, Auckland

The UK

London is the discount-flight capital of Europe, so finding a cheap airfare to Germany shouldn't be tough. The main airlines are British Airways and Lufthansa, with flights several times a day to Frankfurt, Munich, Düsseldorf, Hamburg, Berlin and other cities.

Deregulation has brought some tempting deals to the London-Munich route, and fares seem to be dropping all the time. When we checked, British Airway's Go subsidiary was flying from Stansted (London) to Munich for as little as £88 return; Debonair was advertising £76 for the round-trip Luton (London) to Munich.

CityFlyer Express flies out of Gatwick (London) to Frankfurt, and Air UK flies from Stansted to Düsseldorf. Return tickets from Heathrow or Gatwick to Frankfurt in high season cost between £78 (with British Midland) and £137 (with British Airways/Lufthansa). Ryanair, another cut-rate airline with a handful of aircraft, was advertising a return flight to Frankfurt for a mere £49.50 when we looked. Bear in mind that precious few seats may actually be available at the cheapest prices advertised.

Bucket shops abound in London. They generally offer the cheapest tickets, though usually with restricted validity. However, many may not be registered with the ABTA (Association of British Travel Agents), which guarantees a refund or an alternative if you've paid for your flight and the agent then goes out of business.

The listings magazine *Time Out*, the weekend papers and the *Evening Standard* carry ads for cheap fares. Also look out for the free magazines and newspapers widely available in London, especially *TNT*. You can often pick them up outside main train and tube stations.

Trailfinders' head office is a good place for budget air fares; it also has a travel library, bookshop, visa service and immunisation centre. STA Travel also has branches in the UK. Some useful agents' addresses include:

STA Travel
  (☎ 020-7361 6161 for Europe, or ☎ 020-7361 6262 for long-haul)
  86 Old Brompton Rd, London SW7
Trailfinders
  (☎ 020-7937 5400)
  194 Kensington High St, London W8 7RG
Council Travel
  (☎ 020-7437 7767)
  28a Poland Street, London W1
Usit CAMPUS
  (☎ 020-7730 7285, reservations ☎ 0870-240 1010)
  52 Grosvenor Gardens, London SW1W 0AG

Continental Europe

Discount flights to various airports in Germany are available from many major cities in Continental Europe, especially from Amsterdam and Athens.

Many travel agencies in Europe have ties to STA Travel, where cheap tickets can be bought and STA Travel tickets can be altered free of charge (first change only).

In the Netherlands, NBBS Reizen is a popular agency, with offices at Rokin 38 (☎ 624 09 89) and Leidsestraat 53 (☎ 638 17 26). In Paris, Council Travel (☎ 01 44 55 55 55 65) has its main offices at 22 rue des Pyramides (1er). In Athens, try International Student & Youth Travel Service (☎ 01-383 3767), Nikis 11.

TRAIN

The train is another good way to get to Munich if you're already in Europe, and it's more comfortable than the bus. It's not worth spending the extra money on a 1st-class ticket, since travelling 2nd-class on German trains is almost as comfortable. Note that you'll need to pay a *Zuschlag* (surcharge) for faster trains. This costs more if you wait to buy it on board.

Long-distance trains between major German cities are called IC (InterCity) trains; when they cross national borders they carry the label EC (EuroCity). From Munich, EC trains travel directly to Rome, Milan, Florence, Verona, Prague, Paris, Strasbourg, Salzburg and Zurich. You'll pay a surcharge of DM7 on both IC and EC trains (DM9 if you buy it on the train).

On several German routes, the InterCity-Express (ICE) runs at speeds up to 280km/h. These 'bullet'-type trains are furnished a bit like aircraft, with radio headphone sockets and video screens built into the backs of some seats. The bistros and restaurant cars are pretty sleek, too. The surcharge varies by the route, but usually adds at least 10% to the ticket.

InterRegio (IR) trains cover secondary routes and usually run at intervals of two hours. For journeys of over two hours, you can usually get there faster by switching to an IC or ICE. The IR surcharge is DM3.

Regional Express (RE) trains are local trains that make limited stops and link the rural areas to the national and commuter networks.

Overnight international trains are made up of mostly sleeper carriages, and there may be only one or two carriages with seats. A berth in a four-person compartment will cost an extra DM31 to DM49, it's an extra DM24 to DM38 in a six-person compartment. Extra charges for single-bed sleepers are DM140 to DM221, doubles are an extra DM70 to DM110 per person.

If you have a sleeping berth on an international trip, the train conductor will usually collect your ticket in the evening and hand it back to you in the morning. If you're in a regular seat, however, expect to be woken up by conductors coming aboard in each country to check your ticket.

Be sure to reserve a seat on IC, EC and ICE trains, especially during the peak summer season and around major holidays. Trains get very crowded, and you may find yourself standing in the corridor like a poor relation. Reservations cost DM5 and can be made as late as a few minutes before your departure.

To Prague on the Cheap

If you're going to the Czech Republic, consider buying the Prague Excursion Pass sold by Deutsche Bahn. It covers round-trip travel (and all supplements) to Prague from the Czech border and back within seven days. You can enter from Germany, Austria, Poland or Slovakia, and you don't have to return via the same border crossing when you leave the country. The 2nd-class pass costs DM60 (DM45 if you're under 26) from Deutsche Bahn offices or EurAide. Note that citizens of Australia, South Africa and several other countries must first apply for a Czech entry visa, a process which takes up to two weeks.

Rail Passes

Eurail Available to non-European residents only, Eurail passes are supposed to be bought before arriving in Europe. But they can be purchased within Europe, so long as your passport shows you've been there for under six months. Note that outlets where you can do this are limited and that the passes will be about 10% more expensive. (If you've lived in Europe for over six months, you're eligible for an Inter-Rail pass, which is a better buy.) Eurail passes are valid for unlimited travel on national railways (and some private lines) in 19 European countries. They also cover many ferries, eg from Sweden to Germany, as well as steamer services in various countries.

For people aged 25 and under, a Youth-pass offers unlimited 2nd-class travel for 15 or 21 consecutive days (US$388/499), or for one/two/three months (US$623/882/1089). The Youth Flexipass, also for 2nd-class travel, is valid for freely chosen days within a two-month period: 10 days is US$458 or 15 days is US$599.

For those 26 and older, the equivalent passes provide 1st-class travel. The standard Eurail pass costs US$554/718 for 15/21 days or US$890/1260/1558 for one/two/three months. The Flexipass costs US$654/862 for 10/15 days of travel within two

months. Groups of up to five people travelling together can get a 'saver' version of either pass, saving about 18%. Eurail passes for children are also available.

They can be a great deal if you're covering lots of ground in a limited time. But if you're spending more than a week in Germany, the pass probably doesn't pay: you'll burn through the allotted time on routes that would cost you less if you paid the full fare. You may be better off with a BahnCard (see Fares & Discount Tickets later in this section). Couples and groups should consider the useful Euro-Saver pass, which costs $US470 for two to five adults over the same period.

German Rail A German Rail (or Deutsche Bahn) pass can be a cheaper way of getting around the country, and it allows you to avoid the ticket queues. Passes can be obtained in most non-European countries including Australia, Canada, the USA and Mexico, and at most major train stations in Germany itself (passport required). The pass is valid on all trains, and some river services operated by the Köln-Düsseldorfer Line.

The standard German Rail pass is available to any non-German citizen not resident in Germany, and entitles you to unlimited 1st or 2nd-class travel for four/seven/10 days within a one-month period. The 2nd-class German Rail pass costs US$174/240/306.

German Rail Youth Similar to the German Rail pass is the German Rail Youth pass, limited to 2nd-class travel for passengers aged between 12 and 25. It costs US $138/$174/239 for four/seven/10 days of travel.

German Rail Twin Two adults travelling together should check out the German Rail Twin pass, which costs US$261/360/459 for four/seven/10 days of travel in 2nd-class.

Europass Also for non-Europeans, the Europass gives unlimited travel on freely chosen days within a two-month period. Youth (aged 25 and under) and adult (solo, or two sharing) versions are available, and purchasing requirements and sales outlets are the same as for Eurail passes. They are cheaper than Eurail passes as they cover only France, Germany, Italy, Spain and Switzerland. The youth/adult price is US$233/348 for five travel days, US$253/368 for six days, US$313/448 for eight days, US$363/528 for 10 days and US$506/788 for 15 days. You can also visit one/two of four other 'regions' (Austria and Hungary, the Benelux, Portugal, Greece) in the chosen duration for another US$45/78.

Fares & Discount Tickets

The average price of 2nd-class train travel throughout Germany is currently DM0.27 per kilometre; for 1st-class the average is DM0.41 per kilometre. In this book we round train fares to the nearest DM0.50, and list only 2nd-class fares. Children aged three years and younger travel free, children from four to 11 are half-price.

Although train travel in Germany does offer good value, without a rail pass or a ticket bought through a special offer, it can get expensive: it costs about DM120 for a Munich-Frankfurt ticket on non-ICE service and DM147 on an ICE train.

Tickets can usually be bought from the conductor for a surcharge of DM5 (DM10 for ICE trains), but an increasing number of services (generally slower, regional services) operate without a conductor. For these trains passengers are required to buy a ticket *before* boarding, so ask if you are in doubt. Anyone caught without a valid ticket will be fined DM60.

At many train stations passengers must buy tickets from vending machines for distances under 100km – it's generally more convenient anyway. If you're travelling further than anywhere indicated on the machine, press button 'X' for the maximum fare and contact the conductor on board. Holders of the BahnCard (see later in this section) should press the '½' or 'Kind' (child) button for a half-price ticket.

In addition there are various permanent and temporary reduced-rate ticket offers available, including:

Guten-Abend-Ticket If arriving very late is not a problem, the Good Evening Ticket is good value. It's valid for unlimited train travel from 7 pm until 2 am (from 2 pm Saturday), and costs DM59 in 2nd-class (DM69 in 2nd-class on an ICE train). There are black-out periods around Easter and Christmas – check with DB for details. A flat DM15 surcharge is levied at the weekend.

Schönes-Wochenende-Ticket DB has one of the finest train deals in Europe – the so-called Nice Weekend Ticket. This allows two adults and three children to travel anywhere in Germany from midnight Saturday until 2 am Monday for just DM35. The catch is that you have to use local trains and *not* ICE, IC, ICN (InterCity Night) or IR trains. That's not so bad, though – you can get clear across the country on the slower trains (and no German train is *that* slow).

BahnCard If you plan to travel within Germany for more than a month, the BahnCard is probably cheaper than just buying tickets at the counter. It allows you to buy train tickets (including for ICs and ICEs, but *not* for S-Bahns or U-Bahns) and many regional bus tickets for half-price. A 2nd-class BahnCard costs DM260 (DM120 for those aged from 17 to 22, students under 27, anyone over 60 and card holders' spouses) and is valid for one year. People aged under 17 pay only DM60 for the BahnCard.

Sparpreis The Sparpreis, a return ticket between any two stations in Germany, costs DM249, and accompanying passengers pay only DM125. It is valid for 30 days but the return trip cannot be completed within a single Monday-to-Friday period. The Sparpreis is not valid on ICE trains.

Twen Tickets Passengers aged up to 25 automatically qualify for Deutsche Bahn's cheaper *Twen* tickets, which give a reduction of 25%. Examples of standard one-way Twen fares to/from Munich are:

origin/destination	2nd-class (DM)
Amsterdam	195
Berchtesgaden	38
Berlin	146
Bucharest	210
Budapest	107
Cologne	138
Copenhagen	266
Frankfurt-am-Main	90
Freiburg	102
Heidelberg	78
Garmisch-Partenkirchen	22
Geneva	141
Milan	71
Lindau	43
Nice	202
Paris	219
Prague	72
	(84 overnight)
Rome	95
Vienna	77
Zurich	85

BUS

In some cases, bus travel is a good alternative to the train if you're already in Europe and on your way to Germany. Especially for shorter distances, it's usually, though not always, cheaper than taking the train. The downside is that it's slower. Some of the coaches are quite comfortable, with a toilet, air-conditioning and snack bar. Advance reservations may be necessary at peak travel times. In general, return fares are markedly cheaper than two one-way fares.

Eurolines This is the umbrella organisation of numerous European bus companies (its German arm also operates as Deutsche Touring) with services between major cities across Europe. You'll find their Web site at www.eurolines.com. Offices in Europe include those listed below, although information and tickets are also available from most travel agents.

France
  (☎ 01 49 72 51 51) Gare Routière Internationale, 28 Ave du Général de Gaulle, 75020 Paris
Germany
  (☎ 089-545 87 00) Arnulfstrasse 3 (Hauptbahnhof), 80335 Munich
  (☎ 069-790 32 88) Am Römerhof 17, 60486 Frankfurt-am-Main
Netherlands
  (☎ 020-560 87 87) Amstel Busstation, Julianaplein 5, 1097 DN Amsterdam
UK
  (☎ 01582-404 511) 52 Grosvenor Gardens, Victoria, London SW1 0AU

Buses connect Munich with a host of European cities. There are direct connections to/from Vienna three times a week (one-way/return DM55/100, seven hours); Paris four times a week (DM117/211, 13 hours); Brussels four to five times a week (DM83/143, 13 hours); and London four to five times a week (DM142/218, 22 hours). Cities such as Prague, Amsterdam and Rome can be reached by changing buses within the Eurolines network.

Within Germany, Eurolines bus services include the Romantic Road (which extends from Frankfurt to Füssen) and the Castle Road (from Mannheim to Rothenburg ob

Securely on Track

In recent years, the number of crimes committed on trains – especially at night – has increased. There are horror stories of passengers being robbed after having been drugged or made unconscious by gas blown in through the ventilation ducts. While this should not stop you from using the train, be aware and take a few precautions. Never leave your baggage out of sight, especially the bag holding your personal documents, tickets and money. Lock your suitcases, backpacks or bags; better yet, buy a lock and fasten them to the luggage rack. Travel in the daytime is safer, though it's easier to catch some sleep (and save accommodation costs) on night trains. Sleeping compartments are lockable from the inside (only the guard has a key), and many couchettes can be secured with the aid of a cross-bar.

GETTING THERE & AWAY

der Tauber), as well as a route from Reutlingen to Strasbourg, France. One-way/return fares to/from Munich include Frankfurt (DM116/232, 12 hours) and Würzburg (DM84/168, 10 hours).

If you're under 26 or a student, you get a 10% discount, and kids aged between four and 12 and adults over 60 travel half-price. For frequent travellers, the Eurolines pass offers unlimited travel between 18 cities over either 30 or 60 days. If you're under 26 it costs DM429/529 for 30/60 days in low season and DM559/699 in high season. If you're 26 or over you pay DM529/629 for 30/60 days in low season and DM649/769 in high season.

Eurolines buses stop outside the centre, in the northern suburb of Fröttmaning at the Park & Ride facility next to the underground station U6.

Busabout This is a UK-based budget alternative to Eurolines. Busabout (☎ 020-7950 1661, fax 7950 1662) is at 258 Vauxhall Bridge Road, London SW1V 1BS. Though aimed at younger travellers, it has no upper age limit. It runs coaches along five interlocking European circuits, including one through Munich. You'll find its Web site at www.busabout.com.

The Busabout pass costs £249 (£199 for youth and student-card holders) for 15 days travelling on as many of the five circuits as you like. There are also passes for 21 days (£345/275), one month (£425/325), two months (£595/485) and three months (£895/£720), as well as Flexipasses entitling you to between 10 and 30 days of travel in a two-month period.

The main drawback is that buses on most loops travel in one direction (ie from Salzburg to Munich or from Munich to Stuttgart, but not vice-versa). Moreover, you can't just jump on a bus to the next city without buying one of the above passes.

Busabout has two stops in Munich during summer: The Kurpfalz Hotel (☎ 089-540 98 60), Schwanthalerstrasse 121; and Camping Thalkirchen (☎ 089-723 17 07), Zentrallandstrasse 49 (take the U3 to the Thalkirchen stop). In winter it stops at

Hotel Helvetia (☎ 089-590 68 50), Schillerstrasse 6, about 100m south of Munich's Hauptbahnhof.

BEX BerLinien Bus or BEX (☎ 0130-83 11 44 for travel to Berlin) runs daily buses between Berlin and Munich, via Leipzig, Bayreuth, Nuremberg and Ingolstadt. One-way/return SuperSpar tickets to Berlin from the Munich Hauptbahnhof (north side entrance) for passengers under 26 or over 60 cost DM76/139; full-fare tickets are DM129/ 149. You'll find its Web site at www.berlin linienbus.de.

CAR & MOTORCYCLE

Driving to Munich can be a lot of fun. Generally, the quality of German roads is very high, and having your own vehicle provides you with flexibility to explore outside the city. The disadvantage is that traffic in Munich is horrendous and parking is scarce.

If you're bringing your own vehicle, always carry proof of ownership. Driving licences from most countries are valid in Germany for one year. You must also have third-party insurance. It's compulsory to carry a warning (hazard) triangle and first-aid kit in your car at all times. If you're coming from the UK, the quickest option (apart from the Channel Tunnel) is to take the car ferry or hovercraft from Dover, Folkestone or Ramsgate to Calais, in France; you can be in Germany in three hours from there. At the borders to Poland and the Czech Republic there can be long delays.

Technically, there is no speed limit on autobahns, but in an effort to increase safety and curb noise pollution many segments have limits ranging from 100 to 130km/h. Fuel is expensive: depending on the time of year, prices vary from DM1.55 to DM1.75 per litre for unleaded regular, DM1.65 to DM1.80 for unleaded super and DM1.25 to DM1.45 for diesel (by the way, taxes account for 80% of the bill).

If your vehicle breaks down, you can call the German motoring association ADAC (☎ 0180 22 22 22) from the emergency call pillars next to the autobahn. Follow the pictorial instructions and help will arrive.

BICYCLE

Bicycles can travel by air, which can be surprisingly inexpensive, especially with some charter airlines. The independent charter airline LTU, for instance, charges only DM30 to transport a bicycle. You *can* take them to pieces and put them in a bike bag or box, but it's much easier check it in as a piece of baggage.

On trains, you'll need to purchase a separate ticket for your bike. These cost DM6/12 for distances under/over 100km. Most trains (excluding ICEs) have a 2nd-class carriage at one end with a bicycle compartment.

If you're under your own steam, you'll find Germany has a reasonable network of bike paths. Regional bike maps generally cost DM9.80 at tourist offices and bookshops throughout Germany.

HITCHING & RIDE SERVICES

Hitching isn't entirely safe in any country in the world and we don't recommend it. However, travellers who do decide to hitch shouldn't have too many problems getting to and from Munich via the main autobahns and highways.

Aside from hitching, the cheapest way to the Bavarian capital is as a paying passenger in a private car. Leaving Germany, or travelling within the country, such rides are commonly arranged by *Mitfahrzentralen* (ride-share agencies). The fare you pay comprises a commission to the agency and a per kilometre charge to the driver. It's best to call the driver the night before and again on the morning of departure just to make sure they're still going.

One popular, central agent is the ADM-Mitfahrzentrale (Map 7a, ☎ 194 40), near the Hauptbahnhof at Lämmerstrasse 4. It's open from 9 am to 8 pm daily. Sample fares from Munich (including booking fees) are: Vienna DM42, Berlin DM54, Amsterdam DM74, Paris DM79, Prague DM59 and Warsaw DM88. Staff speak English, but service can be sluggish.

The CityNetz Mitfahr-Service Kängaruh (☎ 194 44), Adalbertstrasse 10–12, just 70m from the Universität U-Bahn stop, is slightly cheaper and also arranges lifts for women with female drivers.

There's a Web site with fares posted at www.mitfahrzentrale-carnet.com. Check also the bulletin board in the university Mensa at Leopoldstrasse 13.

FERRIES

Return tickets are often cheaper than two one-way tickets. Also keep in mind that prices fluctuate dramatically according to the season, the day and time of departure and, for overnight ferries, cabin amenities. All prices quoted below are for one-way fares. For a more complete list of ferry links, see the Getting There & Away chapter in Lonely Planet's *Germany* guide.

The UK

Hamburg-Harwich The car ferry run by Scandinavian Seaways (☎ 040-389 03 71 in Hamburg) operates at least twice weekly year round and takes 20 hours. One-way fares range from DM97 for a berth in an inner four-bed cabin in low season to DM495 for a one-bed outer suite with private bath in high season. Cars up to 6m long are an additional DM80/110 in low/high season.

Sweden

Sassnitz-Trelleborg Scandlines Hansa-Ferry (☎ 0180-534 34 43, or ☎ 0383-926 14 20 in Sassnitz) operates a quick ferry to/from Sweden, popular with day-trippers. There are five departures daily. The trip takes four hours and costs DM30/20 in summer/winter. Cars are DM155 to DM195, including all passengers.

Denmark

Rostock-Gedser Scandlines (☎ 0381-673 12 17 in Rostock) runs its Vogelfluglinie ferries at least nine times daily to Gedser, about 100km south of Copenhagen. The trip (one to two hours) costs DM85 (DM115 in high season) for cars up to 6m in length, DM40 for motorbikes, and DM5 per adult.

Norway

Kiel-Oslo Color Line (☎ 0431-730 00 in Kiel) makes this 19½ hour journey almost

GETTING THERE & AWAY

daily. The fare, including a berth in the most basic two-bed cabin, is DM150 and about 30% more in summer. Students pay half-price in the off-season.

Finland

Travemünde-Helsinki Finnjet-Silja Line (☎ 0381-350 43 50 in Rostock) makes several trips weekly, which take 25 hours and cost from DM250 in four-bunk cabins in summer and DM180 during low season. Students get a 20% discount (50% if booked within a week of departure).

TRAVEL AGENTS

Munich has a wealth of bucket shops offering cheap airfares, but some of the bigger, established agencies have virtues of their own.

ABR Reisebüro (☎ 120 40), at the front of the Hauptbahnhof, is the Bavarian state travel agency. It's good for booking train tickets, rafting tours and other organised tours in Bavaria.

Atlas Reisen is a national chain of travel agencies with outlets in the city's Kaufhof stores, including Kaufingerstrasse 1–5 (☎ 26 90 72). They're particularly good for making bus, ferry and package-tour reservations.

Council Travel (☎ 39 50 22), near the university at Adalbertstrasse 32, offers a wide range of services to students, including details of study abroad and work permits. It also issues ISIC cards (DM17, photo and student ID required).

EurAide (☎ 59 38 89), in the Hauptbahnhof next to track 11, has its finger on the pulse of Deutsche Bahn. Its English-speaking staff can book train travel in Germany or elsewhere in Europe, field complex rail-pass inquiries and find the cheapest train fares.

Just Travel (☎ 747 33 30), Dreimühlenstrasse 29, is an English-speaking agency that offers cheap tours and package deals to mainly European destinations.

STA Travel (☎ 39 90 96), Königinstrasse 49, is another student and youth travel specialist with a well-linked international network.

Travel Overland (☎ 27 27 61 00) is a popular bucket shop with offices at Theresienstrasse 48 (☎ 28 08 50) and Barer Strasse 73 (☎ 27 27 61 00). Flights don't come much cheaper than here.

ORGANISED TOURS

There's a multitude of tour operators with European tours integrating Munich as a stop

of one to two days. It's also worth contacting the German National Tourist Office in your home country (see the Facts for the Visitor chapter under Tourist Offices Abroad).

Of the options available, DER Travel Service in the UK (☎ 020-7290 11 11, fax 629 74 42, 18 Conduit Street, London W1R 9TD) or the USA (☎ 310-479 4140 or toll free 800-937 1235, fax 847-692 4141, 11933 Wilshire Blvd, Los Angeles, CA 90025) has a huge selection of holidays in Munich and Bavaria, they include self-catering, independent package holidays as well as balloon and river cruises. They also offer package tours geared to gay and lesbian travellers. Check out their Web sites at www.der.com (in English) and www.der.de (in German).

Two good special interest operators for Bavaria (both UK-based) include Moswin Tours Ltd (☎ 0116-271 99 22), 21 Church Street, Oadby, Leicester LE2 5DB and the German Travel Centre (☎ 020-8429 29 00), 403–409 Rayner's Lane, Pinner, Middlesex HA5 5ER.

Also in the UK, Holt's Tours (☎ 01304-612 22 48), 15 Market Street, Sandwich, Kent CT13 9DA, offer a yearly rotating agenda of battlefield tours. In 2000 they're featuring Berlin but will redeploy to Munich in 2001.

The German railways (Deutsche Bahn) offer excellent tours including transport and very nice room and board (often from just DM100 per couple per night) for package destinations that include Munich. There are some interesting and unusual options for Bavaria as well, such as steam-train or horseback-riding tours. Deutsche Bahn foreign offices include:

(☎ 020-8390 38 40) Suite 4, The Sanctuary, 23 Oakhill Grove, Surbiton, Surrey KT6 DU

(☎ 310 479-4140 or toll free 800-937 1235) 11933 Wilshire Blvd, Los Angeles, CA 90025

(☎ 2-9248 6129, fax 9248-6217) 321 Kent Street, Sydney, NSW 2000

For information on walking, bicycle and bus/tram tours in Munich see the Organised Tours section of the Getting Around chapter.

WARNING

This chapter is particularly vulnerable to change – prices for international travel are volatile, routes are introduced or cancelled, schedules change, special deals come and go, rules and visa requirements are amended. Airlines seem to take a perverse pleasure in making price structures and regulations as complicated as possible. You should check directly with the airline or travel agent to make sure you understand how a fare (and ticket you may buy) works. The travel industry is highly competitive, and offers many specials and bonuses. You should get opinions, quotes and advice from as many airlines and travel agents as possible before paying. The details in this chapter should be regarded as pointers; they cannot be a substitute for careful, up-to-date research.

GETTING THERE & AWAY

Getting Around

TO/FROM AIRPORT

Munich's Franz-Josef-Strauss Flughafen (airport) is connected by the commuter trains S1 and S8 to the Hauptbahnhof (main train station). The trip costs DM14 with a single ticket or eight strips of a *Streifenkarte* (a 10-strip ticket). The service takes 40 minutes and runs every 20 minutes from 4 am until around 1 am. At the ticket machines (one level above the train station, near the escalators) you might consider buying a *Tageskarte* (day pass) for DM18 for travel on the entire network, or for DM26 a ticket covering up to five passengers.

The Lufthansa airport bus runs at 20-minute intervals from Arnulfstrasse, on the north side of the Hauptbahnhof, between 6.50 am and 7.50 pm (DM16/26 one way/return, children DM6/12, 45 minutes). Its comfy coaches stop at several points at the terminal for passengers of all airlines, and snacks are served on board during the summer months. Call ☎ 13 08 23 33 to reserve a seat, or book through the tourist office.

A taxi linking the airport to Munich's outskirts will cost at least DM50 and to the city centre about DM100.

PUBLIC TRANSPORT

You can't get around much easier than on Munich's excellent public transport network (MVV, ☎ 41 42 43 44). The system has 16 concentric ringed zones around the city, but most places of interest to visitors (except Dachau, Schloss Schleissheim and the airport) are within the four-zone inner-city area (the blue *Innenraum* on maps). The system is modified often, usually involving some subtle spin on zones or prices. New fares, work on the lines and other relevant changes are posted on information boards or at MVV ticket windows (such as those on the first lower level of the Hauptbahnhof).

Tickets & Passes

Short rides (over a total of four stops, with no more than two U-Bahn or S-Bahn stops) cost DM1.80, longer trips cost DM3.60. It's cheaper to buy a strip-card of 10 tickets *(Streifenkarte)* for DM15, and stamp one strip (DM1.50) per adult on rides of two or less tram or U-Bahn stops, two strips (DM3) for longer rides. Passengers aged 15 to 20 can ride on the Streifenkarte for half-price. You can change between trains, buses and trams as often as needed to get where you're going.

The best value is in day passes for the inner zone, which cost DM9 for individuals and just DM13 for up to five people, and three-day inner-zone passes, which are DM22/33. The MVV also sells the weekly *Isarcard*, costing DM15.50 for individuals for one to two zones, DM19 for three zones, and DM22.50 for four zones. The snag is that the Isarcard begins on Sunday, so if you buy it on say Wednesday it's still only valid through to the following Saturday.

You won't always find vending machines that sell the Isarcard (in the Hauptbahnhof, there's one at the entrance to the U1/U2 and to the U4/U5). You can also procure weekly passes from a *Zeitkartenstellen* counter in the first lower level of the Hauptbahnhof, in the Poccistrasse station (U3/U6 line near the Theresienwiese) or in the Ostbahnhof.

Bicycles on the underground cost DM3.60 per trip or DM4.50 for a day pass, but you can't take them on board during the weekday rush hours (6 to 9 am and 4 to 6 pm).

Buying & Using Tickets

Bus and tram drivers sell single and day tickets, but other multiple, weekly or monthly tickets, as well as those for the U-Bahn and S-Bahn trains, must be bought in advance. Most types of tickets are available at the blue MVV vending machines (which also have instructions in English) in U- and S-Bahn stations, at bus stops or from MVV ticket windows at the bigger stations. Some tobacconists and newspaper kiosks also sell tickets.

MVV tickets must be validated before use by time-stamping them in the little machines at station entrances, and on board buses and trams. Failure to do so will put you at the mercy of uniformed (sometimes plain-clothed) ticket inspectors who speak perfect English, who have seen and heard it all before, and who possess Teutonic efficiency when it comes to handing out fines of DM60 for unauthorised travel (you can even be fined on the platform if you can't show a ticket).

Note that rail passes (Eurail etc) are valid on Munich's S-Bahn (but not U-Bahn) trains.

U-Bahn & S-Bahn

The underground is the most efficient way to get around Munich. The U-Bahn and sub-urban S-Bahns cease at around 12.30 am on weekdays and 1.30 am on weekends, but after that you can take a night bus. Timetables are located on the platforms and in the first level above the platforms (it's an idea to look before you descend).

Colour-coded route maps are posted in all stations and carriages (see also Map 1). Many stations also have an orientation map showing locations of pharmacies, post offices and main buildings (such as museums) in the area.

As the train approaches a stop it is announced over the loudspeaker, and at some multi-platform stations the driver will also tell you to get out on the right-hand side (*'bitte Fahrtrichtung rechts aussteigen'*). Choosing the wrong door is like swimming against the tide.

Bus

As a rule, the underground will zip you around town much faster than the bus. There are only a few dedicated bus lanes, so buses tend to get stuck in traffic like every other vehicle. But the odds are that sometime you'll have to take a bus to places not served by the U- or S-Bahn.

Bus stops are marked with a big 'H' (for *Haltestelle*) and the name of the stop. Drivers sell tickets but they're slightly more expensive than from the vending machines, so buy ahead. On its approach, each stop is announced via a loudspeaker or a digital display. If you want to alight, push one of the buttons located on the handrails; you'll need to push another one to open the back doors. And if you only just miss a bus, don't expect the driver to brake and kindly let you get on – it won't happen.

Night buses *(Nachtbusse)* operate after standard hours – very convenient for disco and club-goers – but the routes, hours and schedules change often. Pick up a copy of the latest schedule from any tourist office.

CAR & MOTORCYCLE

Munich is encircled by an autobahn and, closer to the city centre, a six-lane series of roads known as the *Mittlerer Ring* (Middle Ring Road), which bears the brunt of rush-hour traffic. Police with radars are active on the ring (speed limit: 60km/h) and other roads in town, and there are cameras at many intersections. If you're filmed running a red light, expect a nasty fine in the mail.

The city centre is a minefield of one-way streets, pedestrian zones and general traffic congestion. Unless you plan to flee into a car park, you could hunt a long time for a parking spot. Note that ticket enforcement is Orwellian in pay-and-display areas, for which the hourly rate is usually DM2 (DM3 just south of the train station).

Car parks *(Parkhäuser)* cost DM2.50 to DM3.50 per hour, or roughly DM20 to DM25 per day. In the centre you'll find attended parking at the Tiefgarage vor der Oper on Max-Joseph-Platz (☎ 29 41 87), which is open from 7 am to 1 am Monday to Saturday and from 10 am to 1 am Sunday and public holidays. Other car parks include Am Stachus and Am Färbergraben, but both are closed on Sunday and public holidays.

One useful option is Park & Ride (ie free car parks next to U- and S-Bahn stops, signposted 'P+R'). If you're coming from Nuremberg on the A9 autobahn, pass the junction 'München Nord' going towards town and take the first exit to 'Fröttmaning'. The P+R next to the U6 stop is clearly marked, and from there it's a mere 17 minutes by U-Bahn to the Glockenspiel at Marienplatz. (See Map 1 for more P+R locations.)

Germany's main motoring organisation is the Allgemeine Deutscher Automobil Club (ADAC, ☎ 767 60). The main office is at Am Westerpark 8 and there's a big, more central ADAC office at Sendlinger-Tor-Platz (☎ 54 91 72 34).

Car Purchase

Unless you're staying in Germany for a while, this is more hassle than it's worth due to the costs and paperwork involved. European Union nationals must register the vehicle with the ominous-sounding *Ordnungs-und Strassenverkehrsamt* (Public Order & Traffic Office). You'll need proof of ownership, insurance and a passport or ID, and in some cases official translations of foreign documents. You'll also have the pleasure of paying a stiff motor vehicle tax.

If you're not an EU national, forget it – you have to be a resident to buy and register a car. You could ask a friend or relative to buy a car for you, but as that puts their own driving record and insurance rates at risk, it's not a popular option.

But if you're undeterred, there are plenty of used-car bargains to be had in Munich – provided you know what you're doing. Make sure the vehicle has a valid *TÜV* seal of motor-vehicle fitness. See the Shopping chapter for further details.

Car Rental

Some of the best deals around are offered through a US company called AutoEurope, which negotiates low rates with major agencies such as Europcar, Hertz and Budget. There's no need to book ahead, you don't pay extra for one-way rentals or airport drop-offs and there's no charge for cancellations or changes. There's a three-day minimum rental charge, though it could still work out cheaper than with many competitors. The minimum age for renting cars is 19.

The smallest economy car will cost roughly DM125 for the three-day minimum and DM225 for a week, including unlimited kilometres, VAT and third-party insurance, but not collision damage waiver (CDW). The CDW will add about DM25 per day to your rate. Some US credit cards automatically include CDW for rental cars; bear in mind, however, that card-holders may actually have to pay for any damage up front (!) and claim the amount back from the credit-card company – check this out ahead of time.

To reach AutoEurope from Germany, call toll-free ☎ 0130-82 21 98; from North America, it's ☎ 800-223 55 55; from Australia ☎ 1-800-12 64 09; from New Zealand ☎ 0800-44 07 22; and from the UK ☎ 0800-89 98 93.

Some local firms offer good deals from time to time, too. Autohansa (☎ 50 40 64), at Schiessstätterstrasse 12, was advertising a summer special of DM135 for three days and DM225 per week for an Opel Corsa with unlimited kilometres, plus DM75/125 for CDW per three days/week. Swing (☎ 523 20 05), at Schellingstrasse 139, offers similar rates.

All major car-rental firms have offices in Munich. Their standard rates begin at about DM80 per day and DM360 per week, including tax and unlimited kilometres. Some deals include CDW, which can save DM25 or more per day. There are also special weekend rates for rental from noon Friday until 9 am Monday, starting at around DM99. You have to be at least 21 years old. All these firms have offices upstairs in the Hauptbahnhof and at Franz-Josef-Strauss airport.

Avis
   (☎ 550 22 51) Hauptbahnhof
   (☎ 97 59 76 00) Airport
Europcar
   (☎ 549 02 40) Hauptbahnhof
   (☎ 973 50 20) Airport
Hertz
   (☎ 550 22 56) Hauptbahnhof
   (☎ 97 88 60) Airport
Sixt Budget
   (☎ 550 24 47) Hauptbahnhof
   (☎ 0180-526 25 25) Airport

TAXI

Taxis (always bland beige-coloured sedans) are expensive and hardly more convenient than public transport. They cost around DM5 at flag fall plus DM2.20 per kilometre for the first 6km and DM2 thereafter; night fares are about DM0.20 higher per kilometre. For a radio-dispatched taxi ring

☎ 216 10, ☎ 216 11 or ☎ 194 10. Ranks of taxis are at all main train stations and obvious spots throughout town.

Between 5 pm and 1 am you can benefit from a Deutsche Bahn deal called BahnTaxi. A flat-rate ride for two people to most anywhere in the centre costs DM15. You can order one from conductors on the train before you reach Munich, or at the Reisezentrum in the Hauptbahnhof. The taxi rank is at the south-eastern end of the Hauptbahnhof, near the Bayerstrasse exit.

RIKSHA-MOBIL
Riksha-Mobil (☎ 129 48 08), at Gabrielenstrasse 2, has yellow pedicabs seating two people (plus light luggage), and it's a novel way to see the town. But it ain't cheap: a journey of a few minutes costs DM3.80, and a 45-minute jaunt round the sights costs a whopping DM89. Check the fare to your destination before you hop on. Rickshaws depart from in front of the fish fountain on Marienplatz (you can also flag one down).

BICYCLE
You can pick up a free bicycle map booklet called *Rad & Tat* (in German only) from the tourist office on Marienplatz. You'll find it on the open-access information shelves on the right at the rear of the office, so you won't have to queue.

Radius Tours & Bikes (Map 7a, ☎ 59 61 13), at the end of platform No 31 in the Hauptbahnhof, rents three-speed city bikes for DM25/DM45/DM75 per day/two-days/week, mountain and trekking bikes for DM30/54/90. You can also rent bikes by the hour (DM5 for city bikes, two-hour minimum). Rail-pass holders get a 10% discount, and there's a 20% discount from Tuesday to Thursday. It's open from 10 am to 6 pm Monday to Saturday.

Bike and Walk Company (☎ 58 95 89 33) rents city bikes for DM20 for the first day, DM10 for each additional day and DM50 for every week after that. Simply show up at the Neues Rathaus on Marienplatz between 10.30 and 11.30 am or 3 and 3.30 pm from May to mid-September, or phone to arrange a pick-up time.

Aktiv-Rad (☎ 26 65 06), Hans-Sachs-Strasse 7 near the Frauenhoferstrasse U-Bahn station, charges DM18 per day for city bikes. It is open from 9.30 am to 1 pm and 2 to 6 pm Monday to Friday, 9.30 am to 1 pm Saturday.

Guests of the Jugendherberge München hostel can rent bikes for DM22/40/54 for one/two/three days.

ORGANISED TOURS
Walking Tours
Some of Germany's most delightful walking tours are with Munich Walks (mobile ☎ 0177-227 59 01), which runs English-language tours daily from May to December. They last 2½ to three hours and cost DM15/12 for people 26 or older/under 26 (children under 14 free when accompanied by an adult). The Discover Munich tour features witty anecdotes on history and architecture; it leaves at 10 am and 3 pm each day from May to October. The Infamous Third Reich Sites tour covers exactly that, but goes less often: 10.30 am Monday, Thursday and Saturday from May to August; and 2.30 pm on Monday and Saturday during September and October. All tours leave from in front of the EurAide office, track 11 of the Hauptbahnhof.

Bike and Walk Company has rival English-language tours with similar subject matter, but are slightly longer (3½ hours). They cost DM15 (kids under 14 free when accompanied by an adult), and leave from the main entrance of the Neues Rathaus on Marienplatz (under the Glockenspiel). Tours take place at 10.30 am daily from May to October, and at 10.30 am Friday, Saturday and public holidays during April.

Bicycle Tours
Mike's Bike Tours (☎ 651 42 75, mobile ☎ 0172-852 06 60) runs 3½-hour guided city cycling tours in English (DM31). The tours depart at 11.30 am and 4 pm daily from the archway in front of the Toy Museum on Marienplatz. Tours finish at a leafy beer garden, ideal for a glass of the good stuff.

Bike and Walk Tours (☎ 58 95 89 33) are new on the scene, and led by a troupe of

euro currency converter DM1 = €.51

native English speakers. Guides present sparkling tales (Hitler's foiled putsch etc) during a laid-back pedal-tour of the sights that also ends with a *Mass* of brew. Self-promotion is refreshingly absent.

Radius Tours & Bikes (☎ 55 02 93 74) is another option, with a competent three hour tour in English. It costs DM25 and departs from the Radius office in the Hauptbahnhof at 10.30 am daily from 1 May to 3 Oct; from 15 May to 5 Sept, a second tour departs at 2.30 pm. All takers get a free bottle of mineral water.

Bus & Tram Tours

Panorama Tours (☎ 55 02 89 95) runs seven coach tours to various places in the city (one to 4½ hours, from DM17/9 for adult/child, to DM100 per person). The open-topped double-deckers are pleasant in nice weather, but commentary is given in at least two languages so everything takes twice as long to explain. They leave from in front of the Hertie department store, opposite the Hauptbahnhof. Most tours start at 10 am or 2.30 pm.

Circle Line (☎ 26 02 51 83) gives one-hour tours of Munich in English (and seven other languages if need be), they depart from the north side of the Elisenhof, near the Hauptbahnhof. Tickets for the double-deckers cost DM17 (children four to 12 years DM9). Tours depart every hour on the hour from 10 am to 4 pm.

Stattreisen München (☎ 54 40 42 30) runs tram tours (in German only) on weekends. On Saturday there's a tour of 'unknown quarters' that departs from the kiosk next to the cinema at Sendlinger Tor. On Sunday there's a 'city-and-suburbs' tour departing from the fountain in front of the Karstadt Sporthaus, on Neuhauser Strasse. Both tours cost DM12/10 and leave at 2 pm (these are regular trams, so you'll need an MVV ticket).

For a little tour of your own, jump on tram No 17 going south from Karlsplatz, which will take you round the southern edge of the Altstadt and through Lehel to the east side of the English Garden (about 25 minutes). Alight at Tivolistrasse – the Chinese Tower is about half a kilometre to the west.

Things to See & Do

Munich serves up a cocktail of big-city sophistication and relaxed southern *Gemütlichkeit*. This translates into a healthy mix of entertainment, from earthy beer gardens and trendy pubs to world-class opera and avant-garde theatre. The Altstadt (old town) is a pleasure to stroll around, as its historic treasures were painstakingly restored in the aftermath of WWII (many look now like they did towards the end of the 19th century). Its grand avenues and spacious squares recall the glory of Bavaria's monarchy, and plenty of Müncheners will happily do the same if they get the chance.

Munich is compact enough to digest in a couple of days, but you could easily spend several weeks exploring the place without getting bored: the museums alone are large and interesting enough to fill a holiday. The individual districts outside the Altstadt have a life of their own, and it's well worth getting out to them to see how 'real' Müncheners live.

HIGHLIGHTS

According to a joint study, published in 1999, by the City of Munich and automaker BMW, the most visited attractions in Munich are:

1. Olympia Park
2. Hellabrunn Zoo
3. Deutsches Museum
4. State Gallery of Modern Art
5. Olympia Tower
6. Schloss Nymphenburg
7. BMW Museum
8. Hypo-Kulturstiftung Art Gallery
9. Neue Pinakothek
10. Municipal Gallery in the Lenbachhaus

This ranking includes German as well as foreign visitors. (Figures weren't available for the Alte Pinakothek, which was reopened in 1998 after a lengthy renovation.) Our recommendations for visitors read as follows (in no particular order):

- A tall one in one of Munich's fabulous beer gardens

- Poking round the colourful stands of Viktualienmarkt, and buying a weird fruit or two
- A visit to the Deutsches Museum and at least one of the big art museums
- Watching the surfers in the English Garden's *Eisbach*
- Bar-hopping in Schwabing's student district or Haidhausen
- A classical concert at the Gasteig, or a jazz gig in the Bayerischer Hof's Nightclub
- Watching street performers on Marienplatz and in the pedestrian zone
- A visit to Schloss Nymphenburg and its folly-filled garden
- Eating breakfast and watching the world go by at one of Munich's trendy cafes
- Cycling along the banks of the Isar River

WHAT'S FREE

It's easy to spend a fortune enjoying the sites in Munich but some of the most enjoyable things will cost you nothing. The following list of activities and sights are free, and are described in greater detail under the individual sights in this book.

- Visit one of the museums free on Sunday (see the Museums section, later in this chapter)
- Take in the aromas and exotic wares of the Viktualienmarkt
- Watch the Glockenspiel do its thing on Marienplatz
- Marvel at the city's architectural masterpieces, especially along Ludwigstrasse, on Königsplatz and along Maximilianstrasse
- Search for tombstones of the famous in the South Cemetery and Bogenhausen's St George Church
- Stroll or jog through the English Garden or the grounds of Schloss Nymphenburg
- Visit a free organ or classical music recital at one of Munich's churches
- Admire the Jugendstil (Art Nouveau) houses in Schwabing, Neuhausen, Bogenhausen and other neighbourhoods
- Catch the drunken oompah band in the Hofbräuhaus or in the Chinese Tower of the English Garden
- Discover hidden treasure in Munich's many flea markets

Museums

Munich has dozens of museums, but most of the famous ones are concentrated in and around the Altstadt. Most have both a standing collection and changing thematic exhibits, so consult the monthly listings for details.

Display captions are frequently in German only, which can drastically reduce your enjoyment and understanding of the exhibits (unless, of course, you speak the language). Some museums have English-language pamphlets at ticket counters, which you may borrow for free or take with you, or read attached to strings in the exhibit halls. Others have entire guidebooks that are only available for purchase. Some of the larger museums, such as the Deutsches Museum or Schloss Nymphenburg, have taped, self-guided audio tours in several languages (around DM4 to DM5).

Many of the large public galleries have free entry on Sunday, notably the Alte Pinakothek, the Neue Pinakothek, the State Gallery of Modern Art, the Glyptothek and the State Antiquities Collection (Staatliche Antikensammlung). Note that in most of the state-run museums, you *can* take photos if you don't use a flash.

Most of Munich's museums are closed on Monday. The important exceptions are the Deutsches Museum, the Toy Museum, the Siemens Forum and the BMW Museum, as well as the Amalienburg on the Schloss Nymphenburg grounds. For more information about the museums themselves, see the individual entries in this chapter.

Residenz Museums (Map 7)

Within the Residenz palace, the Residenzmuseum (☎ 29 06 71) has an extraordinary array of over 100 rooms displaying treasures of the Wittelsbach dynasty. The museum is so large that it's broken into two sections, which take about two hours each to see. You can do it on your own with a copy of the excellent English-language guide *Residence Munich* (DM6, at the cash desk), which has room-by-room tours with photographs and explanations.

The enclosed **Grotto Court**, one of the first places you'll see when you enter, features the wonderful **Perseus Fountain**. The grotto itself, which frames a rather dilapidated statue of Mercury, is an elaborate post-WWII reconstruction; many of the shells covering the walls were brought back by Germans on beach holidays in the 1950s, following an appeal made by the museum authorities.

Next door is the famous **Antiquarium**, a long, tunnel-like hallway built to house the Wittelsbach's huge antique collection. The **Kurfürstenzimmer** (Elector's Rooms) feature some stunning Italian portraits, and has one long passage with two dozen views of Italy painted by Carl Rottmann, one of Munich's leading Romantic painters.

Other highlights include the **Ancestral Gallery**, remodelled in 1726–30 and including 121 portraits of the rulers of Bavaria (note, in the centre, the larger paintings of Charlemagne and Ludwig the Bavarian).

Also worthy of mention are the **Schlachtensäle** (Battle Halls); the **Porcelain Chambers**, containing 19th century porcelain services from factories in Berlin, Meissen and Nymphenburg; and the **Asian Collections**, with Chinese and Japanese lacquerware, tapestries, carpets, furniture and jewellery.

The museum is open from 10 am to 4.30 pm Tuesday to Sunday; admission is DM7/5 for adults/children (free for children). Two-hour tours (DM8) in German are held at 11 am on Sunday and Thursday, and at 2 pm Thursday and Saturday; each tour starts at Maximiliansplatz, and takes in half the collection.

Schatzkammer The Residenzmuseum entrance is also the entrance to the Schatzkammer der Residenz (Treasury; separate admission of DM6/free), which exhibits an enormous quantity of jewels, ornate goldwork and other precious objects. The mind-boggling treasures in this Aladdin's Cave include portable altars, the ruby jewellery of Queen Therese, amazing pocket watches and 'exotic handicrafts', including applied art from Turkey, Iran, Mexico and India.

The visit culminates in the murkily-lit chamber containing the **Bavarian crown jewels**, made in the early 19th century for Max II Joseph soon after the duchy was made a kingdom by Napoleon.

It's worth the admission price; the English-language guide *Treasury in the Munich Residence* costs another DM6. The Schatzkammer is open from 10 am to 4.30 pm Tuesday to Sunday.

Egyptian Art Museum At the south side of the Hofgarten, the **Staatliche Sammlung Ägyptischer Kunst** (State Collection of Egyptian Art, ☎ 29 85 46), at Hofgartenstrasse 1, has a small but excellent display of Egyptian antiquities, artwork, monuments and statues from the Old, Middle and New Kingdoms (2670–1075 BC). It's open from 9 am to 4 pm Tuesday to Friday (also from 7 pm to 9 pm on Tuesday). Saturday, Sunday and holidays the hours are 10 am to 5 pm (DM5/3). Enter at the north side of the Residenz at the Obelisk.

Königsplatz Museums (Map 7)

The **Glyptothek** and the **Staatliche Antikensammlungen** on Königsplatz are both impressive and often overlooked by tourists. Each costs DM6/3.50, or you can visit both for DM10/6. Try to go on a Sunday when they're free; both are closed on Monday.

Glyptothek This fascinating museum (☎ 28 61 00), Königsplatz 3, contains Greek and Roman sculpture as well as portraits of Greek philosophers, leaders and Roman kings. During a visit to Italy in 1804, Ludwig I acquired a bunch of these wonderful finds; 12 years later, he chose Leo von Klenze in Germany's first architectural competition to build the museum. King and designer discussed the blueprint in over 500 letters, which was the main reason why the place wasn't opened until 1830.

Highlights here include the stunning remains of the Greek **Temple of Aegina**, which had been excavated by German and English explorers in the early 19th century. The place resembles a petrified morgue (eg disembodied heads and headless warriors,

all in armour), and you can take some good flash-less pictures if the sun's out. Don't miss the **Barbarini Faun**, a reclining Adonis-type character in the nude with stunning anatomical detail.

The inner courtyard has a calm and pleasant **cafe**, and classical theatre is also staged here under the stars in summer. The museum is open from 10 am to 5 pm Tuesday to Sunday and to 8 pm on Thursday (DM6/3.50).

State Antiquities Collection The **Staatliche Antikensammlungen** (☎ 59 83 59), at Königsplatz 1, features one of Germany's best assemblies of ancient vases, gold and silver jewellery and ornaments, bronzework, and Greek, Roman and Etruscan sculptures and statues. The building was erected by Georg Friedrich Ziebland from 1838 to 1848, and was initially conceived for mainstream art and industrial exhibits in the time before the Alte Pinakothek.

Although the collection is compared to those of the British Museum and the Paris Louvre, the ground-floor exhibit is poorly lit – not the best environment for oodles of brown vases. The real highlight is the cellar display, which includes some comical Roman masks, helmets, shields and animal-shaped drinking vessels. It's a bit like stumbling across a long-forgotten props room from *Ben Hur*.

The museum is open from 10 am to 5 pm Tuesday to Sunday and to 8 pm on Wednesday (DM6/3.50).

State Ethnology Museum (Map 7)

The Staatliches Museum für Völkerkunde (☎ 210 13 60) has one of Europe's largest Asian and Oriental collections (many of its 350,000 items were personal souvenirs of the Wittelsbach royal family). Don't miss the fantastic Brazil section with artefacts from now-extinct tribes as documented by Bavarian explorers Spix and Martius from 1817 to 1820. Hours are from 9.30 am to 4.30 pm (DM6/3.50).

Lenbach House (Map 7)

Portraitist Franz von Lenbach (1836–1904), a leading *Gründerzeit* painter, used his considerable fortune to construct an Etruscan villa in Munich between 1883 and 1889. It was sold to the city by his widow in 1924, and she threw in a bunch of his works as part of the deal.

Today his fabulous ochre-coloured residence is open as the Museum im Lenbachhaus (☎ 233 03 20), Luisenstrasse 33, featuring a staggering range of 19th century masterpieces by Munich and other German masters and space for exhibitions of international modern art. Much of the place was pummelled during WWII, and only a small upstairs section has been restored to its dark and gloomy original state. You'll also see at least one of Lenbach's 80-odd portraits of Bismarck (see also Painting & Sculpture in the Facts about Munich chapter).

A whole section upstairs is devoted to *Blaue Reiter* (Blue Rider) painters, members of a movement begun in 1911 by Franz Marc (1880–1916) and Wassily Kandinsky (1866–1944), widely acknowledged to be the first abstract painter. The group, which also included Paul Klee, Alexej Jawlenski, August Macke and Gabrielle Münter, is acknowledged as the high point of German expressionism (see the Painting & Sculpture section of the Facts about Munich chapter). The irony here is that von Lenbach vigorously opposed the Secessionist painters, whose works gave impetus to the Blue Rider group.

In the nearby Königsplatz U-Bahn station is the **Lenbachhaus Kunstbau**, a separate display hall with rotating modern art exhibitions.

Both are open from 10 am to 6 pm daily; combined entry is DM8/4. Outside the Lenbachhaus there's a beer garden and a lovely courtyard with fountains.

Mineral Museums (Map 7)

Rock fans should head for the nearby **Museum der Geologischen Staatssammlung** (State Geological Collection, ☎ 21 80 65 13), Luisenstrasse 37, with 20,000 exhibitions on the earth's crust and mineral wealth. It's open from 8 am to 6 pm weekdays (free).

Also popular is the **Museum Reich der Kristalle** (Museum of the Crystal Realm,

☎ 23 94 43 12), Theresienstrasse 41 (entrance at Barer Strasse, across the street from the Alte Pinakothek), with excellent exhibits on the formation of minerals and crystals. It's open from 1 to 5 pm Tuesday to Friday and from 1 to 6 pm weekends (DM2/1).

Alte Pinakothek (Map 7)

The Alte Pinakothek (☎ 23 80 52 16), at Barer Strasse 27 (north entrance), is a treasure trove of the works of European masters between the 14th and 18th centuries. This rather monolithic structure (commissioned by Ludwig I) was reopened in 1998 after an expensive four year renovation; as far as anyone can tell, most of the renovation money went towards a sophisticated alarm system.

The collection reflects the rather eclectic tastes of the Wittelsbachs over four centuries. The works are sorted by schools over two sprawling floors: the early German section is in the left wing of the ground floor, with a continuation upstairs; the lower right wing is devoted to baroque and Renaissance works from around the globe. Upstairs there are Italian, Flemish and Dutch sections on one side, and French and Spanish on the other.

Major displays include Albrecht Dürer's Christ-like *Self-Portrait* and his *Four Apostles*; Rogier van der Weyden's *Adoration of the Magi*; Botticelli's *Pietà*; and Peter Paul Rubens' two-story-high *Judgement Day*. This museum houses, in fact, one of the world's most comprehensive Rubens collections. Look out also for Paulus Moreelse's lascivious *Blonde Shephardess* exposing herself in the Flemish Masters section.

The museum is open from 10 am to 6 pm Tuesday to Sunday, Thursday until 8 pm (DM7/4).

Neue Pinakothek (Map 7)

Just opposite the Alte Pinakothek, at Barer Strasse 29, is the Neue Pinakothek (☎ 23 80 51 95). This modern building (1975–81), by Alexander von Branca, contains an extensive collection of 18th and 19th century paintings and sculpture, from rococo to Jugendstil. The interiors are a bit peppier than those of the Alte Pinakothek, with powerful red and blue backdrops in many rooms and excellent lighting.

Highlights include familiar classics by Impressionists such as Van Gogh's *Sunflowers* or Manet's *Breakfast in the Studio*. Among more off-beat works, don't miss Walter Crane's *The Steeds of Neptune* showing aquatic horses riding waves into the beach, or Goya's chilling kitchen still-life, *Plucked Turkey*.

Some of the early Romantic and neoclassical works look rather tame in comparison. One interesting section for students of German painting is the Biedermeier room, which refers to a late-Romantic trend towards tranquil interiors, middle-class portraits and genre paintings. (The term later came to be used more widely to describe furniture in roughly a French Empire style.)

The museum is open from 10 am to 5 pm Tuesday to Sunday, (to 8 pm Tuesday and Thursday); enter on Theresienstrasse (DM 7/4, free on Sunday).

Pinakothek der Moderne (Map 7)

One block east of the Alte Pinakothek, at the corner of Gabelsbergerstrasse and Türkenstrasse, is a huge construction site where the new, gleaming Pinakothek of the Modern will be unveiled in 2001. The six storey, Bauhaus-like complex will bring together four contemporary museums: the State Gallery for Modern Art (now in the Haus der Kunst), the New Collection of applied arts and the State Graphics Collection (both now in the Bavarian National Museum) and the Architecture Museum. The creation is aimed at rivalling Berlin's Museum Insel development in the year 2000 (although Berlin's is really in a bigger league). A trendy cafe and the inevitable museum shop are also planned.

Hypo-Kulturstiftung Art Gallery (Map 7a)

South of the Theatinerkirche, on fashionable Theatinerstrasse at No 15, is the Kunsthalle der Hypo-Kulturstiftung (☎ 22 44 12), one of Munich's best-loved museums with excellent rotating exhibitions. It's open from 10 am to 6 pm daily (Thursday till 9 pm), closed

Sunday (DM10/8, Monday it's half-price). Check with EurAide or the tourist offices as to what's on when you're in town.

Deutsches Museum (Map 7)

Said to be the world's largest science and technology museum, the Deutsches Museum (☎ 217 91), Museumsinsel 1 near Isartor, to the east of the city centre, takes up eight floors, and you could spend days, if not weeks wandering a 16km path round the displays. Many of the exhibits are hands-on, and it's a wonderful place to take the kids.

The basement is devoted to mining and automobiles, and the ground floor to tunnel construction, railways and aeronautics. The 1st floor has a flimsy and dated section on physics and chemistry, and a wonderful section on musical instruments. The 2nd floor has the over-hyped Altamira cave exhibit. The 3rd floor ranges from geodesy and weights and measures to microelectronics and telecommunications. The 4th to 6th floors are dedicated to astronomy and amateur radio. The roof affords a nice view west over the Isar towards the Altstadt.

Demonstrations take place throughout the day (consult the notice boards by the ticket booths). A popular one is in the electricity section where a staff member is raised in the insulated 'Faraday Cage', which is then zapped with a 220,000V lightning bolt. There's usually a staff musician playing one of the ancient keyboards in the instrument section, which makes for a relaxing interlude from the hordes of visitors elsewhere in the museum.

The museum is open from 9 am to 5 pm daily (DM10/DM4). It's free for children under six and a family ticket costs DM22. A visit to the planetarium is DM3 extra. There's a reasonable restaurant (run by Käfers) on the 1st floor. To reach the museum take any S-Bahn to Isartor, U1 or 2 to Fraunhoferstrasse, or tram No 18 almost to the door.

Forum der Technik In the north-east corner of the Deutsches Museum complex on Museumsinsel, near Rosenheimer Strasse, is the Technical Forum (☎ 21 12 51 83), with a Zeiss planetarium show and an IMAX (big-screen) cinema. Offerings are generally nature-oriented – stampeding elephants or dinosaurs that leap into your lap – and it's absolutely worth the admission price of DM12.50/9.50. A combination ticket for the planetarium and IMAX is DM20.50/15.50.

Several days a week, there are late-night performances of Jean-Michel Jarre, Pink Floyd and other evergreen rock/pop show-masters (DM18.90/14.90). Programs for children run on weekdays (DM6.50) and prices are reduced on Monday, 'cinema day' (DM8.50).

Museum Villa Stuck (Map 6)

Franz von Stuck's lovely Jugendstil (Art Nouveau) villa (☎ 45 55 51 25), Prinzregentenstrasse 60, has changing exhibitions of the classical, modern and contemporary periods. It's being renovated in stages through the end of 2002, but most of the museum's collection remains open to viewing. Hours are from 10 am to 5 pm daily and Thursday till 9 pm (closed Monday). Admission prices vary with the display.

City Museum (Map 7a)

The Munich Stadtmuseum (☎ 23 32 23 70), St-Jakobs-Platz 1, documents city history, as you'd expect, but includes exhibits of brewing, fashion, musical instruments, photography and puppets. You'll also find some very intricate wooden Morris dancers and a model of the city as it was in 1570. There are rotating exhibitions (call ☎ 23 32 55 86 for program information), and films are shown nightly as well. It's open from 10 am to 6 pm Tuesday to Sunday (DM5/2.50).

Modern Art Gallery (Map 7)

The Staatsgalerie Moderner Kunst (☎ 21 12 71 37), Prinzregentenstrasse 1, in the west wing of the Haus der Kunst, displays some great German and international contributions to modern art that were banned by the Nazis. The collection includes some pretty wild paintings by Munch, Picasso and Magritte, as well as funky sculptures and pop art. The upstairs section is devoted to the abstract and avant-garde – one enigmatic work by Joseph Beuys consists of petrified

logs. The museum is open from 10 am to 5 pm Tuesday to Sunday, and to 8 pm on Thursday (DM6/3.50). In 2001 the gallery will be relocated to the Pinakothek der Moderne (see earlier in this section), leaving the Haus der Kunst free for special exhibits (half of it is already used for this purpose). Take bus No 53 from the city centre.

Bavarian National Museum (Map 4)

At the western end of Prinzregentenstrasse, at No 3, the formidable Bayerisches Nationalmuseum (☎ 21 12 41) has the city's biggest collection of Bavarian and other German art, as well as modern, industrial and prehistory artwork from around the world. In the main building, there's folk art and history, including religious and traditional costumes and loads of artefacts.

The ground floor has early-medieval, Gothic, Renaissance, rococo, baroque and neoclassical works; the 1st floor has applied arts, including clocks, ceramics, jewellery and stained glass. The Fine Art Collection has sculptures, carvings and paintings up to the 14th century. It's open from 9.30 am to 5 pm Tuesday to Sunday (DM3/2).

The **Neue Sammlung** (New Collection, ☎ 22 78 44), housed in a side wing of the complex, holds rotating exhibitions from its huge collection of applied and industrial art. You'll find all sorts of everyday items, from toasters to petrol pumps to desktop lamps, all meticulously documented.

In the northern section the **Prähistorische Staatssammlung**, (Prehistoric Collection, ☎ 29 39 11) at Lerchenfeldstrasse 2, is packed with archaeological goodies, including artefacts from the city's first Roman and Celtic residents. It's open from 9 am to 4 pm Tuesday to Sunday, and to 8 pm Thursday (DM5/3).

Take U4 or U5 to Lehel, or tram No 17 or bus No 53 almost to the door.

Schack Gallery (Map 4)

Just east of the Bavarian National Museum, housed in the former Prussian embassy, is the **Schack-Galerie** (☎ 23 80 52 24) at Prinzregentenstrasse 9. It houses the permanent collection of the Schack family, comprising 19th century German masters (Böcklin, Feuerback, Lenbach and others). Hours are from 10 am to 5 pm daily, closed Tuesday (DM4/2.50).

Alpine Museum (Map 6)

The Deutsches Alpines Museum (☎ 211 22 40), in the beautiful white building at Praterinsel 5 (north of the Deutsches Museum), has loads of mountain paintings, graphics, scientific instruments and a detailed history of the German Alpine Association (DAV). It's open from 1 to 6 pm Tuesday, Wednesday and Friday, from 1 to 8 pm Thursday and from 10 am to 6 pm Saturday (DM5/2.50). Take any S-Bahn to Isartor and then tram No 17 to Mariannenplatz, and walk east over the bridge.

Centre for Unusual Museums (Map 7a)

We could make lots of jokes about this place, but to paraphrase Groucho Marx, it doesn't need our help. The Zentrum für Aussergewöhnliche Museen (☎ 290 41 21), Westenriederstrasse 26 (any S-Bahn to Isartor or tram No 17 or 18), is a gathering of bizarre and unusual collections, including bottles, Easter bunnies, chamber pots, corkscrews and locks. There's also a collection of items associated with 'Sissi' (that's how Germans refer to that beloved Empress Elisabeth of Austria). It's open from 10 am to 6 pm daily (DM8/5).

Theatre Museum (Map 7a)

The Deutsches Theatermuseum (☎ 210 69 10), Galeriestrassse 4a, under the Hofgarten arcades, has everything about theatre history – manuscripts, scores, sketches of stage sets, photos and the largest Wagner collection after Bayreuth's. It's open only for rotating exhibitions or by appointment, but the library's hours are always from 10 am to noon and from 1.30 to 4 pm Tuesday and Thursday.

Hunting & Fishing Museum (Map 7a)

The Deutsches Jagd- und Fischereimuseum (☎ 22 05 22), Neuhauser Strasse 2 in the pedestrian zone, is not just for rifle-and-rod freaks, there are rococo hunting sleighs, Stone-Age fishing tackle and Chinese scroll paintings (with hunting motifs, of course). It's housed in the former Augustinerkirche (1290), which was secularised in the early 19th century as a customs hall. The interiors are stunning, with groined ceilings and lavish rococo adornments – not to mention the rooms and rooms of stuffed animals and antlers. It's open from 9.30 am to 5 pm daily, and till 9 pm Monday and Thursday (DM5/3). Look for the big bronze boar out front, a popular meeting spot.

White Rose Memorial (Map 7)

Inside the Ludwig-Maximilian-Universität you will find the **Denkstätte Weisse Rose** (☎ 36 54 45), at Geschwister-Scholl-Platz 1. There's a library dedicated to the WWII resistance movement along with lots of photos and documents about their activities. It's a fitting place for the museum, as Hans and Sophie Scholl were arrested here for distributing anti-Nazi leaflets and were summarily executed. The memorial is in the lower mezzanine behind the entrance hall. It's open from 10 am to 4 pm weekdays, and Thursday till 9 pm. It's closed during August, although you can always call and they'll open it up for you (free).

Siemens Forum (Map 7)

The Siemens Forum (☎ 63 63 26 60) on Oskar-von-Miller-Ring has fascinating exhibits on 140 years of company history: electronics and microelectronics from the telegraph to the multimedia personal computer. It's a fun, hands-on kind of place, housed in a huge modern complex completed in October 1999. There's an audio tour in English and entry is free, so why not? It's open from 10 am to 5 pm weekdays and Sunday.

Take the U4 or U5 to Odeonsplatz or tram No 19.

Toy Museum (Map 7a)

In the tower of the Altes Rathaus, the most amusing thing about the city's Spielzeugmuseum (☎ 29 40 01) is right in front: the wind-powered sculpture that releases pent-up energy every few minutes by clanging and banging. That's a free exhibit. Inside you'll be treated to an assortment of dolls, puzzles, games and more dolls. Unless you're a big doll fan, give this one a wide berth (Barbie's 40th birthday was a big hit here). It's open from 10 am to 5.30 pm daily (DM5/1).

Valentin Museum (Map 7a)

Dedicated to one of Bavaria's most beloved comic actors, this museum (☎ 22 32 66) celebrates the life and work of Karl Valentin and his partner, Liesl Karlstadt. It's in Isartor, the southernmost gate of the medieval fortifications and itself a work of 14th century art, bearing an impressive fresco of Ludwig the Bavarian's triumphant return to the city in 1322.

The museum is full of props and other items from Valentin's films and stage career. The humour, though, is heavy-going and tough to decipher if you don't understand German. There's an OK view of the Isartor and beyond from the rear balcony.

The museum's uproarious opening hours are from 11.01 am to 5.29 pm Monday, Tuesday, Friday and Saturday, and from 10.01 am to 5.29 pm Sunday, closed Wednesday and Thursday (DM2.99/1.99). There's a cafe, too, at the top of the tower with a comical crowd and, if you're lucky, the resident accordionist and tuba-player. Take any S-Bahn to Isartor.

Jewish Museum (Map 7a)

The Jüdisches Museum München (☎ 20 00 96 93), Reichenbachstrasse 27, is an under-visited exhibition on the history of Jews in Munich and Bavaria. You'll see photos and correspondence of some of the long-forgotten voices of the Holocaust. Admission is free, but hours (from 2 to 6 pm Tuesday to Thursday) are limited due to budgetary constraints (donations are encouraged).

Karl Valentin, Germany's Charlie Chaplin

Bertolt Brecht and Hermann Hesse were fans, and bohemian Schwabing wouldn't have been the same without him. Karl Valentin (1882–1948) was the closest Germany came to having its own Charlie Chaplin. Even today his films and records still have a wide following outside Bavaria.

A joiner by profession, Valentin turned to comedy early in his career (you can see the nail upon which he 'hung up his job' in the Valentin Musäum). His routines carried doses of social commentary, and really packed 'em in to classy venues such as the Bayerischer Hof. It wasn't long before the spindly-legged mime artist began experimenting with film, producing silent slapsticks such as *Der Neue Schreibtisch* (The New Desk), with the famous postcard-image of a moustachio'd Valentin sitting under a wreck of a writing-table. All told, Valentin made more than 50 films and 100 recordings.

Valentin's humour can be a bit tough for foreigners to digest. One of his best-known quotes is: 'The Siegestor is a great institution – it's open day and night.' Here's another gem: 'Why does St Peter have eight clocks? So that eight people can tell the time at once.'

Valentin's fortunes declined after WWII, and he died a poor man on *Rosenmontag* (Carnival Monday) in February 1948. His works enjoyed a revival of interest in the 1960s, however, and the two fountains on Viktualienmarkt honour him (on the south side) and his stage partner, Liesl Karstadt (in the beer garden).

MICK WELDON

Bavaria Film Museum

Hard-core film fans and kids shouldn't miss the Bavaria Film Tour (☎ 64 99 23 04) of the Bavaria Film Museum, at Bavariafilmplatz 7, in the suburb of Geiselgasteig. But if you've already taken another film-studio tour (say, in Berlin's Babelsberg) you should give this one a miss. Take the U1 or U2 to Silberhornstrasse then tram No 25 to Bavariafilmplatz.

The tour goes through the sets of *Das Boot*, *Enemy Mine*, *Cabaret* and *The Never-Ending Story*, all of which were made here, but all too often you'll be stuck before video screens and left to watch film clips.

The 90 minute tour runs from March to October (DM17/12). Tickets including the 30 minute 'Action Stunt Show' and the wraparound, Dolby-stereo Showscan Cinema cost DM31/26. Either go early or avoid it during the tourist season as it gets extremely crowded.

Michael Ende Museum (Map 3)

The tiny Michael Ende Museum (☎ 891 21 10) at Schloss Blutenburg in the suburb of Overmenzing has books, photos and personal effects from the author of *The Never-Ending Story*. It's open from 2 to 5 pm on weekends, weekdays by appointment (DM 4/2). See also Schloss Blutenburg, under Western Munich, later in this chapter.

Zoo (Map 5)

The Hellabrunn Zoo (☎ 62 50 80), Tierparkstrasse 30, south of the centre in Thalkirchen, was the first 'geo-zoo' (1928, with distinct sections dividing animals by continents). Today it has about 5000 animals representing 460 different species, including rhinos, elephants, deer, bucks and gazelles. It's absolutely worth the DM10/5 admission if only to gain access to the petting zoo, crawling with sheep, deer and lambs that you can feed (DM0.50 per handful). There's also a huge transparent bird 'tent' covering 5000 sq m with lots of colourful species. Kiddies can ride either ponies or camels for DM3 per 15 minutes (the camel rides start about 3 pm but the ponies run all day). One highlight, in summer, is the daily show of falconry at 12.45 pm (weather permitting), with lots of high-velocity swoops and shredding of (already-dead) mice. Take U3 to Thalkirchen or bus No 52 almost to the entrance.

BMW Museum (Map 3)

Opposite Olympic Park at Petuelring 130 is the popular BMW Museum (☎ 38 22 33 07). Behind the museum, the BMW (Bayerische Motoren Werke) headquarters building (1970–73), with its striking steel cylinders, is an architectural attraction in its own right.

The museum is as immaculate as you'd expect. Exhibits include many BMW cars, motorcycles, planes, concept cars and, near the top, simulators and interactive displays. It's open from 9 am to 5 pm daily, last entry at 4 pm (DM5.50/4).

Take the U3 from Marienplatz to Olympiazentrum. Look for the huge silver towers (and if you're flying overhead, the landing pad with BMW logo). The BMW factory (☎ 38 22 33 06), adjacent to the headquarters and museum, does free tours of the factory line (in German and English).

Altstadt

The Altstadt is the old city centre, and the Marienplatz square is the heart of the Altstadt. The pedestrianised Kaufingerstrasse runs west from Marienplatz to Karlsplatz (also known as Stachus) at the western boundary of the Altstadt. On the eastern side of the Altstadt lies Lehel, a pretty residential district somewhat removed from the tourist rabble, with a few nice restaurants and pubs.

The city's historical centre is encircled by ring roads in the position of the former city fortifications: Sonnenstrasse to the west, Oskar-Von-Miller-Ring and Von-der-Tann-Strasse to the north, Franz-Josef-Strauss-Ring, Karl-Scharnagl-Ring and Thomas-Wimmer-Ring – one road with three named sections – at the east, and Blumenstrasse and Frauenstrasse at the south.

North of Marienplatz is the Residenz (the former royal palace), with the Nationaltheater and Residenz Theatre. Just north is

Odeonsplatz, home to the spectacular The-atinerkirche St Kajetan. East of Marienplatz is the Platzl quarter for pubs and restau-rants, as well as Maximilianstrasse, a fash-ionable street that's fun for strolling along and window-shopping.

Just south of the centre on Museumsin-sel, an island in the Isar, is the Deutsches Museum and the Forum Der Technik.

HISTORIC CENTRE WALKING TOUR – Part I (MAP 7a)

This extensive circuit covers the main sights within the bounds of Munich's historic cen-tre. Starting at Marienplatz, moving north to the Residenz and arching counterclockwise back to the starting point, the tour takes about 1¼ hours if walking at a leisurely pace. It's split into two parts for manage-ability, and allows a detour north into Lud-wigstrasse. If you include visits to all the museums and churches, however, you've got a two day itinerary on your hands.

Marienplatz (Map 7a)

This is the heart and soul of the Altstadt, punctuated by the glowing **Mariensäule** (St Mary's Column), erected in 1638 to cele-brate being spared by both Swedish forces and the plague. At its top is the golden fig-ure of the Virgin Mary, carved in 1590 and originally located in the Frauenkirche. To the west is the start of the pedestrian zone. Our tour of the square starts under the tow-ering spires of the Neues Rathaus.

Neues Rathaus The late-Gothic new town hall (1867–1908) surrounds six courtyards, including the large and leafy **Prunkhof** (Court of Resplendence); there are festivals and events in them throughout the year. The building's blackened facade is festooned with gargoyles and statues, including, at the corner, a wonderful dragon climbing the turrets.

The highlight of the building is, of course, its incessantly photographed **Glock-enspiel** (carillon), which has three levels. Two portray the **Schäfflertanz** (Cooper's Dance) which is held every seven years (the next one is scheduled for 2005), and the

Ritterturnier, a knights' tournament held in 1568 to celebrate the marriage of Duke Wilhelm V. The carillon has been jingling since 1903, although the 40-odd 'acoustic' bells you hear are in fact on a recorded tape. The apparatus springs into action to a won-derfully chimed tune at 11 am (November to April only), noon and 5 pm.

There's a tame night scene featuring the **Nachtwächter** (Night watchmen) with the **Friedensengel** (Angel of Peace) who put the **Münchner Kindl** (Munich child) to bed with a lullaby at 9 pm. (See the Places to Eat chapter under Cafes & Bistros for informa-tion on the two best cafes for viewing the entertaining spectacle – Metropolitan and Café Glockenspiel.)

You can take a lift to the top of the 80m-tall tower (DM3/DM1.50) from 9 am to 7 pm weekdays, and from 10 am on week-ends and holidays. The cashier is on the 4th floor; take the lift inside or, via the stair-case, take a look at the stately corridors and views of the inner courtyard.

Fish Fountain The Fischbrunnen was used to keep river fish alive during medieval mar-kets; later it was used as the ceremonial dunking spot for butchers' apprentices, and

---

Do Not Pass *Los*

If you fantasise about owning a Munich hotel or a row of Schwabing villas, well, you can dream on – with the help of a Ger-man version of the Monopoly board game. The first Munich edition is out (DM89, in German) with lots of desirable property up for grabs from the word *Los* (Go). Oddly enough, addresses out in the suburbs can be dearer than on the central Marienplatz, and other prominent spots such as the Kaufingerstrasse shopping dis-trict are simply missing.

The mystery behind this property scam? The producers were merely playing their own brand of capitalism and charged firms to put their logos on a board space, com-plete with their real-life street names.

today it's a good meeting spot. Local legend says that dipping an empty purse into the water here on Ash Wednesday (and they still do, right after the Carnival festivities) guarantees it will always be full.

Altes Rathaus The rump of the neogothic old town hall (1474) stands forlornly at the eastern end of the square. It's all that remains of the Gothic building constructed by Jörg von Halspach, although the Gothic-era dancehall over the gateway has been restored to its former resplendence, with wonderful ceiling carvings that took 15 years to complete. Emperor Charles V supposedly dined here, and there are copies of the elegant swaying **Morris dancers**, which you can view in the Stadtmuseum.

The old hall was destroyed by bombs in WWII and unveiled in a plainer style with little fanfare in 1972. In its south tower is the city's Toy Museum (see the Museums section earlier in this chapter).

St Peter & Heiliggeist Churches At the southern end of Marienplatz is the **Alter Peter** (also known as St Peterskirche), which was the city's first parish church in the 11th century. The Gothic building you see today was begun in the 14th century, and the high altar (a joint venture by Jan Polack and Erasmus Grasser) is split up in pieces around the church. The flamboyant rococo interior was restored after WWII. You can climb its unique rectangular 92m-tall tower (297 steps, DM2.50/1.50) for the best view of the city and, if there's a warm *Föhn* wind, the Alps will appear in startling detail (although the balcony is fenced in to foil suicide attempts). The tower is open from 9 am to 6 pm Monday to Saturday, and from 10 am to 6 pm on Sunday.

Just east of the Alter Peter, the **Heiliggeistkirche** (Church of the Holy Spirit, 1392) was first built as a hospital in the 13th century. It appears almost economical in design until you look up to see the Asam brothers' amazing rococo ceiling, completed during the interior revamp from 1724 to 1730. This is also Germany's largest Gothic hall church. At the main entrance is

an imposing **bronze statue** of Duke Ferdinand of Bavaria (he's now all but forgotten, but was a big cheese back in 1608).

From Marienplatz to Max-Joseph-Platz (Map 7a)

From the north-eastern end of Marienplatz, Sparkassenstrasse leads north past some exceptional buildings. Near the south end of the street is the **Alter Hof** (Old Court), the Wittelsbach residence until they outgrew it and built the Residenz you'll see later in this tour.

Alter Hof Munich's oldest royal residence, the Alter Hof, became the seat of the ruling Wittelsbachs in 1253. Its severe neogothic style emerged in a 19th century renovation, which saw many of the oldest sections torn down and the entrance tower reduced in height.

One notable story linked to the Alter Hof is that of Catherine of Brabant, the wife of Ludwig the Stern who ruled here in the late 13th century. Ludwig had embarked on a crusade when he heard reports of his wife's alleged infidelity. Furious, the king rushed back to court and had Catherine beheaded on the spot. He later discovered that Catherine had been faithful after all, and to assuage his guilt Ludwig had a monastery built in Fürstenfeld to the east of Munich.

Another anecdote involves primates. The slender timbered gable (Burgstock) of the Alter Hof was supposedly home to a monkey that played in the bedroom of the youthful Ludwig the Stern. When a market pig threatened Ludwig's cradle one day, the monkey grabbed the young royal and brought him to safety on the pinnacle of the Burgstock. The main snag in the story is the fact that the Burgstock wasn't built until a number of years later.

Hofbräuhaus Just opposite the Alter Hof, turn right into Münzstrasse and walk one block to Orlandostrasse (teeming with touristy shops); look to the left-hand corner to see Munich's celebrated Hofbräuhaus, crawling with tourists from opening time at 10 am. The ballroom upstairs was the site of the first large meeting of the National Socialist Party on 20 February 1920; you can visit if the rooms aren't being used for a function. Back downstairs, after guzzling a *Mass* (litre mug) or two of beer (DM11 to DM13 apiece), drivers can check their alcohol level in the coin-op Breathalyzers (DM3) by the toilets.

Return to Sparkassenstrasse, turn right and walk north one block to the former **Münzhof** (Mint). It housed the **Bavarian State Mint** for nearly two centuries until 1983, but before that it served as a royal stable, an art gallery and a library. An inscription on the west side of the building reads *Moneta Regis* (Money Rules).

Max-Joseph-Platz (Map 7a)

From the old mint, walk a few metres west on Pfisterstrasse and take a right in the tiny Hofgraben, which leads one block north into **Maximilianstrasse**. This is Munich's most glamourous shopping street, with splendiferously expensive shops and the grand Kempinski Vier Jahreszeiten Hotel. Turn left, and this avenue leads to the southern end of Max-Joseph-Platz, home to some of Munich's most beloved buildings, among them the **Nationaltheater** (which contains the five-tiered **Opera House**). The lovely classical structure has a tumultuous history: erected in 1818 under Maximilian I, it was destroyed by fire in 1823 and rebuilt by star architect Leo von Klenze. Bombs reduced it to a carbon shell in WWII, but the beautiful beast rose from the ashes to its present state during 1958 to 1963, for the princely sum of DM63 million.

On the north side of the square is the grand-daddy of them all – the Residenz. The focal point is a **statue of Bavarian king Max I Joseph**, who promulgated Germany's first constitution in 1818.

At the southern end of the square is the old **central post office**, on the site of a former palace, with a frescoed Italianate arcade. The place still dispatches mail; enter at the west side.

Residenz (Map 7a)

On the north side of Max-Joseph-Platz looms the oldest section (1571) of the Residenz, the huge palace that housed the Bavarian rulers from 1385 to 1918, and today contains more than 400 years of architectural history. It was here that the Wittelsbachs built a fortress from 1570 to 1620 and moved their seat from the Alter Hof.

Northern wings were added to create several interior courtyards, including the **Emperor**, **Apothecary** and **Fountain courtyards** and two smaller ones, **Chapel** and **King's Tract**. Most of the later work and its emergence as a royal palace were directed by Leo von Klenze, Munich's leading court architect of the 19th century. Badly damaged in WWII, the Residenz was carefully rebuilt in the 1950s and 1960s, and work is still continuing in some sections.

The west side of the building fronts Residenzstrasse and has the entrance to the Egyptian Art Museum and the Altes Residenztheater; the south side of the building, on Max-Joseph-Platz, holds the entrance to the Residenzmuseum and the Schatzkammer (see Museums earlier in this chapter).

Altes Residenztheater The Old Residence Theatre, also known as the Cuvilliés Theatre, is perhaps Europe's finest rococo theatre, with a stunning, lavish interior. While the building was destroyed during bombings in 1944, the interior furnishings had been removed so what you see today is original.

This masterpiece was designed by the talented Belgian François Cuvilliés, who actually began his career as a court jester under Elector Max Emanuel. Cuvilliés showed greater potential by designing defence systems for the military, so he was sent to Paris to study the latest art trends. He returned with a distinctive rococo style, and was a jester no longer.

You can visit, except during state opera and theatre company rehearsals, from 2 to 5 pm Monday to Saturday and from 10 am to 5 pm Sunday (DM3/free). The entrance is at Residenzstrasse 1.

Lion Statues At the entrance to the theatre and the Egyptian Art Museum on Residenzstrasse, note the two lions guarding the gates. Rubbing one of the lions' shields (look for the one that's been buffed to a gleaming shine) is said to bring wealth to the rubber.

Odeonsplatz (Map 7a)

Feldherrnhalle Residenzstrasse leads north along the outer wall of the Residenz to your right; to your left, just north of Viscardigasse, stand the grandiose arches of the Feldherrnhalle (Field Marshall's Hall). A few metres north lies Odeonsplatz, the square which marks the starting point of Ludwigstrasse, a broad Parisian-style boulevard which shoots north past the university to the **Siegestor** (Triumphal Arch), which itself marks the starting point of chic Leopoldstrasse.

Odeonsplatz was the site of one of the earliest putsch attempts by Nazis in 1923, the so-called Beer Hall Putsch that landed Hitler in jail. On the ground near Residenzstrasse on the hall's east side there's a **bronze plaque** commemorating the four Bavarian policemen who died in the clash with Hitler's men. (Hitler later made a Nazi shrine out of the Feldherrnhalle, but this is of course no longer there.)

The Feldherrnhalle, dedicated to the field marshals under the Wittelsbachs, has two major statues. One is of General Johann Tilly, who surrendered Munich to the Swedes during the Thirty Years' War; the other is of Karl Phillipp von Wrede, the chief of the Bavarian troops who allied with Napoleon (but switched allegiances in time to defeat the French at the Battle of Nations in 1815). Between the two stands a memorial to Bavarians who died in the Franco-Prussian war. The hall itself is a near-replica of the Loggia dei Lanzi in Florence, with the exception of the two huge **Bavarian lions** that stand guard on either side of the steps.

Theatinerkirche St Kajetan At the south-west side of Odeonsplatz is the landmark Theatinerkirche St Kajetan (1663–90), built to commemorate the conception (after a lengthy period of trying by Henriette Adelaide) of Prince Max Emanuel. Designed by Italian architect Agostino Barelli, the church's massive yellow towers around a giant cupola are another landmark of

Munich's skyline. The ornate Italian lines end in snail-like flourishes, which isn't surprising as the facade was completed only a century later by François Cuvilliés, the rococo master of the Residenz's theatre.

Inside, the intensely stuccoed high dome stands above the **Fürstengruft** (royal crypt) containing the remains of Wittelsbach family members, including Prince Elector Max Emanuel, his parents Ferdinand and Henriette, Bavarian king Max I Joseph and crown prince Rupprecht of Bavaria. There's another crypt in the St Michael's church, too, that contains Ludwig II's tomb. (See the 'Frauenkirche' section later in this chapter to continue the Walking Tour.)

Hofgarten At the east side of Odeonsplatz, the neoclassical **Hofgartentor** (1816) leads the way to the former royal gardens. To the left (north) of the entrance is the **Café Tambosi**, an expensive street cafe usually chock-a-block with cashed-up tourists. The entrance itself consists of **Klenze's Arcades**, bearing frescoes of Bavarian historical scenes and of the Wittelsbachs.

The Court Garden has humble origins. Although laid out as an Italianate garden from 1613 to 1617, it was used mainly as a vegetable garden for the court until the 18th century. Paths culminate in the centre at the **Diana Temple,** a striking octagonal pavilion that is a favourite spot for impromptu classical recitals. The view of the Theatinerkirche through the temple arches beyond the garden to the east is quite a sight, too.

The southern limit of the Hofgarten is formed by Hofgarten Strasse and the Residenz; the northern boundary is defined by the **Galeriegebäude** (Galerie Building), built by Elector Karl Theodor to house his private art gallery above the Hofgarten arcades. After the Alte Pinakothek was founded in the early 19th century, the building was handed over to the Munich Arts Association, which holds exhibits here. Under the same roof you'll find the **Theatre Museum** (see Museums earlier in this chapter).

At the eastern end of the Hofgarten is the modern **Bayerische Staatskanzlei** (Bavarian chancellor's office, 1992), the last big architectural order by the Christian Socialist Union's (CSU) powerful party chief, Franz-Josef Strauss, before his death in 1988. The old-style cupola is in fact the only remaining section of the ruined Army Museum that was left here as a war memorial. Known in its entirety as the 'glass palace', the combination with the modern wings caused quite a fuss when the blueprint was unveiled. The covered arcade immediately north-west of the Staatskanzlei was originally part of the Renaissance gardens.

Prince Carl Palace Sandwiched between the Staatskanzlei and the busy Von-der-Tann-Strasse stands the **Prinz-Carl-Palais**, the official residence of Bavarian minister-president Edmund Stoiber. The place was an early attempt by Friedrich von Sckell (who helped to lay out the English Garden just to the north) to blend a classical structure with parkland. That noble aim died with the 1980s construction of the Inner Ring Road directly underneath the palace, which is used only for state receptions and other representative functions. A lovely fountain plays in front (Map 7).

Ludwigstrasse To the north of Odeonsplatz leads the wide and impressive Ludwigstrasse, the product of star architect Leo von Klenze. This is one of Europe's classic promenades, commissioned in 1816 by Ludwig I (then still crown prince) to help turn Munich into an 'Athens of the North'. It leads over a kilometre north to the Siegestor, with a remarkable uniformity of neoclassical style and proportions (Map 7).

Klenze was an advocate of planned cities and, with his personal love of severe geometrical lines, threw himself into the project. (Critics now argue that the boulevard is in fact too broad for human dimensions, and the huge volumes of traffic only emphasises its width.) At Odeonsplatz 4 is one of Klenze's earliest works, the **Leuchtenberg Palais** (Map 7), which today houses the Bavarian Finance Ministry (there's usually a guard out front). Originally an exclusive residence, the palace was converted to a hotel during the Revolution of 1848. In front of the palace is a stately **statue of Ludwig I on horseback** from 1862, erected 14 years after his abdication.

The remaining buildings of lower Ludwigstrasse were based on the Leuchtenberg-Palais. Next door at No 3 is a building called the **Odeon**, site of concerts and parties before WWII. Today it's simply another government building, the **Bavarian Ministry of the Interior**.

Bavarian State Library Farther north and on the eastern side of Ludwigstrasse is the **Bayerische Staatsbibiliothek** (Map 7, Bavarian State Library) at No 16, built by Friedrich von Gärtner from 1832 to 1843. The four sculptures standing guard atop the entrance stairway are jokingly referred to as the 'Three Wise Men' – the philosophers Aristotle, Hippocrates, Homer and Thucydides. The library has more than 7 million volumes – the most extensive scientific collection in Germany. On top of that there are 250,000 maps, 800 atlases and over 42,000 periodicals. You can also see the 16th century globes of the earth and cosmos made for Duke Albrecht V, or you can just browse the stacks (see Libraries in the Facts for the Visitor chapter).

Ludwigkirche Just north of the Bavarian State Library stands the **Ludwigkirche** (1829–1844), also by von Gärtner. This is the most striking departure from the austere geometric lines of his predecessor, Leo von Klenze (and from the air, is one of the city's major visual landmarks). Its alabaster towers are done in a Florentine campanile style. Take a peek inside at the huge *Last Judgement* by Peter Cornelius, one of the world's biggest frescoes, which was aimed at rivalling Michaelangelo's. Cornelius painted several frescoes in the church and they've been undergoing a painstaking restoration (Map 7).

Ludwig Maximilian University Farther north, on the west side of Ludwigstrasse, you'll come to **Geschwister-Scholl-Platz** and behind it, the main building of the Ludwig-Maximilian-Universität. Some 75,000 students are registered here, making it the second-largest university after the Free

University of Berlin. Munich is an extremely popular place to study and there aren't enough classrooms to go round; courses are held occasionally in the hallways to deal with the bottlenecks (Map 7).

Founded in 1472 in Ingolstadt under Duke Ludwig the Rich, the university was moved to Landshut in 1800 by Elector Max IV Joseph; finally, in 1826, Ludwig I transferred it to Munich (and Landshut, once bigger and more powerful than Munich, sank into relative obscurity). The design is by von Gärtner (1835–40), and it's definitely worth strolling into the large vaulted **Aula** (assembly hall), as well as the light and airy **Lichthof** (atrium).

For such a relatively young university it has attracted some academic heavyweights over the years. Distinguished staff members have included Friedrich von Schelling, the philosopher; Justus von Liebig, the father of modern scientific agriculture; and Wilhelm Röntgen, the inventor of the x-ray.

The broad surface of the square is anchored by two huge, bowl-shaped fountains on either side of the street, providing welcome relief from the traffic and an interruption of the long, severe facades along Ludwigstrasse. Students and street performers congregate here in summer.

The square itself, which links the university with the priests' seminary opposite, was named at the end of WWII for Hans and Sophie Scholl, students and founding members of the White Rose resistance group (Die Weisse Rose). After handing out anti-Hitler leaflets in the main assembly hall, they dumped a further batch into the stairwell and were arrested for 'civil disobedience'. Four days later the siblings were tried at the Court of Justice on Karlsplatz and executed at Stadelheim Prison in Giesing (a suburb south of Haidhausen).

There is a memorial museum to the White Rose in the main university building (see the Museums section earlier in this chapter).

Siegestor (Map 7)

At the northern end of Ludwigstrasse stands the bombastic **Victory Gate** (1843–52), a triumphal arch (modelled on the Arch of Constantine in Rome) and built by Friedrich von Gärtner. There was little occasion for its construction except to please the Bavarian Army, whose most recent significant victory had been the expulsion of French troops between 1813 and 1815. The structure was badly damaged in WWII, and the upper section was left incomplete but with an added inscription: *Dem Sieg geweiht, vom Kriege zerstört, zum Frieden mahnend* (Dedicated to victory, destroyed by war, urging us to peace).

The figure up top is a smaller version of the **Bavaria statue** on the Theresienwiese, this time in a lion-drawn chariot.

HISTORIC CENTRE WALKING TOUR – PART II (MAP 7a)
Frauenkirche

From Odeonsplatz, our walking tour continues south about 400m down Theatinerstrasse (which turns into Weinstrasse); turn right in the alley opposite the grassy Marienhof and you'll face Munich's trademark, the oxidised copper onion domes atop the clunky late-Gothic **Frauenkirche**

The Devil's Footprint

Local legend has it that Jörg von Halspach, builder of the Frauenkirche, struck a deal with Satan. Halspach needed money to complete the church, and the devil agreed to provide it on the condition that Halspach build the church without a single visible window. When Satan came to inspect the Frauenkirche, he saw the tall Gothic windows from a distance and rejoiced, because he thought he'd won the architect's soul. But Halspach led the devil to a spot in the foyer, from where not a single window could be seen. Furious, Satan stamped his foot and stormed off, leaving a hooved footprint in the pavement of the entrance hall.

Restoration work after WWII means the illusion no longer works, but the outline (which looks more like that of a modern loafer) remains.

(Church of Our Lady, 1468–88). The 99m-high towers have another function, too: they serve as the upper limit for all buildings erected in the Altstadt.

This twin-spired church, built of monotonous red brick and very Bavarian in its simplicity, belonged to the archbishopric of Munich-Freising. Its highlights: the magnificent **St Nepomuk Altar** by Cosmas Damian Asam and Johan Michael Ernst, and the **tomb of Emperor Ludwig the Bavarian** are also simple but elegant. The church was originally supposed to provide space for 20,000 worshippers – a slightly ridiculous plan, as at that point Munich only had 13,000 residents – but a shortage of money shrank the blueprint.

You can climb the south tower (DM4/2) from 10 am to 5 pm Monday to Saturday, April through October.

From Frauenkirche to Karlsplatz (Map 7a)

From the Frauenkirche, walk south through one of the several lanes to Kaufingerstrasse, a busy shopping street. Turn right and continue 200m along what becomes Neuhauser Strasse to the **Michaelskirche** (St Michael's Church), widely acknowledged as Germany's grandest Renaissance church. Built from 1583 to 1597 for Duke Wilhelm V, the staggeringly vast stucco interior is exceeded in area only by St Peter's in Rome. When the first version of the church collapsed prematurely, Wilhelm took it as sign and spent loads of money rebuilding with a fortress-like foundation.

There's a **crypt** underneath containing the tombs of some Wittelsbachs, including Ludwig II's, which is always covered and illuminated with candlelight.

In front is the **Richard Strauss Fountain**: the streams of water recall the *Dance of the Seven Veils* in Strauss' celebrated opera *Salomé*, which shares the name with a piece by Oscar Wilde. Continue west to the corner of Kapellenstrasse, on your right you will find the **Bürgersaal**, an 18th century oratory, built for theology students. It also houses the crypt of Rupert Mayer, a Jesuit priest and noted opponent of the Nazis. The

crypt attracts dozens of pious worshippers (Mayer was declared a saint in 1987).

Just west of here is **Karlsplatz**, punctuated by the medieval **Karlstor**, the western gate and perimeter of the Altstadt, and an enormous modern **fountain**, a favourite meeting point. One of the Germany's largest department stores, Karstadt, has a huge branch here; it's also a major tram, bus, U-Bahn and S-Bahn connection point. Locals refer to the square as **Stachus** because of an ancient dislike for Elector Karl Theodor. Stachus was the name of a beer-garden owner nearby, a certain Eustachius Föderl.

Lenbachplatz (Map 7a)

Just north-east of Karlsplatz is **Lenbachplatz**, location of a number of ornate neoclassical buildings. The edifice at No 2 is home to both Deutsche Bank and the Bavarian Stock Exchange (Börse); while the former just keeps growing, the latter has sunk into near-obscurity due a concentration of equities business in Frankfurt.

Next door at No 3 is the impressive **Bernheimer House**, designed by Friedrich von Thiersch in the late 19th century, as one of the first dual-purpose residential and office buildings. Today its main tenant is the painfully trendy restaurant and bar, **Lenbach**, whose entrance on the rear side (in Ottostrasse) is illuminated by two Olympic-style torches. The place was completely renovated a few years ago by Deutsche Bank, who lent large sums to one-time property speculator Jürgen Schneider (who now resides in a Frankfurt prison).

On the opposite (east) side of the square stands the **Künstlerhaus am Lenbachplatz**, built by Gabriel von Seidl in 1900. The front has been invaded by the Mövenpick restaurant chain, but the interiors are stunning, with a sweeping ballroom styled like an Italian palazzo (and decorated by master portraitist Franz von Lenbach himself). The exterior is brilliantly lit by night.

The real focus of the square, though, is the splendid **Wittelsbach Fountain**, conceived in the late 19th century by Adolf von Hildebrandt. Two groups of figures illustrate the beneficial and destructive power of water.

Father Mayer's Anti-Nazi Crusade

In 1923 the Bürgerbräukeller beer hall organised a discussion entitled 'Can a Catholic be National Socialist?' One of its key speakers was a Jesuit priest, Rupert Mayer, who stunned his audience (mostly SA men) by rejecting any link with the Nazis. Father Mayer was booed off the podium, and for the next 20 years he would remain a marked man for Hitler supporters. His courage was all the more remarkable for someone who had lost a leg in WWI, and who suffered constant pain from poorly-fitting wooden prostheses.

The Nazi leader blamed Mayer for the failure of his coup attempt (now known as the Beer-Hall Putsch) later that year, but Mayer wasn't intimidated. After the Third Reich began in 1933, Mayer condemned Germany's new rulers in sermons at St Michael's Church and other gatherings. "They (the Nazis) love to tell us, 'You should be happy. In Spain they would have put you against the wall long ago' ... but when (the soul) is destroyed before the world, I can think of nothing more terrifying."

The cleric avoided purely political statements, but confrontation was inevitable. In the late 1930s Mayer was arrested, imprisoned and released numerous times; during one stay in Sachsenhausen Concentration Camp, the authorities feared his death would provide opponents with a martyr to rally around. So the priest was moved in 1940 to the Ettal monastery south of Munich, where he remained in isolation until he was freed by US troops in 1945.

Mayer died of a stroke a few months after WWII, and his body was interred in a special crypt in the Bürgersaal on Neuhauserstrasse. The priest was finally beatified in 1987.

From Karlsplatz to Sendlinger Strasse (Map 7a)

Our walking tour resumes from Karlsplatz; double back and turn right into Eisenmannstrasse, where you'll see the ornate **Damenstiftskirche** to your left, and continue south to **Sendlinger Tor**, the 14th century southern portal. From there, bear north-east into the Sendlinger Strasse; about 200m farther on your left, at No 32, is the St-Johann-Nepomuk church, better known as the **Asamkirche** (1733–46), designed and built by the Asam brothers. Above the entrance is a statue of St Nepomuk himself, a Bohemian monk who drowned in the Danube. The church shows a rare unity of style, with scarcely a single unembellished surface; the interior is particularly jaw-dropping (note, as you enter, the **golden skeleton** of Death trying to cut the string of Life to the right).

Carry on about 300m along Sendlinger Strasse and take a right on Rosental, which runs past the **Stadtmuseum** on St-Jakobs-Platz. The outstanding exhibits cover brewing, fashion, musical instruments, photography and puppets (DM5, closed Monday).

There are films shown nightly here as well. (See Museums earlier in this chapter and Cinemas in the Entertainment chapter.)

Viktualienmarkt (Map 7a)

Carry on east down Rosental to emerge at the western edge of the bustling **Viktualienmarkt**, one of Europe's great food markets. Originally the market took place on Schrannenplatz (or Grain Market, the site of today's Marienplatz), but space grew short and some traders set up shop on St Peter's cemetery. This 'godless' behaviour raised such an outcry that the king declared a market on the courtyard of the former Heiliggeist hospital. Viktualienmarkt was born.

It's crowded throughout the year: in summer the place is transformed into one of the finest and most expensive beer gardens around; in winter people huddle for warmth and schnapps in the small *Kneipen* (pubs) around the square. The merchandise and food are of the finest quality, but bargains don't exactly abound (see Self-Catering in Places to Eat for suggestions). On the south side, you'll see a statue of the famous comedian Karl Valentin holding out his hand –

a perfect spot for a Chaplinesque flower (see also Museums earlier in this chapter).

If thirsty, seek out the **Maypole** shooting up from the centre of the square, bearing craftsmen's symbols and the traditional blue-and-white Bavarian stripes. It will invariably point you towards the next beer garden. Marienplatz is just to the north-west.

Königsplatz (Map 7)

North-west of the Altstadt is Königsplatz (U2 or tram No 27), a Greek-revivalist pile commissioned under Ludwig I to house several art museums (see Museums earlier in this chapter). Work was started by none other than architectural giant Leo von Klenze in 1816, but the square was only completed in 1862, 14 years after Ludwig's abdication. This blaze of Greek classicism was meant to recall the 19th century liberation of the country from the occupying Turks and, conveniently, the coronation of Ludwig's first son Otto as king of Greece (who, in a further stroke of fate, was dethroned by the Greeks the year the square was finished).

The square took on a sinister meaning in the 1930s, when Hitler had the lawn paved over with 20,000 granite slabs to create a parade grounds for his brown, leathery troops. Situated at the eastern side of the square, at the intersection, are two foundations (now overgrown with grass) on which two classical 'honour temples' stood in the 1930s. In them were 16 fallen Nazis, killed in the 1923 putsch attempt at the Feldherrnhalle. The US Army bombed the temples in 1945, but it wasn't until 1988 that the slabs were removed and the square grassed over.

The expanse is bordered by the **Glyptothek** to the north and the **Staatliche Antikensammlungen** opposite, designed in the centre like a Corinthian temple (see Museums earlier in this chapter). The centrepiece of the square is the Doric-columned **Propyläen** gateway (1846), which today provides a fantastic backdrop for open-air cinema and rock concerts.

Karolinenplatz (Map 7)

A block east of Königsplatz, on the sweeping circle known as Karolinenplatz (thus named for Max I's wife), stands a 29m-high **obelisk**, a Klenze-designed monument (1833) to the French soldiers who fell during Napoleon's ill-fated Russia campaign. The bronze came from the melted-down armour of Turkish ships sunk in the Battle of Navarino six years earlier. The Amerika Haus (☎ 55 25 37 20) is on the south-west side at Karolinenplatz 3.

Gärtnerplatz (Map 7 & 7a)

South of the bustling Viktualienmarkt begins the **Gärtnerplatz district**, which encompasses lots of alternative bars, pubs and restaurants before melding into the more fashionable Lehel farther north. On the west bank of the Isar is the hulking **St Maximilian Church**, a 19th century Italian Romanesque church that has recently undergone a huge facelift.

The centre of the area is, of course, Gärtnerplatz, flanked by the **Theater am Gärtnerplatz** to the south. Operas and operettas are the main fare here. The building was founded by several rich Munich families as a folk theatre, but when the owners went bankrupt, Ludwig I took the place over himself. Since 1926 this has been the seat of the **State Theatre of Operetta**.

For the record, that revolting glass, steel and cement pile on the western bank of the Isar across from the Deutsches Museum is the modernist **European Patent Office**, which serves to remind us how charming most of the older buildings are. To its immediate north is its smaller cousin, the **German Patent Office**.

Lehel (Map 6 & 7)

North-east of the Gärtnerplatz district lies Lehel. It manages to be part of the Altstadt and yet keep a separate identity, helped by its lovely site between the old city walls (to the west) and the Isar (to the east). The area has many lovely residential buildings from the *Gründerzeit* period (from about 1870), recalling the fact that many poor craftsmen and artisans used to live here. Nowadays, though, only the well-to-do can afford to buy here, although there's a decent budget hotel in Thierschstrasse (see the Places to Stay chapter).

A relaxed atmosphere still prevails, and a good place to sample it is at **St-Anna-Platz**, which is flanked by two pretty churches, the **Church of St Anne** on the northern side and the **Klosterkirche St Anna** (Monastery Church of St Anne), which stands almost hidden behind a line of trees opposite. Built from 1723 to 1733 by Johann Fischer, the Klosterkirche was Munich's first rococo church and is surrounded by a Franciscan monastic complex; you can view the restored interior (a riot of rococo decoration, with an altar by the Asam brothers) from 8 am to 6 pm daily.

The parish **St-Anna-Kirche** (Church of St Anne) opposite, is a much younger creation – late-19th century by Gabriel von Seidl, with chunky neoRomanesque towers on a beautiful tree-lined square. The huge altar and the nave paintings are impressive.

Author Lion Feuchtwanger spent his early childhood here at No 2 St-Anna-Platz; in the 1920s he wrote the novel *Erfolg* (Success), a critique of early 20th century Munich, as well as the classic *Jüd Süss*. At the eastern end of the square is an intimate little restaurant called Gandl, with a pleasant pavement cafe (see the Places to Eat chapter). The whole scene remains one of tranquillity despite the U-Bahn station that opened in 1989.

Just north of the churches, at St-Anna-Strasse 2, is the quirky little monastic-goods store Gutes aus Klöstern (see the Shopping chapter) in an inn by the same name.

Over on the western side of the Isar lies **Mariannenplatz** with the **St-Lukeas-Church**, (St Luke's Church, 1893–96) right by the river. It's been undergoing an extended renovation, but the huge dome and towers continue to mould the skyline in this part of town.

ENGLISH GARDEN (MAP 4)

The Englischer Garten is nestled between the Altstadt, Schwabing and the Isar River. The **Chinesischer Turm** (Chinese Tower), now in the centre of the city's best-known beer garden, was constructed in 1789, which also marked the beginning of the park's construction. Following the storming of the Bastille in the same year, Elector Karl Theodor (Munich's least popular ruler) was looking for something to placate his subjects with, lest the French revolutionary fever prove contagious.

Theodor eventually gave in to his Minister of War, Benjamin Thompson (an American lieutenant-general who had emigrated to Munich) and called in Friedrich von Sckell, the court gardener of beautiful Schloss Schwetzingen near Mannheim. Thompson and Sckell set to work, and Theodor proclaimed that a people's garden would be laid out 'for the purpose of exercise and recreation'. At first he called his project the 'Theodor Garten' but wisely changed the name to Englischer Garten, which was more closely suited to the principles of democratic enlightenment.

The result is Europe's largest city park (measuring 5km by 1.5 km). It's a great place for strolling, drinking, sunbaking and paddle-boating. In balmy summer weather, nude sunbathing is the rule rather than the exception here. It's not unusual for hundreds of naked people to be in the park on a normal working day, with their coats, ties and frocks stacked primly on the grass. There are formal FKK (nude bathing) zones but no-one (not even the police) seems to take much notice. It's a lovely way to spend a sunny afternoon, but keep an eye firmly on your stuff. On the southern edge at Maximilianstrasse there's surfing on the Eisbach (see the Activities section later in this chapter).

Check out one of the four beer gardens here (see the Entertainment chapter), or head out for a little paddle on **Kleinhesseloher See**. Just south of the Chinese Tower is the heavily photographed monument **Monopteros** (1838), which is regularly cleared of graffiti and junkies. Towards the south-west end is a **Japanese Teahouse** (1972), where tea ceremonies are held on the second and fourth weekends of the month; at 3 and 4 pm on Saturday and Sunday.

There are many ways into the park, but the closest point to the central Chinese Tower is from the university on the western side.

The park is not a safe place to spend the night, police patrol frequently and muggers, drug fiends, proselytisers and other colourful characters are everywhere. In other words, forget it.

Western Munich

Hauptbahnhof (Map 7a)

Munich's main train station dates from the 1950s, its grander predecessor (from the mid-19th century, by Friedrich Bürklein) having been blown to bits in WWII. While the nondescript facade remains, the interior has been transformed into a high-tech temple of polished aluminium, glass and marble, with a fancy modern passenger service centre and two storeys of shops and restaurants. You wouldn't go here just for fun, but the new packaging makes the Hauptbahnhof a tolerable place to at least wait for a train.

Old Botanical Gardens (Map 7a)

Schützenstrasse is the unremarkable pedestrian zone that links the Hauptbahnhof to Karlsplatz. Due north across Prielmayerstrasse and Elisenstrasse is the **Alter Botanischer Garten**, once Munich's pride and joy before heavy air pollution in the 19th century led planners to design another one (the Neuer Botanischer Garten) on the more salubrious grounds of Schloss Nymphenburg. The design was laid out by Friedrich von Sckell, including a large and pleasant **Neptune Fountain** in the south-east corner, which is, however, framed in unsightly power lines.

North, across the park, is the **Park Café**, a trendy outside cafe by day and a teeny-bopper's disco with classical columns at night. On the western edge of the gardens is a windy square with some striking huge chess pieces, called the **Kunst-Plattform**; as the name suggests, occasional art events take place here among the oversized pawns and rooks.

Palace of Justice (Map 7a)

The southern edge of the Old Botanical Gardens is bordered by the towering red 19th century **magistrates' court building** and, just to the east on Karlsplatz, the dignified neobaroque **Justizpalast**, which was built by Friedrich Thiersch. It was here that Hans and Sophie Scholl were tried for 'civil disobedience' in 1943 and condemned to death.

Westend (Map 5)

Now practically an appendage of the Hauptbahnhof area, the **Westend** was incorporated into Munich in 1890 as a separate district. Its boundaries are Theresienwiese to the east and Barthstrasse to the west, while the north-south borders are roughly Landsbergerstrasse and the Ganghofer Bridge. As early as 1830, the area was a slum for foreign workers and retired people, and day labourers without citizenship slept under the open air. With the arrival of the railway, halfway through the 20th century, parts of the area gradually turned into 're-spectable' middle-class communities. This element can still be seen in the facades along Schiessstättstrasse, although it failed to set an example for the entire area.

At one stage, it was known as Munich's 'broken-glass district' but nowadays it's better known as 'Little Istanbul' for its large numbers of Turkish immigrants. Other ethnic groups have also settled in the area, however – among them Greeks, Italians and people from the former Yugoslavia. The long, busy boulevard of Schwanthalerstrasse buzzes with electronics stores, produce markets and, as you'd expect near any big-city train station, sex shops.

The area between the Holzapfelstrasse, Westendstrassse and Schwanthalerstrasse is the most venerable part of the neighbourhood. Several breweries are at home here, including **Hacker-Pschorr** and the **Augustiner Brewery** who have easy access to their biggest sales event of the year, the Oktoberfest on Theresienwiese. Augustiner also runs a charming beer hall in front of its brewery on Landsbergerstrasse (see Beer Halls & Gardens in the Entertainment chapter).

At the far west side of the Westend is **Golliersplatz**, a leafy oasis in which the neighbourhood children play. A flea market is held here in summer, and No 83 on bordering Gollierstrasse is home to a pleasant breakfast cafe, Das Gollier.

Theresienwiese The Theresienwiese lost one of its biggest customers in 1998, when the old Trade Fair complex closed down and moved to more modern premises in Riem. What remains is a vast meadow for parking, occasional flea markets and the world's biggest folk festival – Oktoberfest.

Overlooking the grounds is the big greenish statue of the **Bavaria**, designed by Leo von Klenze for Maximilian II. The 19m-tall lady, who was cast in 1850 by foundry artist Ferdinand von Miller, was the biggest thing to be made in bronze at the time. Miller poured it in three parts, finishing just before his workshop burnt to a crisp.

Behind the Bavaria is Klenze's sweeping classical **Ruhmeshalle** (Hall of Fame, 1843–53), commissioned by Ludwig I and containing busts of 70-odd Bavarian rulers and other historical figures. Art historians regard it today as Klenze's crowning achievement. The complex and statue was meant as Munich's answer to the Valhalla in another Hall of Fame near Regensburg (ironically, also designed by Klenze). Its 11m-high base has 60 steps, and it's another 121 steps to the top for a view of the 'Wies'n' (the popular diminutive term for the Theresienwiese).

The field hasn't always been a place for light-hearted boozing. In February 1918, Munich armaments workers went on strike and a huge number of employees from various industries gathered here to call for an end to the war. The following November, Kurt Eisner proclaimed a free Bavarian state to replace royalty, an ill-fated experiment with democracy that spawned chaos and extremism (see the History section in the Facts about Munich chapter).

More recently, a member of a radical neo-Nazi group set off a bomb during the 1980 Oktoberfest, killing 13 and injuring more than 200 people. There's a memorial service every year to commemorate the tragedy.

Directly overlooking the eastern side of the meadow is **St Paul's Church**, a neogothic basilica that takes on a new meaning during Oktoberfest: the best views of the event are from its 70m-high tower. In December 1960, a low-flying airplane clipped the tower and tumbled into Paul-Heyse-Strasse; more than 40 people perished in the accident.

West Park This huge and surprisingly varied expanse, laid out for the International Horticultural Exhibition of 1983, is the newest of Munich's parks. Unfortunately the Middle Ring Road sears right through it, but both sections are linked by pedestrian bridges. Its greatest asset is the illusion that Mother Nature was more creative here than should be possible: ponds and marshes, gentle knolls, rushing waterfalls and a wide assortment of flora abound. The ducks, swans and frogs simply thrive.

Oriental follies give the park an exotic dimension. Nepalese craftsmen were drafted to build a **wooden temple** with adjoining buildings, and close by there's a **Chinese garden** suitable for an un-Bavarian meditation. The curiosity perched on stilts in the pond is the **Thai Pavilion**, another lovely temple without obvious practical use. The park is studded with theme gardens including a **rose garden** and a **hops garden**, and there's also the inviting **Seecafé** for an afternoon drink and snack – the kids will enjoy feeding the swans. Cultural events such as open-air concerts and theatre productions are held on the **Seebühne** (Lake Stage) amphitheatre. For program information call ☎ 32 42 55 66, or any of the advance ticket offices (see the Entertainment chapter).

To get there, take the U6 west to Westpark and cross Krüner Platz and Specklinplatz north into the park – it's a five minute walk from the station.

Neuhausen (Map 3)

North-west of the Hauptbahnhof lies cosmopolitan Neuhausen. It's one of Munich's oldest neighbourhoods dating back to the 12th century in municipal records, although there's evidence that it's even two centuries older. Perhaps it's this long history and association with the royal family that gives Neuhausen an air of relaxed confidence.

Neuhausen's development took a giant leap forward from 1662, when Elector Karl

Ferdinand Maria gave Italian architect Agostino Barelli the job of drawing up plans for a major palace to celebrate the birth of his son, crown prince Max Emanuel. Nearly a century elapsed before the grand **Schloss Nymphenburg** was finished (see that section later in this chapter).

The only other buildings of the day were the servants' quarters, built outside the palace gates. The original village was destroyed by fire in 1794, an event that prompted Maximilian I to have a proper neighbourhood laid out in the early 19th century. From then on Neuhausen became a residential pad for the well-heeled, with the villas along Nymphenburg Canal resembling second-string royal residences.

Nymphenburger Strasse was actually one of the first commuter roads into Munich, put down to ease transport of the royals into town. The city's first tram – a horse-drawn vehicle – served the boulevard from 1876. Neuhausen was already a part of Munich, in spirit, by the time the neighbourhood was absorbed in 1890.

WWII swept away many of Neuhausen's old buildings, and as was the case elsewhere in Munich, their modern successors were less than tasteful. Its sights are scattered but worth exploring; you might conclude the day with a brew in the lovely Hirschgarten beer garden (see the Beer Halls & Gardens section in the Entertainment chapter).

Around Stiglmaierplatz (Map 7 & Map 5)

The broad square called **Stiglmaierplatz** is a good launch point into Neuhausen. The north-east side of the square is watched over by the Bavarian lions of the **Löwenbräukeller**, one of Munich's few genuine beer halls. It also has one of the few cellars you'll have to walk *up* the stairs to reach. The place burnt to a cinder in 1986 but has been so well rebuilt you won't tell the difference.

Continuing up Nymphenburger Strasse will take you past the **Justizbehörde** (Courts of Law) at No 16, with jurisdiction at both state and local levels. Moving west, the next street is Erzgiessereistrasse where the

Bavaria statue was cast (and where Friedrich von Miller's workshop burned down soon afterwards). Von Miller cast the weighty lady in three sections, but it still took three weeks to cart the pieces out to the Theresienwiese.

Continuing west along Nymphenburger Strasse, the rather dour office complex at No 64 is the **Franz-Josef Strauss House**, the headquarters of the Bavarian conservative CSU party that has run the state virtually unopposed since WWII.

If you take a left on Erzgiessereistrasse and head south, you'll meet Arnulfstrasse running parallel to Nymphenburger Strasse. Along here are a number of key entertainment options, including the **Augustiner Keller** beer garden and the seasonal **Circus Krone** (see Theatre in the Entertainment chapter for more details).

Circus Krone has been a fixture in Munich for decades, and its building at the corner of Marsstrasse and Wredestrasse is a parody of itself, shaped like a great circus tent. Performances run from December to March, and then, when it's all over, the circus leaves in a grand procession, with elephants and camels driven along Arnulfstrasse towards the Hauptbahnhof. The hall is left to host rock concerts and other events the rest of the year.

Farther west on Arnulfstrasse is probably Munich's least liked authority, the **Municipal Tax Offices** between Deroystrasse and Marsstrasse. More congenial is the former freight depot opposite, site of large and regular **flea markets** run by the Bavarian Red Cross (see Markets in the Shopping chapter for details) and the **Winter Tollwood Festival** in December, which also sells a bewildering range of gifts.

Around Rotkreuzplatz (Map 3)

Modern, bustling, ugly Rotkreuzplatz is the centre of Neuhausen. The area reverberates with the huge volumes of traffic that pulse through Landshuter Allee, another product of myopic town planners in the 1960s.

Rotkreuzplatz has to put up with several garish buildings. On one side stands the Rot-Kreuz-Schwesternschule (Red Cross Nursing School), linked at the rear to the Red Cross Hospital. Nearby is the huge **Kaufhof** department store with a large furniture department; unlike most German retailers, it also opens on Sunday morning (and the selection isn't bad). The focal point of the square is the **modern fountain** of a corpulent couple whose outstretched hands spurt water. A saving grace of the area is its **Christkindlmarkt** (Christmas market), one of the better alternatives to the seasonal crush on Marienplatz (see Markets in the Shopping chapter for details).

The area around Rotkreuzplatz has plenty of good restaurants, cafes and bars. Ice cream is another major attraction, sold by Eis Ecke Sarcletti at Nymphenburger Strasse 155.

If you're staying in the Youth Hostel (Jugendherberge) at Wendl-Dietrich-Strasse 20, continue east and you'll reach the **Neuhausen Model Housing Estate**, built by Hans Döllgast between 1928 and 1930 with about 1900 middle-class apartments and lush lawns between Rotkreuzplatz and Arnulfstrasse. Although regarded as successful, it doesn't command as much respect as the Borstei (see later in this section).

Maria Trost Church North-west of Rotkreuzplatz is a welcome contrast to the concrete planning sins committed in Neuhausen: the **Maria-Trost-Kirche** on Winthirstrasse. In its cemetery lies the remains of the Irish missionary **Winthir**, who is credited with converting the people of Neuhausen to Christianity around 1000 AD. Some other notable grave tablets include those of Oskar von Miller, founder of the Deutsches Museum, and Johann Baptist Stiglmaier, who helped to cast the Bavaria statue designed by Friedrich von Miller.

Jumping on tram No 12 will take you past **Rondell Neuwittelsbach**, a traffic circle that used to be the hub of Neuhausen's old brewing and working class district, to **Romanplatz**, one of Munich's most exclusive residential areas. Towering poplars and smart villas line the avenue.

Borstei (Map 3)

Up on Dachaustrasse, in the area bordered by Pickelstrasse and Lampadiusstrasse is the **Borstei**, a mecca for architecture students.

Erected in 1900 by private builder Bernhard Borst, this was Munich's first municipal residential complex. Each home had its own sanitary facilities (a revolution back then!). There were shops integrated into the complex and all courtyards and portals were styled individually. Though a bit outdated today, this is still considered to be one of Munich's best-conceived developments.

Olympic Park (Map 3)

More than a quarter-century after the event for which it was built, the Olympiapark (☎ 306 70) remains an integral part of life in the city. In the 19th century this was a practice field for royal riders; in 1909, the first Zeppelin airship landed here; and in 1929, it became the site of Munich's first civil airport at Oberweisenfeld.

The centrepieces today are the 290m-high Olympiaturm (Olympia Tower) and the 75,000-sq-m transparent 'tented' roof covering the west side of the Olympic Stadium, Olympic Hall and the swimming centre. Today the complex is open as a collection of public facilities, and the grounds are the site of celebrations, concerts, fireworks displays and professional sporting matches throughout the year. The 50m swimming pool is open to the public, as is the ice arena (see Ice Skating in the Activities section later in this chapter). Discussions have taken place about a possible face-lift for the stadium, but the administration of Munich mayor Christian Ude was leaning towards building a new football stadium on a separate site.

There are two tours daily from April to October (meet at the information booth at the park's north-east): a soccer tour at 11 am, which visits the Olympic Stadium, VIP area and locker rooms (one hour; DM 8 for adults, DM6 for children under 15), and an adventure tour that covers the entire Olympiapark on foot and in a little train (1½ hours, DM13/8).

If you like heights, go to the top of the **Olympiaturm**, which is open daily from 9 am to midnight, with the last trip up at 11.30 pm (DM5/2.50). The lift travels at so-many jillion metres per second, and you can feel your stomach bounce at the top. When the

euro currency converter DM1 = €.51

weather is good, you'll have stunning views towards the city (although the grounds of the Olympiapark and the BMW museum are better). If you're feeling cashed up and hungry, you can have a meal at the revolving restaurant (☎ 308 10 39).

Olympic Spirit Couch potatoes will love this: whether it's on a ski run, a tennis court, a kayak slalom or the 100m dash – at the press of a button, these simulations of Olympic events (housed in the former Olympic velodrome, next to the main park) are stunningly realistic, and your performance can even influence the outcome. Its **Action Cinema** has a 180° screen – a vicarious, bone-chilling way to experience the downhill. Queasy stomachs can turn sportscaster in a replica of an announcer's booth. Olympic Spirit (☎ 30 63 86 26) is open from 10 am to 6 pm weekdays, weekends and holidays to 7 pm. Regular admission (cinema included) costs DM26, concessions DM18; you can also buy a 'try-out' ticket for DM10, which doesn't include all rides (or the cinema).

Russian Orthodox Chapel Anything but orthodox, this makeshift church was cobbled together by a certain Father Timofei in an overgrown corner to the south of the Olympic grounds. The eccentric cleric has lived here since 1952, and managed to build a church out of miscellaneous building scraps. He then adorned the interior with pieces of silver paper. The city of Munich had a removal order issued when the Olympic Park was being built, as a horse-racing stadium was planned at the chapel's location.

Father Timofei stood his ground and gained widespread public support as the event hit the media. The horse-racing facility, meanwhile, has been built in Riem (which is also the site of the New Fairgrounds). In summer the priest sells produce to passers-by and opens the chapel to anyone who's interested. In 1999 he claimed to have celebrated his 105th birthday.

You won't see the chapel easily, even from the Olympic Tower: it's behind the

Olympiaberg, a former rubble heap from WWII that's been grassed over.

Schloss Nymphenburg (Map 3)

If the Residenz hasn't satisfied your passion for palaces, visit the amazing Schloss Nymphenburg (☎ 179 08/0) north-west of the city centre (tram No 17 or bus No 41). Begun in 1664 as a villa for Karl Ferdinand's wife, Electress Adelaide of Savoy, the castle and formal gardens were continually expanded and built upon, until 1758, to create the royal family's summer residence. Today the castle, porcelain factory and grounds (the surrounding park is worth a long stroll) are open to the public, and the grounds are also home to the **Museum Mensch und Natur** (Museum of Man and Nature, see later in this section), all definitely worth it if you're here with kids.

A combined ticket to everything except the Museum of Man and Nature costs DM8/7. Admission to the Schloss and the Schönheitengalerie is DM5/4; to Amalienburg or Badenburg DM3. Entry to the Museum of Man and Nature costs DM3/1.50.

Palace The main palace building (☎ 179 08/0) consists of two wings to the north and south of the main villa. You can visit from 9 am to 12.30 pm and from 1.30 to 5 pm Tuesday to Sunday. You should allow at least an hour inside the palace.

The rooms are all sumptuously decorated. The circuit begins upstairs in the **Steinerner Saal** (Stone Hall), a two-story dining hall with fantastic frescoes by Johann Baptist Zimmermann. The **Gobelin Room**, with its stunningly detailed tapestries, is almost as good. The tour also takes in the **Wappenzimmer** (Heraldic Room) and the **Chinesisches Lackkabinett** (Chinese Lacquer Room), but take time out to see the cute **chapel** in the west wing.

Our favourite is Ludwig's **Schönheitengalerie** (Gallery of Beauties), in the southern wing, formerly the apartments of Queen Caroline. It's now the repository of 38 portraits of women, all of social standing, whom Ludwig I considered beautiful. The most famous of these is *Schöne Münchnerin*, the portrait of Helene Sedlmayr, daughter of a shoemaker, but you'll also find a smouldering one of court dancer Lola Montez, who cost Ludwig his crown (see the boxed text 'Lola Montez, Femme Fatale' in the Facts about Munich chapter).

Also in the south wing is the **Marstallmuseum** (Royal Stables Museum, ☎ 179 08), with the coaches and riding gear of the royal families. This includes the wedding coach of Ludwig II that was never used after his engagement fell apart. It's open from 9 am to noon and 1 to 5 pm Tuesday to Sunday (DM3/2).

Tours of the palace are only offered to groups; pick up a copy of the unintentionally hilarious English-language translation of the guide *Nymphenburg* (DM5) at the cash desk.

Porcelain Museum The former factory of Nymphenburg Porcelain, on the 1st floor of the Marstallmuseum, is now the Nymphenburger Porzellan Sammlung Bäuml (☎ 17 90 80). Temporarily shut for renovation, the museum was expected to reopen sometime in 2000.

For some material evidence of your visit, there's a fine porcelain shop, the Staatliche Porzellan-Manufaktur (☎ 179 19 70), which is an ideal place to stock up on German *objets d'art*, but you'll need plenty of dosh. Hours are from 8.30 am to 5 pm weekdays, with a half-hour break at noon.

Gardens The Nymphenburg royal gardens are a magnificently sculpted English park. In front (east) of the palace is a long canal, on which locals can be seen curling and ice skating in winter. At the eastern end of the canal is the **Hubertus Fountain**, a huge braying stag that spouts water behind the elaborate trellis. Behind (west) the castle, the royal gardens ramble on around the continuation of the Nymphenburger Canal.

The whole park is enchanting and contains a number of intriguing follies and other buildings. The architect Friedrich Ludwig von Sckell was responsible for the broad design of today's version of the gardens; he softened the original, rather harsh lines of the French layout and modelled the grounds more along the lines of an English landscape garden.

Four of the buildings are open to the public. Electress Amelia had the **Amalienburg**, a small hunting lodge with a large domed central room, built as a kooky hunting lodge between 1734 and 1739 by Franz Cuvilliés the Elder. The place drips crystal and gilt decoration; don't miss the amazing **Spiegelsaal** (Mirror Hall). Amalienburg is open from 9 am to 12.30 pm and 1.30 to 5 pm daily.

The two storey **Pagodenburg** (1717–19) was built as a Chinese teahouse by Prince Max Emanuel; after a lengthy renovation, it was expected to reopen in 2000. Opposite it, the **Badenburg**, by the lake of the same name, was also built by Max Emanuel, as a sauna and bathing house. You can visit it from 10 am to 12.30 pm and 1.30 to 5 pm Tuesday to Sunday.

Elsewhere in the park, there's the **Magdalenenklause**, which served as a retreat for Max Emanuel, and a **witch's cottage** designed around 1800 as a fantasy playroom for the royal offspring.

If you're into plants, however, the high points are the **greenhouses** in the **New Botanical Garden** (Neuer Botanischer Garten) on the northern edge of the grounds. There are wild and wonderful rooms for palms, cactus and loads of colourful tropical varieties. The botanical garden is also spangled with some lovely **porcelain statues**, products of the palace's own factory.

Museum Mensch und Natur This natural history and science museum (☎ 17 64 94) is a fun place to bring the kids. Interactive, if aged, displays in German, provide kids with quizzes, but mostly they'll be racing to the upstairs exhibits on animals and the earth. There are rotating exhibitions in addition to the permanent collection, and a nice cafe downstairs. It's open from 9 am to 5 pm Tuesday to Sunday. Admission is DM3/1.50, kids under six free.

Schloss Blutenburg (Map 3)
West of Nymphenburg, in the suburb of Obermenzing, stands the picturesque Schloss

Blutenburg (☎ 891 21 10), sited on an island in the Würm River. Once the summer residence of the Wittelsbachs, this idyllic 15th century palace was used for trysts by Agnes Bernauer and her future husband, Duke Albrecht III (see the boxed text 'The Tragedy of Agnes Bernauer'). The chapel features a lovely late-Gothic altar by Polish artist Jan Polak. Concerts are held in the inner courtyard several times a year, and there's a pleasant little beer garden on the island next to the moat.

Among other things, Blutenburg houses the **Internationale Jugendbibliothek** (International Youth Library, ☎ 891 21 10) with 400,000 children's titles in 110 languages. It's open from 9.30 am to 4 pm weekdays (to 2.30 pm on Friday).

Also out here is the tiny Michael Ende Museum (☎ 891 21 10) with books, photos and personal effects of the author of *The Never-Ending Story*. (You really need to be a Michael Ende fan to enjoy it.) See the Museums section, earlier in this chapter, for details.

To get to Schloss Blutenburg, take the S1 or S2 to Obermenzing and then bus Nos 73 or 75 to Pippinger Strasse. There is also a bus stop for the Nos 73 and 75 buses on the northern side of the Nymphenburg gardens,

at a roundabout nearly 500m west of the Botanical Garden.

Hirschgarten (Map 3)

Much more than just a beer garden, the **Hirschgarten** was laid out by Elector Karl Theodor ostensibly as a zoological garden in 1780. In the event, this enormous green park was used primarily as a fallow-deer pen for the royal hunts. Beer-drinkers have replaced the royals but the wildlife remain, and children love to pet the furry critters over the fence (feed is available for DM0.50). See the Entertainment chapter for other Beer Halls & Gardens.

The towering chestnuts and oaks make a great shady spot for the **Magdalenenfest**, a fun festival held every July with a kiddy carousel and lots of gift and food stalls.

Southern Munich

Planners still aren't sure how to describe the sprawling, fragmented area to the south of the Altstadt. The district immediately south of Sendlinger Tor is technically called **Isarvorstadt** but Munich residents' geography is geared more by the genuine neighbourhoods of **Schlachthof** and **Glockenbach**.

Sendlinger Tor (Map 7a)

The Sendlinger Gate was once the portal that marked the beginning of the salt route to Italy. The gate is one of the outcomes of Germany's first architectural competitions, launched in February 1808 to develop the area to the west and south-west of the city. It's the last old 14th century town gate, but all that's left is a large archway, finished in brick, which replaced the original triple-arch in 1906.

To the east is the lively Sendlinger Strasse with the Asam Church and a plethora of shops; south-west, down Lindwurmstrasse, you will find the Schlachthof quarter.

Schlachthof Quarter (Map 5)

South of the old city walls, the racetrack-like Lindwurmstrasse leads south-west towards

---

The Tragedy of Agnes Bernauer

Star-crossed love always makes for a good story. Karl Albrecht III, heir to the duchy of Bavaria, had Schloss Blutenburg built in 1431 as his summer residence, and secretly married the beautiful commoner Agnes Bernauer. They lived there happily until the old duke found them out, he tricked his son into leaving town and had Agnes tried for witchcraft. The girl was sentenced to death and drowned in the Danube in 1435, and her fate has been related in folk songs and stories ever since. Every four years the Bavarian town of Straubing holds a theatre festival to illustrate the tragic tale. After the deed, Karl's father suffered so much guilt that he had a memorial chapel erected in Agnes' memory.

the autobahn, passed the Schlachthof (Slaughterhouse) quarter. Once a key trade route in and out of Munich, the road is still important for meat and produce trucks that transport raw material to Munich's restaurants from Europe's biggest wholesale market, the **Grossmarkthalle** (see also Markets in the Shopping chapter). It's also a runway for Müncheners keen to get out of town fast on Friday evening.

The right-hand-side of Lindwurmstrasse, up to Goetheplatz, is dominated by the **Klinikum Innenstadt der Ludwig-Maximilian-Universität** (Hospital on the Left Bank of the Isar), the main clinic of Munich's Ludwig Maximilian University. Just south on Goetheplatz is a large and imposing post office, completed in 1933; the structure was the final instalment in a program designed to give Munich a harmonious chain of post offices. Several good-value hotels and pensions are scattered around Goetheplatz (see the Places to Stay chapter).

Kapuzinerplatz (Map 5)

To the south-west of Goetheplatz lies **Kapuzinerplatz**, which is the location of two superlative buildings. On the south side of the square is a monstrous red-brick pile that is Munich's **Arbeitsamt** (Employment Office), completed in 1987. This place assembled all of the agency's staff under one roof, and is in fact the largest employment office in all of Germany.

Those who'd rather not apply for work can cross to the north side of Kapuzinerplatz to the **Paulaner Bräuhaus**, a large and cosy Bavarian restaurant and beer garden founded in 1892. Beer is still brewed in the centre of the inn, providing Munich with some of its best and freshest *Weissbier*.

Without any apparent policy link, the **Schlachthof** is located just behind the Arbeitsamt. This huge abattoir (the largest in southern Germany) was built over a century ago under the supervision of noted hygienist Max Pettenkofer, and set a new standard in its day. Unfortunately they haven't done much about the stink, and depending on the wind the area can smell like, well, a big butcher's shop. Here too is the **Schlachthof**

music hall, from where concerts are broadcast weekly (see Rock in the Entertainment chapter).

Directly west of Kapuzinerplatz, at No 12 in the Adlzreiterstrasse, there's a **commemorative plaque to Albert Einstein**, whose family lived here from 1885 to 1894. The house and courtyard were destroyed in WWII. Einstein had a tough time in Munich; his father's electronics shop eventually went bust and the family moved to Switzerland.

South Cemetery (Map 7)

The Alter Südfriedhof teems with prominent ghosts, although many are familiar only to Müncheners. Painter Carl Spitzweg, chemist Justus Liebig, and Joseph von Fraunhofer are among those buried here – just look at the list by the north (main) gate. If you can overlook its morbid aspects, the cemetery is actually a lovely place to stroll; you can spend hours absorbing details of Munich's past on the gravestones.

The Alter Südfriedhof was originally established as a simple plague cemetery, opened in 1563; but when the Elector Karl Theodor outlawed all central cemeteries in the 17th century, the place was promoted to Munich's chief graveyard. Enough family lines have been broken that the cemetery is mostly unkempt, and many markers have subsided or been attacked by undergrowth.

Glockenbach (Map 5)

The area between the Südfriedhof and the Isar is roughly defined as Glockenbach. The name means 'bell brook', which, not surprisingly, comes from a bell foundry that was located on one of the various streams nearby. Many of the city's carvers and woodworkers lived here, giving rise to street names such as Baumstrasse and Holzstrasse.

The loveliest spot is undoubtedly the path along the babbling brook, the **Westermühlbach**, which runs south along Pestalozzistrasse. It's the only survivor of a network of creeks that once criss-crossed Munich; the rest have been rerouted or paved over.

Nowadays Glockenbach is becoming more and more an extension of the gay scene just to the north; here you'll find gay-and-mixed places such as **Café Glück** at Palmstrasse 4. Holzplatz is the starting point for a high-heeled race during the Christopher Street Day festival (see also Public Holidays & Special Events in the Facts for the Visitor chapter). To the south, you'll find the pricey colonial cuisine of the **Makassar** restaurant on Dreimühlenstrasse.

Moving north you'll encounter bunches of closet boutiques and second-hand shops along **Fraunhoferstrasse**, **Müllerstrasse** and **Hans-Sachs-Strasse**. The last street was listed as a public monument in 1981 thanks to its clutch of neo-Renaissance and baroque buildings. If you find you need a chartreuse lampshade or leather tulip-chair cover, this is where it will be. The area around Müllerstrasse is the heart and soul of Munich's gay district, and has some funky cinemas such as the **Werkstattkino**, which is part of the **Fraunhofer pub**, a favourite haunt of night owls and theatre-goers.

Eastern Munich

Haidhausen (Map 6)

The oldest settlement on Isar's eastern bank, Haidhausen has staged a remarkable recovery since the beginning of the 20th century. This used to be a refuge for vagrants, prostitutes, the mentally ill and anyone else who couldn't get citizenship to live in Munich – an undignified station in history for a prime location on the salt route established by Henry the Lion in the 12th century.

Back then, Haidhausen was home to wheelwrights, masons, blacksmiths and other tradesmen. But it sank into poverty as the salt trade dried up and after several centuries as Munich's doormat, Haidhausen was lifted by the establishment of the **Maximilianeum**. This grand building was designed by Frederick Bürklein as a school for gifted students in 1876. (Today it houses the talented representatives of the Bavarian parliament – see also the Royal Boulevards Walking Tour, later in this section.)

Haidhausen is changing. Yuppie hotels, fashion shops and expensive flats are encroaching where folksy shops and corner stores were once the norm. It's not all bad: Haidhausen has a lively pub and restaurant scene, and by some measures it outranks Schwabing as Munich's best entertainment quarter.

Gasteig Culture Centre The hub of the district is the **Kulturzentrum Gasteig**, a huge and boxy glass-and-brick complex that caused no end of controversy before its completion in the early 1980s. The classy Munich Philharmonic Orchestra has its home here, as well as the Richard Strauss Conservatory and one of Germany's largest municipal libraries. It also has an intimate, less formal theatre called the **Black Box** (see Theatre in the Entertainment chapter).

The back section of the Gasteig houses the **Volkshochschule**, or adult education centre, which offers (among other things) good and cheap German language courses. Next door on Rosenheimer Strasse is the **City Hilton**. On almost the same spot stood the **Bürgerbräukeller**, the beer hall where Hitler narrowly escaped an assassin's bomb in 1939.

On the south side of the busy Innere Wiener Strasse (opposite the Gasteig) is a prim little church called the **Nikolai and Loretto Chapel**, half-submerged in the dense woodland of the Isar embankment. Just west is the lovely **Müllerisches Volksbad**, a swimming pool with a fantastic Art Nouveau interior (and definitely worth a look whether you swim or not), as well as the giant **Muffathalle** concert hall.

Continue up Innere Wiener Strasse and you'll reach the **Hofbräukeller**, a wonderful restaurant-cum-beer garden that once housed the state-run brewery of the Hofbräuhaus. The brewery was badly damaged by fire in 1987, and the luxury flats that sprang up on part of the site prompted speculation that it was arson rather than accidental.

Wiener Platz In front of the Hofbräukeller is one of Munich's most charming markets on Wiener Platz, a single mass of stalls and restored lodging houses crowned with a maypole. If you haven't already stocked up at Viktualienmarkt, there's a wonderful assortment of cheeses, breads, fish and veggies, and it's open every day (except Sunday). Just a few metres farther north, the smart turreted houses on Grütznerstrasse stand in stark contrast.

East of Wiener Platz stands the slender red pinnacle of the **Johanniskirche**, which in English bears the cumbersome title of Church of St John the Baptist. Dubbed 'Haidhausen's Cathedral' after being built from 1852 to 1874, the Johanniskirche boasts 21 neogothic windows decorated with a wonderful cycle of religious paintings. The surrounding square is pleasant, with its leafy park and townhouses, and well shielded from the traffic noise of busy Max-Weber-Platz just to the north.

One architectural gem nearby is the incongruous, timber-framed **Kriechbaumhof** at Preysingstrasse 71. Restored to its original 17th century form, it's home today to a youth centre; the impression is one of a cottage plucked from an Alpine meadow. Directly across the road is the **Üblacker House**, a WWI-era labourer's flat that's been turned into a standing exhibit.

French Quarter From Preysingstrasse, turning east on **Wörthstrasse** will bring you past the lovely Café Voilà (see Breakfast Places in the Places to Eat chapter) to the green elongated square called **Bordeauxplatz**, which with a little imagination (OK a *lot* of imagination) conjures up a town square in the south of France. Many of the area's streets and features bear French names, a fad that dates from Germany's victory in the Franco-Prussian War (1870–71). Some Müncheners still call this area the **French Quarter**, although you can argue about the flair.

Turning south-west down Metzstrasse leads to **Weissenburger Platz**, a sunny, circular expanse with streets radiating from all sides. The square is framed in trees and flowerbeds and anchored by a monumental **three-tiered fountain**, the only surviving part of Munich's one-time Crystal Palace. (Constructed for the 1854 Industrial Exhibition, the German replica of the British landmark burned down in 1931.) The adornments help

you forget the discount stores and junk shops in the side streets. On the southern side of the square is a good Australian bar-restaurant – the only in Munich – called **Outland** (see the Places to Eat chapter). Not far to the east is **Pariser Platz**, built in a similar fashion.

Still farther eastwards, on the broad half-crescent of **Orleansplatz**, stands the **Ostbahnhof**, a local hub of commuter traffic on the U- and S-Bahn networks. This marks the eastern border of Haidhausen; on the other side of the tracks lies the huge disco and entertainment complex of **Kunstpark Ost** and the south-eastern suburb of Berg am Laim.

Bogenhausen (Maps 4 & 6)

From the late-19th century, Bogenhausen became an exclusive residential quarter for the rich. Elegant villas with elaborate facades sprang up from the 1870s onwards, and the rise of Art Nouveau later that century made itself felt throughout the area – for example, in the Holbeinstrasse and the Mühlbauerstrasse, as well as in the main Prinzregentenstrasse. Bogenhausen is bordered on the west by the Isar and the towering **Friedensengel** (Angel of Peace), one of Munich's most photographed monuments (see also the Royal Boulevards Walking Tour later in this chapter).

Branching north-east from the Europa-Platz near the Friedensengel is Möhlstrasse, a chic street peppered with exclusive villas built for Munich's super-rich. Many of them are occupied today by lawyers' offices and consulates. Crossing east down Siebertstrasse leads to **Holbeinstrasse**, which contains some of Munich's finest Art Nouveau houses (and they're all listed monuments). No 7 is a particularly fine example.

Bogenhausen's other main landmark is the **Prinzregententheater** built by Max Littman for Prinz-Regent Luitpold from 1900 from 1901 in a combination of Art Nouveau and neoclassical styles. It housed Munich's opera company until the Nationaltheater was finally restored in 1963; by that time, the Prinzregententheater had fallen into such a state of disrepair that it was closed. Renovation wasn't completed until 1988, and the final stage of work was only completed in 1999, when the theatre was reopened to the strains of Wagner's *Tristan and Isolde*.

Up near the Max-Joseph-Brücke, Thomas Mann lived for nearly 20 years in the *Allee* (boulevard) on the Isar that is named after him (many local scenes appeared in his works before he emigrated in 1933). Few writers can afford to live in Bogenhausen today, however: this is a district of brass nameplates and security cameras, and the bulk of the action is in dog-walking. Nonetheless, Bogenhausen remains one of Munich's prettiest neighbourhoods.

Church of St George In the extreme north of Bogenhausen stands a charming little 18th century church, the baroque **St Georgkirche** (Church of St George) on Kirchplatz. Here lie buried some of Munich's key cultural figures, including writers Erich Kästner, Annette Kolb, Oskar Maria Graf and film director Rainer Werner Fassbinder, and it's fascinating to read the inscriptions. Kirchplatz was the centre of the original village of Bogenhausen, and harks back to a world much simpler than that of Mercedes-Benzes and poodle shampoos.

The north-east corner of Bogenhausen is home to a marvel (some would say monstrosity) of modern architecture – the Hypo-Bank's main administration building. This gleaming 113m tower (1975–81) seems to hover over visitors – or press down upon them, depending on your point of view. Judge for yourself: it's at the Richard Strauss stop on the U4.

The surrounding area is a generic-looking subdivision called **Arabellapark**, begun in 1965 in a greenfield site and now home to more than 60,000 Munich residents. There's a dramatic wave-motion pool at the end of the U4, the **Cosimabad** complex (see Swimming & Sauna under Activities later in this chapter), but other than that there's not much to lure you out here.

Royal Boulevards Walking Tour (Map 5)

This walk takes in two of Munich's grandest royal boulevards. It begins in the eastern part of the Altstadt on Maximilianstrasse before crossing the Isar River into the sprawling Maximilian-Anlagen (also known as the Europapark) and snaking up to the eastern side of Prinzregentenstrasse, another 19th century masterpiece. An alternative route is described from just east of the Friedensengel monument running south to Max-Weber-Platz. Each partial circuit takes about an hour to walk, and ends near a U-Bahn station for easy return transport (if need be).

Starting point is the **Nationaltheater**, one of Germany's most important classical theatres, which, as an added bonus, houses the prestigious Bavarian State Opera. The huge avenue before you is the Maximilianstrasse, whose buildings were designed largely by Friedrich von Bürklein between 1852 and 1875. King Max II (who commissioned all this) wanted a mish-mash of Bavarian, Italian and English Gothic, and the result became known as Maximilian Style.

Moving east along Maximilianstrasse you'll cross a roaring thoroughfare called Thomas-Wimmer-Ring, one of Munich's post-war planning sins, before reaching on your right the watchful stone sentries of the Staatliches Museum für Völkerkunde (State Ethnology Museum). Directly opposite is the **Regierung von Oberbayern** (Upper Bavarian Administration building), which is illuminated at night (lest you forget its importance). At this point you should already see, looming on the eastern horizon, the red-golden wings of the **Maximilineum**, seat of the Bavarian parliament.

Max II Monument Before you reach the Isar, take a gander at the **Max II Monument** in the middle of a cobbled traffic circle at the intersection of Thierschstrasse. The base of this dark bronze statue displays four rather stern-looking 'children' who embody the German tribes from Bavaria, Franconia, Swabia and the Rhineland-Palatinate. King Max II towers over them all, balding and framed in tram lines that gracefully circumvent the statue. On the north side of the monument and hidden behind a leafy square is the **Kleine Komödie**, a long-standing temple of laughs.

Carry on east across the **Maximiliansbrücke**, designed from 1903 to 1905 by Friedrich von Thiersch, with the worn, incessantly photographed statues. One of them, the **Pallas Athène**, replaced a lamppost on the eastern link of the bridge in 1906. The bridge spans the Isar and, in the middle, the Praterinsel, a magnet for nude bathers and site of a former schnapps distillery that's been remodelled into an art and cultural centre, the Riemerschmid. The view is fantastic: upstream you'll glimpse the tower of the Art Nouveau **Müllerisches Volksbad**, while due north are the gently graded, foaming waterfalls on the Isar.

The traffic gets heavy at this point, so our tour seeks solace in the woods. On the east side of the Isar, cross to the northern side of the circular Max-Planck-Strasse (which goes around the Maximilineum on both sides) and continue north through the Maximilian-Anlagen, an undulating park that is a bonanza for cyclists in summer and tobogganists in winter.

Friedensengel Walk about half a kilometre along the leafy paths before emerging by the 6m-high **Friedensengel** statue, or Angel of Peace, on Prinzregentenstrasse. The graceful gilded lady is a replica of the Nike figure on the Greek mountain of Olympia, supported by a 20m-high column. She recalls the 1871 Treaty of Versailles, which ended the Franco-Prussian war. The covered base contains some lovely golden frescoes, and is a popular gathering spot for New Year's celebrations. It's a wonderful vantage point west over the city, too.

Turn east at the Friedensengel and proceed along the wide green concourse, which narrows at Maria-Theresia-Strasse. At this point you can go south through a lovely and quiet neighbourhood of *fin-de-siècle* villas, inhabited by lawyers, doctors and professional associations, before reaching Einsteinstrasse and the nearby U-Bahn station at Max-Weber-Platz. Or, you can carry on east, from the Friedensengel, down Prinzregentenstrasse, the dividing line between ritzy, residential Bogenhausen to the north, and the lively former workers' quarter of Haidhausen.

The Prinzregentenstrasse was laid out from 1891 to 1912 in a gesture of self-promotion by Prince-Regent Luitpold. Today it serves as a main traffic artery, a showcase for several fine museums and a theatre. Moving east you'll reach, on your right, the **Museum Villa Stuck** (1897) founded by leading Jugendstil painter and rebellious artist Franz von Stuck. It's being renovated in stages through the end of 2002, but the museum remains open.

A few streets farther east you'll see the fancy **Feinkost Kafer** delicatessen on the north side of Prinzregentenstrasse, at the east corner of Trögerstrasse. Have a peek inside, even if you feel you can't afford anything, as the gourmet decorations (spread over two floors and multiple theme shops) are a real treat. For those on expense accounts there's a restaurant upstairs.

On the right-hand-side, behind the high walls, is the **Prinzregentenstadion**. This anachronism of a pool complex attracts a strange mixture of fashion models and senior citizens, and in winter it becomes an ice skating rink. The changing rooms are a riot.

Prinzregententheater Proceed 200m east past a recumbent, ill-maintained **statue of Richard Wagner** to reach the wedding-cake facade of the **Prinzregententheater**, opened in 1901 with a performance of Wagner's *Die Meistersänger*. Although it was erected during the heyday of Art Nouveau, the building is more a neoclassical copy of Bayreuth's opera house. Its interiors rumble with dark Renaissance motifs (grotesque masks and goblins).

On the north side of Prinzregentenplatz there's a little Indian restaurant called Swagat, a perfect spot for a cheap and tasty lunch (see the Places to Eat chapter). Our tour ends at the U4 station entrance, on the broad square beyond the massive fountain. You can also take bus No 53 back towards the city centre.

Schwabing

Until 1890 Schwabing was its own little peaceful village north of Munich, where the bourgeoisie built marvellous villas for their weekend retreat from the commerce of the city centre. This was instrumental in Schwabing's transformation from sleepy village to Munich's bohemian district: money mixed with art. From that point onward, Schwabing became a kind of *Schwabylon*, as its residents described it with obvious delight. Foreigners regarded it much like New York's Greenwich Village or Paris' Left Bank community. During the period until WWI there emerged the *Künstlerlokale* (artists' bars and pubs) where Rainer Maria Rilke, Thomas Mann and Karl Valentin would drown their sorrows.

Sadly, much of this creative flair has disappeared from Schwabing today, although its restaurant and bar scene retains the youthful spark of the university district. By some measures, Schwabing loosely takes in the area from Odeonsplatz past Münchener Freiheit and north to the artery called Frankfurter Ring. Beyond that lie the suburbs of Milbertshofen and Freimann (although some people assert that Schwabing runs all the way to the northern city limits).

In 1896 the red bulldog became the symbol for *Simplicissimus*, the bitingly satirical periodical, and for its sibling *Die Jugend*, which printed withering caricatures of leading political figures. The magazine's flowing illustrations in a deceivingly innocent style inspired the German term *Jugendstil*, which is better known under the French label *Art Nouveau* in English. Some Schwabing artists were arrested after their sketches made fun of Kaiser Wilhelm II (see also Literature in the Facts about Munich chapter).

Much of what remains of this era is cliche, and the areas around Türkenstrasse, Barerstrasse and Amalienstrasse really derive their life from the student population, not artists. Still, there are plenty of used bookshops, emporiums, and interesting pubs and cafes, which lend Schwabing a special flair, especially on the western side of Leopoldstrasse. (The establishments on the other side tend to cater to tourists.)

Leopoldstrasse (Map 4)

For many Müncheners it's the local *Champs Élysées*, filled with reaching poplar trees,

chic bars and ice-cream shops and in the summer, impromptu pavement art markets. Despite its torrents of cars, no other street captures the buzz of Schwabing quite like Leopoldstrasse, even if the illusion has become reality in too many of its pretentious bars and restaurants. On Sunday afternoon, natives and tourists take to the broad promenades to stroll, drink coffee and, above all, 'people watch'.

The street begins at the southern **Siegestor** (Victory Gate), which was commissioned by Ludwig I and was built by Friedrich von Gärtner. Immediately to your left (west) on Akademiestrasse is the **Akademie der bildenden Künste** (Academy of Fine Arts), a three storey Italian Renaissance building from the late 19th century. The facade is festooned with arched windows and, as one would hope, fine artwork.

As you move north, you'll see some attractive neoclassical buildings both on your left and right that have been usurped by big German insurance companies. The giant white alien striding out of No 36 is the famous **Walking Man** statue by American artist Jonathan Borofsky (1995), commissioned by the world's biggest reinsurance company, Munich Re, in the block behind.

At the corner of Martiusstrasse you'll really feel that you've entered the upmarket cafe district, with seas of pavement tables filled with beautiful people scrutinising passers-by. On the right corner is the **Roxy**, the ringleader of trendy spots here. A couple of doors farther on is the **Gaststätte Leopold**, an attractive Bavarian restaurant, which, by all accounts, is best enjoyed via its earthy panelled interiors and lighting, rather than its food or service.

On the right a few metres to the north is the Hertie department store, with the thumping rooftop disco, Skylight, after dark. This leaves us at Münchener Freiheit, the departure point for a walking tour through Schwabing's old section.

Old Schwabing Walking Tour (Map 4)

This walk sweeps through the old bohemian district of Schwabing, covering a circuit from Münchener Freiheit. The charms of the district are chiefly architectural, aside from the many pubs and restaurants. The tour takes about an hour at a leisurely pace.

Begin the walk at the U-Bahn station at **Münchener Freiheit**, a wide patchwork of green areas, concrete and busy streets. This is the heart of Schwabing, which beat more vigorously before the square was ripped up during the underground's construction in the early 1970s. Focal points are the usually overcrowded Café Münchener Freiheit and the outdoor chessboard a few steps to the south (filled with retirees and the unemployed).

The first stop is on the north side of the square, the church with the bold clockface. The **Erlöserkirche** (Church of Salvation), built by Thomas Fischer in 1900, was a rejection of the high sacral features of the Romantic period and was an attempt at a village church with modern and Art Nouveau traits.

From the Erlöserkirche carry on eastward down Haimhauserstrasse and take the second right into Occamstrasse. In the 1970s this was a popular place for a pub crawl, and you can smell the beery aromas that waft out of the seedy (but colourful) establishments. At Wedekindplatz, take a left into Feilitzschstrasse towards the English Garden; on the left is the smoky **Hopfendolde bar**, site of occasional flea markets and better known nowadays as **Paddy's Irish pub**.

This area is home to some of Munich's cabaret theatres. In the first street on the left, past Paddy's, is the **Münchner Lach und Schiessgesellschaft** (roughly, Munich 'Laughing and Shooting Company'), Ursulastrasse 9. Close by you'll also find two notable Spanish restaurants, El Cortijo and Don Quixote (see the Places to Eat chapter).

At the end of Feilitzschstrasse, on the right-hand-side, stands the former parish **Church of St Sylvester** (1811), one of Schwabing's old, pretty and sleepy village-style churches. Ascend the steps into the raised courtyard, an oasis of peace a world away from the bar district a few metres to the west.

At this point you can take time out for a brew in the English Garden at the **Seehaus**

on the northern shore of the lake (see Beer Halls & Gardens in the Entertainment chapter). Our tour continues south in Mandlstrasse along the western fringe of the English Garden, admiring the many old villas before turning right into Seestrasse. On your right, at the corner of Werneckstrasse, is the **Werneck-Schlösschen**, one of Munich's last summer palaces to be built (early 18th century). It's named after a small town between Paris and Versailles where German Elector Max Emanuel resided for a short time in exile.

Turn left into Werneckstrasse and immediately right into Nikolaistrasse, where on the south side stands the **Seidlvilla**, a smart, castle-like residence that has served as a community centre and art gallery since 1991 (see Where to Shop in the Shopping chapter). The gate's usually shut but check the opening times – you should be able to buzz and just stroll in.

From Nikolaistrasse our route winds higgledy-piggledy towards Leopoldstrasse: take the first left into the Siegesstrasse and the first right into Maria-Josepha-Strasse, which feeds into the Trautenwolfstrasse. From here we cross over the broad, well travelled avenue of Leopoldstrasse into **Ainmillerstrasse** to discover some of Munich's finest Art Nouveau architecture.

Ainmillerstrasse was home to some of the founding members of the *Blauer Reiter* (Blue Rider) group of artists: Paul Klee at No 32 and Gabriele Münter and Wassily Kandinsky at No 36. Poet Rainer Maria Rilke lived at No 34. The crowning glory of the street is No 22, a vintage Art Nouveau facade with wonderful blue-and-gold arches topped with the helmed heads of Roman soldiers, and with Adam and Eve reclining under the Tree of Knowledge. The flowery cream-and-grey block next door is also spectacular.

Take a right into Friedrichstrasse to see Munich's first Art Nouveau block of tenements, at No 3. The gilded artwork clearly indicates that Schwabing wasn't home to just artists and revolutionaries at the beginning of the 20th century. Friedrichstrasse runs north into the square dominated by the

St Ursula Church, which in 1897 took over from the Church of St Sylvester as Schwabing's new parish church. Its style is striking Florentine, reflecting a revival of popularity of cross-domed churches during the period.

At St Ursula Church turn east into Kaiserstrasse, where Lenin lived during his exile in an unremarkable flat at No 46 (it's not marked with a memorial plaque or such). Under the alias of Meyer, the Soviet leader-to-be published two periodicals, the influential underground *Der Funke* (The Spark) as well as *Die Morgenröte* (The Dawn), and wrote some essays and articles under the name Lenin for the first time. His Munich works include a seminal essay *What is to Be Done?*, which laid down principles for the October Revolution of 1917. The row of old workers' tenements has been buffed to a shine, and looks wonderful today.

The street butts into Leopoldstrasse, with the only superficially exclusive Lardy nightspot on your right (see the Entertainment chapter). Proceed north along Leopoldstrasse, and you'll end up where we began, at the Münchener Freiheit U-Bahn station.

Activities

Munich makes a perfect base for a range of outdoor and leisure sports activities. For information about hiking and climbing, contact the Deutscher Alpenverein (Map 7a, German Alpine Club, ☎ 14 00 30), which has an office two blocks east of the Hauptbahnhof at Bayerstrasse 21.

For gear, the Sport Schuster, Rosenstrasse 1–5, and the better Sport Scheck (Map 7a, ☎ 216 60), nearby at Sendlinger Strasse 6, both have multiple floors of everything imaginable for the adventurer, from simple camping equipment to expedition wear, plus excellent bookshops. There's a discount Sport Scheck store at the Ostbahnhof selling discontinued merchandise.

For details about tickets to sports events (soccer, tennis, ice hockey, horse racing and more), see Spectator Sports in the Entertainment chapter.

Billiards

Munich's most traditional pool hall is the Schelling-Salon (Map 7, ☎ 272 07 88) at Schelling-strasse 54. Supposedly Hitler and Lenin were among the characters who racked their balls here, which is possible as the place was founded in 1872. There are 13 pool and five snooker tables, several table tennis tables in the cellar, and bunches of hard-drinking locals playing cards. There's even a little billiard museum in the back, it's open from 6 to 8 pm on weekends or by appointment (free). The salon is open from 6.30 am to 1 pm daily; closed on Tuesday and Wednesday.

There's a great pool hall in the Ostbahnhof called Billiard World (☎ 48 56 49). Open from 9 am till 1 am, it has dozens of pool and snooker tables with playing fees ranging from DM13 to DM15 per hour, depending on the time of day.

Back in the city centre, the Billiard Café (Map 7a, ☎ 22 63 00) at the corner of Rumfordstrasse and Klenzestrasse is a clean, relaxed place with 6 pool and 5 snooker tables and a bar. Hours are from 11 am to 1 am.

Boating

There are several places in town to take a little tootle with a boat; the most popular spot is the English Garden's Kleinhesseloher See, where rowing/pedal boats cost DM10/12 per half-hour for up to four people. It's generally less crowded at the Olympiapark, which rents paddle boats for DM10/18 and rowboats for DM7/12 per half-hour/hour.

Cycling

The Bavarian office of the Allgemeiner Deutscher Fahrradclub (German cycling association, or ADFC) puts out a *Radwegkarte* map (DM8.50) that displays all bike routes in Munich. It's available at bookstores or from the ADFC office (Map 7a, ☎ 55 35 75) at Landwehrstrasse 16 near the Hauptbahnhof. It's open from 2 to 6 pm weekdays and from 10 am to 4 pm Saturday.

You can also get a more basic but adequate bike path map of Munich, *Münchner Radlstadtplan*, for free, at the Umweltladen,

Rindermarkt 10 just south of Marienplatz (enter on Pettenbeckstrasse).

Remember that bicycles can be taken on the U- and S-Bahns all day at weekends, but not during rush hour on weekdays (6.30 to 8.30 am and 3 to 6.30 pm).

One excellent and easy tour you can do without a map begins at Wittelsbacher Brücke on the western bank of the Isar (south-east of the South Cemetery). From here you can cycle south into the greenery of the Isarauen (Isar Meadows), past the leafy and inviting Flaucher beer garden (see the Entertainment chapter), and on to the Thalkirchner Brücke by the zoo. Cross the bridge east and return north along the other side – you can do this easily in an hour (without stops).

Fitness

Most fitness studios in Munich are facilities that you can't just stroll into; you'll usually have to sign a contract for at least a few months, and it can work out to be an expensive proposition.

Of the few exceptions is Der Sport Studio (Map 3, ☎ 57 34 79), Landsbergerstrasse 191, which has lots of weight training and body-building equipment. A day card costs DM20. To get there take tram Nos 18 or 19 from the Hauptbahnhof west to Elisenheimerstrasse.

The Gesundheitspark (Health Park) in the Olympic stadium is run by the Munich Volkshochschule and has 20 to 40 hours of courses weekly. Some are on a drop-in basis. Call ☎ 30 61 01 60 for details or pick up their brochure from tourist information. Take the U3 to Olympiazentrum.

The municipal Sportamt (☎ 65 01 47) runs gymnastics programs at more than 25 locations around town; the brochure *Freizeitsport* from tourist information lists the addresses. The cost is DM5 per hour, or DM20 for a strip of five tickets. Two locations with fitness equipment are at Sieboldstrasse 4 (take any S-Bahn to Rosenheimer Platz) and Memeler Strasse 53 in Bogenhausen (take the U4 to Arabellapark). Hours are from 10 am to 10 pm weekdays, and from 1 to 8 pm on weekends.

Ice Skating

When it's freezing you can skate for free on Nymphenburg Canal and the Kleinhesseloher See in the English Garden. But for year-round fun, the best place is the Olympia Eisstadion (☎ 30 67 21 50) in the Olympia-park, which has a varied program (figure skating to informal mass races), although there are fixed times for recreational skating. These are from 10 am to noon weekdays, from 2 to 4 pm Wednesday and Friday, as well as from 8 to 10 pm Thursday and Sunday (DM5/3). See also Inline-Skating later in this section.

Rafting

Rafting on the Isar River is a wonderful thing to do. On warm spring and summer days, many Munich residents take advantage of a little loophole in the law that allows free camping on the banks of the river (as long as you don't make a fire in protected areas). The shores of the Isar resemble an army camp on some summer evenings – but don't despair, there's more space around the next bend.

The usual route is to begin between 25km and 50km south of Munich, at either Wolfratshausen or Bad Tölz, and make your way back with the current. There's a really easy starting point 100m from the Wolfratshausen S-Bahn station, and in good weather you'll just need to follow the crowds. There are several places along the river where you'll have to take the raft out of the water and carry it around dams or locks, but for the most part it's just a lazy, wonderful trip. For a couple it can be the most romantic part of a trip to Munich.

Nude bathing along the route is not only permitted, it would seem to be the rule (though for some of the folks you'll see standing on the riverbank clothing *should be* mandatory). Make sure to use plenty of sunscreen on places not ordinarily exposed to the sun.

To get started you'll need a reasonable-quality inflatable rubber raft (available at Kaufhof, Sport Scheck or Schuster, though the first is cheapest) for about DM150 to DM250. Get on S-Bahn No 7 and head for

Wolfratshausen (the last stop) or change trains for Bad Tölz. You'll need food, four litres of water per person per day plus something waterproof to hold all your gear (a second little kiddy raft tied to your raft works well, but make sure your sleeping bag and clothes are secure and in sealed plastic bags).

As evening approaches, find a nice quiet stretch of riverbank on which to bed down, take the raft out of the water and set up your camp. It's quiet, peaceful and if you have a camping stove, you can probably get away with cooking up some dinner. It's usually not bug-infested, so you won't need a tent.

Do not attempt this if it's rained heavily in the few days previous. The Isar, while shallow, is very cold and swells to dangerous levels after rainstorms, creating fast and unstable currents. Call for weather reports (☎ 0190-11 69 58, DM1.20 per minute) and check the newspapers before heading out. The best rule of thumb is to watch the locals and follow warning signs along the route.

For more information on river trips and rowing in the area, contact the Bayerische Kanu Verband (☎ 15 70 24 43), and ask for a copy of its *Wanderführer Bayern*, which lists routes and regional rental outlets. It's also available in bookshops.

Raft Tours Organised tours down the Isar aboard huge rafts are really fun, and if you're not into buying a raft and doing it all yourself, this is a great way to spend an afternoon. They usually start at Wolfratshausen for groups (though individuals can join some), and they're a real hoot: usually accompanied by an oompah band and at least a keg of beer, the rafts stay out for several hours. The price (from DM50 to DM150 per person) includes transport, beer and lunch. The tours are extremely popular and often book out months in advance. To book, call or visit ABR (Map 7a, ☎ 120 42 37), the official Bavarian travel agency, in the front of Munich Hauptbahnhof, or call the Wolfratshausen tourist office (☎ 08041-50 52 38/48).

Inline-Skating

The coolest thing in inline-skating is Skate 'n' Fun (☎ 49 00 13 13), in Kunstpark Ost at Grafingerstrasse 6 behind the Ostbahnhof. It's a safe and clean indoor stunt park with ramps, shells and skating areas for people of all ages. Rented gear, including complete protection (pads, helmets and the like), costs from DM8, plus the DM5 entry fee. You can rent both standard skates and those with extra stunt protection for DM30 a day or DM40 for the weekend. Courses are run daily.

The endless concrete surfaces of the Olympiapark make for great skating, and it's slightly cheaper than at the Ostbahnhof. You can borrow inline skates at the Eisstadion for DM6 for two hours, and for DM2 for every additional two hours. Protection gear rents for DM3 per item. You'll need an ID or passport plus DM100 deposit. The shop in the Eisstadion is Holiday Sport, Spiridon-Louis-Ring 3 (☎ 30 77 94 52).

Swimming & Sauna

It's not recommended to swim in the Isar River due to its relatively high bacteria content, but a lot of Müncheners do. In summer you'll see plenty of them frolicking off the pebbly shores that line the river within the city limits, such as off the Praterinsel north of the Deutsches Museum.

There are nine indoor swimming pools in town, most of them with sauna facilities. As you may have noticed in the English Garden, Germans aren't at all prudish and saunas are usually mixed and nude, so check your modesty in at the front desk.

Aside from fantastic 25m and 50m pools and awe-inspiring diving towers, the Olympia-Schwimmhalle (☎ 30 67 22 90) in the Olympiapark has an elaborate sauna complex that includes a steamy 'grotto'. Entry is DM5 (DM4 for under 18s); add a sauna and the price is DM15/11. Tanning beds (DM5) are available as well. It's open daily in varying sessions from 7 am to 10.30 pm.

The spectacular Müllerisches Volksbad (☎ 23 61 34 29), Rosenheimer Strasse 1, is a riot of Art Nouveau style and worth visiting even if you don't swim. It has a large pool, sauna, steam baths and public baths; the cost is DM3.50/2.50 per hour, or with a private cabin (in which to take a hot bath)

DM7.50. It's open to women only on Tuesday and Friday, men only on Wednesday and Thursday. Hours are from 7.30 am to 11 pm on weekdays and from 9 am to 11 pm on weekends.

Out in Arabellapark is Munich's most modern indoor swimming complex, the Cosima-Wellenhallenbad (☎ 91 17 90) at Cosimastrasse 5. Weekdays from 2 pm the wave-motion machine is switched on for 10 to 15 minutes every hour – they're almost big enough to white-cap. It costs DM5 per 1½ hours, and another DM1 for every extra half-hour; a day pass is DM10. It's open from 7.30 am to 11 pm daily.

Of Munich's 19 open-air swimming pools, one of the most charming is the Prinzregentenstadion (Map 6, ☎ 23 84 93 22), Prinzregentenstrasse 80. It has ageing but elegant facilities (the same might be said of its patrons), and the place becomes an ice skating rink in winter. It's open from 8 pm to 7.30 pm daily (DM4.50/DM3), with a flat fee of DM2 after 5 pm.

The Dantebad (Map 3, ☎ 23 61 79 81), at Dantestrasse 6 in Neuhausen, is the only heated swimming facility (32 degrees in the warmest pool) where you can also swim outdoors year-round. The facility was modernised and reopened in October 1999. Opening hours are from 8 am to 11 pm daily (DM5/ 4).

Surfing in the English Garden Some of the most bizarre surfing you'll see takes place in the tiny, chilly and fast-moving Eisbach, an arm of the Isar that runs north through the English Garden. It all started just after WWII when a GI from the occupying US forces waxed down a makeshift board and set off to find some breakers. What he discovered was a rapid called the 'permanent wave' in the Eisbach just north of Maximilianstrasse, between the Haus der Kunst and the Bavarian National Museum.

Spectators crowd along the bridge daily in summer to watch the action. Right next to the bridge is a commemorate plaque to Count Rumford. The more skilled surfers can stay up for five minutes or more. If you want to have a go yourself, rent surfboards from Sport Scheck, Sport Schuster and other sport suppliers from about DM30 per day plus deposit.

Tennis & Squash
Tennis has boomed in Germany ever since an awkward carrot-top named Boris Becker burst onto the scene in the 1980s, and Munich has plenty of indoor and outdoor facilities. Indoor tennis courts charge from about DM25 to DM40 per hour in the winter but are slightly cheaper in summer, while outdoor courts cost from about DM12 to DM40 per hour, depending on the day and time of day. Squash courts charge about DM30 to DM45 per hour. Many tennis clubs have English-speaking coaches, which ask about DM40 per hour for lessons.

The Olympiapark (☎ 30 67 26 90) has four all-weather outdoor courts, which on weekdays cost a reasonable DM13 for unlimited play between 7 and 10 am, and DM16 between 10 am and 4 pm. After that it jumps to DM23, which is also the flat all-day rate at weekends. Court lighting costs an extra DM3.

Sport Scheck has two indoor court facilities: Allwetter Nord (☎ 95 10 16) at Münchnerstrasse 15 in the northeastern suburb of Unterföhring (take the S8 towards the airport), and Allwetter Süd (☎ 78 10 18) at Meglingerstrasse 6 south-west of town in Forstenried (take the U3 to Forstenreid, then bus No 69 two stops to Munckstrasse, direction Solln). Opening times and prices vary, but you can pick up a brochure at Sport Scheck's shop at Sendlingerstrasse 6.

Squash Centre Schwabing (Map 4, ☎ 308 35 16), Winzererstrasse 47b, is a popular student location charging DM28 per hour. Take the U2 to Hohenzollernplatz and walk east five minutes (cross four streets) to Winzererstrasse.

LANGUAGE COURSES
Goethe Institute
The Goethe Institute is a nonprofit, government-subsidised organisation that promotes German language and culture abroad. Besides offering a comprehensive course program, they also stage some 10,000 events

year round, including theatre performances, symposia, lectures, film and music festivals.

Goethe Institute language courses cater to all age groups and stages of proficiency – from absolute beginner to professional level. The program is divided into three general levels: *Grundstufe* (basic), *Mittelstufe* (intermediate) and *Oberstufe* (advanced); each is further divided into sublevels.

Intensive courses cost DM3140 (eight weeks), DM1690 (four weeks) and DM1360 (two weeks). Accommodation costs DM1700/1400 for a single/two-bed room over eight weeks, or DM850/700 for the four week course. The institute also runs three-week summer programs for children and youths aged 10 to 20 years, from DM3250.

Course information can be obtained from German embassies or consulates abroad and from the Goethe Institute's central registration office (Map 7a, ☎ 159 21 24 94, fax 15 92 12 37, email brehm@goethe.de),

Helene-Weber-Allee 1, 80637 Munich. You can also visit its more central office at Sonnenstrasse 25 (☎ 551 90 30). Information is available on the Internet at www.goethe.de.

Volkshochschule Courses offered at the Münchner Volkshochschule (VHS, or adult education centre, ☎ 48 00 60), at Rosenheimerstrasse 5 in the Gasteig, are good value and open to everyone. It offers classes in German at all levels, which begin twice a year. The courses usually last three or four months and include an examination and certificate; they cost around DM30 per teaching hour. One popular option is to combine au pair work with a German course.

Ludwig-Maximilians-Universität Munich's main university (☎271 26 42) offers day and evening courses at different levels year-round. Prices are similar to those charged by the Volkshochschule.

Places to Stay

Munich crawls with tourists from May to September, so be sure to reserve accommodation well ahead of time during the summer. The flow thins considerably from November to March (apart from during the Christmas and New Year's holidays), when many hotels flog their empty rooms at lower rates (check your travel agent or the Munich Hotel Verbund, see later in this chapter).

Accommodation tends to be expensive. Even if you book through EurAide or the city tourist offices (see later in this chapter), you'll be lucky to find anything under DM60/90 for a single/double in a hotel or pension. The DJH and independent hostels are the cheapest options for a bed, bearing in mind that an age limit of 26 generally applies (exceptions are listed).

German hotels and pensions are almost always clean, even the down-at-heel ones. Television and room phones aren't standard in the cheapest category, and some of the older places might not have a lift; if these things are important, check before you book. Note that only the more expensive hotels might have air-conditioning, which is something to consider for the summer.

One great German custom is the inclusion, in most cases anyway, of breakfast in hotel room rates. This is commonly an all-you-can-eat buffet of bread and rolls, cheeses, cold cuts, jams and honey, cereals and a 'bottomless' cup of coffee or tea. A good feasting at breakfast could easily keep you going until mid-afternoon. Speaking of food, the term *hotel garni* means your host doesn't have a restaurant, but probably serves breakfast.

Some hotels have parking in their own garages or inner courtyards, and you should expect to pay about DM10 to DM25 per night per vehicle. At smaller establishments, you may have to seek a spot on the street or in a public garage. For the latter, you can reckon on paying DM20 to DM25 per day.

As a rule, reserve if possible and say if you're arriving after 6 pm, when many places begin to cancel unconfirmed bookings. Note that rates in city hotels can rise about·10 to 15% during the summer; prices rocket during Oktoberfest (increases of 50% or more aren't unheard of).

Bookings The main tourist office at the Hauptbahnhof (Map 7a, ☎ 23 33 02 57/58, fax 23 33 02 33, email tourismus@ muenchen.btl.de), left of the main entrance, has a room-finding service for DM5. You'll have to make a 10% down-payment which will be deducted from your bill (keep the receipt). Hours are from 9 am to 8 pm Monday to Saturday, and from 10 am to 6 pm Sunday. There's a second branch of the tourist office on Marienplatz, open from 10 am to 8 pm weekdays and from 10 am to 4 pm on Saturday. Both offices are often crowded so expect to queue during summer, or you can write ahead of time to: Fremdenverkehrsamt München, Sendlinger Strasse 1, 80331 München.

The Munich Hotel Verbund (Map 3, ☎ 30 77 50 50, fax 30 77 50 55, email info@ muenchen-hotel.de), Karl-Theodor-Strasse 81, in the north of town, is a private hotel association which runs a free booking service for Munich's 300-odd hotels in all price categories. They can often give you better rates than if you booked yourself. You'll need to leave a credit card number – it's standard procedure. It's a 24-hour service so you can ring or fax your request at any time.

EurAide (Map 7a, ☎ 59 38 89), near platform 11 in the Hauptbahnhof, has a skilful room-finding service for a DM7.50 fee. It's often a good alternative to fighting the crowds in the city tourist offices. In summer, it's open from 7.45 am to noon and 1 pm to 6 pm daily, and mornings only on Saturday. In winter, the office closes at 4.30 pm on weekdays.

Munich Key The city tourist office has organised a nifty deal called Munich Key, which includes hotel accommodation, a public-transport pass (MVV) in the city centre during your stay, and a voucher booklet for discounts to many sights and museums. The deal covers all price ranges, but isn't available during major trade fairs or Oktoberfest. On the other hand, in August (for instance) you could book rooms with private bath/WC in a budget hotel from as low as DM64/98. Reservations are binding, so you'll pay a hefty fee if you cancel at short notice (ie 60% the day before your arrival). Write or call the Munich tourist office for a rates calendar and list of participating hotels.

PLACES TO STAY – BUDGET
Camping

The most central camping ground is *Campingplatz Thalkirchen (Map 5,* ☎ *723 17 07, fax 724 31 77, Zentralländstrasse 49)*, south-west of the city centre with a pretty location on the Isar. It's close to the zoo and the hostel on Miesingstrasse. Open from mid-March to late October, it can get incredibly crowded but there always seems to be room for one more tent. The price is DM8.40 per person plus DM5.50 per tent, and DM8.50/4 per car/motorcycle. An extra charge of DM7 is levied during Oktoberfest. There are laundry facilities on the grounds. Take U3 to Thalkirchen and bus No 57 to Thalkirchen, the last stop (about 20 minutes from the city centre).

The *Jugendlager am Kapuziner Hölzl* (see DJH Hostels) also has camp sites costing DM7 per person and DM7 per tent.

A bit farther away and west of the city centre is *Waldcamping Obermenzing (Map 3,* ☎ *811 22 35, fax 814 48 07)*, on the outskirts of an upscale neighbourhood at Lochhausener Strasse 59. Take the S2 to Obermenzing and then bus No 75 to Lochhausener Strasse. It charges DM6 per night, another DM3.50 to DM5 per tent, and DM5 per car.

Langwieder See (☎ *864 15 66, fax 863 23 42)* has a great location on a man-made lake, but can only be reached by car on the autobahn A8 towards Augsburg. It's open from early April to the end of October. Prices are roughly the same as at Obermenzing.

DJH Hostels

Munich's summer budget favourite is the *Jugendlager am Kapuziner Hölzl (Map 3,* ☎ *141 43 00, fax 17 50 90)*, on In den Kirschen, north of Schloss Nymphenburg. Nicknamed 'The Tent', this mass camp is only open from mid-June to early September. There's no night curfew, but the usual 26-year age limit applies (with priority given to people under 23) and you can only stay three nights. The cheapest 'beds' (a thermal mattress and blanket in the big tent) cost DM14 with breakfast; showers are available. Bunk-style beds are DM18. Take U1 to Rotkreuzplatz, then tram No 12 to the Botanischer Garten, and then walk down Frank-Shrank-Strasse.

Most central is the sparkling *Jugendherberge München (Map 3,* ☎ *13 11 56, fax 167 87 45, Wendl-Dietrich-Strasse 20)*, north-west of the city centre. One of the largest hostels in Germany, it is relatively loud and busy, but very popular and friendly. Beds cost from DM25.50 (DM23 if you're willing to sleep in a room with 36 others!). There's no curfew or lock-out. The hostel has a cute pub/restaurant (built partly in an old tram), a garden, laundromat and bicycles for rent (see the Getting Around chapter). Take the U1 to Rotkreuzplatz.

Still fairly accessible to the city centre, and a better deal, is the more modern *Jugendgästehaus München (Map 5,* ☎ *723 65 50/60, fax 724 235 67, Miesingstrasse 4)*, south-west of the city centre in the suburb of Thalkirchen. Costs per person are DM26 in dorms, DM28 in triples and quads, DM31.50 in doubles, and DM36.50 in singles. There's a 1 am curfew. Take the U3 to Thalkirchen, then follow the signs.

Jugendherberge Burg Schwaneck (☎ *793 06 43, fax 793 79 22, Burgweg 4–6)*, is in a great old castle in the southern suburbs. Ludwig I used the place for costume balls in the early 19th century. Dorm beds cost from DM22.50 and singles/doubles DM31.50/63. To get there take the S7 to Pullach and walk for 10 minutes.

The spanking new *Jugendherberge Dachau (*☎ *08131-32 29 50, fax 322 95 50, Rosswachtstrasse 15)*, is a worthy alternative to the Munich hostels when the latter are booked solid. Staff are very friendly and breakfast is superb. Dorm beds cost DM32. Take the S2 to Dachau (20km north-east of Munich), and then bus Nos 726 or 720 to John-F-Kennedy-Platz.

Independent Hostels

Munich has quite a few non-DJH hostels or hotels that offer cheap dormitory accommodation as well as simple rooms. A newcomer is the 24-hour *Euro Youth Hotel (Map 7a, ☎ 59 90 880, fax 59 90 88 77, email info@euro-youth-hotel.de, Senefelderstrasse 5)*, still wearing the decor of the grand Hotel Astoria it once was, until WWI. Beds in a 30-person dormitory cost just DM25 each, in a three and four-bed room DM36, and in a double room DM42. Tapped half-litres of Augustiner (the brewery owns the place) cost just DM3.60; breakfast costs DM7.90.

At the *CVJM-YMCA Jugendgästehaus (Map 7a, ☎ 552 14 10, fax 550 42 82, email muenchen@cvjm.org, Landwehrstrasse 13)*, you don't have to show a religious bent but it helps, given the restrictive mood of the place. Singles/doubles/triples cost DM48/41/38 (or DM53 for a larger single), but prices are 16% higher for guests over 26. Smoking and alcohol are forbidden outside the house restaurant, which is closed Monday.

Somewhat scruffy but clean and pleasant, the *Haus International (Map 3, ☎ 12 00 60, fax 12 00 62 51, Elisabethstrasse 87)*, is a 'youth hotel', not a hostel, so travellers of any age can stay. It has more than 500 beds in all; prices range from DM40.50 in five-person dorms to DM55/104 for small and simple singles/doubles, to DM85/144 for clean singles/doubles with all the mod cons. There's a pool, disco, beer garden and cafeteria. Take the U2 to Hohenzollernplatz or tram No 12 to Barbara Strasse.

Jump In (Map 6, ☎ 48 95 34 37, no fax, Hochstrasse 51) charges from DM29 per person in multi-bed rooms (beware the thin floor mattresses) and from DM45/70 for more comfortable singles/doubles with hall shower. There's no curfew or age limit. Communal cooking facilities and washing machine are available. Take any S-Bahn to

Karlsplatz, then tram No 27 (direction Schwanseestrasse) and get off at Ostfriedhof. Hochstrasse is at the bottom of the hill on the right side.

The *Kolpinghaus St Theresia (Map 3, ☎ 12 60 50, fax 12 60 52 12, Hanebergestrasse 8)*, is a 10 minute walk north of Rotkreuzplatz (or via U1). Beds in single/double/triple rooms cost DM49/36/34.

Women aged under 26 can try the Catholic *Jugendhotel Marienherberge (Map 7a, ☎ 55 58 05, no fax, Goethestrasse 9)* behind the poorly-marked black door (look for the tiny buzzer). Beds in common rooms start at DM30 and singles/doubles cost DM40/70. There's a midnight curfew.

4 you münchen (Map 7a, ☎ 552 16 60, fax 55 21 66 66, email info@the4you.de, Hirtenstrasse 18) just north of the Hauptbahnhof, bills itself as an ecologically-correct hostel. It's often full, but our last visit found the place to be poorly cleaned and maintained. If you're undeterred, dorm beds cost from DM31.50 and singles/doubles start at DM61.50/92. Guests over 26 pay about 15% more. Its organic breakfast costs DM7.50.

Hotels & Pensionen

You'll find a slew of budget pensions and hotels – some a bit seedy and claustrophobic, others quite OK – clustered around the Hauptbahnhof. Note that many of the places along Schwanthalerstrasse have an excellent view of the Oktoberfest opening parade, but they fill up months (or even a year) in advance at this time. The area (and its hotels) becomes gradually nicer moving south, towards the residential section, east of Theresienwiese.

Around Hauptbahnhof In a morass of sex shops, *Hotel Monaco (Map 7a, ☎ 545 99 40, fax 550 37 09, email Hotel.Monaco@ netplace.de, Schillerstrasse 9)* rises above it all with a floral elegance. Take the lift to the 5th floor, where you'll find artful paper roses in the halls and rooms. It's a bargain from DM55/70 for simple singles/doubles and DM138/158 for rooms with all amenities.

Hotel Eder (Map 7a, ☎ 55 46 60, fax 550 36 75, Zweigstrasse 8), is tucked away in a

euro currency converter DM1 = €.51

PLACES TO STAY

quiet street just south-east of the Hauptbahnhof. Rooms and the downstairs breakfast/reception area are panelled with rustic Bavarian pine, and service is exceedingly friendly. Bathless rooms start at DM65/75, while those with private shower cost from DM75/100. Breakfast is included.

Hotel Jedermann *(Map 5,* ☎ *53 36 39, fax 53 65 06, email hotel-jedermann@ cube.net, Bayerstrasse 95)* can be highly-recommended and is only five minutes walk from the Hauptbahnhof. Renovated in 1998, its attractive rooms start at DM65/95 with shared facilities, and DM95/130 for ones with private bath, including a buffet breakfast. Staff speak English, and guests can surf the Web (free) on a dedicated terminal.

Hotel Helvetia *(Map 7a,* ☎ *590 68 50, fax 59 06 85 70, Schillerstrasse 6)* is primarily a backpackers' hotel, but others can sample its charms a minute's stroll from the Hauptbahnhof. After a recent facelift, all windows are sound-proofed, most rooms have phones and there's a laundry service (big loads DM8.50). Beds in 4/6/10 bed dorms cost DM33/35/22. Singles/doubles with hall shower are DM55/78, and there are doubles with private bath from DM99. Breakfast is included. The Busabout stop is just outside the door (see the Getting There & Away chapter).

The carpets have seen better days at **Pension Marie-Luise** *(Map 7a,* ☎ *55 25 56 60, fax 55 25 56 66, Landwehrstrasse 35)*, but the rooms are all right from DM55/85. There's a useful common room. Reception is next door at **Andi (Comfort) Hotel** (see Places to Stay – Mid-Range). Nearby, **Pension Alpina** *(Map 7a,* ☎*/fax 538 07 22, Landwehrstrasse 49)*, offers very basic rooms from DM45/68. Breakfast costs extra at both places.

Alfa Hotel *(Map 7a,* ☎ *545 95 39, fax 545 95 32 99, Hirtenstrasse 20)* just north of the Hauptbahnhof, has cramped but clean quarters from DM65/95, a passable bar and courtyard parking.

East of Theresienwiese *Hotel Pension Mariandl (*☎ *53 41 08, fax 54 40 43 96, Goethestrasse 51)* on Beethovenplatz has

old-world charm, friendly staff and clean, pleasant rooms. Singles/doubles cost DM70/ 95, or DM65/90 if you book through the city tourist office (not EurAide) at the Hauptbahnhof. Downstairs, the restaurant has live jazz or classical music every night at 8 pm (see the Places to Eat and Entertainment chapters).

Hotel-Pension Utzelmann *(Map 7a,* ☎ *59 48 89, fax 59 62 28, Pettenkoferstrasse 6)*, near Sendlinger Tor, is a model budget hotel, and unfortunately it's no secret. It's run by a friendly English-speaking family, has bright, cheery rooms with four-poster beds, charges DM50/95/130/160 for one to four-bed rooms with hall shower (DM125/ 145/175/180 with private bath and WC). There are no telephones in the rooms.

An ideal compromise of location, price and cleanliness is **Pension Haydn** *(Map 7,* ☎ *53 11 19, fax 54 40 48 27, Haydnstrasse 9)*, near the Goetheplatz U-Bahn station and within walking distance of the Hauptbahnhof. Don't be put off by the ugly corrugated metal balconies, as it's quite homey inside. Rooms without bath start at DM60/90.

Hotel-Pension Schmellergarten *(Map 5,* ☎ *77 31 57, fax 725 68 86, Schmeller Strasse 20)*, is run by a friendly English-speaking couple in a quiet residential area south of Sendlinger Tor. It charges from DM65/90 for singles/doubles with hall shower, DM75/115 for rooms with a private shower, and DM85/125 for ones with private shower and WC. All rooms were recently refurbished; breakfast is included. Take the U6 to Poccistrasse.

Near pretty Kaiser-Ludwig-Platz, **Pension Schubert** *(*☎ *53 50 87, Schubertstrasse 1)*, has functional rooms without bath for DM50/85, while a fully equipped double isn't bad for DM95.

Westend *City Pension (Map 5,* ☎ *54 07 38 64, fax 500 46 65, Golierstrasse 36)*, has simple, cheerful and bright rooms a whopping four flights up (no lift) for DM60 to DM70 (singles) and DM100 to DM130 (doubles), plus DM10 for breakfast. Reception isn't always staffed, so it's a good idea to ring first.

Kurpfalz Hotel *(Map 5, ☎ 540 98 60, fax 54 09 88 11, email Hotel-Kurpfalz@ Munich-Online.de, Schwanthalerstrasse 121)*, has pleasant Bavarian-style rooms, satellite TV, and an Internet terminal for guests. You'll get a 10% discount if you book via its Web site (www.munich-spe-cials.de). Take tram Nos 18 or 19 to Holzapfelstrasse (three stops); it's a five-minute walk from there. Busabout stops here in the winter months.

The friendly ***Hotel Westend*** *(Map 5, ☎ 508 09 00, fax 502 58 96, Landsberger Strasse 20)* is a fabulous deal that belies the GDR-like facade: spacious rooms for DM65/90, and DM90/120 for cavernous ones with private facilities. Walk or take tram Nos 18 or 19 three stops from the Hauptbahnhof to Holzapfelstrasse.

Another good deal is the ***Hotel Petri*** *(Map 5, ☎ 58 10 99, fax 580 86 30, Aindorfer-strasse 82)*. Rooms have distinctive antique furniture and a TV, and there's a garden and small indoor swimming pool. Bathless singles cost DM95, while singles/doubles with shower and WC start at DM115/175. Take the U4 or U5 to Laimer Platz.

Altstadt *Hotel-Pension am Markt (Map 7a, ☎ 22 50 14, fax 22 40 17, Heiliggeist-strasse 6)*, overlooking the Viktualienmarkt, is excellent value for money. The owner's favourite opera singers adorn the walls. Simple rooms start at DM60/110; rooms with bath and WC cost from DM116/160.

Hotel Blauer Bock *(Map 7a, ☎ 23 17 80, fax 23 17 82 00, Sebastiansplatz 9)* is clean, comfortable, central and has reasonably spacious rooms. Rooms with private shower and WC start at DM100/150, or DM70/100 with communal facilities. A buffet breakfast is included and garage parking is available.

Of a similar standard and price is ***Hotel Arosa*** *(Map 7a, ☎ 26 70 87, fax 26 31 04, Hotterstrasse 2)*, with simple bathless rooms from DM77/102 and smarter ones from DM112/152, including breakfast.

The run-down but friendly ***Hotel Atlanta*** *(Map 7a, ☎ 26 36 05, fax 260 90 27, Sendlinger Strasse 58)*, is located between Sendlinger Tor and the Asamkirche; go through the creepy door and up the creepy stairs to clean (brown) rooms priced from DM50/89, or DM79/98 with facilities.

Schwabing *Pension Frank (Map 7, ☎ 28 14 51, fax 280 09 10, Schellingstrasse 24)*, is run by a friendly ex-estate agent who caters to young fashion models. It has lovely wrought-iron beds, a small collection of novels in English, a communal kitchen (note the sagging sink) and bathless rooms from only DM65/85. It's pleasant but often overrun by Anglo-Saxons. Take the U3 to Universität.

The eclectic ***Am Kaiserplatz*** *(Map 4, ☎ 34 91 90, no fax, Kaiserplatz 12)* has interiors ranging from down-home Bavarian to bordello velvet. It's run by an engaging old lady who rents the comfy, spacious rooms for just DM49/79 with hall shower. Take the U3 to Münchener Freiheit.

Hotel-Pension am Siegestor *(Map 7, ☎ 39 95 50/52, fax 34 30 50, Akademiestrasse 5)*, has the three upper floors in an old villa right by the Siegestor. Many rooms overlook the pretty Art Academy across the street. The lift is a delightful old Art Deco contraption. Singles/doubles begin at DM65/95, all with shared facilities in the hall. Take the U3 or U6 to Universität.

Lehel *Hotel-Pension Beck (Map 6, ☎ 22 57 68, fax 22 09 25, email pension.beck@ bst-online.de, Thierschstrasse 36)*, is a bit disorganised but endearing with its reception-area parakeets and Bavarian pinewood in the middle of fashionable Lehel. And it's cheap, from DM40 for beds in a multi-bed room and DM56/82 for simple singles/doubles. Doubles with all amenities cost from DM108. Prices include breakfast. Take any S-Bahn to Isartorplatz, or tram No 17 (direction Effn-erplatz) and alight at Mariannenplatz.

Neuhausen Comfortable but a bit out of the way, the ***CA Comfort Aparthotel*** *(Map 3, ☎ 15 92 40, fax 15 92 48 00, email CAM@blattl.de, Dachauer Strasse 195–99)*, caters to the business crowd with modern, well-appointed rooms and nice staff. Singles/doubles with

euro currency converter DM1 = €.51

PLACES TO STAY

facilities start at DM79/98 at weekends, jumping to DM135/160 during the week. Take bus Nos 20 or 21 towards Moosach.

PLACES TO STAY – MID-RANGE

'Mid-range' in Munich can mean paying over DM200, but you may do far better by joining a package tour or booking through a travel agent. Also, many hotels will come down if you merely ask if there's anything cheaper.

Around Hauptbahnhof North of the train station is a veritable package-tourist heaven, with several hotels lining Arnulfstrasse. All seem to offer the same thing: moderately clean, moderately well-appointed rooms, and staff used to groups of up to 100; these can be an excellent bargain if you can get yourself booked into a group, so don't scoff at the idea.

Rack rates for these hotels – the *Regent (Map 7a, ☎ 55 15 90, fax 55 15 91 54, Seidlstrasse 2)*; the *REMA-Hotel Esplanade (Map 7a, ☎ 55 13 90, fax 59 34 03, Arnulfstrasse 12)*; and the *Astron Hotel Deutscher Kaiser (Map 7a, ☎ 545 30, fax 54 53 22 55, Arnulfstrasse 2)* – all range between DM135 and DM230 for singles and DM185 and DM318 for doubles.

Hotel Kraft (Map 7a, ☎ 59 48 23, fax 550 38 56, Schillerstrasse 49) in a quiet area near the university hospital, has dated furniture but is otherwise top notch, with cable TV and a trouser press in every room, lest the creases catch you unawares. Singles/doubles with breakfast, start at DM140/170.

Behind the ghastly purple facade, the *Hotel Mirabell (Map 7a, ☎ 549 17 40, fax 550 37 01, Landwehrstrasse 42)* has attractive rooms of a high standard, with soundproofed windows, light wood panelling and pleasant wall prints. Singles/doubles/triples go for DM100/140/180, including breakfast.

Not far south of the Hauptbahnhof are two options run by Best Western. We recommend only one of them: the *Hotel Cristal (Map 7a, ☎ 55 11 10, fax 55 11 19 92, Schwanthalerstrasse 36)*, with huge rooms from DM215/250 and friendly staff. Prices go down dramatically at weekends.

Andi Comfort Hotel (Map 7a, ☎ 55 25 56 60, fax 55 25 56 66, Landwehrstrasse 35), has quiet, nicely-equipped rooms from DM95/155. Breakfast and pleasant banter at reception are included.

Just north of the Hauptbahnhof sits the *Amba Hotel (Map 7a, ☎ 54 51 40, fax 54 51 45 55, Arnulfstrasse 20)*, which offers simple rooms from DM80/120 and rooms with all facilities from DM140/180. It's clean, well-run and perfect for catching an early train.

East of Theresienwiese One of our enduring favourites is *Hotel Uhland (Map 5, ☎ 54 33 50, fax 54 33 52 50, email Hotel_Uhland@compuserve.com, Uhlandstrasse 1)* in a lovely villa just east of the Theresienwiese. It has relaxed English-speaking staff, large comfy rooms (some with a tiny balcony), and an Internet terminal for guests. Rooms with shower and WC start at DM110/160, and there's even a waterbed in one. Rates are about 10% lower if you book via email. Walk or take the U3 or U6 to Goetheplatz.

The *Westfalia (Map 5, ☎ 53 03 77/78, fax 543 91 20, Mozartstrasse 23)* occupies another palace-like house in an idyllic spot. It has lovely big rooms from DM85/120 (DM110/170 with private amenities). It's in high demand during Oktoberfest, especially as the folklore parade marches right under the balconies on the second day.

The *Olympic (Map 7, ☎ 23 18 90, fax 23 18 91 99, Hans-Sachs-Strasse 4)*, is just south of the Altstadt in one of Munich's prettier streets. It has quiet, well-furnished rooms on a picturesque little courtyard. Singles/doubles start at DM155/215, but can be cheaper in slow periods.

Westend Two places that overlook the Oktoberfest grounds can be bargained down out of season. *Hotel Krone (Map 5, ☎ 50 40 52, fax 50 67 06, email hotel-krone@gmx.de, Theresienhöhe 8)*, has worn English-style interiors and rack rates of DM120/140 for singles/doubles. For stays of a few days, try offering DM80/110 for one of the three rooms in the separate wing.

Next door, *Hotel Seibel (Map 5, ☎ 514 14 20, fax 54 01 42 99, email Hotel-Seibel@ t-online.de, Theresienhöhe 9)*, has a pleasant atmosphere, very friendly staff, lovely wrought-iron beds and hardwood furniture. It charges from DM99/139 for rooms with all amenities. Rooms at the back are quieter, away from the busy thoroughfare out front.

Altstadt & Around The 400-year-old *Hotel Schlicker (Map 7a, ☎ 22 79 41, fax 29 60 59, email schlicker-munich@t-on-line.de, Tal 8)* occupies an ideal spot near Marienplatz, and is a pretty good deal for the comfort it provides. Spacious, modern, newly- renovated singles/doubles start at DM130/ 190. Prices *don't* go up in the summer or at Oktoberfest, but the place is very popular so book ahead.

The *Advokat (Map 7a, ☎ 21 63 10, fax 216 31 90, email advokathot@aol.com, Baaderstrasse 1)* is Munich's first design hotel, with an attitude to match. Housed in a renovated 1930s apartment block, the place is a minimalist temple – simple but tasteful lighting, comfy but sparing beds and furniture, with few facilities outside the private bath/WC. Literature readings are sometimes held in the lobby. Rooms start at DM155/215.

Escape the tourist rabble at *Am Gärtner-platz-Theater (Map 7, ☎ 202 51 70, fax 20 25 17 22, Klenzestrasse 45)*, which has antique-filled rooms from DM80/100 (DM110/140 with private bath) in a cool part of town.

Around English Garden The aptly-named *Gästehaus am Englischen Garten (Map 4, ☎ 383 94 10, fax 38 39 41 33, Liebergesellstrasse 8)*, is located in a romantic *fin-de-siècle* mansion near the Klein-hesseloher See. Its antique-filled rooms start at DM127/154 with shared bath, and from DM151/180 with private amenities. Reserve as far ahead as possible. Take the U3 or U6 to Münchener Freiheit.

East of the Isar Just 10 minutes from the city centre, *Pension Fischer (Map 6, ☎/fax 697 30 92, Tegernseer Landstrasse 69)* is a well-tended little place on a quiet courtyard,

with polished wood furniture in every room (but no private telephones). It charges DM80/140 for bathless singles/doubles, and DM120/160 for rooms with all amenities. Note that its loyal Oktoberfest clientel book early. Take the U2 to Silberhornstrasse (it's on the corner near the station).

Blattls Hotel Altmünchen (Map 6, ☎ 45 84 40, fax 45 84 44 00, email HAM@ blattl.de, Mariahilfplatz 4), is cosier inside than its ultra-modern exterior suggests. All rooms have comfy furniture, private bath, modem plugs and for polyglots, trilingual TV. Rooms normally cost DM150/185, but there are weekend deals as low as DM89/118. The Auer Dult fair takes place on the square opposite three times a year. Take any S-Bahn to Marienplatz, and then bus Nos 52 or 56 toward Haidhausen (four stops).

Other Districts The *Jagdschloss (Map 3, ☎ 82 08 20, fax 82 08 21 00, Alte Allee 21)*, is a renovated, century-old hunting lodge in a western suburb with lots of rustic Bavarian hardwood. It retains the relaxed air of a place in the woods, an attitude reflected in the staff's traditional garb. There's a nice beer garden, too. Rooms with private bath start at DM114/179.

The decorators had a ball at the new *Seibel Park Hotel (Map 3, ☎ 829 95 20, fax 82 99 52 99, email Seibels-Park-Hotel@ t-online.de, Maria-Eich-Strasse 32)* in the western suburb of Pasing. It's laden with flowers and Art Deco trimmings and charges the same rates as its hospitable sibling in the Westend (from DM99/139). Take any S-Bahn to Pasing, and then bus No 70 to Maria-Eich-Strasse – it's about 25 minutes from the Altstadt.

PLACES TO STAY – TOP END
Hotels at the top of the heap are what you'd expect: luxurious and very expensive. Again, cheaper weekend deals can ease the financial damage.

Around Hauptbahnhof The *Hotel Ex-celsior (Map 7a, ☎ 55 13 70, fax 55 13 71 21, email Excelsior-Muenchen@t-online.de, Schützenstrasse 11)* is just a few hundred metres from the train station, but inside it's a world away: hushed voices, fancy lighting, antique furniture and an atmosphere reminiscent of pre-WWII. Singles/doubles start at DM265/330, and breakfast is another DM27.

On the edge of the Altstadt, overlooking Karlsplatz, lies *Hotel Königshof (Map 7a, ☎ 55 13 60, fax 55 13 61 33, email Koenigshof-Muenchen@t-online.de, Karlsplatz 25)* the even classier big brother of the Excelsior. The salons are large enough to get lost in. Room rates begin at DM355/400; add DM32 for a royal breakfast.

Around English Garden The *München Park Hilton (Map 4, ☎ 384 50, fax 38 45 18 45, email fom_munich-park@hilton.com, Am Tucherpark 7)*, is the 'bargain' of the top-end range. It has classy rooms from DM195/215, with a bevy of facilities including a heated outdoor pool, sauna, and a lovely view of the Isar from its terrace restaurant. Every room in this modern 15-story tower has picture windows, and the view of the leafy environs is lovely. Oddly enough, it has one star more than the Munich City Hilton but lower rack rates.

Lehel The *Opera Garni (Map 7a, ☎ 22 55 33, fax 22 55 38, St-Anna-Strasse 10)* just off Maximilianstrasse, is an elegant place decorated in Italian style. Read the morning newspaper in its over-the-top courtyard (marmoreal pillars and Roman busts). Singles/doubles with all amenities start at a stylish DM260/280.

Schwabing The *Hotel Carlton (Map 7, ☎ 28 20 61, fax 28 43 91, Fürstenstrasse 12)*, is within striking distance of Schwabing's bars and restaurants and, for diplomats, the US and British consulates. Its rooms aren't hanger-sized, but do have soft-toned Italian interiors and in some cases, balconies. Rates start at DM140/170 (rising to DM440/510 for a sprawling suite).

The *Holiday Inn Crowne Plaza (Map 4, ☎ 38 17 90, fax 38 17 98 88, Leopoldstrasse 194)* in the heart of Schwabing, is a tower hotel built for the 1972 Olympic Games. It

has a chic lobby and rooms as nice as you'd expect from a high-class hotel chain. The service is excellent. Singles/doubles start at DM330/362.

Altstadt One of the grand dames of the Munich hotel trade is the lovely *Bayerischer Hof (Map 7a, ☎ 212 00, fax 212 06 33, email hbh@compuserve.com, Promenadeplatz 2–6)*, with singles/doubles for DM343.50/477, and suites from DM410/595. It boasts a lovely location, right behind Marienplatz, a pool and a great jazz club downstairs (see Entertainment).

The most famous hotel in town is the *Kempinski Vier Jahreszeiten München (Map 7a, ☎ 212 50, fax 21 25 20 00, email reservation.hvj@kempinski.com, Maximilianstrasse 17)*, with a grand facade featuring statues of the managers, the four seasons, and the four continents known at its construction in 1857. Rooms here, with not as many amenities as you'd expect, start at DM430/510, and suites range from DM495 to DM770.

If that's not dear enough for you, try the *Rafael (Map 7a, ☎ 20 09 80, fax 22 25 39, email info@hotelrafael.com, Neuturmstrasse 1)*, in a gorgeous renovated villa just around the corner from the Hofbräuhaus. Service is polite almost to a fault. Chambers here start at DM508/756, excluding the roll of notes you'll need for tipping the liveried servants. Garage parking and breakfast cost another DM36 and DM38 per day respectively.

East of the Isar The *München City Hilton (Map 6, ☎ 480 40, fax 48 04 48 04, email fom_munich-city@hilton.com, Rosenheimerstrasse 15)*, is slightly less elegant than its counterpart, the Munich Park Hilton, but appeals to business-people for its central location (next to the Gasteig) and ultra-modern conference rooms. There's no swimming pool. Singles/doubles start at DM222/243. The Sunday breakfast deal is fantastic (see Places to Eat – Breakfast Places).

The *Palace Hotel (Map 6, ☎ 41 97 10, fax 41 97 18 19, email Hotel_Palace_Muc@compuserve.com, Trogerstrasse 21)* is an intimate hotel near the Prinzregententheater.

Rooms and suites are all furnished in a lofty pseudo-French style, with marmoreal baths and Louis XIV chairs. The wonderful panelled bar was carted, piece by piece, from France. Most rooms look out onto a peaceful courtyard, and are equipped with modem plugs. Singles/doubles start at DM245/335 and junior suites at DM450. Breakfast costs another DM29.

GAY & LESBIAN HOTELS

Deutsche Eiche (Map 7a, ☎ 21 16 60, fax 23 11 66 98, Reichenbachstrasse 13), is a century-old Munich institution. A few years back it was saved from the wrecker's ball through the intervention of German film director Rainer Fassbinder and some Hollywood stars. Its modern rooms are all equipped with TV, telephone and private shower/WC, and there's a big sauna and roof terrace. Singles/doubles start at DM120/170, including breakfast.

Pension Eulenspiegel (Map 7, ☎ 26 66 78, Müllerstrasse 43a), is a small and cosy guesthouse in a quiet back courtyard in Munich's gay district. Singles/doubles with all amenities are priced at DM88/130, breakfast included.

Best Western's K+K Hotel am Harras (Map 5, ☎/fax 76 97 98 08, email kkhoel@ muc.kkhotels.de, Albert-Rosshaupter-Strasse 4), in the south-west suburb of Sendling, is a modern chain hotel (it's not strictly gay, but gay-friendly) charging from DM125/170 for singles/doubles. Non-smoking quarters are also available.

PRIVATE ROOMS & LONG-TERM RENTALS

If you plan to stay in Munich for a month or longer, you might consider renting a room or flat through a *Mitwohnzentrale* (flat-sharing agency), which acts as an agent between people looking to let their digs temporarily and folks in need of a temporary home. Bear in mind that housing is tight in Munich, and that you'll have plenty of rivals for the cheaper options. In most cases the agency will give you the name and contact number of a flat-owner, and let you do the rest. You may have to pay a deposit,

and it helps to already be in Munich so you can look at places at short notice.

The *City Mitwohnzentrale (Map 7a, ☎ 194 30, fax 194 20, Lämmerstrasse 4),* on the north side of the Hauptbahnhof, lets furnished or unfurnished flats and rooms, from four days to indefinitely. Prepare to pay a fee for long-term rentals of up to 1½ months rent. Generally speaking, a room in a flat costs from DM500 per month, an apartment starts at DM800; some are cheaper, many are more expensive. Commission is about 15% based on the rent due. They'll send you a form in English; fill it out and fax it back along with a photocopy of your ID/passport and credit card, or drop by with your documents.

Home Company (Map 7, ☎ 194 45, fax 271 20 19, email HomeCompanyMuen chen@t-online.de, Georgenstrasse 45) is a well-organised rival based in Schwabing. Sign-up procedures are similar to the City Mitwohnzentrale, but commission is higher at around 20% of rent due.

The *Mitwohnzentrale an der Uni (Map 7, ☎ 28 6 60 60, fax 28 45 16, Kaulbachstrasse 61),* has very friendly staff and a huge selection of rooms in the summer months. Best of all, you can browse their Web site (www.mwz-munich.de) to see what's on offer before you even ring up. Commission is 15% of rent due. There's another office in the U-Bahn station Universität (exit Adalbertstrasse).

Mr Lodge (Map 7, ☎ 50 38 38, fax 28 55 28) shares offices with the Mitwohnzentrale an der Uni but deals only in stays of a month or longer. Commission is 15% of rent due but the standard is pitched higher, so the rents tend to be higher, too.

Antje Wolf Bed & Breakfast Munich (Map 3, ☎ 168 87 81, fax 168 87 91, Schulstrasse 36), arranges apartments and guest rooms with or without breakfast from a day to a month.

The nun-run *Jugendhotel Marienherberge* (see Independent Hostels) rents out single/double rooms to women aged under 26 for DM550/960 per month, including breakfast. In August, rates are DM100 cheaper per head. The midnight curfew applies.

euro currency converter DM1 = €.51

PLACES TO STAY

Places to Eat

Germans generally tend to make lunch their main meal of the day, but in urban centres like Munich dinner takes on a more prominent role. One in four residents is a foreigner, which guarantees a large number of ethnic eateries, and Munich's wealthy, cosmopolitan residents like to go out to eat. Most neighbourhoods have a spate of restaurants in various price classes, so chances are you won't have to go far; if you do, public transportation will likely get you where you need to go within half an hour.

Bavarians eat supper from as early as 5 pm, so if you're heading to a traditional German place before 7 pm it's a good idea to reserve a table. Many other restaurants only really get going after 7 pm, and some of the trendy eateries and Mediterranean offerings (eg Spanish, Italian, or Greek) are packed after 9 pm.

Most restaurants only figure on one or two seatings per night, so don't feel you have to pay up and leave right after your meal. Many diners stay on for another hour or so nursing a drink, chatting and enjoying the atmosphere. The bill will only be sent when you request it (unless there's a change of waiters on shift).

Eateries come and go. This, along with the screaming popularity of many places, means you should try to call ahead to book a table. Otherwise, you may find yourself stuck at the house bar (if there is one), to await a free table.

Cost

Eating cheaply in Munich is much like anywhere else in Germany: Excellent Turkish fast food is the leader of the snack pack. The area south of the Hauptbahnhof is full of little places selling doner kebab from DM5 to DM6, which are large enough to constitute a meal. The smaller Turkish pizzas (lahmacun) cost from about DM3.50. As for cheap sit-down options, pizzerias are reliably good, and you should be able to get away with spending DM20 or less per head.

Even at the fancier places, going out to dinner can be quite affordable as long as you stick to one main course and a single beverage. One way to trim your food bill is to target the midday specials, which can be half the price of the regular menu, and pick up something simple for supper.

Cafes are also great places to eat cheaply, offering lots of bistro-type dishes such as lasagne, salads, quiches and soups for DM10 or less. They're often cosy, relaxed places that are ideal for lingering over a newspaper or writing postcards.

FOOD
Breakfast

German breakfasts are a veritable feast, consisting of white and whole-grain rolls, different types of sliced bread, jam, meats (ham, salami, mortadella etc) cheese and eggs (usually boiled), plus coffee, tea or hot chocolate. If you're staying at a hotel it'll most likely be an all-you-can-gorge affair – enough to keep your belly filled until mid-afternoon. There are lots of breakfast cafes in Munich, but many don't start serving before 9 am.

Munich Specialities

Munich (and Bavarian) food is hearty, thigh-slapping fare which has only a distant relationship to anything vegetable. Many local menus focus on combinations of pork, potatoes and cabbage. The dishes meant to be extra special are billed as *Schmankerl*, for which you'll pay a bit extra.

As elsewhere in Germany, high-quality *Wurst* (sausage) is to be found in a bewildering variety. A *Wurstteller* is a generous spread of sausage served with a couple of slices of bread and a minuscule garnish, while a *Schlachtplatter* (literally, 'slaughter platter') includes liver and blood sausage. The culinary flagship of Munich is the *Weisswurst*, a chunky veal sausage that's supposed to be eaten before midday (see boxed text 'The Weisswurst Legend').

Another local favourite is *Leberkäse* (literally, 'liver cheese'), a comical name as it contains neither liver nor cheese. It's actually a smooth spicy meatloaf, served in thick, juicy slabs and generally delicious. You'll find it simmering under the orange lamps at many an *Imbiss* (snack bar) around town.

Other mainstay dishes include *Schweinebraten mit Knödel* (pork roast with dumpling), *Rippchen* (spare ribs), which are especially popular in beer gardens, *Hendl* (chicken), sold roasted in halves or whole, and *Schweinshax'n* (pork knuckles). You'll have trouble escaping boiled or chipped potatoes (*Kartoffeln*) and sauerkraut, which are common side dishes.

That's not forgetting the famous *Brez'n*, the huge pretzels laced with rock salt, available in beer halls or gardens with the hidden aim of making you drink more (see also Beer Halls & Gardens in the Entertainment chapter).

As for dessert, if you stumble across *Dampfnudeln* (steamed dumplings) on the menu, steer clear – unless you enjoy a bland, doughy mass sprinkled with cinnamon or poppy seeds and drowned in custard sauce for safe keeping. An apple strudel with ice cream is a safer bet.

DRINKS
Nonalcoholic
Tap water is safe to drink anywhere in Germany and is free at restaurants, but you'll get strange looks if you order it. Waiters would rather bring you the bottled *Mineralwasser* which most Germans prefer, and it costs something. *Stilles* is without bubbles, while *mit Kohlensäure* means it's carbonated.

Soft drinks are widely available but diet versions are only slowly trickling into German restaurants. If they taste different from what you're used to, it's because the formula has been rejigged to German tastes.

Coffee is a staple, and usually fresh and strong (though you'll miss the burnt or darker brands that are popular, say, in France or Italy). It comes in cups (*Tassen*) or pots (*Kännchen*), and condensed milk and sugar are served alongside. In smarter places you'll see people nursing a big bowl of steaming *Milchkaffee*, which is akin to 'half-and-half'. By the way, the 'bottomless cup' hasn't yet made it to Germany; you pay by the cup (DM4 to DM5 each in cafes).

As for tea, if you don't want a pot ask for *ein Glas Tee*, and it'll be served with a tea bag, sugar and maybe a slice of lemon. If you want milk, ask for *Tee mit Milch*. Herbal teas are available, but only as an exception.

Alcoholic
Beer Bavaria is the most productive beer region in the world, and the locals have made a science out of brewing. All beers adhere to the *Reinheitsgebot* (Purity Law) passed in 1516. You'll have a stunning choice, including *Pils* (pilsener), which is a good standby even if occasionally bitter. Also common is the pale ale called *Helles*, its darker counterpart known as a *Dunkles*, and *Schwarzbier*, a stout similar to Guinness (but without the creamy foam). *Starkbier* and *Bockbier* are strong varieties brewed mostly in springtime.

A popular Bavarian brew that has caught on elsewhere in Germany is *Weissbier* (known as *Weizenbier* farther north). It's made with wheat instead of barley malt and served in tall, half-litre glasses. Weissbier comes pale or dark, and also as a cloudy variety called *Hefeweissbier*, with a layer of still-fermenting yeast on the bottom of the bottle.

If you want to go easy on the brew, order a sweetish *Radler* which comes in half or full litres and mixes pale ale and lemonade. A *Russen* ('Russian') is generally a litre-sized concoction of Weissbier and lemonade.

Wines You'll find wines from around the world in Munich supermarkets, restaurants and bars. Varieties from France, Italy and Spain are as common as German wines. 'New World' wines from places like Chile and South Africa have caught on, and cheaper vintages from Eastern Europe are beginning to make inroads.

The bulk of Bavarian output come from Franconia in the fat-bellied *Bocksbeutel* bottles, and here you'll find some delightfully crisp varieties that don't make it onto

PLACES TO EAT

the export lists. For further insight, see Wine in the Shopping chapter.

RESTAURANTS
Restaurant Etiquette
The concept of 'service' is not widespread in Germany. Even in quite smart places you will probably, at some point, suffer long waits, lukewarm food, inattentiveness or just plain rudeness. Critical articles on this topic make the German press on a regular basis, but the message hasn't got through to the restaurant trade.

A service charge is always included in the bill, and German waiters tend to be well-paid. A customary tip is around 5% of the bill, which you just add on to the total when you pay. Most people just round up, and this is done verbally: If the waiter says 'DM46', you might answer with, say, 'DM50'. Don't be afraid *not* to tip if the service was abominable.

If it gets crowded you may occasionally be asked to share your table with another party. It's the done thing, but you're not expected to socialise with your table mates. Only in the most formal restaurants (and some American places) are tables restricted to one party.

Though declining in popularity, smoking is still common in German restaurants, and non-smoking sections are rare or ineffective. Polite smokers in your immediate vicinity *might* just ask if you mind before they light up.

American
Bobolovsky's (Map 4, ☎ 39 73 63, Ursulastrasse 10) is a trendy restaurant-bistro in Schwabing close to the English Garden. The best deal here is the Monday all-you-can-eat buffet (from 8 pm) – burgers, chicken wings, ribs, enchiladas and other stuff. It also does a good rump steak (DM22.50) and has a long breakfast menu (see the Breakfast Places section later in this chapter).

The *New World Cafe (Map 7a, ☎ 260 56 66, Utzschneiderstrasse 8)* is an upmarket diner that's dedicated to beautiful people. Signed pictures of supermodels line the walls, and even the main dishes bear the names of models and fashion designers. With all this glamour, food becomes somewhat secondary. Main courses cost around DM20 (eg sweet and sour lentils 'Vivienne Westwood' for DM19). It's open from 9 am to 9 pm daily.

Asian
Mangostin Asia (Map 5, ☎ 723 20 31, Maria-Einsiedel-Strasse 2) in Thalkirchen near the zoo, is a very chic place with Thai, Japanese and Indonesian food. It's popular, but service can be reprehensible, and the food varies from good to despicable depending on the night. Hours are 10 am to midnight daily.

Vinh's (Map 3, ☎ 123 89 25, Leonrodstrasse 29) near the corner of Landshuter Allee, is a tiny place that does spectacular Vietnamese food, with rice dishes from DM15 to DM18. The house specialities range from DM21 to DM35 (don't miss the roast duck for DM22.50). If he likes the crowd, the eccentric owner will dress up in silver duds and perform magic tricks. Hours are from 11.30 am to 2.30 pm and 5.30 to 11.30 pm Monday to Friday; weekends it's open from 5.30 to 11.30 pm only (phone ahead to reserve a table). Take U1 to Rotkreuzplatz or bus No 33 or tram No 12 to Albrechtstrasse.

Co-Do (Map 6, ☎ 448 57 97, Lothringer Strasse 7), in Haidhausen, snubs traditional Asian decor, going instead for black and white photos on bare walls. It has first-rate food, with delicious aromas and mysterious spices, and the service is excellent – but the portions could be a bit bigger. Main dishes start around DM17. It's open from 6 pm to 11.30 pm daily.

Shida (Map 7, ☎ 26 93 36, Klenzestrasse 32), is a very good and very intimate Thai place (it's small, so reservations are essential). Main courses range from DM18 to DM30. It's open from 6 pm to 12.30 am daily.

Australian
Outland (Map 6, ☎ 48 99 78 80, Weissenburger Platz 3), in Haidhausen, is done up like a rough kiosk in the outback (it was once called 'Outback' but had to change

when a former owner won rights to the name). The food is wild too, with highlights including kangaroo fillet (DM18.50), shark steak (DM16.50) and a Bush Burger with Razorbacks (hot chips) for DM12.50. Of course there's Foster's and some classic Aussie wines. It can get pretty raucous after 10 pm, when the drinks get cheaper. It's open from 4 pm to 1 am weekdays, from noon to 1 am Saturday and from 10 am to 1 am Sunday.

Bavarian/German

For German food, it's best to go local at the less touristy beer halls and restaurants, or at one of the many markets. See also the Self-Catering section below and Beer Halls & Gardens in the Entertainment chapter.

Andechser am Dom (Map 7a, ☎ 29 84 81, Weinstrasse 7a), behind the Frauenkirche, serves lovely monastery beer with its reasonably priced fare (eg beef tips with horseradish and potato salad, DM19.80). The courtyard is wonderful for dining in summer. Look for the photo of Bavarian premier Edward Stoiber, who looks like Paul Newman at a distance. It's open from 10 am to 1 pm daily.

The *Hundskugel (Map 7a, ☎ 26 42 72, Hotterstrasse 18)*, right in the centre, is Munich's oldest restaurant, founded in 1440. It's a famous place to go with family and friends. The food's perfectly fine, if pricey for an evening meal, although lunch specials can cost under DM20. It's open from 10 am to midnight daily.

Boeuf à la Mode (Map 7, ☎ 53 47 79, Thalkirchner Strasse 50) in the Glockenbachviertel does great Bavarian-style food. The Angus roast loin with noodles and salad (DM26.50) is a highlight. Starters average DM13 to DM18, and main dishes DM22 to DM32. There's a lovely beer garden out the back. Hours are from 6 pm to 1 am daily.

Half-hidden behind the Viktualienmarkt is *Zum Alten Markt (Map 7a, ☎ 29 99 95, Dreifaltigkeitsplatz 3)*. It's decked out in hunting-lodge decor, and gets packed to the hilt so reserve ahead. The terrace is charming in summer. Salads start around DM16 and main courses at DM24; the pork medallions

with spinach noodles and fried onions cost DM29. It's open from 11 am to midnight daily (closed Sunday).

Right next door is the *Bratwurstherzl (Map 7a, ☎ 29 51 13, Heiliggeiststrasse 3)*, with more cosy panelling. The specialties here are Franconian; 10 Nuremberg sausages cost DM10, and taste better than at its touristy rival by the Frauenkirche. It's open from 10 am to 11 pm Monday to Saturday.

The *Weisses Bräuhaus (Map 7a, ☎ 29 98 75, Tal 10)* is one of Munich's best-loved Bavarian restaurants. Try the upstairs section where the *real* locals hang out. All of the meat dishes are excellent (mostly DM12 to DM28), and the *Weisswurst* here sets the city standard. You can also consume parts others throw away (brain, lung etc). It's open from 8 am to midnight daily.

Chinese

A good-value option is *Der Kleine Chinese (Map 7, ☎ 202 11 32, Fraunhoferstrasse 35)* with cheap sit-down meals from around DM11 and very friendly service. It's open from 10 am to 11 pm daily.

China Pham (Map 3, ☎ 350 73 04, Georgenschwaigstrasse 25) in northern Munich has generous portions of steaming Chinese fare including lemon-grass chicken (DM18) or the delightful 'Drunk Duck', which is flambéed in rice wine (DM21.50). Most dishes cost between DM17 and DM25. Take the U2 to Milbertshofen. Hours are from 11.30 am to 3 pm and from 5.30 to 11.30 pm daily.

Fish & Seafood

The Viktualienmarkt has any number of fish stands where you can put together a full meal (see Self-Catering below). Bona-fide seafood restaurants in Munich tend to be on the expensive side.

Close by, the *Poseidon (☎ 28 59 38)*, on Dreifaltigkeitsplatz, is a lovely French-run seafood bar with fantastic graved or smoked salmon (DM16), bouillabaisse (DM19) and mussels with melted cheese (DM17). It's open from 10 am to 9 pm daily.

The *Hunsingers Pacific (Map 7a, ☎ 55 02 97 41, Maximiliansplatz 5)* on the corner of

PLACES TO EAT

The Weisswurst Legend

Müncheners have made an art out of their beloved *Weisswurst*, a white veal sausage flecked with parsley. According to a popular tale, Weisswurst was invented in the pub 'Ewiges Licht' (Eternal Light) on Marienplatz in 1857. The pub owner and butcher, Sepp Moser, supposedly ran out of skins for making veal sausage and used finer pork skins instead. And instead of frying he chucked them into a potful of hot water (by some accounts this was an accident). In any case his guests were delighted and Bavaria's national dish was born.

In Germany, strict rules apply for preparing and eating Weisswurst. The Munich Sausage Controls Board (yes, there is one) has ruled that Weisswurst must contain at least 70% veal, with the remainder made up of brains, hide, spleen and other yummy ingredients. It must be simmered but *never* boiled, peeled before eating and consumed with sweet, grainy mustard. Mid-morning is the traditional 'Weisswurst break', and the only drink that can possibly do it justice is a foamy Weissbier.

Peter Lill, author of the book *The Legend of the Weisswurst*, claims that much of this ritual is based on, well, baloney. He says that Herr Sepp couldn't possibly have invented Weisswurst because he took over the pub in 1860. Lill also debunks the idea that the fat links must be eaten before the midday bells chime – modern refrigeration means it keeps all day.

'Real' Müncheners seem to take little notice of Lill's work. They scorn the outsiders who, say, prefer to cut the sausage lengthwise or (horror of horrors) to eat the skin. Unlike Bavarian beers, Weisswurst has few friends north of the border, and some Germans still refer to that Bavarian frontier as the '*Weisswurst Line*'.

Max-Joseph-Strasse, is a renowned seafood restaurant with a strong offering of Asian dishes. Most mains cost between DM20 and DM35. Hours are from 11.30 to 1 am daily (from 6 pm to 1 am Sunday).

The name brings fast food to mind, but *Italfisch (Map 5, ☎ 77 68 49, Zenettistrasse 25)* near the Schlachthof, is actually an expensive place with fine seafood and fantastic service. You can expect to pay upwards of DM60 for an exquisite daily special. It's open from 11.30 am to 3 pm and from 6 pm to 1 am weekdays, and from 6 pm to 1 am Saturday (closed Sunday).

French

The top restaurants in Munich usually serve (what else?) French food, and few are really *bon marché*. One notable exception is *La Marmite (Map 6, ☎ 48 22 42, Lilienstrasse 8)*, an intimate little place geared to Alsatian cuisine, and it's reasonably affordable. The two and three-course set meals are a bargain at DM35 or less. Make sure you reserve a table, as the place fills up fast. It's open from 7 pm to 1 am Monday to Friday.

Le Bousquerey (Map 6, ☎ 48 84 55, Rablstrasse 37) in Haidhausen, east of the Isar River, is a splendid French place that specialises in seafood. The restaurant is small and intimate (reservations suggested). There's a good French and German wine list; set menus are about DM60 to DM70 per person, main courses average DM20 to DM35.

Another very good but expensive French place is *Rue des Halles (Map 6, ☎ 48 56 75, Steinstrasse 18)*, south of the centre in Mittersendling, with a very light, modern interior, comfortable atmosphere, and slick but attentive service. Count on spending about DM150 per person without wine. It's open from 6.30 pm to 1 am daily.

The restaurant upstairs at *Alois Dallmayr (Map 7a, ☎ 213 51 00, Dienerstrasse 14–15)* near Marienplatz, is renowned for its excellent French and Continental food and great service; main courses range from DM30 to DM60. Look out for its unbeatable Tuesday special (two five-course meals for the price of one). It's open from 9.30 am to 6.30 pm Monday to Wednesday, from 9.30 am to 8 pm

Thursday and Friday and from 9.30 am to 4 pm Saturday.

Greek

Paros *(Map 6, ☎ 470 29 95, Kirchenstrasse 21)*, in Haidhausen, is a gem of a place. The simple wooden tables and large photos of earthy Greek islanders belie just how sophisticated the food is. The lamb roast stuffed with fetta cheese (DM20) will melt in your mouth. You can have a tasty three-course meal for about DM35, and the service is excellent. It's open from 5 pm to 1 am daily (on Sunday it opens at 11.30 am).

A cheap hole-in-the-wall with good food is **Bei Meri** *(Map 7, ☎ 28 80 88 39, Theresienstrasse 56)* in Schwabing. Wash down a tasty *papoutsabsi* (eggplant with melted cheese and vine leaves stuffed with minced meat, DM10) with a Weissbier (DM3.50) and chat with the friendly owners. It's open from 8 am to 10 pm daily (closed Sunday).

Simera *(Map 4, ☎ 35 53 80, Kaiserstrasse 55)* is another good Greek place in Schwabing, with huge and tasty portions of meat and fish (DM20 to DM36). Daily specials costs just DM11.50 before 5 pm. The desserts are tempting – try the honey, nut and pastry creations for DM7.50. Hours are from 11.30 am to 1 am daily.

Ice Cream

Eis Ecke Sarcletti, at the southern end of Rotkreuzplatz (Map 3), may well have the best Italian ice cream in the city, and the crowds know it. It's about DM1 per scoop, and there's a little outdoor cafe as well.

The **Eis Boulevard** *(Map 4, ☎ 34 76 87, Leopoldstrasse 52)* is a trendy alternative.

Indian

Maharani *(Map 7, ☎ 52 71 92, Rottmannstrasse 24,)*, diagonally opposite the Löwenbräukeller at Stiglmaierplatz, is the best bet for dependable, authentic Indian food, and they'll make it spicy if you ask them to. Main courses average DM23 to DM31. It's open from noon to 3 pm and from 6 pm to midnight, daily.

Bombay *(Map 5, ☎ 272 44 54, Geyerstrasse 22)*, south of the Hauptbahnhof, is a cosy little place with nice Indian food. The curries and any dishes with chicken are good. Most mains cost around DM20. It's open from 5.30 to 11.30 pm Monday to Friday, and from 11.30 am to 11.30 pm weekends.

Another recommendable option with pleasant decor is **Ganga** *(Map 7a, ☎ 201 64 65, Baaderstrasse 11)*. Try the chicken tikka with rice (DM21) and a mango lassi (DM5.50). It also has a good range of vegetarian dishes. Hours are from 11.30 am to 3 pm and from 5.30 pm to midnight daily.

Swagat *(Map 6, ☎ 47 08 48 44, Prinzregentenplatz 13)* in Bogenhausen, has some great lunch specials from about DM13, and a nice outdoor section in summer. It's open from 11.30 am to 2.30 pm and 5.30 pm to 1 am daily.

International

'International' has the snob appeal of 'Nouvelle Cuisine' a few years back, and the meals tend to be priced accordingly.

In a lovely spot by St Anne's Church in Lehel, **Gandl** *(Map 6, ☎ 29 16 25 25, St-Anna-Platz 1)*, is a bit like a cosy flat with a hearth. There's a daily 'three-minute' dish for people on the run (eg lasagne for DM12.50). The menu is semi-Italian, with creative salads and pastas from DM9 to DM19, and the steaks and fish dishes are superb from about DM30. There's also a little wine shop in the front. Service can get a bit testy when it's busy. It's open from 9 am to 10.30 pm daily (closed Sunday).

Königsquelle *(Map 7a, ☎ 22 00 71, Baaderplatz 2)* really deserves more attention than it gets on the local restaurant scene. The dishes aren't terribly complex (eg a veal chilli or a Wiener schnitzel), but the ingredients are fresh and the cooking is 1st-class. The dark hardwood interior is relaxing, too. Most mains cost about DM20 to DM30. Hours are from 5 pm to 1 am daily (from 7 pm on Saturday).

Dukatz im Literaturhaus *(Map 7a, ☎ 291 96 00, Salvatorplatz 1)* is a trendy, spacious place that holds readings (Salman Rushdie was a recent guest) and doubles as an art gallery. Service is good and the food of high standard. Mains average about

PLACES TO EAT

euro currency converter DM1 = €.51

DM25 but cost up to DM45. You'll discover quotes at the bottom of cups (such as 'More eroticism, please!'). It's open from 10 to 1 am daily.

Kleinschmidtz (Map 7, ☎ 260 85 18, Fraunhoferstrasse 13) is an offbeat restaurant-cum-wine-shop with changing art exhibits. The cuisine is ambitious but not pretentious, and everything's prepared with organic ingredients. They do a lovely creamed veal and melted cheese over chipped potatoes for DM18; most meals cost DM25 or more. Hours are from 11 am to 10 pm Monday to Saturday and from 5 to 10 pm Sunday.

In the south of town near the Schlachthof, *Makassar (Map 5, ☎ 77 69 59, Dreimühlenstrasse 25)* is a fancy French-Creole-International place that lures the jet set (Brad Pitt, Boris Becker and Joe Cocker among them). It's run by the former chef of Jacque Cousteau's *Calypso* research ship, and the menu is full of his African and Caribbean recipes. A good mid-priced dish is the breast of duck in honey-mustard sauce with veggies (DM32). It's open from 5 pm to 1 am daily.

A well known top-end place is the *Garden-Restaurant (Map 7a, ☎ 212 09 93, Promenadeplatz 2–6)*, behind the Hotel Bayerischer Hof. The luxurious decor borders on kitsch, but the food and service are excellent. You'll likely pay from DM75 per head for a three-course meal with a glass of wine. Hours are from noon to 3 pm and from 6 pm till midnight daily.

Tantris (Map 4, ☎ 36 19 59 16, Johann-Fichte-Strasse 7) regularly gets top marks among Munich's luxury restaurants. Meals are very expensive but very good, so it's easy to forgive the 1970s decor and dragon sculptures in the forecourt. Mains start around DM40, and a three-course evening meal with wine could easily set you back DM200. It's open from noon till 3 pm and from 6.30 pm to 1 am Tuesday to Saturday.

Italian

Italian cuisine is especially good value in Munich. The city's proximity to Italy means that there is a huge number of options, from the dozens of small, corner pizzerias to mid-range *osterias* to, well, more pretentious establishments.

Lunches don't come much cheaper than at *Heller's Trattoria (Map 6, ☎ 25 38 29, Sternstrasse 14)*, a cosy little eatery in Lehel. All spaghettis cost just DM10, and the house wines cost from just DM3 pér glass. It's open from 11 am to 3 pm and from 5 to 11 pm daily (closed Sunday).

The great thing about *Il Mulino (Map 7, ☎ 523 33 35, Görrestrasse 1)* is that you can order fantastic pizzas for DM10 to DM15 in what's actually a classy little restaurant. There are good pastas and more expensive meat dishes. The leafy beer garden gets packed in summer. Service is snappy. It's open from 11.30 am to 1 am daily.

Café Osteria La Vecchia Masseria (Map 7a, ☎ 550 90 90, Mathildenstrasse 3) south of Landwehrstrasse, is one of the best-value places in Munich, and perfect for a romantic evening. The beautiful atmosphere comes with great service and nice touches like fresh aniseed bread on ceramic tiles. Pizzas cost from DM9 to DM11, pastas from DM9 to DM14, and there are some fine three-course meals from DM40. The beer garden in the courtyard in lovely, too. Hours are from 11.30 am to 1 am daily.

Also south of the Hauptbahnhof is the small *Trattoria La Fiorentini (Map 7a, ☎ 53 41 85, Goethestrasse 41)*, a local hang-out that does good pizzas from DM7 to DM14. The menu, which changes daily, has main courses that average DM14 to DM18. Staff can get snooty if it's crowded, but the food's good. It's open from 11 am to midnight daily.

Cipriani (Map 7a, ☎ 260 43 97), in Asamhof, occupying a small courtyard off Sendlinger Strasse behind the Asamkirche, has pastas from DM12 to DM14. The outside area is lovely in summer. Happy hour is from 5 to 9 pm daily, when cocktails are DM6. It's open from 11 am to midnight daily (closed Sunday).

The *Piccolo Osteria (Map 7, ☎ 28 44 74, Amalienstrasse 39)* is a cosy, family-run place in Schwabing with fresh salads, pastas and excellent fish dishes. We enjoyed the tagliatelle with salmon and shrimp

(DM24.50), but the fish and rucola salad (DM17.50) also looked tasty. There's a good wine list. Hours are from 5 pm to around midnight daily.

Hippocampus (Map 6, ☎ 47 58 55, Mühlbaurstrasse 5) is a trendy and upscale Italian place right near the Prinzregententheater. Set menus range from DM60 to DM80, and many of its main courses (such as shark Genua style, DM35) have neat combinations. It's open from noon to 2.30 pm and from 6 to 11 pm daily.

Japanese

Maitoi (Map 7, ☎ 260 52 68, Hans-Sachs-Strasse 10) south of Sendlinger Tor, is a very slick, simple Japanese restaurant with takeaway sushi. Special evening prices apply after 7 or 9 pm, when everything is 25% cheaper. It's opening hours are from 12.30 to 2.30 pm and from 6.30 pm to midnight Monday to Saturday.

A top-rate sushi restaurant is *Tokami (Map 7, ☎ 28 98 67 60, Theresienstrasse 54)* in Schwabing. As you'd expect the fish dishes are superb but most of 'em aren't cheap. Starters cost DM3 to DM12.50, soups and salads DM6 to DM8, and the mixed sushi platters DM32 to DM48. The menu also offers interesting Japanese pastas and a good spread of wines. Hours are from noon to 2.30 pm and from 6 pm to 1 am daily.

Jewish

There's more than bagels and lox at *Cohen's (Map 7, ☎ 280 95 45, Theresienstrasse 31)*. Tucked away in a back courtyard, its owners manage to blend eastern European and Middle Eastern flavours with homey New York style kosher food. The place is nicely lit, with polished wood floors and big windows. There's a huge array of appetisers, best sampled as a platter (DM16), and the portions are massive. Many main dishes are in the DM20 to DM25 range. It's open from 12.30 pm to around midnight daily.

Mexican

What passes as 'Mexican' or 'Tex-Mex' in Germany is often a far cry from the real thing. But as it's regarded as slightly 'exotic', these restaurants are on the trendy side and the menus are priced accordingly. 'Spicy' dishes tend to be on the mild side; try asking for *extra scharf* (extra spicy) if you want more heat.

Joe Peña's (Map 7a, ☎ 22 64 63, Buttermelcherstrasse 17), part of a national chain, is regarded as Munich's best Tex-Mex place. It's dressed up as a cantina with a long and useful bar, but can get very loud. The food's reasonable, although we thought DM22 to DM25 a bit high for enchiladas or burritos. The margaritas are superb, and all cocktails cost DM7.50 before 8 pm. Hours are from 5 pm to 1 am daily.

Sausalitos (Map 7, ☎ 28 15 94, Türkenstrasse 50), close to the university, is the 'in' Mexican place for students. After 8 pm it's full of fashion victims and is usually standing room only. You can watch how everything's cooked in the open-front kitchen. Salads start at DM14, steaks at DM16, and enchiladas from DM20. It's open from 5 pm to 1 am daily.

The *Escobar (Map 6, ☎ 48 51 37, Breisacherstrasse 19)*, in Haidhausen, does decent Tex-Mex mains for DM14 to DM23 and salads from DM11 to DM18. It also has Munich's wackiest ceiling fan – something straight out of *Mad Max*. Fill up at the Tuesday night all-you-can-eat buffet for DM16. Hours are from 6 pm to 1 am daily.

Spanish & Latin American

The *Casa de Tapas (Map 3, ☎ 27 31 22 88, Bauerstrasse 2)* in Schwabing, serves lots and lots of the delectable starters for DM5.50 (stuffed olives, cheeses, fried zucchini slices and more). The main courses are good, too, and run between DM12 and DM25. Cocktails, at the bar, cost just DM6.50 between 4 and 8 pm. Reserve ahead or forget about a table. It's open from 11 am to 1 am daily (except Sundays, when it's open from 4 pm).

Mediterranean meets multi-media at *Bar-Tapas Teatro (Map 6, ☎ 48 00 42 84, Balanstrasse 23)* in Haidhausen. There's little decoration as special projectors show fantastic images on the walls, and the place

euro currency converter DM1 = €.51

is otherwise candlelit. The food keeps step with the presentation. Tapas start at DM5.50, served in simple clay dishes. Daily meat dishes cost around DM25, and fish around DM30; a carafe of house red wine costs DM12.50. It's open from 5 pm to 1 am daily.

El Cortijo (Map 4, ☎ 33 11 16, Feilitzschstrasse 32), also in Schwabing, has a good selection of fish, meat and chicken dishes for DM15 to DM30. We enjoyed the garlic chicken (DM16.50) and manchego cheese (DM9.50), and the caramel pudding with whipped cream (DM6.50) was a show-stopper. Service is sharp, and you'll get a glass of port thrown in as a *digestif*. It's open from 5.30 pm to 1 am daily.

We've heard conflicting reports about *Don Quijote (Map 4, ☎ 34 23 18, Biedersteiner Strasse 6)* on the edge of the English Garden in Schwabing. Regarded by some as the best Spanish place in town, there have also been complaints about pitiful service and uninspired cooking. The decor is inviting, but that may not justify a visit. Sample dishes include pheasant in sherry almandine (DM18) and rabbit in butter and onion sauce (DM25). It's open from 6.30 pm to 1 am daily (reserve ahead).

Theme

Relive the 16th century at the *Welser Küche (Map 7a, ☎ 29 65 65, Residenzstrasse 27)* behind the Feldherrnhalle. The staff don medieval costume, and you'll have to eat with your hands a lot during the three-hour proceedings. It's terribly cliched of course, but fun to do once. Four, six or even 10-course meals cost DM36, DM50 and DM70 respectively. Reservations are required. It's open from 6 pm to midnight daily.

There's always the *Planet Hollywood (Map 7a, ☎ 29 03 05 11, Platzl 1)* opposite the Hofbräuhaus. The personal effects of stars are fun (eg a Judy Garland dress under glass in the foyer), but you're paying mainly for the hype – the food itself is unremarkable and expensive. Burgers and trimmings start at DM16, and a hickory-smoked half-chicken with salad and fries will set you back DM24.50. Hours are from 11 am to 1 am daily.

Turkish

Dersim (Map 3, ☎ 123 54 54, Jutastrasse 5), in Neuhausen, is light years away from the kebab stands of the city centre but still affordable. Its delicious starters cost from DM6.50 to DM11.50, and its forte is lamb (from about DM16 to DM22). The aromas are wonderful as most everything's bought fresh from the markets. It's open from 5.30 pm to 1 am daily.

Vegetarian Restaurants

Vegetarians tend to have a tough time in Germany, a meat-eater's land. Fortunately a few vegetarian places have sprung up in Munich and most places have at least a token vegetarian meal on the menu.

Prinz Myschkin (Map 7a, ☎ 26 55 96, Hackenstrasse 2) gets rave reviews in the local press. It offers gourmet vegetarian cooking, blending East Asian, Indian and Italian influences. Daily menus and main courses cost DM18.50 to DM23.50; pizzas are expensive at DM16.50 to DM19.50. The sophisticated salads are a real treat, between DM7.50 and DM17.50. It's also a great place for a wine or coffee. It's open from 11 am to midnight daily.

Freedom of choice reigns at *Buxs (Map 7a, ☎ 22 94 82, Frauenstrasse 9)* with 45 different kinds of soups, salads and antipasti at its self-serve counter. Weigh your appetite carefully, as the salads are priced at DM3 per 100g. There are also 13 kinds of coffee and 10 different teas. It's open from 11 am to 8.30 pm weekdays and from 11 am to 3.30 pm Saturday.

Café Ignaz (Map 7, ☎ 271 60 93, Georgenstrasse 67), in Schwabing, is a non-smoking eatery with vegetable quiches, pastas, soups and salads. Most dishes cost just DM12 or less. It's open 10 am to 10 pm daily (9 am on Sunday). See also Cafes & Bistros later in this chapter.

Another fine option is the *Das Gollier (Map 5, ☎ 50 16 73, Gollierstrasse 83)* with a big range of casseroles, pizzas, crepes and grain dishes at good prices. It's open from noon to 3 pm and from 5 pm to midnight weekdays, from 5 pm to midnight Saturday and from 10 am to midnight Sunday.

CAFES & BISTROS

Cafes are a great German institution. Not quite as decadent as, say, their Viennese counterparts, they're still havens of peace and wonderful places to relax over a cup of coffee with a newspaper. Once reserved for the older coffee-and-cake crowd, nowadays cafes are casual eateries for people of all ages and walks of life.

Numerous cafes change their identities over the course of a day, starting out as breakfast places, then offering a smallish lunch menu and cakes in the afternoon before turning into a restaurant-bar or just a bar at night. Many of the cafes listed here, in fact, would fit just as well into the Restaurant section or the Pubs & Bars section of the Entertainment chapter.

City Centre

Centrally located cafes cater to tourists and trendoids, and therefore tend to be expensive. One exception that serves excellent home-made sweet and savoury pastries is the stand-up *Höflinger (Map 7a)*, at the corner of Sendlinger-Tor-Platz and Sonnenstrasse. Another fine option is *Ziegler (Map 7a, Brunnstrasse 11)*.

The *Stadtcafé (Map 7a, ☎ 26 69 49, St-Jakobs-Platz 1)* at the Stadtmuseum, is a popular haunt for Munich's intellectual types, especially in summer when the lovely courtyard opens. Some of the dishes are a bit too 'intellectual' but everything is well prepared. It's open from 11 am to midnight daily.

The newly-renovated *Kandil Restaurant (Map 7a, ☎ 54 82 82 52, Landwehrstrasse 8)*, near the Hauptbahnhof, serves a wide selection of cafeteria-style meals from DM8.50 to DM13 (see also Breakfast Places, later in this chapter).

The *Gap (Map 7a, ☎ 54 40 40 94, Goethestrasse 34)*, is an artsy, somewhat esoteric *cantina culturale* with exhibits and occasional folk and classical music. A soup and sandwich combo costs DM7.50, and there are groovy daily specials (such as a veggie platter with lentil mousse) for about the same price. It's open from 10 am to midnight daily.

The *Interview (Map 7a, ☎ 20 23 94 21, Gärtnerplatz 1)*, has a pleasant sidewalk cafe with a nice view of the theatre and Italian set lunches for DM16.50 to DM17.50. Hours are from 10 am to 1 am daily (except Sunday when it's open from 10 am to 7 pm).

At Marienplatz, one of the best places to watch the Glockenspiel as it does its thing is the bistro at the *Metropolitan (Map 7a, ☎ 230 97 70, Marienplatz 22)* on the 5th floor. It's open from 9 am to 11 pm daily. Next door, *Café Glockenspiel (Map 7a, ☎ 26 42 56, Marienplatz 28)* has much the same thing but is far more downmarket (open from 10 am to 11 pm daily).

Across the square on the west side is *Café Am Dom*, from where the view is just so-so but the atmosphere is nicer outside in summer.

On the Viktualienmarkt, seek out *Löwenbräu Stadt Kempten (Map 7a)* at No 4 (closed Sunday). There, you'll get a half-litre of Löwenbräu for DM5.20, and the daily set-menus start at around DM13.

Haxenbauer (Map 7a, ☎ 29 16 21 00, Sparkassenstrasse 8), with the pig on a spit in the window, is a mid-range inner-Munich establishment offering hearty four-course menus from DM48 per person, and very cheap fast food like *Schweinshax'n* (pork thigh) for DM5.80 in the snack-room or for takeaway.

Neuhausen

Near Rotkreuzplatz, a really nice and untouristed place to sit and chat is *froh & munter (Map 3, ☎ 18 79 97, Artilleriestrasse 5)*. Despite the hokey Christmas lights, this cafe does excellent snacks, soups and great Spanish-style tapas for around DM5, and filled tortillas, risottos, and ratatouilles for DM13 to DM18. It also serves up half-litres of organically brewed *Unertl* (DM5.20), some of the best Weissbier in town. Food is served from 6 to 11 pm daily and the service is always friendly.

Ruffini (Map 3, ☎ 16 11 60, Orffstrasse 22) is best known for its extensive (organic) wine list and roof-top terrace, but it also does excellent Italian salads and pastas for about DM15 to DM20. It's open from 10 am

PLACES TO EAT

to midnight Tuesday to Saturday and from 10 am to 6 pm Sunday (closed Monday).

Café Zauberberg (Map 3, ☎ 18 99 91 78, Hedwigstrasse 14), a 10 minute walk east of Rotkreuzplatz, is an upscale cafe and bar. It's popular for its low-key, tasteful decor, friendly service and consistently splendid food. Chicken, schnitzels and steak dishes cost DM20 to DM35. There's a lovely terrace for dining out the front. Reservations are essential. It's open from 11 am to 2.30 pm and from 5 pm to midnight Tuesday to Friday, from 3 pm to midnight Saturday and from 9.30 am to midnight Sunday.

Schwabing

Among the many lively student hang-outs in Schwabing are the *Vorstadt Café (Map 7, ☎ 272 06 99, Türkenstrasse 83)*, and the *News Bar (Map 7, ☎ 28 17 87, Amalienstrasse 55)*. Both are open until at least until 1 am daily, and the News Bar sells English magazines.

The cafes that line Leopoldstrasse are more for socialising, being seen and looking fabulous than for eating, but food is available in spite of it all. Don't expect it to be good and do expect it to cost: they're all similar, but a notable entry is *Café Roxy (Map 4, ☎ 34 92 92, Leopoldstrasse 48)*, with burgers for DM14.50 and sandwiches from DM8.50 to DM13.50. It's open from 8 am to 3 am daily.

The *Kaffeehaus Restaurant Alt Schwabing (Map 7, ☎ 273 10 22, Schelling-strasse 56)*, is a blast from the past, with high, stuccoed ceilings, a quaint old bar and frilly glass lamp covers. The prices have also stood still: pastas and salads start at DM11, and nary a dish is over DM16. It's also good for breakfast (see that section). Hours are 8 am to 1 am on weekdays, and 9 am to 1 am on weekends.

Egger (Map 4, ☎ 39 85 26, Friedrich-strasse 27), is a fine place with large plates and two-course lunch specials from DM11.50 to DM15. At dinner, vegetarian main courses average DM12 to DM15, meat dishes from DM14 to DM21. It's open from 10 am to 1 am daily.

Alter Simpl (Map 7, ☎ 272 30 83, Türkenstrasse 57) close to the university is a packed old student hang-out with good jazz and a reasonable menu. Writers, artists and performers used to meet here at the turn of the century, and the place retains an alternative feel. You can easily have a main course and drink for under DM20. It's open from 11 am to 3 am daily.

The *Café Reitschule (Map 4, ☎ 33 34 02, Königinstrasse 34)* is a chic place near the English Garden. Its gimmick is horses – you can watch them being trained through the glass in the inner courtyard, and the rear terrace has a view of another practice pitch. It's a fine place for a midday meal (mostly international dishes, starting at DM15). The crowd gets seriously pretentious at night. Hours are from 9 am to 1 am daily.

The *Café Monopteros (Map 4, ☎ 33 12 62, Königinstrasse 43)* is just the thing after lolling around in the English Garden all afternoon. A generous slice of cake with ice cream and coffee will cost you just DM7.50, and it does some lovely pastas DM15 or less. It's open from 9 am to 9 pm daily (closed Sunday).

Westend

The nicely renovated *Stoa (Map 5, ☎ 50 70 50, Gollierstrasse 38)*, is a fine place for lunch or dinner. It has a comfortable atmosphere, tapas from DM7.50 to DM15.50, and varied main courses like penne in a three-cream sauce from DM13.30. From Monday to Saturday it has a cheap 'happy hour meal' from 4.30 to 7 pm, when dishes normally up to DM15 cost just DM10. Sundays there's a two-for-the-price-of-one meal offer until 11 pm. It's open from 11 am to 11 pm daily (Sunday from 5 pm).

Gay & Lesbian

The *Café Glück (Map 5, ☎ 201 16 73, Palmstrasse 4)* is a relaxed, esoteric locale with chic sofas on one side and tables on the other. Check out the eyeball chandelier. It does decent salads and main meals for DM15 to DM17 and has a good wine list. It's open from 4 pm to 1 am weekdays, and from 10 am to 1 am weekends. See also Gay & Lesbian under Pubs & Bars in the Entertainment chapter.

BREAKFAST PLACES

When your train drops you at Hauptbahnhof at 7 am, and everyone in the station is drinking large glasses of beer and eating Currywurst, get out of there before you join them.

If you absolutely must eat in the station, try the *bakery* on the ground level next to Sussmann's international bookshop or the kiosk at the head of Track 14, which does fine cappuccinos for DM3. The *cafeteria* is pleasant enough, with boiled eggs for DM1.30. And there's always *Burger King*, upstairs in the main hall, which serves a breakfast of sorts.

Around Hauptbahnhof

South of the train station, breakfast is cheaper than in the expensive hotels to the north and east. Two good spots here are *Sultan (Map 7a)*, on the corner of Schwanthalerstrasse and Goethestrasse, and *Kandil Restaurant (Map 7a, ☎ 54 82 82 52, Landwehrstrasse 8)*, which does rolls with butter, marmalade and coffee for DM5.50. Both places are open from 7 am to 11 pm daily.

Café am Beethovenplatz (Map 7a, ☎ 54 40 43 48, Goethestrasse 51) at the Hotel Pension Mariandl (see Places to Stay), does breakfast from 9 am for DM8.50 to DM17, and on Sunday morning from 11 am (when prices are similar but there's live jazz as well). It's open from 9 am to 1 am daily.

Wiener's buffet (Map 7a), at the corner of Sendlinger-Tor-Platz and Sonnenstrasse next to *Höflinger*, does great breakfasts (eg ham and eggs, rolls and coffee for DM8.50) starting at 8 am.

East of the Isar

Atlas (Map 6, ☎ 480 29 97, Innere Wiener Strasse 2) is a cool cafe near the Gasteig with a big breakfast menu. The American one with pancakes, bacon, fried egg and toast is a bargain for DM15.50. It does bagels and health food, alongside its lunch and evening fare. Hours are from 9 am to 1 am daily.

The *Munich City Hilton*, Rosenheimerstrasse 5 (see also Places to Stay), has a wonderful breakfast buffet from 10 am to 3 pm every Sunday. The designer china, silverware and piano music are a nice complement to the splendid food – we really went overboard on the French cheeses and Norwegian smoked salmon. It costs·a stiff DM70 per head, but that's including a bottle of sparkling wine *Sekt*.

Haidhausen

Café Voilá (Map 6, ☎ 23 74 82, Wörthstrasse 5) has an extensive breakfast menu from DM8 to DM20, and starts serving at 8 am. The high ceilings and huge picture windows make it a great place to watch the world go by. Take any S-Bahn to Rosenheimerplatz or the U4 or U5 to Max-Weber-Platz.

Neuhausen

The painfully trendy *Café am Platz der Freiheit (Map 3, ☎ 13 46 86, Leonrodstrasse 20)*, has very good *Milchcafé* (coffee with milk), served steaming hot in giant bowls, and three eggs with ham for DM8.50, but the service is terrible. It's open from 9 am to 1 am daily.

Schwabing

Treszniewski (☎ 28 23 49, Theresienstrasse 72), in Schwabing, does a dozen-odd kinds of breakfast from which start at about DM6 to DM20. The food is always beautifully served and the bread rolls particularly good, although service can be sluggish. It's open from 8 to 3 am daily (till 4 am on Friday and Saturday).

Bobolovsky's (Map 4, ☎ 29 73 63, Ursulastrasse 10) has a great deal on weekdays from 9 am to 4 pm: any breakfast costs DM9.90 (normally it's up to DM15.40). The choices are named after American film stars. (See also Cafes & Bistros.)

Westend

Speisecafé West (Map 5, ☎ 50 54 00, Tulbeckstrasse 9) in the Westend is a stylish place with a dazzling breakfast menu for DM7.50 to DM15.50. Bacon and eggs costs DM9.50 and French toast DM11.50. Too bad it doesn't open earlier (hours are from 10 am to 1 pm daily).

STUDENT CAFETERIAS & FAST FOOD

Student-card holders can fill up for around DM4 in any of the university *Mensas*, (Mensa comes from the Latin word for 'table' and has nothing to do with the intellectual society). They don't always check ID, so if you're nearly skint it's worth a try.

The best Mensa is on Schillerstrasse (Map 7a), just north of Pettenkoferstrasse, and there are others at Leopoldstrasse 13, at Arcisstrasse 17 (in the Technical University), and at Helene-Mayer-Ring 9 (Map 3, in the Studentenstadt, a huge student housing complex). They're all open from 11 am to 2 pm Monday to Thursday and from 11 am to 1.45 pm Friday.

For quick snacks, any *Müller Bakery Stehcafé* offers coffee for around DM2 and pretzels or bread rolls covered with melted cheese (about DM3) or with bacon or ham (DM3 to DM4).

Throughout the city, branches of *Vinzenzmurr* have hot buffets and prepared meals; a very good lunch (like Schweinbraten with Knödel and gravy) can be as low as DM8, and pizza and hamburgers average about DM4. There's a good one on the west side of Sonnenstrasse, just south of Kaufhof (Map 7a).

Around Hauptbahnhof

Doner and pizza rule the fast-food scene in Munich. Opposite the Hauptbahnhof on Bayerstrasse there are lots of tourist traps, but you can grab a quick cheap bite at *Pizzeria Cadoro's* street pizza window (Map 7a), where large slices are DM3.50 to DM4. *Don't* go inside – it's a tourist trap.

Just south of the Hauptbahnhof are about a dozen places doing doner kebab. Two favourites are the *Gute Stube (Map 7a)* at the corner of Schwanthalerstrasse and Schillerstrasse, with great ones for DM6, and the tiny *Kebab Antep (Map 7a, ☎ 53 22 36, Schwanthalerstrasse 45)*, with the entrance on Goethestrasse, where they cost DM5. There's also spinach pie and other vegetarian offerings.

Thai fans absolutely must head for *Jinny's Thai Food (Map 7a, ☎ 55 07 99 48,*

Schillerstrasse 32) just south of Landwehrstrasse, where exquisite soups (DM4.90) along with daily specials (DM9.90 to DM10.90) await. They're fantastic and the staff are really friendly, too.

Altstadt

Cheap eating is also available in various department stores in the centre. Right opposite Karlsplatz (Map 7a), on the ground floor of Kaufhof, are three good options next to each other: a *Müller* bakery, *Nordsee* seafood and *Grillpfanne* doing sausages. Also at Karlsplatz is a seemingly always-crowded *McDonald's* (Map 7a).

The *Münchner Suppenküche (Map 7a, ☎ 52 38 94 42, Schäfflerstrasse 7)* north of the Frauenkirche, has meat and vegetarian soups from DM3.50. It's open from 10 am to 4.30 pm Monday to Thursday, from 10 am to 3 pm Friday and from 11 am to 3 pm Saturdays (during the Christmas market only).

You won't find game dishes much cheaper than at *Zerwirkgewölbe (Map 7a, ☎ 22 68 24, Ledererstrasse 3)*. Its cellar shop has a stand-up snack bar. Soups start at DM4, and the venison with *spätzle* noodles is a bargain at DM15. It's open from 8.30 am to 6 pm weekdays and from 8.30 am to 1 pm Saturday.

Katty-cornered from the Hofbräuhaus is *Shoya (Map 7a, ☎ 29 27 72, Orlandostrasse 5)*, selling takeaway sushi from DM7 to crowds of locals and tourists. It's open from 10.30 am to midnight daily.

Barely south of the Altstadt is *Der Kleine Chinese (Map 7, ☎ 202 11 32, Fraunhoferstrasse 35)*, which does spring rolls from DM4 and full takeaway meals from about DM8 (see also Asian under Restaurants).

Neuhausen

A spectacular deal for lunch is *Vinh's* (see under Asian Restaurants earlier in this chapter) with super set-lunch specials from DM7.50 (between 11.30 am and 2.30 pm daily).

Schwabing

Reiter Imbiss (Map 4, Hohenzollernstrasse 24), has heaps of meaty stuff for cheap prices, as well as changing daily specials. There are *McDonald's* outlets along Leopoldstrasse.

Right next to the Haus International youth hotel is the ***BP filling station***, with excellent and cheap sandwiches.

SELF-CATERING
Supermarkets

Grocery stores and supermarkets large and small can be found throughout the city (the Turkish ones can be particularly cheap). Bear in mind that at the checkout you will have to pack away the purchases yourself, in either a bag you buy from the till (around 30 pfennigs) or one you've brought yourself. And don't tarry – you're expected to clear out and not hold up the queue.

If you're staying at the hostel in Wendl-Dietrich-Strasse, there's a huge and cheap *Penny Markt (Map 3)* just 50m to the east.

Norma and *Aldi* supermarkets, with outlets throughout the city, are other good places to buy staples. For a last-minute stock-up before your train leaves, hit the slightly dearer ***Tengelmann*** at Bayerstrasse 5, just opposite the Hauptbahnhof.

The supermarket in the basement of the Kaufhof department store opposite Karlsplatz has a far more upscale selection, plus goodies like fresh mozzarella, superb sliced meats and cheeses, and a good bakery.

Koschere Spezialitäten (☎ 22 80 02 58), at the east end of Viktualienmarkt, near the Buxs restaurant, has kosher and Israeli goodies including matzo balls in a zillion variations, filled bagels and Golan Heights wine (from DM18 per bottle).

Bakeries & Other Options

In Neuhausen and close to the hostel is one of Munich's best bakeries, the tiny ***Schneider's Feinbäckerei*** *(☎ 26 47 44, Volkartstrasse 48)*, between Albrechtstrasse and Artilleriestrasse just east of Landshuter

Allee. They bake indescribably good bread rolls, other breads and cakes.

More prosperous picnickers might prefer the legendary ***Alois Dallmayr*** *(Map 7a, ☎ 213 51 00, Dienerstrasse 13–14)*, one of the world's greatest (and priciest) delicatessens, with an amazing range of exotic foods imported from every end of the earth (see also International Restaurants earlier in this chapter). ***Käfers*** *(Map 6, ☎ 416 82 47, Prinzregentenstrasse 73)* is its chief rival, with huge and lavish departments as well as expensive picnic gear.

British Shop *(Map 7, ☎ 542 02 70, Schellingstrasse 100)*, is Munich's leading purveyor of Brit groceries and home goods. It's open from 9.30 am to 7 pm Monday to Friday, and from 9 am to 2 pm Saturday.

Winfield Australia Shop (Map 3, ☎ 542 83 91, Dachauer Strasse 109) caters to Aussies with cravings for Vegemite, Foster's, Akruba hats and Lonely Planet Australia guides. The ostrich meat isn't bad either. Hours are from 9 am to 7 pm Monday to Friday and from 9 am to 2 pm Saturday.

At Viktualienmarkt (Map 7a), just south of Marienplatz, you can put together a picnic feast of breads, cheeses and salad to take off to a beer garden for DM10 or less per person, but it's so good that chances are you'll get carried away and the price will soar. Make sure you figure out the price before buying, and don't be afraid to move on to another stall.

Among the market's mainstays, ***Nordsee***, in a new replica of its original turn-of-the-century shop, has fantastic seafood from cheap to ridiculous; ***Thoma*** is a wonderful cheese and wine shop behind which you'll find the ***Juice Bar***, with great fruity concoctions from DM3 to DM6. Right next to the maypole, look for the ***Oliven & Essiggurken*** stand, with olives and pickles plus pickled garlic and loads more.

Entertainment

Munich's entertainment scene offers a wealth of opportunities. Apart from discos, pubs and beer halls, try not to miss the city's excellent classical and opera venues – the jazz clubs aren't bad either.

Not surprisingly, beer drinking is an integral part of Munich's entertainment scene. According to Berlin government statistics, Germans drink an average of 127L of the amber liquid per person per year, while Munich residents average over 150L. If you're keen to keep up with the locals, a key investment is Larry Hawthorne's *Beer Drinker's Guide to Munich*, available locally, which lists and rates many of Munich's better beer gardens and brews.

Munich nightclub bouncers are notoriously rude and 'discerning', so dress to kill (or look, as locals say, *schiki-micki*) and keep your cool.

Listings The best sources of information are the free *in München*, available at bars, restaurants, ticket outlets and other venues, and the tall, thin, yellow monthly *München im...* (DM3), which is an A to Z listing of almost everything the city has to offer (except discos). Both publications cover new museum exhibitions, festivals, concerts and theatre.

Another great German guide (available at any newsstand) is the monthly *Münchner Stadtmagazin* (DM3), which is probably the most complete guide to bars, discos, clubs, concerts and nightlife in the city.

Bigger newsstands and shops sell *Munich Found* (DM4.50), an English-language city magazine with somewhat useful listings.

Tickets Tickets to entertainment venues are available at official ticket outlets *(Kartenvorverkauf)* throughout the city, but these often specialise in certain genres. The exception is the *Zentraler Kartenvorverkauf* (☎ 26 46 20), which sells tickets to everything, including theatre, ballet, opera, rock concerts and all special events. Its office is

conveniently located at Marienplatz, underground in the S-Bahn station.

BEER HALLS & GARDENS

Many people go to beer halls and beer gardens to drink rather than to eat – especially given the quality of the 'food' is often a secondary consideration, after beer. Despite popular belief, there's actually only a handful of genuine beer halls in Munich, including the Löwenbräukeller and two of the three Augustiner establishments.

Most of the places listed below are gardens or gardens-cum-restaurants; almost all of them open from 10 am to at least 10 pm daily.

Even in the touristy places, be careful not to sit at the *Stammtisch*, a table reserved for regulars (there will be a brass plaque). You won't get served unless you belong there.

Munich beer gardens allow you to bring food but not drinks, and everyone in town does just that: stock up (see Self-Catering in the Places to Eat chapter) and show up for the evening. A few have live music (from oompah to Dixieland) but the main thing is being outside with the beer. Periodic attempts to curb opening times for beer gardens cause an uproar in Bavaria, and locals scornfully tag them 'Prussian' measures. Places in town tend to close their gardens by 11 pm, as a concession to the neighbours.

You sometimes have to pay a *Pfand* (deposit) for the glasses (usually DM5). Beer costs DM9 to DM12 per litre. Food includes roast chicken (about DM15 for a half), spare ribs (DM16 to DM20, and probably not worth it except in Taxisgarten), huge pretzels (about DM5) and Bavarian specialities including *Schweinebraten* (roast pork) and schnitzel (DM17 to DM22). There's both self-service and waiter service.

Radi is a huge, mild radish that's eaten with beer; it's cut with a *Radimesser*, which you push into the centre of the radish. You then twist the handle round and round, creating a radish spiral. Buy a Radimesser at any department store and buy the radish at a market, or buy prepared radish for about DM7. If you do it yourself, smother the cut end of the radish with salt until it 'sweats' – this reduces bitterness (and increases your thirst!).

Obazda (pronounced 'oh-batsdah') is Bavarian for 'mixed up' – this cream-cheese-like beer garden speciality is made of butter, Camembert and paprika (about DM8 to DM12). Spread it on *Brez'n* (a pretzel) or bread. If you hate it while sober, you may like it when inebriated.

City Centre

Most celebrated is the cavernous *Hofbräuhaus (Map 7a, ☎ 22 16 76, Am Platzl 9)*. The artificial cheer is turned on daily and stoked by a raucous Bavarian folk band. This museum piece is generally packed with tipsy tourists, and the food and service leave much to be desired, but the interior's lovely and worth a look. The beer garden in the inner courtyard is slightly less hokey. There's an alcohol Breathalyzer out the back (DM3) if you succumb to the dubious charms of the place. It's open from 9 am to midnight daily.

The sprawling, leafy beer garden at *Augustiner Keller (Map 3, ☎ 59 43 93, Arnulfstrasse 52)*, a 10 minute walk along the north side of the Hauptbahnhof, has a laid-back atmosphere ideal for recreational drinking. Motorised carts come by to clear the empties. Its 5000 seats get very packed in summer and many hard-drinking customers stay on until twelve midnight. There's a good mix of food stands selling sausage, chicken and *Steckerl* (roast mackerel on a stick). Kids can romp around in the playground while you quaff. Hours are from 10 am to 1 am daily.

Southeast of the Hauptbahnhof, *Augustiner Bräustuben (Map 5, ☎ 50 70 47, Landsberger Strasse 19)*, is our favourite tavern in all of Munich. The atmosphere is fantastic: old barrel lids line the walls, service is quick and attentive and the food's decent. At the back you can view Oktoberfest drawhorses through the glassed-in stable door (names include 'Rambo' and 'Tango'). And above all, the beer's cheap (DM8.20 for a litre of Augustiner) from the

brewery next door. Its only real drawback is that there's no beer garden. It's open from 10 am to about midnight daily.

Augustiner-Grossgaststätte (Map 7a, ☎ 55 19 92 57, Neuhauser Strasse 27), has a less raucous atmosphere than the Hofbräuhaus (not to mention decent food), yet it's a more authentic example of an old-style Munich beer hall. Many people never get past the sidewalk service area to marvel at the medieval frescoes and Gothic-tined ceilings inside, pepped up with Italian rococo trimmings. It's open from 9 am to midnight daily.

Viktualienmarkt (Map 7a, ☎ 29 75 45, Viktualienmarkt 6), is a wonderful place right in the city centre (just north of the Maypole on the square). Shaded by a few enormous chestnut trees, the Viktualienmarkt gets packed to the hilt when the market's in full swing. Also see the Viktualienmarkt entry under Self-Catering in the Places to Eat chapter. It's open from 9 am to 10 pm daily (closed Sunday and holidays).

Löwenbräukeller (Map 7, ☎ 52 60 21, Nymphenburger Strasse 2), deserves another mention here for its many earthy locals, a relative dearth of tourists and a grand main hall (which seats 2000) with regular Bavarian music and heel-slapping dances on stage. You'd never guess the place was pummelled in WWII, it's so lovingly restored. There's a large and labyrinthine beer garden that borders the entire complex. It's open from 9 am to 1 am daily.

Braunauer Hof (Map 7a, ☎ 22 36 13, Frauenstrasse 42), near the Isartor, has a pleasingly warped beer garden for such a conventional locale. In the snug courtyard there's a hedge maze, a fresco with a bizarre bunch of historical figures and a golden bull that's illuminated at night. It's open from 10 am to 11 pm daily.

English Garden

This sprawling park has four beer gardens; the two in the northern section (Hirschau and especially Aumeister) tend to attract fewer tourists and more down-home types. See Map 4 for all English Garden venues.

The classic *Chinesischer Turm (Map 4, ☎ 950 28, Englischer Garten 3)*, has a weird

ENTERTAINMENT

mixture of businessfolk, tourists and layabouts, all entertained by what has to be the world's drunkest oompah band (in the tower above the crowd, fenced in á la *The Blues Brothers*). The place seats around 7000 but there's always room for more. It also has a carousel just for kids. Hours are from 10 am to 1 am daily.

The nearby **Seehaus** beer garden *(Map 4, ☎ 381 61 30)*, on the banks of the Kleinhesseloher See, caters to a more upmarket crowd (besides ribs and chicken, there's frozen yoghurt and light beer), but despite the pretentions it's a joy to sit with a brew at the water's edge. There's a boat rental place next door. Seehaus is open from 9 am to 1 am daily.

Just north of Seehaus, via the pedestrian bridge over Dietlindenstrasse, is **Hirschau** *(Map 4, ☎ 36 99 42, Gyslingstrasse 15)*. By day it's a traditional place frequented by Lederhosen types, but later it's transformed into an open-air disco (from 8 pm Tuesday through Saturday, from 3 pm Sunday). The socialites take over when the thumping starts. Hours are from 11 am to 1 am daily (but it's only open on Monday in good weather).

Aumeister *(Map 4, ☎ 32 52 24)*, on Sondermeierstrasse, is the northernmost stop in the English Garden. It's comfy and familiar, with umbrella-clad tables and self-service food stalls, and the crowd (mostly north-Munich residents) is just as relaxed. Take the U6 to Studentenstadt and walk 10 minutes east into the greenery. It's open from 9 am to 11 pm daily.

Schwabing

Max-Emanuel-Brauerei *(Map 7, ☎ 271 51 58, Adalbertstrasse 33)*, is a strange beast: a cosy student pub in the heart of Schwabing with a Latin-American dance floor in the rear (cover charge is DM5 several times a week). Out back there is a shaded courtyard beer garden with heavy oak tables. You'll find lots of budding lawyers here, as a law school cramming course takes place next door. It's open from 10 am to 1 am daily.

Neuhausen

The **Hirschgarten** *(Map 3, ☎ 17 25 91, Hirschgartenallee 1)*, is a beautiful place on a formal royal hunting preserve just south of Schloss Nymphenburg (take the S-Bahn to Laim). It's packed with locals and few tourists. The shady garden is enormous, and you can sit next to the deer that wander just on the other side of the chain-link fence. There's even a retractable marquee in case of a sudden shower. It's open from 10 am to 11 pm daily.

Taxisgarten *(Map 3, ☎ 15 68 27, Taxisstrasse 12)*, north of Rotkreuzplatz, is another peaceful place with mainly local families. The building was originally a meeting point for veterans of WWI, and you can still see a helmeted German soldier over one of the doorways. It also has some of the best ribs in town (DM16.50). Take bus No 177 from Rotkreuzplatz to Klugstrasse. It's open from 10 am to 10 pm daily.

Eastern Munich

Not to be confused with its better-known cousin in the city centre, **Hofbräukeller** *(Map 6, ☎ 448 73 76, Innere Wiener Strasse 19)*, south of Max-Weber-Platz, is a sprawling restaurant and beer garden. Many of the historic rooms retain an early 20th century appeal, thanks to meticulous rebuilding after a 1987 fire. It's popular with urbanites east of the Isar. Take the U1 or U4 to Max-Weber-Platz. Hours are from 9 am to midnight daily.

Sankt Emmerams Mühle *(Map 4, ☎ 95 39 71, Sankt Emmeram 41)*, is a charming 'local haunt' on the eastern side of the Isar. The site drips history: in 1158, Henry the Lion destroyed a nearby toll bridge, an event that led to Munich's founding, and there's a reconstructed paper mill (originally from the 14th century) behind the beer garden. Take a look at the guest book – it's filled with the signatures of rock and pop stars from Abba to Led Zeppelin. Take the U6 to Studentenstadt and then bus No 37 to Sankt Emmerams. It's open from 10 am to 11 pm daily.

Southern Munich

Waldwirtschaft Grosshesselohe *(Map 5, ☎ 79 50 88, Georg-Kalb-Strasse 3)*, via the S7 to Grosshesselohe, is in one of the most expensive neighbourhoods in town. The

continued on page 151

OKTOBERFEST

Try to get to Munich for the Oktoberfest, one of Europe's biggest and best parties (see also the boxed text 'Oktoberfest'). It runs from mid-September to the first Sunday in October. Note that there are no parking facilities in the immediate vicinity (given the drunks, it wouldn't be a good idea to park there anyway).

The festival is held at the Theresienwiese (Map 5), a 15 minute walk south of the Hauptbahnhof, and is served by its own U-Bahn station. If you're asking directions, say 'd'wies'n' ('dee-veez-en'), the nickname for the grounds, and follow the tourists who wear funny hats. Trams and buses heading that way, however, have signs that say '*Zur Festwiese*' ('to the Festival Meadow').

The Oktoberfest runs from about 10.30 am to 11:30 pm daily. Midday to mid-afternoon is the least busy time, and it's best to leave the fair by about 9 or 10 pm, as crowds can get a bit touchy when the beer and schnapps supplies are turned off. Every Thursday is Children's Day, when all children's rides and attractions are half price.

No entrance fee is charged but most of the fun costs something, particularly food and drink. Some 5.5 million litres of beer (costing about DM11 to DM12 per litre) are consumed, along with more than 600,000 chickens, 90,000 pork legs and 80 full-grown oxen. It's Munich's most important tourist attraction, bringing in nearly DM1.5 billion.

Oktoberfest

The world's biggest beer festival dates back to October 1810, when Bavarian Crown Prince Ludwig I married Princess Therese of Saxon-Hildburghausen. His royal highness commissioned horse races as well as an enormous party in front of the city gates. Müncheners loved it so much that they began to celebrate it every year, and this drunken melee became known as Oktoberfest, a 16-day extravaganza that now attracts nearly seven million people a year. The event has spawned imitators throughout Germany and the world (the US city of Cincinnati, Ohio, has a fast and furious one, held over a single weekend).

During the event, the Theresienwiese fairgrounds are practically a city of beer tents, amusements, rides – including a giant ferris wheel and roller coasters (just what beer drinkers need after several frothy ales) – and kiosks selling snacks and sweets. Much of the fun is in becoming mates with people of all nationalities, as about one-third of festival-goers come from outside Germany (Australians, Americans, British and Italians are very well represented).

The action takes place on the 15 days prior to the first Sunday in October (that's 16 September to 3 October 2000 and 22 September to 7 October 2001).

Title page: Paulaner beer tent with loads of people (Martin Moos)

Above right: Smiley face Oktoberfest version (Martin Moos)

MARTIN MOOS

DAVID PEEVERS

Top: Rolling out the barrels

Bottom: Happy hour!

JEREMY GRAY

Left: The many faces of Oktoberfest

There's not a whole lot you can do about the beer prices, but the food is where they really get you at the Oktoberfest tents. After a litre or two of amber liquid, the reluctance to part with DM20 for a beer and a chicken leg tends to waver significantly, so make sure you eat before you arrive.

Self-catering is one way to cut your food bill (see Self-Catering in the Places to Eat chapter). Useful options include several Turkish shops at the western end of Schwanthaler Strasse, which (even during Oktoberfest) sell cheap and tasty doner kebabs, pizzas and filled pastries.

Reserve accommodation as early as you can (like a year in advance). Hotels book out very quickly and their prices skyrocket during the fair. If you show up during Oktoberfest, expect to find only very pricey rooms in Munich, if any at all. Consider staying in the suburbs or nearby cities – Augsburg, Dachau and Garmisch-Partenkirchen are all under an hour away.

You don't have to reserve tables in one of the 14 Oktoberfest beer tents, but it helps if you want to be sure of a spot. The brewers begin accepting reservations months ahead of time, and the Munich tourist office can send you a list of the brewers' contact details (see the Facts for the Visitor chapter).

Major Oktoberfest events include:

Brewer's Parade

A spectacular parade of brewery owners and Oktoberfest waiters – the *Einzug der Festwirte* – takes place at 11 am on the first day of the festival, leading from Sonnenstrasse to the fairgrounds via Schwanthaler Strasse. If you've missed them up to now, this is *the* place to witness large numbers of fresh-faced (read: flushed) Bavarians in traditional garb, swinging their beer mugs atop horse-drawn floats or marching in oompah bands (about 1000 people take part). If you managed to get a hotel room looking into Schwanthaler Strasse, great; if not, you might try taking a late breakfast at the Burger King at the corner of Schwanthaler Strasse and Sonnenstrasse, which has a great upstairs view of the procession.

At noon, the lord mayor stands before the thirsty crowds at Theresienwiese, and with due pomp, he slams home a wooden tap with a mallet. When the tap breaks through the cask's surface and beer gushes forth, he exclaims, '*Ozapft ist!*' ('It's tapped!').

Folklore International

About 500 participants from the Costume Procession (see the following entry) stage musical, dance and folklore performances in the Circus Krone building on Arnulfstrasse at 8 pm on the first evening of Oktoberfest (Map 3). Most likely you'll also sight individual groups performing in the pedestrian zones before and during the festival.

Costume Procession

On the second day, a young girl dressed as the 'Münchner Kindl' on horseback leads 7500 performers from all over Europe (who wear pretzel bras and other traditional drunkenwear) through the streets of the city centre. This is called the *Trachten- und Schützenzug* and is a more relaxed event, starting at 10 am and lasting three hours or more. Ethnic and community groups from all over Germany take part, but you'll also see legions of strangely-clad folks from throughout Europe and as far away as Japan.

Gay Meeting

There's a big gay meeting on the first Sunday of Oktoberfest at the Bräurosl tent, with legions of butch-looking guys in leather pants. It is timed to coincide with a gay leather convention; it's huge fun and open to all.

MICK WELDON

Bavaria Concert

On the second Saturday of the festival, a concert with all the Oktoberfest bands is held on the steps of the Bavaria statue at 11 am. (If the weather's bad they try again a week later.)

Oktoberfest Services

The city maintains extra facilities on the Theresienwiese during Oktoberfest, to keep the crowds healthy, happy and cashed up. By the entrance to the Theresienwiese U-Bahn station you'll find a Deutsche Bank ATM, which is perpetually mobbed, a left-luggage office (DM2.50 per item, last pick-up 11.30 pm) and some of the festival's 60 card-operated telephones (five of these take international credit cards).

On the Theresienwiese itself, you'll find a lost-and-found office behind the Schottenhamel tent. For cuts, bruises, or worse, the Bayerisches Rotes Kreuz (Bavarian Red Cross) has emergency medical services at three points (marked by floating white balloons).

continued from page 146

wealthy residents decided that all the racket (Dixieland music, mainly) was too downmarket for their taste and tried to shut it down. The resulting citywide brouhaha became headline news and the counter-movement is written in Munich history as the 'Beer Garden Revolution' of 1995. It was, of course, successful. It's open from 10.30 am to 10 pm daily.

Menterschwaige (Map 5, ☎ 64 07 32, Menterschwaige Strasse 4), is a secret favourite of many Müncheners, not far from the Bavaria Film Studios. It once belonged to the royal estate of Ludwig I, the man who authorised the first Oktoberfest. The beer garden is still more upscale than most, and its impressive (and expensive) food stalls have a bigger selection than at many other beer gardens. Take the U2 to Silberhornstrasse and tram No 25 to Menterschwaige Strasse. It's open from 11.30 am to 10 pm daily.

Flaucher (Map 5, ☎ 723 26 77, Isarauen 8), is a brilliant stop during a bike ride or hike along the Isar canal. It's located in a secluded corner of the woods, with a good assortment of snack options and a playground for kids. Take the U3 to Brudermühle Strasse and then bus No 45 one stop to Schäftlarn Strasse, walk east across the bridge and follow the signs. Opening times are 10 am to 11 pm daily.

Northern Munich

Insel Mühle (Map 3, ☎ 810 10, Von Kahr Strasse 87), is on a tiny island in the tiny (but fast-moving) Würm River. The old millwheel still stands like a sentry at the entrance. Its key charm is that few locals and even fewer tourists know about the place. But it also has an unbeatable special: on weekdays, a litre of *helles* (pale ale) costs just DM6.90 until 5 pm (normally it's DM9.50). Take the S2 to Allach, then bus No 177 to Friedhof Untermenzing, and walk about 500m west on Von Kahr Strasse. Hours are 10 am to 10 pm daily.

Bamberger Haus (Map 3, ☎ 308 89 66, Brunnerstrasse 2) in Leopoldpark is primarily a mediocre restaurant but there's a

lovely shaded terrace outside for drinking. Have a peek inside – the villa's lovely rococo decor is worth a look. Take the U1 or U2 to Scheidplatz. Opening hours are 11 am to 1 am daily.

PUBS & BARS
City Centre

Right in the centre, *Nachtcafé (Map 7, ☎ 59 59 00, Maximiliansplatz 5)*, is open from 9 pm until 6 am daily. On trendy nights they won't let you in unless you're *tres* chic, female and dressed in a tight black dress, or throwing Deutschmarks around. Other nights there's big band jazz (trumpeter Al Porcino is a frequent guest) and everyone's welcome (see the Jazz section later in this chapter).

Master's Home (Map 7, ☎ 22 99 09, Frauenstrasse 11), is a wonderfully quirky place just east of Viktualienmarkt. It's decked out like a colonial-era home – one room's a study, another has a bathtub, and the restaurant is in the living room with animal skins on the walls. Reliable sources say the food is missable. The bar stays open from 11.30 am until 3 am daily.

Far more homey Bavarian is *Jodlerwirt (Map 7, ☎ 467 35 24, Altenhofstrasse 4)*, in an alley just north of Marienplatz. It's a nice, relatively untouristed place with good Ayinger beer and a pleasant atmosphere. The upstairs bar vibrates with yodelling sessions, and you can join in regardless of talent. Hours are from 5 pm to 1 am Monday to Saturday and from 6 pm to midnight Sunday.

Just east of the Altstadt, *Baader Café (Map 7, ☎ 201 06 38, Baaderstrasse 47)*, is something of a literary think-and-drink place, with snacks and a happy hour from 6 to 8 pm (when all drinks cost DM8 and all meals DM10). The drinks and atmosphere are tops, the food's not. Hours are from 11 am to 1 am Monday to Thursday and Sunday and from 11 am to 2 am Friday and Saturday.

Schumann's (Map 7, ☎ 22 90 60, Maximilianstrasse 36), has built up an awesome reputation for serving Munich's finest cocktails (DM9 to DM20). It draws a lot of custom from the nearby theatres, opera house and five-star hotels, so you'd better look

ENTERTAINMENT

smart. Hours are from 5 pm to 3 am Monday through Friday and from 6 pm to 3 am Sunday (closed Saturday, believe it or not).

Eastern Munich

Julep's (Map 6, ☎ 448 00 44, Breisacherstrasse 18), in Haidhausen is a New York bar with Mexican trimmings, featuring great drinks and a very rowdy crowd. It has very good steaks, burgers and cocktails (happy hour is 5 to 8 pm, when drinks cost DM7.50). Opening hours are from 5 pm to 1 am.

The *Dreigroschenkeller (Map 6, ☎ 489 02 90, Lilienstrasse 2)*, next to the Museum-Lichtspiele (enter on Zeppelinstrasse), is an enormously cosy and labyrinthine cellar pub. All rooms have something to do with the dramatist Bertolt Brecht's play *Die Dreigroschenoper*, ranging from a prison cell to a red satiny salon. Besides great beer and wine, there's an extensive food menu (mostly hearty German stuff). Opening hours are from 4 pm to 1 am Monday to Friday and from 10 am to 1 am weekends.

Schwabing

The area along and around Leopoldstrasse, between the university and Münchener Freiheit U-Bahn station, is the bar district; the backstreets are teeming with places, big and small, and there's something to suit every taste.

Lardy (Map 6, ☎ 34 49 49, Leopoldstrasse 49) is a quasi-exclusive bar, but the bouncers at the door are really there just to limit capacity. There are DJs on Thursday and Friday nights, and English-speaking staff. It's open till 3 am.

Towards Königsplatz is *Treszniewski (Map 7, ☎ 28 23 49, Theresienstrasse 72)*, a chic spot that attracts lots of people in black and intellectual types. It's open from 8 am till 3 am (till 4 am Friday and Saturday).

While *Munich's First Diner (Map 6, ☎ 33 59 15, Leopoldstrasse 82)*, is truly a diner (complete with diner food and waiters on rollerblades), it's better known by the expat set as a great place for imported beer and cocktails. It's a fun flashback to the US of A, if that's what you're after. It's open from 9 am to 1 am daily (till 3 am Friday and Saturday).

Neuhausen

Aside from some nice cafes (see the Places to Eat chapter), this neighbourhood has some intimate local pubs that most tourists don't get to.

Kreitmayr's (☎ 448 91 40), on Kreitmayrstrasse, just east of Erzgiessereistrasse, is a real bar crawler's bar: bar food, good drinks, a pool table, Kegeln (a sort of bowling), darts and pinball, and live music on Thursday (from Irish folk to jazz). It also has a beer garden in summer. It's open from 5 pm to 1 am Sunday to Thursday and from 5 pm to 2 am Friday and Saturday.

The *froh & munter (Map 3, ☎ 18 79 97, Artilleriestrasse 5)*, is the best place for good Weissbier, with a great crowd of locals and good snacks as well. Hours are from 6 pm to 1 am Sunday to Thursday and from 6 pm to 3 am Friday and Saturday (see Cafes & Bistros in the Places to Eat chapter).

DISCOS & CLUBS

Cover prices for discos change often, sometimes daily, but average between DM5 and DM15.

Kunstpark Ost

Kunstpark Ost (Map 6, ☎ 49 00 27 30, Grafinger Strasse 6), is a driving force in Munich's nightlife, with a multiple disco-restaurant-bar-cinema complex behind the Ostbahnhof in the former Pfanni dumpling factory. Discos often host live and very large concerts. Sadly, the landlords have been eyeing plans for a space-age shopping centre on the grounds, so the entire place might be bulldozed at the end of 2001.

It's swarmingly popular at weekends, and some places keep buzzing until 6 am. (During the week only about five places are open, and get jam-packed as a result.)

All that gyrating burns up the calories, and there's a number of grungy fast-food places and eateries if you can't hold out for something better in town. Watch your valuables in the side alleys, where some very unsavoury characters have been known to hang out.

Discos come and go, but one reliable evergreen is the *Bongo Bar (☎ 49 00 12 60)*, with 1950s-style weirdness, go-go dancers and kitsch extraordinaire (chandeliers and thick heavy curtains). Hours are from 9 pm to 4 am Wednesday to Sunday.

New York Tabledance (☎ 61 36 94 09) features lots of tanga-clad girls and muscle boys who do their thing right in front of your face (a 'Don't Touch' rule applies). It has a broader appeal than you might think. Keep banknotes handy for tips (tuck them into the strings). Hours are from 10 pm to 5 am Wednesday to Sunday.

Milch + Bar Faltenbacher (☎ 49 00 35 17) is a cruising ground for a leather-clad 20s crowd. The program is soul and funk. Hours are from 10 pm to 6 am daily.

The enormous ***Babylon*** (☎ 450 69 20), the biggest joint here, attracts big-name concerts and 'parties with thousands' at weekends. Friday nights are 'Fruit of the Room', with 70s and 80s stuff and Schlager, popular updates of treacly German folk songs. It's open from 10 pm to 5 am Friday and Saturday only.

Starsky's (☎ 49 04 21 90) is a mainstream bar and disco with soul-and-funk nights. It's also one of the few places out here that doesn't have a cover charge. It's open from 9 pm to 4 am Tuesday to Saturday.

At the very back of the grounds is ***Shockers*** (☎ 26 02 52 85), a 'horror' bar and disco spread over 14 rooms, with staff dressed up as zombies and ghosts. Look for the coffin at the front entrance. Hours are from 10 pm to 4 am Thursday to Saturday.

Other discos

Another large complex is ***Muffathalle*** (Map 6, ☎ 45 88 75 00 00, Zellstrasse 4), which holds large concerts and, in summer, an open-air disco on Friday with drum 'n' bass, acid jazz and hip-hop (always crowded, so expect long queues). Hours are from 9 pm to 5 am Thursday to Saturday.

P1 (Map 7, ☎ 29 42 52, Prinzregentenstrasse 1), on the west side of the Haus der Kunst, is *the* see-and-be-seen place for Munich wannabes, with extremely choosy and effective bouncers. Hours are from 11 pm to 4 am Sunday to Thursday, from 11 pm to 5 am Friday and Saturday.

Opera (Map 3, ☎ 32 42 32 42, Helmholtzstrasse 12), west of the Hauptbahnhof and off Arnulfstrasse, is a fun place with a strong 30s contingent, and lots of theme nights, such as metal, underground and oldies. Saturday there's black beat and soul. Hours are from 9 pm to 4 am Thursday to Saturday.

Backstage (Map 3, ☎ 33 66 59, Helmholtzstrasse 18), is another concert place and disco; crossover, psychedelic, hip-hop, trash and other freaky music is the rule. Hours are from 9 pm to 4 am Wednesday to Sunday.

Nachtwerk Club (Map 5, ☎ 578 38 00, Landsberger Strasse 186), next to Nachtwerk (see Rock later in this chapter), has middle-of-the-road house and dance-chart music. The gallery bar is a renowned flirt market. It's open from 10 pm to 4 am daily.

Party on the rooftop in Schwabing at ***Skyline*** (Map 4, ☎ 33 31 31, Leopoldstrasse 82), with soul and hip-hop on top of the Hertie department store; it's right next to the Münchener Freiheit U-Bahn station. Nasty critics call it a secretary's disco. It's open from 9 pm to 4 am daily.

Far Out (Map 7a, ☎ 22 66 61, Am Kosttor 2), near the Hofbräuhaus, has mixed theme nights (every night), attracting legions of twisting-and-gyrating under-30s. Thursday is funk and soul, on Friday it's hip-hop and on Saturday there's a house party. Hours are from 10 pm to 4 am Wednesday to Sunday.

The Nazis once danced in the ***Park Café*** (Map 7a, ☎ 59 83 13, Sophienstrasse 7), in the Alter Botanischer Garten. The place now caters to suburban teenies with too much money, but it's worth a look for its classical pillars and crystal chandeliers. Hours are from 10 pm to 4 am Tuesday to Thursday and from 10 pm to 6 am Friday and Saturday.

GAY & LESBIAN VENUES
Listings & Information

Much of Munich's gay and lesbian nightlife is centred in the area just south of Sendlinger Tor. Information for gay men and lesbians is available through Schwules Kommunikations und Kulturzentrum, dubbed *'the sub'*

ENTERTAINMENT

(☎ 260 30 56, Müllerstrasse 43), open from 7 to 11 pm Sunday to Thursday, to 1 am on Friday and Saturday nights. It's a very cool gay community centre, with two floors (a bar downstairs and a library upstairs) that are home to extensive gay resources and support groups.

The *Rosa Seiten* (Pink Pages, DM5) is the best guide to everything gay and lesbian in the city; order it by mail from 'the sub' or take the U2 to Theresianstrasse, where *Weissblauer Gay Shop* (☎ 52 23 52) is just outside the station. An alternative is the *Black Jump shop* (Map 6, ☎ 448 10 73, Orleansstrasse 51); go via the U-Bahn to Sendlinger Tor. These places also hand out free copies of *Our Munich*, a monthly guide to gay and lesbian life.

Lesbians can also contact LeTra/Lesben-Traum (☎ 725 42 72, Dreimühlenstrasse 23), open from 10.30 am to 1 pm Tuesday, from 2.30 to 5 pm Wednesday and from 7 to 10 pm Thursday. A women-only teahouse, the *Frauentee-stube* (Map 5, ☎ 77 40 91, Dreimühlenstrasse 1), is at the corner of Isartalstrasse, south of the city centre (closed Wednesday and Saturday).

Pubs & Bars

There's great service, good food and cocktails at *Morizz* (Map 7, ☎ 201 67 76, Klenzestrasse 43), which looks a lot like a Paris bar: lots of mirrors, very quiet early in the night with lots of theatre types from Gärtnerplatz, but the later it gets, the rowdier it becomes. Hours are from 7 pm to 2 am Sunday to Thursday and from 7 pm to 3 am Friday and Saturday.

Another popular place is *Iwan* (Map 7, ☎ 55 49 33, Josephspitalstrasse 15), a once ultra-chic place that's 'democratised' its crowd. Its two low-lit floors host a very mixed crowd, and in summer there's a nice outside area. There's also a decent vegetarian menu. Hours are from noon to 2 am Monday to Thursday, noon to 3 am Friday and Saturday and from 5 pm to 2 am Sunday.

Ochsengarten (Map 7, ☎ 26 64 46, Müllerstrasse 47), was Germany's first 'leather' bar. It has a forbidding entrance, rustic interior, lots of boots hanging from the ceiling, and a 30s to 40s crowd. Hours are from 10 pm to 3 am daily. Leather lovers also head 'straight' to *Löwengrube* (Map 7, ☎ 26 57 50, Reisingerstrasse 5), a small, exclusively gay place jammed with a tight-Levis-and-rubber crowd. Hours are from 6 pm to 1 am Tuesday to Thursday and Sunday, and from 8 pm to 3 am Friday and Saturday.

Old Mrs Henderson (Map 7, ☎ 26 34 69, Rumfordstrasse 2), on the corner of Müllerstrasse, is a wacky transvestite bar with a stage act. The crowd is mainly gay and curious heteros, and the decor is classic kitsch. There's a show at 9.30 and 11 pm (DM15 cover). It's open from 9 pm to 3 am daily, closed Monday and Tuesday.

A good exclusively lesbian bar is *Bei Carla* (Map 7, ☎ 22 79 01, Buttermelcherstrasse 9), with a mixed-age crowd and snack foods. It's open from 4 pm to 1 am Monday to Saturday and from 6 pm to 1 am Sunday.

There's a mainly lesbian crowd at *Karotte* (Map 7, ☎ 201 06 69, Baaderstrasse 13), just south of the centre, which also serves food from a daily menu. Hours are from 4 pm to 1 am Sunday to Friday, and from 6 pm to 1 am Saturday.

Deutsche Eiche (Map 7, ☎ 231 16 60, Reichenbachstrasse 13), is a very comfortable large bar with a mixed gay-and-straight crowd. Hours are 7.30 am (repeat: am) to 1 am Sunday to Thursday, and from 7.30 am to 3 am Friday and Saturday. Upstairs there's a gay hotel (see Gay & Lesbian Hotels in the Places to Stay chapter).

Discos & Clubs

The Stud (Map 5, ☎ 260 84 03, Thalkirchner Strasse 2), is a leather-Levis place with a dark, coal-mine-like interior and lots of butch guys with no hair. The clientele is gay and lesbian (in fact, they're always looking for more lesbians, so if that fits, head on over). It's open from 11 pm to 4 am Friday to Sunday, and drinks start at DM5. On Sunday they put in a labyrinth (men only).

Fortuna Musikbar (Map 7, ☎ 55 40 70, Maximiliansplatz 5), in the Reginahaus, changes its spots: Wednesday to Friday it's exclusively gay and lesbian, Wednesday is film night, Thursday it's house and live-music parties, and on Saturday it's lesbians only. Hours are from 10 pm to 5 am Wednesday to Monday (closed Tuesday).

Together Again (Map 7, ☎ 26 34 69, Müllerstrasse 1), has live shows from 10 pm Sunday to Thursday, and a disco on Friday and Saturday nights. Hours are from 10 pm to 4 am daily.

NY NY (Map 7, ☎ 59 10 65, Sonnenstrasse 25), is a slick joint with a bar on the ground floor and a high-tech disco with a mixed crowd upstairs. Hours are from 11 pm to 4 am Sunday to Thursday, 11 pm to 5 am Friday and Saturday.

At the two level *Soul City (Map 7, ☎ 59 52 72, Maximiliansplatz 5)*, there's a bar and cafe on the 1st level, while the 2nd level has a disco and dance floor with a young, and extremely mixed, 20s crowd of gays and straights. It's a Munich institution, but some say it's getting a bit stale. It's open from 7.30 pm to 1 am Monday to Wednesday, from 10 pm to 5 am Thursday to Saturday and from 10 pm to 4 am Sunday.

Nil (Map 7, ☎ 26 55 45, Hans-Sachs-Strasse 2), is a cruise joint for all ages. Look for the sleek, wide Venetian blinds, which are generally shut to prying eyes. It's open from 3 pm to 3 am daily.

ROCK

Large rock concerts are staged at Olympiapark. Most other rock venues are also listed earlier in this chapter under Discos & Clubs, including *Muffathalle (Map 6, ☎ 45 88 75 00 00, Zellstrasse 4)*, which also holds jazz, salsa, African and world music and other concerts as well; *Nachtwerk Club (Map 5, ☎ 578 38 00, Landsberger Strasse 186)*; and *Babylon (Map 6, ☎ 450 69 20)* at Kunstpark Ost.

There are concerts held regularly at the *Schlachthof (Map 5, ☎ 765 44 8, Zenettistrasse 9)*, via U-Bahns to Poccistrasse, right in front of a huge abattoir complex. It also hosts a regular TV show called *Live aus dem Schlachthof* with Marc Owen, and comedy nights. It attracts a thirty-something crowd. There's a pleasant-looking beer garden out back, but the area smells of animal feed.

JAZZ

Munich is also a hot scene for jazz; *Jazzclub Unterfahrt (Map 6, ☎ 448 27 94, Einsteinstrasse 42)*, behind the Unions-Bräu restaurant near Max-Weber-Platz, is perhaps the best-known place in town. It has live music from 9 pm (except Monday), and jam sessions open to everyone on Sunday night. It's open from 6 pm to 1 am Sunday to Thursday, and from 6 pm to 3 am Friday and Saturday.

There are also daily concerts in Munich's smallest jazz club, *Mr B's (Map 5, ☎ 53 49 01, Herzog-Heinrich-Strasse 38)*, not far from Goetheplatz. It's open from 9 pm to 3 am Thursday to Sunday.

Go a bit more upmarket with jazz shows at *Night Club (Map 7, ☎ 212 09 94, Promenadeplatz 2–6)*, in Hotel Bayerischer Hof, which has regular jazz and other concerts including reggae, blues and funkabilly. Hours are from 8 pm to 3 am daily. An upscale spot for open-air concerts is in the *Brunnenhof der Residenz (Map 7, ☎ 29 68 36, Residenzstrasse 1)*, which hosts a broad range of concerts including rock, jazz, swing, classical and opera. There's a jazz brunch on Sunday at *Café am Beethovenplatz (Map 7, ☎ 54 40 43 48, Goethestrasse 51)*, at Hotel Pension Mariandl. Hours are from 9 am to 1 am daily.

Backstage Aluminium (Map 3, ☎ 18 33 30, Helmholtzstrasse 18), right at the S-Bahn Donnersberger Brücke station, is a very popular jazz venue, with lots of live performances. Hours are from 7 pm to 3 am Sunday to Thursday and from 9 pm to 5 am Friday and Saturday.

For something more informal try *Café Vogler (Map 7, ☎ 29 46 62, Rumfordstrasse 17)*, with live music several times a week (cover charge is usually DM5) and a happy hour from 7 to 8 pm. It's open from 7 pm to 1 am Sunday to Wednesday, and from 7 pm to 3 am Thursday to Sunday.

Nachtcafé (Map 7, Maximiliansplatz 5) has occasional big band and other jazz concerts. It's open from 9 pm to 6 am daily (see the earlier Pubs & Bars entry).

Munich's most infamous Dixieland venue (it also plays jazz) is the *Waldwirtschaft*

euro currency converter DM1 = €.51

ENTERTAINMENT

Grosshesselohe (Map 5, ☎ 79 50 88, Georg-Kalb-Strasse 3), which plays nightly to the consternation of local residents. Hours are 10 am to 1 am.

FOLK & TRADITIONAL MUSIC

Aside from the oompah bands in some beer halls and the occasional Bavarian music concert in the Nationaltheater, you'll find that the local folk music scene relies heavily on two imports: Irish and Country & Western.

Irish

Munich has a huge Irish expatriate population, and most of its haunts have live music at least once a week.

In Schwabing, two very cool underground cellar bars are *Günther Murphy's Irish Tavern (Map 4, ☎ 39 89 11, Nikolaistrasse 9a)*, and *Shamrock (Map 4, ☎ 33 10 81, Trautenwolfstrasse 6)*. Both are fun, loud, boisterous and crowded every night. Get ready to be jostled and come early if you want a table.

Also in Schwabing, *Shenanigans (Map 4, ☎ 34 21 12, Ungererstrasse 19)*, has karaoke. It's bigger and less crowded than most of the other places mentioned here, and often has live music. Hours are from 5 pm to 1 am daily (except for Tuesday, when it's open from 2 pm to 1 am).

A divey atmosphere prevails at *Paddy's (Map 4, ☎ 33 36 22, Feilitzschstrasse 17)*, in Schwabing, with locals and other interesting folks with interesting smokes. It's open from 11 am to 1 am Monday to Saturday and from 9 am to 1 am Sunday.

Country & Western

Rattlesnake Saloon (Map 3, ☎ 150 40 35, Schneeglöckchenstrasse 91), via the S-Bahn to Fasanerie-Nord, has live country & western or blues from 7 pm Thursday to Sunday.

Oklahoma Country Saloon (Map 5, ☎ 723 43 27, Schäftlarnstrasse 156), is reachable by the U-Bahn to Thalkirchen. It features bluegrass, rockabilly and country & western artists, evenings from 7 pm Tuesday to Saturday.

Both of these places, as you might guess, are 'wild-west style' bars.

CLASSICAL MUSIC, OPERA & BALLET

With its history of sponsorship from the royal courts, Munich has an expectedly vibrant classical music and performing arts scene. Tickets may be purchased at the individual venues or from the advance ticket offices around town; prices range from less than DM10 to almost DM400 per seat.

The Munich Philharmonic Orchestra performs at the *Philharmonic Hall* within the *Gasteig (Map 6, ☎ 48 09 80)*, which is Munich's premier classical-music venue (see the Theatre entry later in this chapter). James Levine is its mega-salaried director. It's also home to the Bayerischer Rundfunk's orchestra, which performs on Sunday throughout the year. You can buy tickets from the Glashalle on the ground floor, from 9 am to 6 pm weekdays and from 9 am to 2 pm Saturday. The Philharmonic season starts in September and runs till July.

The famous Bayerische Staatsoper (Bavarian State Opera) performs at the *Nationaltheater (Map 7, Max-Joseph-Platz 2)*, which is also the site of many cultural events. Tickets are available at regular outlets, at the theatre box office at Maximilianstrasse 11 (from 10 am to 6 pm Monday to Friday, to 1 pm Saturday), or by telephone ☎ 21 85 19 20. During the opera festival in July, you can also pick up cheap tickets (from DM15) at the box office at the last minute (provided, of course, that you're in suitable evening dress. If not, there are always live concert broadcasts via a huge television screen on the square out front.

There are occasional classical concerts at *Theater am Gärtnerplatz (Map 7, ☎ 201 67 67, Gärtnerplatz 3)*, via the U-Bahn to Fraunhoferstrasse, but this is more an opera and operetta venue (some operas are very good, some not).

Small classical concerts are often held in the lovely *Altes Residenztheater (Map 7)*, within the Residenz, in either the Herkulessaal for orchestral pieces, or the Max-Joseph-Saal for chamber music.

Deutsches Theater (Map 7, ☎ 55 23 44 44, Schwanthalerstrasse 13), also puts on the odd operetta and ballet (see also Theatre, later in this chapter).

In summer, concerts are also held in Schloss Schleissheim, Schloss Nymphenburg and in the church of the Schloss Blutenburg.

CINEMAS

Call or check any listings publications for show information; admission is between DM12 and DM15. Note that foreign films in mainstream cinemas are almost always dubbed (Westerns in German can be quite a hoot), and that popcorn in German cinemas is often sweet, not salty.

Two larger cinemas that show first-run (sort of) films daily, in English, are *Museum-Lichtspiele (Map 6, ☎ 48 24 03, Lilienstrasse 2)*, and the excellent *Cinema (Map 7, ☎ 55 52 55, Nymphenburger Strasse 31)*. Films are shown nightly in the *Filmmuseum (Map 7, ☎ 233 55 86)*, in the Stadtmuseum, usually in the original language, with subtitles.

Other cinemas that show English-language movies in their original form include the following:

Amerika Haus
   (Map 7, ☎ 552 53 70)
   Karolinenplatz 3
Atelier
   (Map 7, ☎ 59 19 18)
   Sonnenstrasse 12
Atlantis
   (Map 7, ☎ 55 51 52)
   Schwanthalerstrasse 2
Cinerama
   (Map 6, ☎ 49 91 88 19)
   Grafinger Strasse 6
British Council
   (Map 7, ☎ 22 33 26)
   Bruderstrasse 7
Neues Arena
   (Map 7, ☎ 26 72 97)
   Hans-Sachs-Strasse 7

THEATRE

Munich has a lively theatre scene and, in fact, has the largest number of small, independent theatre houses in the country.

The two biggest companies are the Staatsschauspiel and the Kammerspiele. The Staatsschauspiel performs at the *Residenztheater (Map 7)*, at the intimate rococo *Cuvilliés Theater* (also within the Residenz) and at *Marstall Theater*, at Max-Joseph-Platz 2, behind the Nationaltheater (Map 7).

Kammerspiele (Map 7, ☎ 23 33 70 00, Maximilianstrasse 26), stages large productions of serious dramas from German playwrights or works translated into German. (These are the folks who said that Shakespeare sounded 'better' in German.) You can reserve tickets from 10 am to 6 pm weekdays and from 10 am to 1 pm Saturday, but you have to collect the tickets at least two days before performances. There's also a smaller venue here called *Werkraum*, specialising in works by up-and-coming writers and directors.

Deutsches Theater (Map 7, ☎ 55 23 44 44, Schwanthalerstrasse 13), is Munich's answer to London's West End: touring road shows (usually light musicals) perform here. The season runs all year, with the occasional operetta and ballet thrown in for good measure.

Gasteig (Map 6, ☎ 48 09 80, Rosenheimer Strasse 5), via the S-Bahn to Rosenheimerplatz or tram No 18, is a major cultural centre, with theatre, classical music and other special events in five halls. Theatre is performed here in the Carl-Orff-Saal and on the far more intimate Black Box stage.

Other large venues include *Prinzregententheater (Map 6, ☎ 26 46 20, Prinzregentenplatz 12)*, via the U4, and *Neues Theater München (Map 6, ☎ 65 00 00, Entenbachstrasse 37)*, via the U-Bahns to Kolumbusplatz.

There's regular comedy in the chic *Komödie im Bayerischen Hof (Map 7, ☎ 29 28 10)*, Passage Promenadeplatz, via tram No 19, and at *Kleine Komödie am Max II (Map 7, ☎ 22 18 59, Maximilianstrasse 47)*, via the U-Bahn to Lehel.

Among the smaller alternative venues, *Theater Rechts der Isar (Map 6, ☎ 47 08 42 42, Einsteinstrasse 42)*, stages soul-searching

ENTERTAINMENT

works by Fassbinder and other modern (not just German) playwrights. It's in the Kulturzentrum Einstein, next door to the Jazzclub in Unterfahrt.

Children's Theatre
A big hit with kids is *Circus Krone (Map 3, ☎ 545 80 00, Marsstrasse 43)*, with performances from Christmas to April. For puppet theatre, try *Marionettenstudio Kleines Festspiel (Map 7, Neureutherstrasse 12)*, with its entrance on Arcisstrasse (free admission; take the U-Bahn to Josephsplatz), or *Das Münchner Marionettentheater (Map 7a, ☎ 26 57 12, Blumenstrasse 29a)*, via the U-Bahn to Sendlinger Tor. There are performances (including puppet shows and children's theatre) throughout the year at *Münchner Theater für Kinder (Map 7, ☎ 59 38 58, Dachauer Strasse 46)*; take the U-Bahn to Stiglmaierplatz.

SPECTATOR SPORTS
Munich has a decent (if not overwhelming) range of regular sporting events. Check the monthly listings in *München im...*, *Munich Found* or the daily press for what's on. Naturally, the Olympiapark hosts a huge number of large-scale events including football matches (soccer). Aside from the events listed below, competitions are held for athletics, shooting, canoeing, rowing, water and volleyball, inline skating, bicycling and other sports at the Olympiapark. Check the listings for details of dates and entrance

fees. You can pick up tickets at most of the advance ticket offices.

Football
Munich has two major-league football teams, FC Bayern München and TSV 1860 München, who usually play at the Olympiastadion (Olympic stadium at Olympiapark). Games start at either 3.30 or 6 pm, and are held on weekends (Map 3).

Horse Racing
Place your bets for the equine dashes at München-Riem stadium east of town (only in the warm summer months). Entry is DM9 for adults (DM15 on multiple-race days), and students with ID pay a flat DM6. In addition, trotting races are held several times a week at the München-Daglfing racetrack at Rennbahnstrasse 25. Tickets cost DM5 for adults and DM3 for students. Kids under 15 get in free, as do all women for the weekday races.

Tennis
The Olympiahalle at Olympiapark hosts a number of tennis tournaments, mostly second-string ones (but with good prize money) such as the Compaq Grand Slam in September.

Field Hockey
The German national leagues, for both men and women, battle it out in summer at several venues around the city.

Shopping

The first stop for most shoppers is the central pedestrian zone in Munich's Altstadt, comprising Kaufingerstrasse, Neuhauser Strasse and the area around Marienplatz. Here the mainstream department, clothing and shoe stores are located. Just to the north are the more elegant jewellery and garment shops in Maximilianstrasse and Brienner Strasse – the broad avenues are also good for seeing and being seen. Im Tal and other streets around Viktualienmarkt are packed with intriguing antique, decorating and speciality shops.

Outside the Altstadt, especially in Schwabing and Haidhausen, you'll find that the shops (and clientele) are decidedly more offbeat, with some very good deals. In Schwabing, Schellingstrasse, Türkenstrasse and Hohenzollernstrasse have quirky boutiques, galleries, bookstores and import shops; in Haidhausen, the area between Wiener Platz and Rosenheimer Strasse has some marvellous boutiques and hole-in-the-wall shops that make for great browsing.

Note that the end-of-season sales are held in late January *(Winterschlussverkauf)* and late July *(Sommerschlussverkauf)*; some smaller shops begin sales unofficially a few weeks earlier. The rest of the year, markdowns are generally pretty tame ('15% off' becomes a big deal).

Munich shopping hours are 9 am to 8 pm Monday to Friday and from 10 am to 4 pm Saturday. These times apply to the following unless otherwise stated.

WHAT TO BUY
Antiques
Munich has over 200 antique shops. You'll find top-end places in the central Brienner-strasse, Prannerstrasse and Hans-Sachs-Strasse; prices tend to be lower in Schwabing and around the Viktualienmarkt (such as in Im Tal). The flea and antiques markets (see Markets later in this chapter) are also good for bargains.

Even if you don't need an old Tottenham Hotspur football, a wooden propeller or a safari hat, it's worth taking a look in Squirrel (Map 7, ☎ 272 09 29) at Schellingstrasse 54. It also has English leather suitcases and bags, snuff boxes, ink wells and other dated items you'll never use. Hours are from 11 am to 6 pm Monday to Friday, and from 11 am to 1 pm Saturday.

Kunst-Oase (Map 4, ☎ 39 68 75), Hohenzollernstrasse 58, is more kitsch than the 'art' in its name implies, but it's still cute – old street lamps, sideboards with animal feet, and fancy mirrors. It's open from 9 am to 6.30 pm Monday to Friday, and from 9 am to 1 pm Saturday.

Century Box (Map 6, ☎ 48 16 62) at Steinstrasse 73 has lots of quaint stuff dating from 1900 to 1969. The advertising plaques (such as the one with the 'Persil' washing-powder lady) are especially good. Hours are from 10 am to 6 pm Monday to Friday, and from 10 am to 2 pm Saturday.

Books
Hugendubel is a heavyweight among German book retailers. If it's in German and in print, you'll probably find it here. The cultural, English-language and travel sections (plenty of Lonely Planet titles) are excellent. You can lounge on comfy sofas and read before you buy; some outlets also have a cafe. Locations are at Karlsplatz (Map 7a, ☎ 48 44 84), Marienplatz 22 (Map 7a, ☎ 238 90), Salvatorplatz 2 (Map 7a, ☎ 21 03 64) and Nymphenburger Strasse 168 (Map 3, ☎ 130 74 00). Opening hours are from 9.30 am to 8 pm Monday to Friday, and from 9.00 am to 4 pm Saturday.

Lehmkuhl (Map 4, ☎ 380 15 10), Leopoldstrasse 45 in Schwabing, is a well-stocked and renowned Munich bookshop that's strong on history and culture and nice for browsing. It also has some novels and guidebooks in English. Hours are from 9 am to 6.30 pm weekdays, and from 9 am to 2 pm Saturday.

Booox (Map 7, ☎ 82 16 66), Schellingstrasse 34, is a fun place with regular special offers (such as half-price or better for paperbacks) from the big German publishers. Novels in English are often a bargain. It's open from 10 am to 6 pm weekdays, and from 10 am to 2 pm Saturday.

Buchhandlung am Gasteig (Map 6, ☎ 45 87 99 09), Rosenheimer Strasse 12, is a cramped but cosy general bookshop with very helpful staff. If they don't have it, they'll tell you who does. Hours are 9.30 am to 6 pm weekdays and 9.30 am to 2 pm Saturday.

English-Language Bookshops Brace yourself: new books in English are priced at least one-third higher in Germany than in Anglo-Saxon countries, and mark-downs are legally restricted.

The wacky Anglia English Bookshop (Map 7, ☎ 28 36 42), Schellingstrasse 3 in Schwabing, claims to be the best-stocked English bookshop in Germany. It has bestsellers, children's titles, fiction and non-fiction, videos, you name it – but things can be hard to find. Better organised is Words' Worth Booksellers (Map 7, ☎ 280 91 41) in the pretty courtyard at Schellingstrasse 21a, with a nice National Trust section. Both shops are open from 9 am to 6.30 pm weekdays, and from 10 am to 2 pm Saturday.

Sussmann International Presse (Map 7, ☎ 55 11 70), in the Hauptbahnhof across from track 24, is handy but expensive. It has titles in English and French, newspapers, magazines and Calvin & Hobbes collections (check its 'bargain' basket for special offers). It's open from 7 am to 10.45 pm daily, and there's another in the Ostbahnhof (☎ 48 90 83 61).

EurAide (Map 7, ☎ 59 38 89) in the Hauptbahnhof (see Tourist Offices in the Facts for the Visitor chapter) has a small selection of well-thumbed English-language paperbacks for a DM2 'donation'.

Travel The best travel bookshop in town is Geobuch (Map 7, ☎ 26 50 30), opposite Viktualienmarkt at Rosental 6, with a dizzying array of maps, guidebooks and other travel literature (mostly in German). Staff are knowledgeable but the place can get *very*

crowded. It's open 10 am to 7 pm weekdays and from 10 am to 4 pm Saturday.

Hugendubel has a pretty good travel section of its own (see the earlier entry), with a huge map selection. Därr's Travelshop (Map 7, ☎ 28 20 32) at Theresienstrasse 66, is another good source of maps and atlases (see also Camping & Outdoor Gear later in this chapter).

Gay Max&Milian (Map 7, ☎ 260 33 20), at Ickstattstrasse 2 near Frauhoferstrasse U-bahn, is the best established gay and lesbian bookshop in Munich. It also has titles in English and French. Hours are 10.30 am to 2 pm and 3.30 to 8 pm weekdays, and from 11 am to 4 pm Saturday.

You might also try the smaller Apacik & Schell (☎ 62 42 04 04), Ohlmüllerstrasse 18 (enter from Entenbachstrasse). It's open from 9.15 am to 1.30 pm and from 2.30 to 6.30 pm weekdays (to 6 pm Thursday); and from 9.15 am to 1 pm Saturday.

Clothing

Traditional Loden-Frey (Map 7, ☎ 21 03 90), a specialist department store at Maffeistrasse 5–7, stocks a wide range of Bavarian wear. Expect to pay at least DM400 for a good leather jacket, Lederhosen or a women's Dirndl dress, but it'll last forever. Kids will enjoy the slide into their basement section. There's a cheaper Loden-Frey Discount in the north of town (see Factory Outlets later in this chapter). Both are open 10 am to 7 pm weekdays and 10 am to 4 pm Saturday.

Wallach (Map 7, ☎ 22 08 71), Residenzstrasse 3 near the opera house, has traditional dress (especially nice women's stuff with embroidery) but also porcelain mugs, bedclothes and other household goods. It's open from 10.30 am to 6 pm weekdays (till 8 pm Thursday) and from 10.30 am till 4 pm Saturday.

For second-hand clothes, try the wonderfully named Holareidulijö (Map 7, ☎ 271 77 45), Schellingstrasse 81, which carries used Lederhosen and other folkwear. The stuff is in good condition and worth the asking price (though it's still not dirt cheap).

Opening hours are 10 am to 7 pm weekdays and from 10 am to 4 pm Saturday.

Designer Blu Cotton (Map 3, ☎ 271 38 85), Hohenzollernstrasse 65, has fashionable Italian styles for men and women, and it's mostly affordable. You'll also find chic hats, scarves and handbags (including the little ones for male 'continentals'). Hours are 10 am to 7 pm Monday to Wednesday, 10 am to 8 pm Thursday and Friday, and 10 am to 4 pm Saturday.

Another good tip is Designer Discount (Map 3, ☎ 12 78 92 45), tucked away in the courtyard at Birkerstrasse 6 in Haidhausen. There's a huge range of marked-down Italian designer clothing for both sexes. Hours are from 11 am to 7 pm Monday, Wednesday and Friday, 11 am to 8 pm Tuesday and Thursday and 10 am to 4 pm Saturday.

For women, Culta Fashion (Map 7, ☎ 22 12 88), Briennerstrasse 11, offers some high-end labels, from Gucci to Jil Sander, at reasonable prices. New lines are delivered once a month, and old ones are marked down.

Bogner (Map 7, ☎ 290 70 40), Residenzstrasse 15, is a label found on evening dresses and tight-fitting ski garments from Aspen to the Zugspitze. Smart buyers take the S-Bahn to the factory outlet (see Factory Outlets later in this chapter).

Avant-gardists will love Susanne Bommer (Map 6, ☎ 489 22 68) at Steinstrasse 19 in Haidhausen. The speciality here is transparent clothing (capes, wrap-around blouses etc) for the cashed-up female. Just browsing is fun. It's open 10 am to 7 pm weekdays and 10 am to 3 pm Saturday.

Pedestrian-zone options include Hirmer (Map 7, ☎ 23 68 30), Kaufingerstrasse 22, a good, five floor clothing store for men; Hallhuber (Map 7, ☎ 26 02 14 50), Kaufinger Strasse 9, for 'young' fashion at moderate prices (see also Factory Outlets later in this chapter); and Ludwig Beck (see Department Stores under Where to Shop).

Clubwear Rag Republic (Map 4, ☎ 33 35 55), Marktstrasse 1 in Schwabing, has trendoid gear at OK prices – jeans, T-shirts, sweaters and jackets with zips in odd places. It's open from 11 am to 8 pm weekdays, and from 10.30 am to 4 pm Saturday.

Zannantonio (Map 4, ☎ 38 68 18), Ungererstrasse 65, makes dresses exclusively from latex (but they're lined with comfy silk). It's quality work, with price tags to match. Hours are from 1 to 6 pm weekdays (closed Saturday).

Leather One of Munich's best leather shops (the conventional kind) is Leder Wirkes (Map 4, ☎ 359 93 50), Taunusstrasse 51, in the northern suburb of Milbertshofen. Wild boar, deer or cow, suit yourself – there are new and second-hand jackets, skirts and trousers in all price categories. It's open from 10 am to 7 pm Monday to Wednesday, from 10 am to 8 pm Thursday and Friday and from 9 am to 4 pm Saturday.

Leder Erdmann (Map 6, ☎ 48 14 20), Rosenheimer Strasse 6, is famous for its motorcycle jackets, but also makes nice wallets and gloves. It's open 9 am to 6.30 pm weekdays and 9 am to 1 pm Saturday.

Shoes If you absolutely *must* buy a pair of Birkenstocks, try Schuh Seibel (Map 7, ☎ 55 58 92), Landwehrstrasse 2. It's got a huge selection of shoes and sandals, and will even ship them home. Tretter (☎ 51 99 21 55), Neuhauser Strasse 2, has some beautiful Italian footwear, solid German lines and a few bargains if you look hard.

Eduard Meier (Map 7, ☎ 22 00 44), Residenzstrasse 22, is Germany's oldest shoe shop. It's expensive but is first-class, and a tempting place during the season sales. Hours are 10 am to 8 pm weekdays and from 10 am to 4 pm Saturday.

Cars & Bicycles

You don't see very many old cars on German roads. That implies a huge turnover on the used-auto market, and the classified sections in newspapers prove it. In Munich, the best sources are *Abendzeitung*; *Süddeutsche Zeitung*; and *Kurz & Fündig*, a free small-ads paper that comes out Tuesday and Friday. Car prices start from DM1500, but for a Golf, Corsa or Uno in reasonable shape, expect to pay from DM3000 to DM5000. As always you'll need to know something about cars or risk landing a lemon.

Check that the vehicle has a valid TÜV (Technischer Überwachungs-Verein) certificate of roadworthiness; most used car ads will say when it expires. You should also see a little round TÜV seal on the number plates with the month of expiry (*not* the one marked 'ASU', which is for emissions control).

Kurz & Fündig is also good for used bicycles; basic models start at around DM110 and three-speed touring bikes at about DM225. Muskelkater (Map 3, ☎ 308 97 27), Belgradstrasse 19 in Schwabing, has a wide selection of well-serviced second-hand bikes, which, however, are more expensive than those in the papers. Expect to pay from DM275 for a solid three-speed bike.

Eccentric & Specialty

The Tiger Store (Map 6, ☎ 489 11 47), Lilienstrasse 7, pays homage to the big cats: rugs, lampshades, jackets, even bikinis bear fiery orange stripes. The gag is, it's all imitation fur. Part of the proceeds go to the World Wildlife Fund. It's open 3 to 7 pm weekdays and from 11 am to 4 pm Saturday.

Gutes aus Klöstern (Map 6, ☎ 21 93 93 21), Tattenbachstrasse 20 in Lehel, proves that religion is good business. You'll find shoe polish, noodles, mouthwash and other blessed products from monasteries and convents around the country. Opening times are from 10 am to 6 pm weekdays and from 10 am to 1.30 pm Saturday.

Linkshänderladen (Map 7a, ☎ 26 86 14), Sendlinger Strasse 17 in the Asampassage, sells everything for lefties (scissors, knives, can-openers etc). It's open from 10 am to 1.30 pm and 2.30 to 6 pm weekdays, from 10.30 am to 2 pm Saturday.

Bottles (Map 7a, ☎ 26 31 35), Josephspitalstrasse 6, has drinking glasses, preserving jars, and wines – not to mention hundreds upon hundreds of, you guessed it, bottles. It's open 10 am to 7 pm weekdays and from 10 am to 4 pm Saturday.

On the other hand, Die Zahnbürste (Map 7a, ☎ 29 16 16 77), Frauenstrasse 17, carries nothing but toothbrushes and dental accessories. Hours are 10 am to 6 pm weekdays, and from 10 am to 2 pm Saturday.

Green Hope (Map 7, ☎ 260 68 09), Jahnstrasse 42, is a hemp textile and clothing store. You can even buy seeds with a How-to-Grow book, but note that it's illegal to smoke your harvest in Germany. Hours are from 2 to 6 pm Tuesday to Friday and from 11 am to 2 pm Saturday.

Spanisches Fruchthaus (Map 7a, ☎ 260 65 97), Rindermarkt 10, has tonnes of exotic dried fruits and other Mediterranean treats from around DM2 per 100g. One look in the window and you're hooked. It's open 10 am to 6.30 pm weekdays and from 10 am to 1 pm Saturday.

Home Goods & Furnishings

Ali Baba (Map 6, ☎ 489 11 68), Johannisplatz 13, sells furniture, lamps and home accessories in Moroccan and colonial style. The briar-wood items (such as jewellery boxes) are good value. Hours are 10 am to 6.30 pm weekdays and from 10 am to 1 pm Saturday.

Who's Perfect (Map 4, ☎ 36 14 70), Neusser Strasse 9 in north Schwabing, has an enormous showroom of designer furniture with minor flaws (most you can't see) and going cheap. Call the shop or check the papers for sales, which take place only 10 days a month.

Kochgut (Map 6, ☎ 470 28 06), Schlossstrasse 5, is a well-stocked kitchen shop with lots of high-quality (and hi-tech) cooking and dining accoutrements. That Porsche pepper mill will go down well at home. It's open 10 am to 6.30 pm weekdays and 10 am to 2 pm Saturday.

Jewellery

Cada (Map 7a, ☎ 29 60 14), Maximilianstrasse 13, is known for its designer jewellery made of cool matte gold, but it's pricey. Hours are from 10 am to 6 pm weekdays, from 10 am to 1 pm Saturday.

Lafayette (Map 6, ☎ 448 12 22), Weissenburger Strasse 21, is a cross between a gallery and jewellery shop, its speciality being amazingly detailed silver pins, earrings and necklaces. Hours are from 3 to 6 pm Monday, from 10 am to 1 pm and 3 to 6 pm Tuesday to Friday, and from 10 am to noon Saturday.

Music

You have to wonder how Zweitausendeins (Map 7, ☎ 272 42 78), Türkenstrasse 67, makes money (eg 100 classical music CDs for DM99 and other great offers). There's also cut-rate jazz, pop and rock – but never the latest releases. Hours are 9.30 am to 7 pm weekdays and from 10 am to 4 pm Saturday.

The biggest selection in town is at World of Music (WOM; Map 7a, ☎ 235 05 70), Kaufingerstrasse 15. You can listen on one of 500-odd headphones before you buy; few bargains are to be had, except in the 'Nice Price' sections (DM10 or less for golden oldies).

Ludwig Beck on Marienplatz has an excellent classical and jazz CD section (see Department Stores later in this chapter).

CD Börse (Map 7a, ☎ 22 25 40), Aventinstrasse 10, is a great place to pick up used CDs (or unload your own for a little cash). Good thing they don't scratch easily. It's open from noon to 6.30 pm weekdays, from 10 am to 2 pm Saturday.

Porcelain & Gifts

Staatliche Porzellan-Manufaktur (Map 3, ☎ 179 19 70) at Schloss Nymphenburg is *the* place to buy that royal tea service or Bavarian lion for the den. You'll need a princely income too (simple glazed teacups are from about DM150). Hours are from 8.30 am to 5 pm weekdays, with a half-hour break at noon.

Bayerische Kunstgewerbeverein (Bavarian Artisans' Association), Pacellistrasse 6, runs a craft shop in the Galerie für angewandte Kunst (see Art Galleries later in this chapter). It has an impressive selection of jewellery, glass, ceramics and wood carvings, at museum-shop prices.

Glashaus (Map 7a, ☎ 26 31 35), Josephspitalstrasse 1, has legions of household breakables and some very good buys. It's open from 10 am to 7 pm weekdays and from 10 am to 2 pm Saturday.

Amid its beer-mug candles, Bavarian flags and cowbells, I-Düpferl (Map 7a, ☎ 291 95 70), Im Tal 31 near the Isartor, has some nice gifts and souvenirs at decent prices. The bargain basement is always worth wading through.

Beer steins and *Mass* glasses are available at all department stores (see Department Stores later in this chapter), as well as from the beer halls themselves.

Toys

Obletter Spielwaren (Map 7a, ☎ 231 86 01), Karlplatz 11, has five floors stuffed with fine playthings, including the handpainted wooden items for which Germany is famous. Look out for Märklin model trains and the beautiful Steiff teddy bears, which cost a small fortune but appreciate in value over time. It's open from 9 am to 7.30 pm weekdays and from 9 am to 4 pm Saturday.

Spiel Art (Map 7, ☎ 260 65 97), Müllerstrasse 39, is almost an antiques store. Here you'll find toys from all eras, from wind-up tin cars to Barbie dolls. Hours are 10 am to 6 pm weekdays and from 9.30 am to 1 pm Saturday.

Camping & Outdoor Gear

Sport Scheck (Map 7a, ☎ 216 60), at Sendlinger Strasse 6, has multiple floors of everything imaginable for the adventurer, from simple camping equipment to expedition wear, plus an excellent book section. There's a discount Sport Scheck at the Ostbahnhof, selling discontinued merchandise.

Sport Schuster (Map 7a, ☎ 23 70 70), nearby at Rosenstrasse 1–5, is a slightly more conservative version of Sport Scheck, with a good mountain-climbing and hiking section.

Därr's Travelshop (see the Travel entry under Books earlier in this chapter) at Theresienstrasse 66 sells specialist bits and pieces for expeditions to the corners of the earth. You'll find not only freeze-dried eggs Benedict but also the usual sleeping bags, backpacks and outdoor clothing. It's open 10 am to 6 pm weekdays and from 9.30 am to 4 pm Saturday.

Sport Köpf (Map 7a, ☎ 260 30 54), Sendlinger-Tor-Platz 6, is especially good for skis, snowboards and ski outfits, and has very friendly service. Hours are 9.30 am to 7 pm weekdays and from 9.30 am to 4 pm Saturday.

Photo Supplies

Germany makes some of the world's finest optical goods (Leica, Hasselblad, Zeiss), although you'll be pressed to find a bargain.

Sauter Photographic (Map 7, ☎ 551 50 40), Sonnenstrasse 2 off Sendlinger-Tor-Platz, has a fantastic selection of new and used cameras, lenses and flash equipment. Check out the rotating carousels in the shop window for the latest offerings. It's open from 9.30 am to 7 pm weekdays, from 9 am to 4 pm Saturday.

Foto Reparatur Schnell Service (Map 7, ☎ 59 50 72), Landwehrstrasse 12, is run by a congenial Frenchman who has some very good second-hand stuff (eg as-new cameras for well below list price). Hours are 10 am to 1 pm and 2 to 6 pm weekdays, and from noon to 2 pm Saturday.

Wine

Jacques Weindepot (Map 4, ☎ 36 35 30), Leopoldstrasse 130, is Germany's largest chain of wine stores. It has a huge range of reasonably-priced French and Italian vintages, but also interesting 'New World' wines. You can sample everything (they'll open up bottles just for you) with a slice of baguette. It's open 4 pm to 6.30 pm Tuesday to Thursday, from 2 to 6.30 pm Friday and from 10 am to 2 pm Saturday.

Garibaldi (Map 7, ☎ 272 09 06), Schellingstrasse 60, carries a wide range of Italian wines, grappas and other flammable delights, priced from cheap to ridiculous. Hours are 9.30 am to 6.30 pm weekdays and from 9.30 am to 2 pm Saturday.

The cellars of Geisel's Vinothek (Map 7, ☎ 55 13 71 40), Schützenstrasse 11 next to the Hotel Excelsior by the Hauptbahnhof, has a wide selection of German, Austrian, French and Italian wines. It's a pretty swanky place, but you are welcome to try a glass at the restaurant bar before investing more. The shop is open from 10 am to 1 am daily.

WHERE TO SHOP
Art Galleries

Munich has nearly 300 art galleries, with the greatest concentration in the Altstadt and Schwabing. They're located in lovely old courtyards, sprawling villas and showrooms in the swanky shopping districts, but also in former factories and WWII bunkers. A few places that routinely sell artwork are listed here; check in the listing section of *Munich Found*, *In München* or *München im...* to see what's on.

In early September, a group of 65 Munich galleries holds a free event called 'Art Weekend', with guided tours of their collections. There's also a free bus service between venues. For details, call ☎ 29 20 15 a few weeks before the event.

Galerie Dany Keller (Map 7, ☎ 22 61 32), Buttermelcherstrasse 11, specialises in works by young African and Munich artists. Open from 2 to 6 pm Tuesday to Friday, and 11 am to 2 pm Saturday.

Galerie für angewandte Kunst (Map 7, ☎ 290 14 70), Pacellistrasse 6, is a huge state-run gallery and showcase for local artists. The crafts sold in the shop are pretty good, too. Open from 10 am to 6.30 pm weekdays and 10 am to 4 pm Saturday.

Galerie Helmut Leger (Map 4, ☎ 39 39 30), Herzogstrasse 41, shows paintings and isn't averse to the experimental. Open from 2 to 6 pm Tuesday to Friday and noon to 4 pm Saturday.

Galerie Karin Sachs (Map 7, ☎ 201 12 50), Buttermelcherstrasse 16, features the works of abstract 'new media' and computer artists. Open from 2 to 6 pm Tuesday to Friday and 11 am to 2 pm Saturday.

Galerie Klewan (Map 7, ☎ 202 16 06), Klenzestrasse 23, has rotating exhibits of modern masters (eg Giacometti), photography and, if you believe the critics, kitsch. Open from 2 to 6 pm Tuesday to Friday and 11 am to 3 pm Saturday.

Galerie der Künstler (Map 7, ☎ 22 04 63), Maximilianstrasse 42, features quality work by local professionals and up-and-comers from the Munich Art Academy. Open from 11 am to 6 pm Tuesday to Sunday.

Kunstverein (Map 7, ☎ 22 11 52), Galeriestrasse 4, is dedicated to the contemporary European avant-garde, and has a broader appeal than you might think. Open from 11 am to 6 pm Tuesday to Sunday.

Right: Horses, harmonies and high-flyers

Top: Theresienwiese at night
Centre: Collection of steins
Bottom: Legs in Lederhosen

JEREMY GRAY

DAVID PEEVERS

JEREMY GRAY

Produzentengalerie (Map 6, ☎ 228 38 40), Adelgundenstrasse 6, is run by Munich artists who display their own work. You'll find some good bargains. Every other month they rent the place out to other exhibitors, so phone for details. Open from 2 to 7 pm Wednesday to Friday and 11 am to 2 pm Saturday.

Seidlvilla (Map 4, ☎ 33 31 39), Nikolaiplatz 1b, is a beautiful old city-owned villa that exhibits modern painting and photography, but also some very conventional stuff. Open from 2 to 8 pm daily.

Verein für Originalradierung (Map 7, ☎ 28 08 84), Ludwigstrasse 7, presents modern graphic art – sketches, photos, screen prints and more. Open from 3 pm to 6.30 pm Thursday and Friday.

Department Stores

Ludwig Beck A Munich institution since 1861, Ludwig Beck (Map 7, ☎ 23 69 10), Marienplatz 11, is pretty pricey between season sales but its six floors are still great for a browse: apart from men's and women's clothing, there's ceramics, an excellent CD shop, kitchenware, cosmetics, a Thai restaurant, a coffee bar and a branch of Heinemann's, which makes some of Germany's finest filled chocolates. The window decorations are stunning at Christmas time. It's open from 9.30 am to 6.30 pm weekdays and from 9 am to 2 pm Saturday.

Karstadt This is Munich's nicest all-round emporium, and a cut above its chief rival, Kaufhof, in tone and variety. The Karstadt Haus Oberpollinger am Dom (Map 7, ☎ 29 02 30), Neuhauserstrasse 18, carries kitchen appliances, books and household furnishings, while the Karstadt am Karlstor (Map 7, ☎ 29 02 30) has mostly clothing, cosmetics and fabrics. The Oberpollinger branch also has an Atlas Reisen travel agency and an Internet-access shop called Cyberb@r (see Post & Communications in the Facts for the Visitor chapter).

Others Germany's largest department store chain, Kaufhof has branches on Marienplatz (Map 7, ☎ 23 18 51) and Karlsplatz 2 (Map 7, ☎ 512 50). You'll probably end up here sometime to buy an everyday item, but it's really just another big department store.

One of the few things Kaufhof has that Karstadt doesn't is a well-stocked but expensive supermarket (in the basement).

Hertie (Map 7, ☎ 551 20), at Bahnhofplatz 7, is a sprawling place that extends almost from the train station to Karlsplatz. Owned by Karstadt but slightly more downmarket, Hertie has the grocery store that Karstadt lacks, and another Cyberb@r upstairs. The basement Markthallen, run by Käfer's delicatessen, sells some tasty snacks.

Factory Outlets

Some of these places are out of the way, but it's worth the trip; you can get stunning reductions at most outlets.

Loden-Frey Discount (Map 3, ☎ 149 00 80), at Triebstrasse 36–38, sells its famous loden jackets, trousers and other garments for 20–40% off normal price, with mostly unseen flaws. It's open from 9.30 am to 6 pm Tuesday to Friday, and from 9 am to 2 pm Saturday. Take the U3 to Olympia Zentrum, and then bus No 41 to Triebstrasse.

Bogner Extra (☎ 903 75 64), Poinger Strasse 2 in Heimstetten, stocks lots of discontinued women's clothing and current styles with minor flaws. Prices are often 50% off. The outlet also has an Etienne Aigner shop with gorgeous handbags, belts and leather goods for 20 to 30% below list price. It's open from 10 am to 6 pm Monday, Wednesday and Friday, and from 10 am to 2pm Saturday. Take the S6 to Heimstetten – it's about 150m from the S-Bahn station.

Hallhuber (Map 4, ☎ 359 70 27), Taunusstrasse 49, has jeans, stretch trousers, blazers and other 'leftovers' from labels such as Armani, Joop and Chevignon for up to 50% off. It's open from noon to 6.30 pm Monday and Tuesday, from noon to 8 pm Wednesday to Friday and from 10 am to 4 pm Saturday. Take the U2 to Frankfurter Ring.

Markets

Flea & Antique Markets The Auer Dult, a huge flea market on Mariahilfplatz in Au, has great buys and takes place three times a year. The bargains come in droves for china, household goods and all kinds of lurid objects from old postcards to beat-up portraits of Ludwig II. As for antiques, the vendors pretty much know when they're onto something valuable, so true bargains are rare. Look out for 'Der Billige Jakob', who sells off big packets of combs, brushes and other items in a thick Franconian dialect for next to nothing. There are also carnival rides, food stands and lots and lots of beer. The Mai Dult takes place at the end of April, the Jakobi Dult in late July and the Herbst Dult two weeks after Oktoberfest.

Other flea markets that take place regularly include:

Flohmarkt des Bayerischen Roten Kreuzes, Arnulfstrasse 31. Tables are set up in a former freight depot west of the Hauptbahnhof. Go on Saturday, when most vendors show up and the relation of treasure-to-junk rises sharply. Proceeds go to the Bavarian Red Cross. It's on from 7 am to 5 pm every Thursday, Friday and Saturday (Map 3).

Floh- und Antikmarkt at Kunstpark Ost, Grafinger Strasse 6. Here you'll find some neat artwork mixed in with the usual hopeless knick-knacks. Many sellers are amateurs, so you ought to have some luck bargaining. In summer, it's on every Friday from 9 am to 8 pm and from 7 am to 6 pm Saturday; it closes two hours earlier in winter. Take any S-Bahn to the Ostbahnhof (Map 6).

Antiquitäten- und Raritätenmarkt, Neusser Strasse 21. Prices tend to be a bit higher here, as only 'genuine' antiques and rarities are supposed to be on offer (ha-ha). But you'll find some nice furniture, lamps and books. It's open from 10 am to 5 pm Friday and Saturday. Take the U6 to Alte Heide. (Map 4)

Flohmarkt in the Hopfendolde pub, Feilitzstrasse 17, is a cosy little affair with just 20 stalls. It's held from 9 am to 3 pm every Sunday. Take the U3 or U6 to Münchner Freiheit (Map 4).

Flohmarkt Riem, at the Neue Messe (New Fairgrounds), is a sprawling event on the grounds of the old airport, with everything from furniture to used spark plugs (still good, you understand). Profits go to charity. It's held from 6 am to 4 pm Friday and Saturday. Take the S6 to Riem and then bus No 91 to Flohmarkt Riem.

Produce Markets You can't beat the Viktualienmarkt (Map 7) for variety of fresh and exotic vegetables, fruits, meats, fish, spices,

breads and other mouth-watering items. Given the hordes of tourists it's a wonder that this outdoor market retains some of its 150-year-old traditions. Try testing a tomato for freshness, which should unleash a torrent of earthy dialect from one of the legendary *Marktfrauen*. Sure, it's expensive, but where else would you find that Dijon hen or Mexican chili pepper? The tourist office has a free pamphlet, *Viktualienmarkteinkaufsführer*, showing the location of the permanent stands; also see the Self-Catering section in the Places to Eat chapter. It's open from 7.30 am to 6 pm weekdays, and from 7.30 am to 1 pm Saturday.

The Elisabethmarkt at Schwabing's Elisabethplatz is a smaller version of the Viktualienmarkt, but prices are mercifully lower. Stands tend to be more seasonal (especially for fruits and vegetables), but you'll also find a lovely assortment of cheese, wine and sausage. It's on from 7 am to noon weekdays, and from 7 am to 1 pm Saturday.

Another small but charming daily market is at Wiener Platz, north-east of the Isartor, selling cheese, vegetables, fish, flowers and meat. It's held from 7 am to 6 pm weekdays, and from 7 am to 1 pm Saturday.

Known to locals as 'Munich's stomach', the wholesale Grossmarkthalle in Thalkirchen attracts lorries from throughout Bavaria and as far afield as northern Italy to haul away tonnes of meats, vegetables and fruit at the crack of dawn. Hordes of Munich restaurateurs also buy here but *you* won't be able to; you might also have to pay a small fee just to browse. It's open from 5 to 10.30 am Monday to Saturday. Take the U3 to Fürstenried West.

Weekly markets include Neuhausen at Rotkreuzplatz, from 1 to 6 pm every Thursday; Haidhausen at Weissenburger Platz from 8 am to 6 pm Tuesday; and Johanneskirchen's at Fritz-Meyer-Weg, from 1 to 6 pm Tuesday and Friday. Check the daily newspapers for times and locations of other markets.

Christkindlmarkt This traditional market, second only to Nuremberg's in fame, is detested by the locals because it blocks

Marienplatz for four weeks before Christmas and attracts legions of tourists. Predictably, you'll find heaps of kitsch on the stands, but after a cup of *Glühwein* (mulled wine) it all starts to look better. You *will* find some quality nativity scenes, children's toys and carved figures, but they're often expensive; smaller markets such as those on Rotkreuzplatz in Neuhausen or on Münchener Freiheit in Schwabing are cheaper and less touristy. The Christkindlmarkt is open from 9 am to 7.30 pm Monday to Satürday (to 8.30 pm Thursday), and from 10 am to 7.30 pm Sunday.

Excursions

DACHAU

'The way to freedom is to follow one's orders; exhibit honesty, orderliness, cleanliness, sobriety, truthfulness, the ability to sacrifice and love of the Fatherland'

Inscription from the roof of the concentration camp at Dachau

Dachau was the very first Nazi concentration camp, built by Heinrich Himmler in March 1933. It 'processed' more than 200,000 prisoners, and 31,531 were reported killed here. In 1933 the Jewish population in Munich numbered 10,000. Only 200 survived the war.

The camp is now one of the most popular day trips from Munich, though the experience can be so disturbing that we don't recommend it for children under age 12.

Just outside the main exhibition hall is a monument, inscribed in English, French, Yiddish, German and Russian, that reads 'Never Again'. Nearby are large stakes from which prisoners were hanged, sometimes for days, with their hands shackled behind their backs.

Inside the main hall, as you enter, is a large map showing camp locations throughout Germany and Central Europe. Indicators show which were the extermination camps. The exhibit inside shows photographs and models of the camp, its officers and prisoners and of horrifying 'scientific experiments' carried out by Nazi doctors. There's also a whipping block; a chart showing the system for prisoner identification by category (Jews, homosexuals, Jehovah's Witnesses, Poles, Romas and other 'asocial' types); documents relating to the camp and the persecution of 'degenerate' authors banned by the party; and exhibits on the rise of the Nazi party and the establishment of the camp system.

Also on the grounds are reconstructed bunkers, an extermination gas chamber disguised as showers, and a (never used) crematorium. Outside the gas chamber building is a statue to 'honour the dead and warn the living' and a Russian Orthodox chapel. Nearby are churches and a Jewish memorial, erected after WWII.

Guided tours in English are essential if you don't understand German, and a good idea even if you do. If you take the tour, consider buying a copy of the catalogue, which has detailed descriptions of all the exhibits in the museum as well as a written history. The DM25 goes directly to the Survivors Association of Dachau. An English-language documentary is shown at 11.30 am and 3.30 pm (and often at 2 pm). The camp is open from 9 am to 5 pm every day except Monday, and admission is free. Expect to spend two to three hours here.

Organised Tours Dachauer Forum and Action Reconciliation (☎ 08131-710 07) runs free two-hour tours in English at 12.30 pm on Saturday and Sunday (daily from June through August). They are excellent and informative; the bigger the group the longer the tour.

Beer Garden Food and drink may be the last thing on your mind after seeing the concentration camp. If not, take bus Nos 704 or 705 from Dachau train station to the Rathaus (a five minute ride, or a 15 minute walk), and follow the signs towards the Schloss, which has a pleasant beer garden next door. The slightly run-down ***Brauerei Schlossberg Dachau*** (☎ 08131-725 53), Schlossstrasse 8, charges DM9.50 for a *Mass* of house brew and cooks up hearty German fare (eg pork roast for DM12).

Getting There & Away

The S2 to Dachau leaves Munich Hauptbahnhof three times an hour at 16, 36 and 56 minutes past. The trip takes 19 minutes and requires a two-zone ticket (DM7.20, or four strips of a Streifenkarte), including the bus connection.

Change for local buses in front of the Dachau train station; bus No 726 (from

Monday to Saturday) and bus No 724 (on Sunday and holidays) are timed to leave the station about 10 minutes after the train arrives. Show your stamped ticket to the driver. The driver will announce the stop (KZ-Gedenkstätte); then follow the crowds – it's about a five minute walk from the bus stop to the entrance of the camp. Return buses leave from near the camp car park every 20 minutes. By car, follow Dachauer Strasse straight out to Dachau and follow the KZ-Gedenkstätte signs. Parking is free.

SCHLEISSHEIM
☎ 089 • pop 11,500

Just north of Munich, the suburb of Schleissheim is home to several castles that compete with anything in the heart of the city.

Neues Schloss Schleissheim (☎ 315 87 20), in Oberschleissheim, is a spectacular castle, built under the orders of Emperor Max Joseph in 1701, and modelled after Versailles. Inside, above the staircase, you'll see the vaulted ceiling, with frescoes by Cosmas Damian Asam.

To get there take the S1 in the direction of Freising to Oberschleissheim, then bus No 292, which runs weekdays only. The grounds are equally impressive (bring a picnic). It's open from 10 am to 12.30 pm and 1.30 to 5 pm Tuesday to Sunday (DM2/1.50).

Nearby, the **Altes Schloss Schleissheim** (☎ 315 52 72) was a splendid Renaissance palace completed in the 17th century for Duke Maximilan. It was obliterated in WWII, and the reconstructed rump you see today houses a museum of religion which includes a huge selection of cribs and Easter eggs from across the globe (DM5/3, free on Sunday).

The third castle here, on the grounds of Altes Schloss park, is **Schloss Lustheim** (☎ 315 87 20). It contains amazing frescoes and a stunning baroque interior, and is now home to the **Meissner Porzellan Sammlung** – said to be the largest collection of Meissen chinaware in Germany. It's open the same hours as Neues Schloss Schleissheim (DM3/2). A combination ticket to both the Neues Schloss Schleissheim and Schloss Lustheim costs DM4/2.50.

Flugwerft Schleissheim

After Germany's defeat in WWI, the maximum power of German aircraft was heavily restricted. German engineers began a 'ground-up' approach to aerodynamics in an effort to increase performance and speed, and in doing so revolutionised the design of modern aircraft.

This museum (☎ 315 71 40), a 7800-sq-m display within three halls (including a renovated hanger built between 1912 and 1919), is the aviation branch of the Deutsches Museum and stands on the original training grounds of the Royal Bavarian Flying Corps (founded 1912). On exhibit are aircraft from around the world, including the USA, the former Soviet Union, Sweden, Poland and Germany, there's also a great collection of 'alternative' glider kits.

The museum is open from 9 am to 5 pm daily (DM6/4 for adults/students, kids under six free).

Getting There & Away

Take the S1 (direction: Freising) to Oberschleissheim. It's about a 15 minute, signposted walk from the station along Mittenheimer Strasse towards the palaces. By car, take Leopoldstrasse north until it becomes Ingolstadter Strasse. Then take the A99 to the Neuherberg exit, at the south end of the airfield.

STARNBERG
☎ 08151 • pop 22,000

Once a royal retreat, Starnberger See (Lake Starnberg), just 30 minutes by the S6 from Munich (two zones or four strips of a Streifenkarte), is a fast and easy way to get away from the urban bustle of Munich.

The city of Starnberg, at the northern end of the lake, is the heart of the Five Lakes district. Starnberger See, about 22km long, 5km wide and between 1m and 100m deep, is a favourite spot for Munich windsurfers, who also skittle over nearby Ammersee, and the much smaller Wörthsee, Pilsensee and Osterseen.

The tourist office (☎ 90 60 60, fax 90 60 90, email info@starnberger-fuenf-seen-land) is at Wittelsbacherstrasse 2c, and is open

EXCURSIONS

from 8 am to 6 pm Monday to Friday, and also from 9 am to 1 pm on Saturday from June to October. The office gives out and sells maps of the entire area (including maps of hiking trails); and can help you plan public transport to other lake towns. It also books accommodation in the entire Five Lakes District for free.

Starnberg is best known as the place where Ludwig II was found dead; drowned along with his physician, in 1m of water. Ludwig had been brought here under arrest, in an effort to remove him from power, due to insanity. The circumstances of his death remain a mystery, it was known that Ludwig was a good swimmer, and that his doctor was perhaps the only person who could vouch for his sanity.

Conspiracy theorists have a ball with the story. The spot where Ludwig's body was found, near the **Votivkapelle** in Berg, is now marked with a cross erected in the water.

The Bayerische Seen Schiffahrt company runs electrically-powered tour boats across the lake from their docks right behind the S-Bahn station (three hours costs DM23.50 in a two-seater). There are one-hour tours (DM12.50) to the five castles around the lake's edge, also passing the site of the Ludwig II cross. Tours operate daily in summer at 8.50, 9.30 and 10.35 am and 12.15, 1.15, 2.30 and 4.30 pm.

There are several boat-rental booths just west of the train station, where you can rent rowing/pedal/electric-powered boats for DM12/15/20 per hour. The electric boats have about enough power to get you a third of the way down the lake and back.

ANDECHS

A short bus ride from Herrsching, on the east side of the Ammersee (from Munich take S5 to the last stop), is the Benedictine monastery of Andechs (☎ 08152-37 60), rebuilt in 1675 after the Thirty Years' War left it in ruins.

The lovely hill-top rococo structure has always been a place of pilgrimage – the hundreds of offertory candles and relics locked up in the Holy Chapel prove it. But an overwhelming majority of today's visitors are after the beer that the monks have been brewing here for over 500 years. It's excellent beer, but the place is so overrun by tourists it's easy to forget that you're in a religious institution, pious as your love for brew may be. One-hour German-language tours of the entire monastery are at 4 pm Tuesday and Thursday (DM5).

The *Klosterbrauerei* serves a litre of light (DM8), dark (DM9.40) and Weissbier (DM9) in the monastery restaurant, whose overpriced food, service counters and turnstiles bring train stations to mind. Yet the terrace is lovely, with a sweeping view of the valley.

From Herrsching train station, take the Rauner bus (DM3, kids DM2.50), which leaves at least once an hour between 7.55 am and 4.35 pm and returns from 9.55 am to 6.45 pm. Or walk for 3km on the well-marked footpaths (be sure to stick to the path, for it's a steep drop in spots).

FÜSSEN
☎ 08362 • pop 17,000
Nestled in the foothills of the Bavarian Alps, Füssen has a medieval monastery, a town castle and some lovely baroque architecture. But most people flock here to see the famous castles nearby: Neuschwanstein, Hohenschwangau and Linderhof, all legacies of mad King Ludwig II (see the Around Füssen and Around Garmisch-Partenkirchen sections, later in this chapter).

Orientation & Information
Füssen's train station is at the western end of the city, about a three-minute walk from the tourist office, the slick Kurverwaltung Füssen (☎ 938 50, fax 93 85 20, email kurverwaltung@fuessen.de) at Kaiser Maximilian Platz 1. The town's Web site is at www.fuessen.de, it has a decent English-language section.

Neuschwanstein and Hohenschwangau are 4km to the east, while Linderhof is an hour's drive towards Garmisch-Partenkirchen.

Museums
The **Museum of Füssen**, in the Rathaus, houses local folk art (paintings, carvings,

pottery), historical and cultural artefacts of the area, and has an exquisite baroque interior. It's open from 11 am to 4 pm April to October, the rest of the year from 2 to 4 pm (DM5/4).

The **St Anna Kapelle**, is the oldest wing of the medieval monastery's church, and is entered through the museum. On a hill above the town is the **Staatsgalerie im Hohen Schloss**, the former residence of the prince-bishops of Augsburg, now a museum of religious artwork. It's open from 11 am to 4 pm Tuesday to Sunday, April to October; from 2 to 4 pm in winter (DM4/3).

Cable Car

Tickets for the Tegelbergbahn (☎ 983 60) are a bit steep at DM25 but worth it for the dazzling view of the Alps and Forggensee. The mountain station is also a launch point for hang-gliders. After an apple strudel in the **restaurant**, it's a wonderful hike down to the castles (follow the signs to Königsschlösser) in two to three hours. The cable car runs from 8.30 am to 5 pm in summer, and from 9 am to 4.30 pm in winter (last ascent/decent: half an hour before closing). To get there, take the RVA No 9713 bus from Füssen train station to the Tegelbergbahn valley station.

Places to Stay

Camping There are several camping options near the castles. From Schwangau, bus No 9715 takes you to *Campingplatz Bannwaldsee* (☎ 810 01, fax 82 30, Münchner Strasse 151), with camp sites from DM13 right on Forggensee lake. By car, the best bet is *Brunnen am Forggensee* (☎ 82 73, fax 817 38, Seestrasse 81) at the southern end of the Forggensee, which charges DM10.50 per person and DM10.50 per site.

Hostel The Füssen *DJH hostel* (☎ 77 54, fax 27 70, Mariahilferstrasse 5), is by the train tracks, 10 minutes' walk from the station (follow the signs). Dorm beds cost DM20 plus the *Kurtaxe* (resort tax, DM1.20 to DM3) and curfew is a tourist-unfriendly 10 pm. The hostel is closed from mid-November to Christmas. Book ahead, as showing up without a reservation is really pushing your luck.

Private Rooms & Hotels The tourist office has lists of private rooms from DM30 per person. In Füssen there's a Kurtaxe of DM3 per person per night (DM2.40 in the off-season).

The central *Hotel Alpenhof* (☎ 32 32, no fax, Theresienstrasse 8), has attractive rooms from DM40/75.

Hotel zum Hechten (☎ 916 00, fax 91 60 99, Ritterstrasse 6), is in a fine spot near the main square and has a quiet rear courtyard, with rooms from DM60/100.

Places to Eat

Schinagl (☎ 61 39, Brunnengasse 20), is a great bakery with wonderful pastries and breads. Weigh in at *Infooday (Ritterstrasse 6)*, where 100g of hot buffet food costs just DM2.55. It's open until 6.30 pm weekdays and until 1 pm Saturday.

For restaurant dishes, check out the old *Franziskaner Stüberl* (☎ 371 24), on the corner of Ritterstrasse and Kemptener Strasse. Earthy dishes include roast trotters in beer sauce with rye bread (DM11).

Next to the old fire station, *Weizenbierbrauerei* (☎ 63 12) has great beer and Bavarian specialities served by friendly staff. House specials range from DM13 to DM17, *Schweinebraten* (pork roast) from DM12.50 and daily lunch specials from DM12 to DM14. It's closed on Friday.

Getting There & Away

From Munich (DM34, 2½ hours), the best train to catch to beat the crowds leaves at the ungodly hour of 4.57 am, with a 6.31 am change at Biessenhofen and arrival at 7.23 am in Füssen. The most popular early train (No 5862) leaves at 6.50 am, changing at Buchloe for the 7.46 am, arriving in Füssen at 8.57 am; subsequent departures include trains at 7.52, 8.52 and 10.52 am; return trains run at five minutes past the hour until 11.05 pm. Check schedules before you go.

Getting Around

Bus The RVA (Regionaler Verkehrsverbund Ammergau) buses go to the Neuschwanstein and Hohenschwangau castles (see Getting There & Away in the next section).

EXCURSIONS

Bicycles The cheapest rental is Hohenrainer Alwin (☎ 396 09), in the Altstadt at Hintere Gasse 13, with city, mountain and trekking bikes from DM10 per day (open daily).

AROUND FÜSSEN
Schloss Neuschwanstein & Schloss Hohenschwangau

These castles provide a fascinating glimpse into Ludwig II's state of mind. They're practically next to one another, so you can visit both on the same day. Hohenschwangau is where Ludwig lived as a child, but more interesting is the adjacent **Neuschwanstein**, which appears through the mountain-top mist like a kooky mirage.

Ludwig's own creation, Neuschwanstein is, perhaps, the world's best-known castle; the fantastic pastiche of architectural styles inspired Walt Disney's Cinderella Castle. Begun in 1869 and never finished, the grey-white granite castle was an anachronism from the start; by the time Ludwig died in

1886, people were drinking soft drinks in America and the first skyscrapers were being built. For all the money spent on it (see boxed text 'Ludwig's Crazy Castles'), the king himself spent just 100-odd days there.

The initial blueprint for the castle was laid out by a theatre designer rather than an architect, which accounts for its dramatic packaging. Ludwig got the idea of a high-standing castle from a visit to the Wartburg in Thuringia, where the bards used to hold singing competitions.

Neuschwanstein was thus built at a lofty 200m above the valley floor, and its centrepiece became the lavish **Sängersaal** (Minstrels' Hall) where Ludwig could feed his obsession with Wagner and medieval knights. (Wall frescoes in the hall depict scenes from the opera *Tannhäuser*.)

Other sections include Ludwig's bedroom, a gaudy **artificial grotto** (another Wagner allusion), the sleeping chamber is dominated by a huge Gothic-style bed which bears a

Ludwig's Crazy Castles

Few monarchs evoke an image as romantic (and ludicrous) as Ludwig II (1845–86), the last member of the Wittelsbach dynasty which ruled Bavaria for nearly 800 years. As an arts patron, technology freak, recluse – and, above all, builder of impossibly lavish castles, Ludwig was ready-made for the state tourism industry.

Ludwig's obsession with French culture and the 'Sun King' Louis IV, inspired the fairy-tale fantasies of Neuschwanstein, Linderhof and Herrenchiemsee – incredibly lavish projects which spelled his undoing.

The castles ate up Ludwig's own fortune and substantial amounts of the state budget. Ministers and relatives arranged a psychiatric test and in January 1886, Ludwig was declared mentally unfit to rule.

That June he was removed to Schloss Berg, an asylum on Lake Starnberg. One evening the dejected bachelor (at 41, he was friendless, throneless and toothless) and his doctor, took a lakeside walk and were found drowned, several hours later, in just a few feet of water. In Munich, people wept on the streets when the news broke. The exact cause was never determined, although one theory implicates Prince-Regent Luitpold (who ruled after Ludwig's death).

That summer the authorities opened Neuschwanstein to the public to help pay off Ludwig's huge debts. Today the three *Königsschlösser* are among Bavaria's biggest money-spinners – not to mention all those Ludwig T-shirts, beer mugs and ash trays.

MICK WELDON

wood carving of a skyline; and the Byzantine **Thronsaal** (Throne Room), which is, in fact, throne-less, as Ludwig was removed before one could be constructed.

For a great view of Neuschwanstein and the plains beyond, walk for 10 minutes up to the Marienbrücke (Mary's Bridge) which spans the spectacular Pöllat Gorge. Down the other way lies the aquamarine Schwansee lake, a nature reserve.

Hohenschwangau was originally built by 12th century knights, but the current form of the castle stems from the 1830s. It's much less ostentatious than Neuschwanstein, sporting a yellow neogothic facade atop a modest hill just south of its grander cousin, and the interior has a distinct lived-in feeling. After father Maximilian II died, Ludwig had stars painted on the ceiling of his royal bedroom; these were illuminated with hidden oil-lamps while His Nuttiness slumbered.

Tickets & Tours The guided tours get awfully crowded after about 9.30 am, when tourists from Munich arrive by train, so go early to avoid the crush. Tickets to both Neuschwanstein and Hohenschwangau cost DM12/9 each. At Neuschwanstein, get in the queue of the language of your choice; tours (obligatory to visit) leave when there are enough people.

Neuschwanstein is open from 9 am to 5.30 pm April to September, and from 10 am to 4 pm October to March. Hohenschwangau is open from 8.30 am to 5.30 pm mid-March to mid-October, and from 9.30 am to 4.30 pm mid-October to mid-March.

The expense of an organised tour is worth it. EurAide's excellent two-castle tours cover Neuschwanstein, Linderhof and the Wieskirche. It's the best deal around – DM70 per person, including transportation – and leaves every Wednesday in summer from the EurAide office in Munich.

If all that isn't enough Ludwig for you, the Musical Theatre Neuschwanstein stages an evening production in Füssen on the life and times of the fairy-tale King. To reserve tickets (costing a regal DM85 to DM230 for the three-hour performance), call ☎ 01805-58 39 44.

Getting There & Away

Train Munich connections are listed under the Füssen section for Getting There & Away.

Bus From Füssen's Hauptbahnhof, take the RVA bus No 9713 (10 minutes, DM4.80 return), share a taxi (around DM14) or walk the 5km.

From the bus stop, it's a 20 to 30 minute walk up the hill to Neuschwanstein, or a slightly longer trip by horse-drawn carriage (DM8 uphill, DM4 downhill). From Garmisch-Partenkirchen train station, take the bus to Hohenschwangau (two hours, single DM13, five per day).

GARMISCH-PARTENKIRCHEN
☎ 08821 • pop 27,000

The resort towns of Garmisch and Partenkirchen were merged by Adolf Hitler to host the 1936 Winter Olympics. With access to four ski fields, including ones on Germany's highest mountain, the Zugspitze (2963m), the town is a very popular destination for skiers, hikers, snowboarders and mountaineers.

The huge ski stadium on the slopes right outside town has two ski jumps and a slalom course; it hosted more than 100,000 people for the 1936 Winter Olympics and is still used for professional competitions today.

About 20km west of town is Ludwig II's charming Schloss Linderhof (see the Around Garmisch-Partenkirchen section, later in this chapter).

Orientation & Information

The railway tracks that divide the two towns run right down the centre to the Hauptbahnhof. From here, turn east on St Martin Strasse to get to Garmisch and west on Bahnhofstrasse to get to Partenkirchen.

The tourist office (☎ 18 06, fax 18 07 55, email tourist-info@garmisch-partenkirchen.de), on Richard-Strauss-Platz, is open from 8 am to 6 pm Monday to Saturday, and from 10 am to noon Sunday and holidays. The town's Web site, with English sections, is at www.garmisch-partenkirchen.de.

EXCURSIONS

The post office is across the street from the Hauptbahnhof. Change money at the Commerzbank on Marienplatz 2a.

Activities

Skiing The tallest mountain peak in Germany, the Zugspitze, offers some of the most breathtaking views around. In winter, of course, it has some amazing skiing and in summer, spectacular hiking. Other than climbing the mountain (see Hiking, later in this section), there are two options for ascending – a cable car and a *Zahnradbahn* (cog-wheel train) both are a lot of fun.

On a standard day ticket, the cost for the two is the same; there are some discounts available for the train in conjunction with a train trip from Munich (ask at the Munich Hauptbahnhof).

Both are jam-packed at peak times in winter (around Christmas, New Year and festivals) and through much of the summer. Skiers may find it easier, if a little slower, to lug gear up on the train, which offers exterior ski racks. Call ☎ 79 79 79 for a weather or snow report.

Ski Areas Garmisch borders on four separate ski-fields: the Zugspitze plateau (the highest), the Alpspitze/Hausberg (the largest), and the Eckbauer and Wank areas (and yes, Wank residents do say '*Ich bin ein Wanker*').

Day ski passes cost DM61 for Zugspitze (though this includes the cable car or Zahnradbahn ride up to the top), DM47 for Alpspitze/Hausberg, DM33 for Wank and DM28 for Eckbauer. The Happy Ski Card covers all four areas, but it's available for a minimum of three days (DM143, DM190 for four days).

Cross-country ski trails run along the main valleys, including a long section from Garmisch to Mittenwald.

Ski Hire Flori Wörndle (☎ 583 00) has the cheapest rates for ski hire (and has convenient outlets at the Alpspitze and Zugspitze lifts). For skiing information and downhill instruction you can contact the Skischule Garmisch-Partenkirchen (☎ 49 31), Am

Hausberg 8, or for cross-country instruction, the Skilanglaufschule (☎ 15 16), Olympia-Skistadion. Sport Total (☎ 14 25), at Marienplatz 18, also runs skiing courses and organises numerous outdoor activities like paragliding, mountain biking, rafting and ballooning, as well as renting a wide range of gear.

Cable Car What a high: the 10 minute journey aboard the Eibsee cable car is as breathtaking as the fare (DM61 for adults, DM43 for teens aged 16 to 18, DM37 for kids). The car, packed to the brim with people, sways and swings its way up from the base to the **Panorama Observation Terrace**; the ride is not for the faint-hearted!

Zahnradbahn Built from 1928 to 1930, this charming narrow-gauge railway makes its way from the mountain base up to the Zugspitzplatt station, where you can switch for the Gletscherbahn cable car that takes you to the summit of the Zugspitze. Included in a day pass, this is the more scenic, but slower, way up the mountain. If you don't have a day pass, the fares are the same as for the Eibsee cable car (see earlier).

Hiking The best way to get to the top of the Zugspitze (for the fit and adventurous) is to hike (two days). A recommended hiking map is *Wettersteingebirge* (DM7.50) published at 1:50,000, by Kompass. For information on guided hiking or courses in mountaineering call the Bergsteigerschule Zugspitze (☎ 589 99), Dreitorspitz-Strasse 13, Garmisch.

A great short hike from Garmisch is to the narrow Partnachklamm gorge, via a winding path above a stream and underneath waterfalls. Take the cable car to the first stop on the Graseck route (DM5 per head) and follow the signs. Entry to the gorge costs DM3/1.50 at the gate at the southern end, but it's free after 6 pm, and if you come from the northern side.

Places to Stay

The camping ground nearest to Garmisch is *Zugspitze* (☎ 31 80), along highway B24.

Take the blue-and-white bus outside the Hauptbahnhof in the direction of the Eibsee. Sites cost DM8, plus DM9 per person and DM5 per vehicle.

The **hostel** (☎ 29 80, fax 585 36, Jochstrasse 10), is in the suburb of Burgrain. Beds cost DM21 (including Kurtaxe) and there's an 11.30 pm curfew; it's closed from November until Christmas. From the Hauptbahnhof take bus No 3, 4 or 5 to the Burgrain stop.

Five minutes' walk from the station is the quiet **Hotel Schell** (☎ 957 50, Partnachauen Strasse 3), it has singles/doubles from DM45/90 across from a babbling brook.

In the centre of Garmisch, **Haus Weiss** (☎ 46 82, Klammstrasse 6), **Gasthaus Pfeuffer** (☎ 223 8, Kreuzstrasse 9), and the nearby **Haus Trenkler** (☎ 34 39, Kreuzstrasse 20), all offer simple but pleasant rooms for around DM35/70.

Places to Eat

Snacks & Fast Food Schnönegger Käsealm (☎ 17 33, Mohrenplatz 1), has friendly staff and cheese sandwiches from DM2 to DM5; it also sells a variety of delicious all-natural yoghurt (DM6/4.50 with/without fruit) as well as fresh butter and honey.

Perhaps the best value in town is the excellent **Cafeteria Sirch** (☎ 21 09, Griesstrasse 1). It's not much to look at but it has excellent half chickens for DM6.20, schnitzels for 7.20, and beef goulash and noodles for DM8.30.

Bavaria Grill (☎ 33 08, Am Kurpark 16) in Garmisch (entrance on the little alley), is a lot friendlier than it looks from the outside. Fill up on sausage dishes from DM6.90 to DM9.50, and add some excellent fries for DM4.50.

Konditorei Krönner (☎ 30 07, Achenfeldstrasse 1), with an entrance on Am Kurpark, is a beautiful, if pricey, place for coffee and cakes, but the attached takeaway bakery is far more reasonable; try their speciality Mocha creme and almond Agnes Benaur torte for DM3.20.

Bistros & Restaurants The local pizza and pasta guru is **Da Renzo** (☎ 41 77,

Rathausplatz 6), with 100 varieties for DM10 to DM13. Service is snappy, and the toppings are thick.

Chapeau Claque (☎ 713 00, Mohrenplatz 10), is a very cosy wine-bar/bistro with soft lighting and great service. Good snacks include bagels with salmon and cream cheese (DM9.80) baked potato with bacon and onions (DM11.80) or stir-frys for DM14 to DM16.

On the south side of the river, near the Alte Kirche in Garmisch, are two local favourites. The **Bräustüberl** (☎ 23 12, Furstenstrasse 23), is about as Bavarian as you can get, complete with enamelled coal-burning stoves and Dirndl-clad (but sometimes curt) waitresses. The dining room is to the right, beer hall to the left; main courses (nary a vegetable to be seen) are DM10.50 to DM26.50, though the average is about DM17.

The **Gasthaus zur Schranne**, a pleasant old tavern at Griesstrasse 3, has three-course evening menus from just DM12.80. The **Hofbräustüberl** (☎ 717 16), on the corner of Chamonixstrasse and Olympiastrasse, has home-made Hungarian specialities like *hajducki cevap* (skewered and grilled meat with paprika, DM18).

Isi's Goldener Engel (☎ 566 77, Bankgasse 5) is a cavernous place with frescoes, stags' heads and a golden vaulted hall. The menu is huge, ranging from a simple pork thigh with potato dumplings (DM19.80) to game dishes in the DM30 to DM40 range (closed Wednesday).

Getting There & Away

Garmisch is serviced from Munich by hourly trains (DM26, 1½ hours). A special return train fare from Munich for DM68 (DM84 on weekends) includes the trip up the Zugspitze (or a day ski pass). The A95 from Munich is the direct road route.

Getting Around

Bus tickets cost DM2 for journeys in town. Rent bicycles at the Trek Pro Shop (☎ 795 28), Schnitzstrasse 1, near Rathausplatz, DM18 (three gears), or DM25/32 for trekking/mountain bikes.

EXCURSIONS

AROUND GARMISCH-PARTENKIRCHEN
Schloss Linderhof

About 20km west of town is Schloss Linderhof, Ludwig II's hunting palace and the only one of his royal residences to be completed. Nestled at the crook of a steep hillside, it is fronted by formal French gardens with fountains, pools and follies as odd as you'd expect from a nutty monarch.

In the front entrance is a statue of Louis XIV, the Sun King, with the inscription *Nec Pluribus impar*, 'I'm the Greatest'. It's a sample of the themes that occupied Ludwig during his eight years here – the glory of French absolutism, Wagner, mystical German legends, and swans (and occasionally peacocks).

Although the smallest of Ludwig's residences, Linderhof boasts its share of unbelievable treasures. The royal **bedroom** is a shower of colourful ornaments set around an enormous 108-candle **chandelier** weighing 500kg. (It's checked regularly by the national safety board, so go ahead and stand beneath it.)

The dining room recalls the king's fetish for new inventions: a **dumb-waiter table** that rises from the kitchen below so that Ludwig wouldn't actually have to see his servants. The man lived like a hermit, and although he had a special piano-harmonium made for Wagner to play at Linderhof, the composer never dropped by to play.

On the grounds are more Francophilia, and the best part is that the sunnier the weather, the fewer the visitors. Don't miss the oriental-style **Moorish Kiosk** which Ludwig picked up at the 1876 World's Fair in Paris, or the **Venus Grotto**, an artificial cave used as a stage set for Wagner's *Tannhäuser*.

It's open from 9.00 am to 5.30 pm daily, between Easter and mid-October, and from 9.30 am to noon and 1 to 4 pm the rest of the year. Admission is DM10/7 in summer and DM7/4 in winter (when only the main palace is open). A return bus fare from Garmisch-Partenkirchen costs DM11.

Getting There & Away
Train & Bus From Munich, there's an hourly train service to Oberammergau with a change at Murnau (DM26, 1¼ hours); then take the hourly RVA bus No 9606 from the train station to Linderhof (20 minutes, DM9.20 return). A bus from Füssen takes 90 minutes (DM36).

Car & Motorcycle Linderhof is about 20km north-west of Garmisch-Partenkirchen on the rural B23.

OBERAMMERGAU
☎ 08822 • pop 5400

Some 20km north of Garmisch-Partenkirchen lies the picturesque little alpine village (read: tourist trap) of Oberammergau. It's celebrated for its Passion Play, performed every decade since the townsfolk made a deal with God after having been ravaged by the Black Plague in 1633 (see the special section on the Passion Play).

The piece is still performed, as in the original, by amateur actors which lend it an innocent charm. Tickets went on sale for the 2000 performance in 1998 and promptly sold out. But you can visit the **Passionstheater**, which will reopen in spring 2000 after refurbishment. Tours (in German and English, DM5) include a history of the play and a peek at the costumes and sets.

The city tourist office (☎ 10 21, fax 73 25, email info@oberammergau.de), Eugen-Papst-Strasse 9a, books accommodation as well as horse-drawn carriage rides to Schloss Linderhof (DM30). For more on the town and the Passion Play, check the Web site www.oberammergau.de.

Things to See & Do
Highlights of the town include the *Lüftmalerei*, or *trompe l'oeil* paintings on the facades of buildings, these were designed to impart an aura of wealth. Several houses have fairy-tale motifs, like *Hansel & Gretl* and *Little Red Riding Hood*. The rococo **Pfarrkirche** (Pastor's Church) on Pfarrplatz carries another set of wondrous frescoes.

The crowning glory of the town's Lüftmalerei is that on the front of the **Pilatushaus** (Pilate's House, ☎ 16 82) in Ludwigthomstrasse, just off Dorfstrasse. Inside, you can observe local craftsmen at work – potters, sculptors, painters and woodcarvers who've been trained in the village woodcarving school. Opening hours are from 10.30 am to 6 pm Monday to Friday and from 10.30 am to 12.30 pm Saturday (free entry).

The **Heimatmuseum** (☎ 941 36), Dorfstrasse 8, has historical displays of the town and a remarkable collection of cribs, some of them quite colourful and dating from the 18th century. It's open from 2 to 6 pm Tuesday to Sunday, mid-May to mid-October, and the rest of the year from 2 to 6 pm on Saturday only (DM3/1.50).

To rise above it all, take the cable car from the eastern end of town to the Laberjoch (1680m), there's a smashing view of Oberammergau and environs (DM13/19 for single/return tickets).

Shopping Oberammergau is also known for its intricate woodcarvings, and workshops throughout the village make everything imaginable, from beautiful creche scenes to items you wouldn't accept as a gift (eg corkscrews with religious icons as handles). The best (and oldest) shops include Tony Baur (☎ 821), at Dorfstrasse 27, with the village's biggest collection of carvings, and Josef Albl (☎ 64 33), Devrientweg 1, whose work focuses on religious and hunting scenes. The simplest pieces at either place will go for around DM20, but a complicated bas-relief will set you back many thousands of Deutschmarks.

Places to Stay

Hostel The *DJH Jugendherberge* (☎ 41 14, fax 16 95, Malensteinweg 10), is in a wonderful spot 10 minutes' walk from the train station, on the banks of the Ammersee (follow the signs). It charges DM20 per night (including breakfast) in clean four- and six-bed rooms. Mind the 10 pm curfew.

Private Rooms & Hotels The tourist office can refer private rooms from about DM40 per head. If you're coming during the Passion Play, however, set up accommodation well ahead of time. Guests in town are allowed to stay only one or two nights during the performances, when hotel prices shoot up.

The *Hotel Alte Post* (☎ 91 00, fax 91 01 00, Dorfstrasse 19) is a huge chalet in the centre of town, with rustic rooms and four-poster double beds. The restaurant serves good Bavarian specialties (see Places to Eat). Singles/doubles start at DM80/120, including breakfast.

At *Hotel Turmwirt* (☎ 926 00, fax 14 37, Ettalerstrasse 2), most rooms have balconies with stunning mountain views. This 18th century inn gleams with rich wood panelling, and its singles/doubles are, arguably, a bargain from DM100/140.

Hotel Wolf (☎ 30 71, fax 10 96, Dorfstrasse 1), is another gabled place adorned with wooden trim, balconies and boxes of geraniums. It also has a sauna, an outdoor swimming pool, a solarium and plenty of American guests. Singles/doubles cost from DM70/110.

Places to Eat

Bäckerei Ulrich Rommy (Schnitzlergasse 2) sells cheap snacks, sandwiches and scrummy cheese rolls (just DM1.20). The *Gasthaus Weisses Rössl* (☎ 926 84, Dorfstrasse 28) does half-chickens for DM6.50 from the takeaway window and simple meals (eg pork thigh and potatoes) from DM7.50.

The *Hotel Alte Post* (see Places to Stay) does classic Bavarian meals from just DM15, such as a juicy pork roast and oversized dumplings. In summer, meals are served in the pleasant beer garden on the square.

Ammergauer Stubn (☎ 10 11, Dorfstrasse 21) is a comfy little tavern near the train station. Its specialty is schnitzel (DM13) and international dishes, only the steaks cost DM20 or more (closed Wednesday).

Getting There & Away

There are regional trains to/from Munich (DM38, two hours). Rail links to Garmisch-Partenkirchen from Oberammergau are impractical (DM12.20, 1¼ hours via Murnau). There is also a fast service from Frankfurt via Munich (DM159, 5½ hours).

An 'Oberammergau' bus leaves from the Garmisch-Partenkirchen Hauptbahnhof (DM4.80, 40 minutes). A bus from Füssen takes 90 minutes and costs DM13.

euro currency converter DM1 = €.51

EXCURSIONS

For motorists, Oberammergau is on the north-south B23 from Garmisch-Partenkirchen; from Munich, take the autobahn A95 and exit at Eschenlohe.

PRIEN AM CHIEMSEE
☎ 08051 • pop 8700

Blessed with a lovely setting and a stop on the Munich-Salzburg rail line, the harbour town of Prien is an ideal base for exploring the Chiemsee. Munich residents have a special place in their hearts for this lovely lake, an hour east of Munich. So did Ludwig II, who liked it so much he built his homage to Versailles on an island in the centre.

Most tourists pass through en route to the Neues Königsschloss, but the lake's wealth of natural beauty and the multitude of water-sports justify a stay of a night or two.

The are two tourist offices in town which act as information centres for the entire lake district. There's a good branch at the Prien am Chiemsee train station, open from 12.45 pm to 5.45 pm Monday through Friday, in July to September only. The main office (☎ 690 50, fax 69 05 40, email info@ prien.chiemsee.de), Alte Rathausstrasse 11, is open from 8.30 am to 6 pm Monday to Friday, and from 9 am to noon Saturday. Their Web site is at www.prien.chiemsee.de.

There's a bicycle rental at Radsport Reischenböck (☎ 46 31), Bahnhofsplatz 6, a minute's walk east of the station, behind the Sparkasse. It charges DM12/20 per day for city/mountain bikes.

Schloss Herrenchiemsee
Begun in 1878 on the site of an Augustinian monastery on the island Herreninsel, the Schloss Herrenchiemsee provides insights into Ludwig's bizarre motivations. In a glorification of absolutist monarchy, the palace was meant to emulate the French 'Sun King' whom Maximilian II (Ludwig's father) had once supported. There's a portrait of Louis XIV in a more prominent position than any of the shy Ludwig himself, who is represented only by an unfinished statue.

The palace is both a knock-off and an attempted one-up of Versailles, with larger rooms, the immense Ambassador Staircase and the positively dazzling **Hall of Mirrors**, which runs the length of the garden (98m). The 44 candelabra and 33 great glass chandeliers of the castle's main room took 25 servants half an hour to light; candlelit concerts were held here until a few years ago, when the soot damage to the interior became alarmingly apparent. When cash ran out in 1885, only this central section had been completed.

Ludwig spent less than a month in the place. When he *was* in he was rarely seen, as the king normally read during the night and slept all day. The bedrooms are even more fantastic than at the other palaces; the **Paradeschlafzimmer** (Parade Bedroom) resembles a chapel, with the canopied bed standing altar-like on a ledge behind a golden balustrade. We especially enjoyed the **Kleines Blaues Schlafzimmer** (Little Blue Bedroom), with a big blue glass bubble perched on top of a wildly extravagant golden pedestal, looking much like an eclipsed moon.

The palace also contains the **König-Ludwig-II-Museum**, with a display that includes Ludwig's christening and coronation robes, blueprints for other projects and his death mask (DM10/6 as a combination ticket with the palace). The spacious garden is a lovely place for a walk, and there's a reasonable cafeteria in the lobby.

Return ferry fare is DM10 (kids DM5); admission to the castle is DM8/5. The obligatory guided tour is a half-hour rush, full of statistics – how much gold-leaf was used, how many embroiderers wore their fingers out making the frescoes, etc.

The palace is open from 9 am to 5 pm daily from April to October; from 9.30 am to 4 pm in winter. Note that the last ferry for the guided tour departs Prien at 3 pm.

Fraueninsel
This island is home to the Frauenwörth, a 12th century Benedictine monastery. Benedictine monks returned to the area in the 1980s and founded another monastery, which functions today. The island also contains a memorial to (and the remains of) Irmengard of Fraueninsel, the great-granddaughter of

Charlemagne; and the **Torhalle** (DM3), the gateway to the monastery (mid-9th century), inside is a chapel. Return ferry fare, including a stop at Herreninsel, is DM12.50 (kids DM6).

Activities

Swimming & Boat Rental The most easily accessed swimming beaches are at Chieming and Gstadt (both free), on the lake's east and north shores respectively. Fees for boat rental, available at many beaches, vary from roughly DM7 to DM40 per hour, depending on the type. In Prien, the Bootsverleih Stöffl (☎ 20 00), in front of the Westernacher am See restaurant, has 2-seater paddleboats for DM8 per hour, and a huge array of electric-driven vessels for DM17 to DM36.

The new Prienavera, a weak pun on the Italian word for 'spring', will house an enormous pool complex suitable for families with sauna, steam baths and solarium. It was due to open near Prien harbour in the autumn of 1999.

Places to Stay

The closest camp site is *Campingplatz Hofbauer (☎ 41 36, fax 626 57, Bernauerstrasse 110)* on the main road to Bermau, a 10 minute walk south of town. Charges are DM10.50 per adult, plus DM10 per tent/car. It's open April to October.

The tourist office can set up private quarters in the centre from just DM20 a person. Beds at the HI youth hostel (☎ 687 70, fax 68 77 15, Carl-Braun-Strasse 66), a 15 minute walk from the train station, cost DM24 with breakfast.

With a nice view of the lakefront, the *Hotel Garni Möwe (☎ 50 04, fax 648 81, Seestrasse 111)*, offers a reasonable deal at DM60/120 for singles/doubles.

For something really special but relatively cheap, head over to the *Bonn Schlössl (☎ 890 11, fax 891 03, Kirchplatz 9)*, a mock Bavarian castle in Bernau, a town just 2km south of Prien and largely overlooked by tourists. Take the hourly RVO bus 9505 from Prien train station, and alight at the Bernau minigolf course near

the hotel. The latter is run by the excellent restaurant *Der Alte Wirt* at the same address (see Places to Eat). Singles/doubles start at DM90/170.

Pride of place, however, goes to the *Yachthotel Chiemsee, (☎ 69 60, fax 51 71, Harrasserstrasse 49)*, a ritzy place south of Prien harbour with a sauna and its own three-masted yacht. Rooms here start at DM187/249.

Places to Eat

For a quick bite, the best bet is *Metzgerei Schmid (☎ 15 62, Bahnhofstrasse 7)*, with yummy sandwiches, pizza, and fresh lasagne for DM3 to DM8. The *Scherer SB Restaurant (☎ 45 91, Alte Rathausstrasse 1)*, is a self-service cafeteria, serving hearty dishes and salads for DM9 to DM19.

The best vistas in town are at *Westernacher am See (☎ 47 22, fax 96 84 93, Seestrasse 115)*, with a great garden on the promenade for people-watching. The food's not bad, either (try the trout in garlic butter for DM18.90).

For truly great Bavarian cuisine with swift service, drop by the old-world *Der Alte Wirt*, a massive half-timbered inn in nearby Bernau (see Places to Stay, earlier in this section, for directions). Main dishes average DM15 to DM25, with the misleadingly named *Leberkäse* (a smooth pork sausage without an ounce of liver) the star of the menu. The waitresses dart round the dining halls as if on wheels.

Getting There & Around

From the Prien am Chiemese train station (hourly service from Munich, DM22.40, one hour), walk down the stairs and through the tunnel to Chiemsee Bahn station, where you catch the historic steam train (1887) to the ferry terminal at Prien/Stock (Hafen). One-way costs DM3.50/1.50, 10 minutes, DM5.50/2.50 return. From there, Chiemsee Schiffahrt (☎ 60 90), Seestrasse 108, operates boats that ply the waters of the lake with stops every hour at Herreninsel, Gstadt, Fraueninsel, Seebruck and Chieming.

It is possible to circumnavigate the entire lake and make all of the stops mentioned

EXCURSIONS

here (get off and catch the next ferry that comes your way), for DM17.50.

BERCHTESGADEN
☎ 08652 • pop 8200

Arguably the most romantic place in the Bavarian Alps, the resort of Berchtesgaden enjoys spendid isolation created by centuries of monastic self-rule. The surrounding area is known as the Berchtesgadener Land, a droplet of German terrain which would belong to Austria but for the influence of the Holy Roman Empire. Nowadays visitors (including Americans in their tens of thousands) flock to nearby Obersalzberg to see the infamous Eagle's Nest, a mountain-top tea-house built for entertaining Hitler's foreign guests.

Orientation & Information

The tourist office (☎ 96 70, fax 633 00, email marketing@berchtesgaden.de), is just across the river from the Hauptbahnhof at Königseer Strasse 2, it is open from 8 am to 6 pm on weekdays, from 8 am to 5 pm on Saturday, and from 9 am to 3 pm on Sunday and public holidays in summer. Throughout the rest of the year it opens from 8 am to 5 pm on weekdays and from 9 am to noon Saturday.

Accommodation is surprisingly cheap (private rooms start around DM25) and the booking service is free. The town has a decent Web site, including an accommodation listing, at www.berchtesgadener-land.com.

The post office and bus station are at the Hauptbahnhof, perhaps the most grandiose surviving Nazi-era train station. To change money, try the Hypovereinsbank on the main square at Weihnachtsschützenstrasse 2½ .

For bicycles, the Big Pack Country Store (☎ 94 84 50), Maximilianstrasse 16, rents two-wheelers from DM10 per day.

Salt Mines

A tour of the **Salzbergwerk** (☎ 600 20) is a must. Visitors change into protective miners' gear before descending into the depths of the salt mine for a 1½ hour tour. It's open from 9 am to 5 pm daily between 1 May and 17 October, and from 12.30 to 3.30 pm

Monday to Saturday during the rest of the year. Admission is DM21 for adults and DM11 for children.

Eagle's Nest

The area's most sinister draw is at Mount Kehlstein, a sheer-sided peak in Obersalzberg where Martin Bormann, a Hitler confidante, engaged 3000 workers to build a diplomatic meeting-house for the Führer's 50th birthday. Better known as the Eagle's Nest, the Kehlsteinhaus occupies one of Germany's most breathtakingly scenic spots. Nowadays it houses a restaurant (☎ 29 69), open from late May to early October, that donates its profits to charity.

Hitler's holiday home, the so-called 'Berghof', was located nearby, with a labyrinthine bunker complex drilled into the alpine rock. While the Eagle's Nest was spared – or perhaps plain overlooked – by Allied bombers, the Berghof was reduced to ruins. US troops blew it up again in 1952 to discourage pilgrimages.

Kehlstein is reached from Berchtesgaden by RVO bus to Hintereck (No 9538), then by special bus to the Kehlstein car park, where a lift whooshes 120m, through solid rock, to the summit (open mid-May to October). Admission and car-park cost DM24 with a *Kurkarte* (discount pass), but a ticket with return bus fare from Berchtesgaden train station costs just DM26.80. (Reserve a seat for the way down.) On foot, it's a 30 minute wheeze from the Kehlstein car park to the summit, and two to three hours from Berchtesgaden.

The creepy history of the place is best told by Berchtesgaden Mini Bus Tours (☎ 649 71 or ☎ 621 72). At DM55, the four-hour guided tour (in English) plus admission, is tremendous value (kids go half-price). Buses depart 1.30 pm from mid-May through October from the tourist office; reserve ahead of time. It's the only historical tour of the area, as the local authorities prohibit German-language tours for fear of attracting neo-Nazis.

Documentation Centre The Obersalzberg Documentation Centre (☎ 94 79 60) presents a detailed history of the Third

THE PASSION PLAY

Name the world's longest-running play: is it *The Mousetrap*, the famous 'whodunnit' by Agatha Christie? A Shakespeare classic perhaps? The unlikely answer is the deeply religious *Passionsspiele* (Passion Play), which can be viewed during the summer of 2000, in the tiny Bavarian town of Oberammergau, 20km north of Garmisch-Partenkirchen.

When the Black Plague struck Oberammergau in 1633, survivors made a deal with God and vowed to forever stage a play depicting the passion, death and resurrection of Christ – if, in return, they could only be rid of the epidemic. The appeal seemed to work: after the premiere of the play, in 1634, there were no more plague deaths even though many locals had shown early signs of the illness. The town continued to stage the play every 10 years (with a few exceptions), and although passion plays were commonplace in the 17th century, Oberammergau's has been the only one to endure.

It's a drama of Wagnerian proportions, lasting from 9 am to 5.30 pm with a three-hour break for lunch. The cast consists of 2200 shaggy

THOMAS KLINGER

Right: Jesus is scourged.

Passion Play

THOMAS KLINGER

locals (haircuts are forbidden months ahead of time) – with as many as 250 amateur actors on stage at once. The play has changed with the times: in 1990, the part of the Virgin Mary was awarded to a mother of two, shocking the traditionalists. (The same actor plays Mary in 2000.)

The 100-odd performances between May and October 2000 sold out over a year ahead of time, and unless you know someone, you aren't likely to get tickets for the performance in 2000 (although scalpers are said to make a fortune close to the event). Demand for the 470,000 tickets – costing DM65 and DM110 each, and coupled mostly with local hotel bookings – exceeded supply several times over; the Passion Play draws more tourist buses than many an Andrew Lloyd-Webber evergreen. Move over, Jesus Christ Superstar.

THOMAS KLINGER

Above left: Stephan Reindl as Jesus Christ.

Left: The Last Supper

Reich, including a wealth of fascinating photos, correspondence and film footage. The contrasts are chilling: in one section you'll see a relaxed-looking Hitler and girl-friend Eva Braun strolling around the Eagle's Nest on holiday, in the next are displays devoted to Nazi terror campaigns.

Opened in autumn 1999, the centre (until 1996 a leisure facility for the US military) also embraces part of Hitler's labyrinthine bunker under the Eagle's Nest. It's open from 9 am to 5 pm Tuesday to Sunday, May to October; from 10 am to 3 pm the rest of the year (closed Monday). Last admission is one hour before closing time. Entry costs DM5 for adults and DM3 for seniors, but students get in free. To get there, take the same buses from Berchtesgaden as you would for the Eagle's Nest (see that section earlier in this chapter).

Königssee

Framed by steep mountain walls, the beautiful, emerald-green Königssee lies like a misplaced fiord 5km to the south of Berchtesgaden. There are frequent electric-boat tours (DM18, 1½ hours), in all seasons, to the quaint onion-domed chapel at St Bartholomä, which we all know from the glossy tourist leaflets.

In summer, boats continue to the far end of the lake. If you're lucky, the boat will stop and the guide will play a flügelhorn towards the amazing **Echo Wall**. In the valley, about one hour's hike from the dock at St Bartholomä, is the **Eis Kapelle** – as snow gathers in the corner of the rocks here, a dome emerges that reaches heights of over 200m; in summer, as the ice melts, the water erodes tunnels and creates a huge opening in the solid ice.

Skiing

The Jenner area (☎ 958 10), at Königssee, is the most popular of Berchtesgaden's five ski fields. Daily/weekly ski-lift passes for its intermediate to advanced pistes cost DM37/155. The Gutshof and Hochschwarzeck are gentler and better suited to families, with day passes DM22/16 and DM27/18.50 for adults/children.

The Skischule Treff-Aktiv (☎ 667 10), Jennerbahnstrasse 19, rents skiing and snowboarding equipment at good rates. The Outdoor Club (☎ 50 01), Am Gmundberg 7, organises a vast range of activities and courses, from hiking and mountaineering to paragliding and rafting.

Places to Stay

Camping Of the five camping grounds in the Berchtesgaden area, the nicest are at Königssee: *Grafenlehen* (☎ 41 40) and *Mühleiten* (☎ 45 84). Both charge DM10 per site plus DM8 per person.

Hostel The *hostel* (☎ 943 70, fax 94 37 37, Gebirgsjägerstrasse 52), charges DM22 (including Kurtaxe and breakfast) for a bed. From the Hauptbahnhof, take bus No 3 to Strub, alight at the 'Jugendherberge' stop and follow the signposted footpath for a few minutes. The hostel is closed from early November to late December.

Hotels The newly-renovated *Hotel Watzmann* (☎ 20 55, fax 51 74, Franziskanerplatz 2), is just opposite the chiming church in the Altstadt. Simple singles/doubles cost just DM33/66 (DM39/78 in summer). The hotel closes in November and December.

Only 10 minutes' walk from the Hauptbahnhof but with wonderful views over the valley is the *Pension Haus am Berg* (☎ 949 20, fax 94 92 30, Am Brandholz 9), where singles/doubles start at DM38/76, breakfast is included.

Rooms at the *Gästehaus Alpina* (☎ 25 17, fax 21 10, Ramsauer Strasse 6) near the Hauptbahnhof, range from DM38 to DM45, and some have nice views to Kehlstein, Jenner, Göll and Brett.

Also near the station, the *Hotel Floriani* (☎ 660 11, fax 634 53, Königsseer Strasse 37), has rooms with bath, cable TV and minibar from DM40/80 for singles/doubles. Some rooms have balconies.

The *Hotel Rosenbichl* (☎ 944 00, fax 94 40 40, Rosenhofweg 24) in the middle of the protected nature zone, is exceptional value with singles from DM58 to DM85 and doubles from DM116 to DM170. Non-smokers

EXCURSIONS

find solace here. There's also a sauna, whirlpool, solarium and a library (mainly German stuff).

The *Hotel Vier Jahreszeiten* (☎ *95 92, fax 50 29, Maximilianstrasse 20)* close to the centre, has panoramic views of the Alps, a good restaurant and singles/doubles from DM75/130.

Places to Eat

There's a good weekly *market* at Weihnachtsschützenplatz from 8 am to 11 am every Friday from April through October, with an incredible array of fresh produce and meats. It's joined by a farmer's market on the last Friday of the month.

For a quick bite, the *Express Grill* (☎ *23 21, Maxmilianstrasse 8)*, sells half-chickens for DM5.80 and burgers from DM3.50, while the butcher's *Fritz Kastner* (☎ *23 39, Königseerstrasse 3)*, right across from the tourist office, does unbeatable filled rolls from DM3.50.

Grassl's Bistro-Cafe (☎ *25 24, Maximilianstrasse 11)*, is an ideal spot for lunch among all those cute porcelain jugs, with tasty soups, sandwiches and daily specials from DM10 to DM17. It's open from 9 am to 6 pm, closed Sunday.

Hotel Watzmann (see Places to Stay) deserves another mention for its well-priced dishes served to outside tables. The *Hubertus Stuben* (☎ *95 20)*, part of Hotel Vier Jahreszeiten on Maximilianstrasse, offers vegetarian dishes alongside venison and sirloin steak specialties, from around DM18.

Gasthaus Bier-Adam (☎ *23 90, Markt 22)*, has a good range of traditional fare to suit all budgets, a nice dark beer and cheerful service. The nearby *Gasthaus Neuhaus* (☎ *21 82, Markt 1)*, features old-style Bavarian cuisine with occasional folk music and a nifty terrace.

The *Bräustübl* (☎ *14 23, Bräuhausstrasse 13)* is a huge beer hall that caters to carnivores, putting on a heel-whacking Bavarian stage show every Saturday night.

Getting There & Away

For the quickest train connections to Berchtesgaden it's usually best to take a Munich-Salzburg train and change at Freilassing. It's a 2¾ hour train trip from Munich (DM48), but just an hour from Salzburg (DM12.20). Berchtesgaden is south of the Munich-Salzburg A8 autobahn.

SALZBURG
☎ 43662 • pop 143,500

The city that delivered Mozart to the world has much to recommend it, even though the nearby hills are nowadays more alive to *The Sound of Music*. Mozart's influence is felt everywhere: at Mozartplatz, the Mozarteum, Mozart's Birthplace, and in those confectionary delights called *Mozartkugeln* (sometimes unwittingly translated as Mozart's Balls). But even the eminent composer must take second place to the powerful archbishops who turned Salzburg into a showcase of the Italian Renaissance, with its spacious plazas and wedding-cake architecture.

Orientation

The city centre is split by the clear cold waters of the River Salzach. The old town (mostly a pedestrian precinct) is on the left (south) bank, in the shadow of the hilltop Hohensalzburg Fortress. Most of the attractions are on this side of the river. The new town and business districts are on the right (north) bank, along with most of the cheaper hostels.

Information

Tourist Offices There are several tourist offices in Salzburg (☎ 889 87, email tourist@salzburginfo.or.at). For hotel reservations call ☎ 88 98 73 14, fax 889 87 32; a commission of AS30 is charged. The central office, at Marktplatz 5, is open from 9 am to 7 pm daily, April to September (8 pm in July and August); it closes at 6 pm from October to March and on Sunday. The regional information section (☎ 84 32 64) in the same building is open from 9 am to 6 pm Monday to Saturday.

Other information offices, open throughout the year, can be found in the Hauptbahnhof on platform 2a; in the airport; at Mitte; Münchener Bundesstrasse 1; and in the south at Park & Ride Parkplatz (Alpensiedlung Süd, Alpenstrasse). The office in

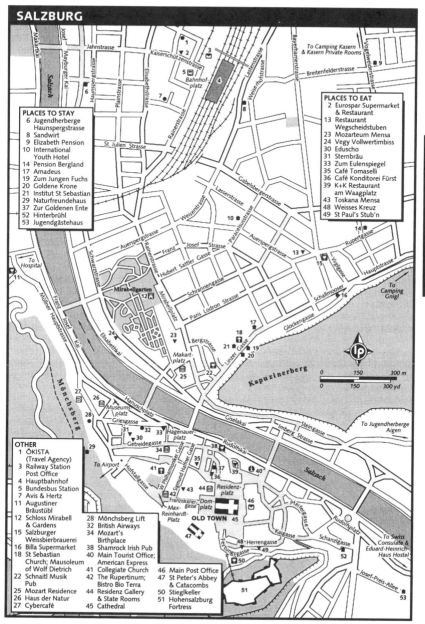

SALZBURG

PLACES TO STAY
6 Jugendherberge
   Haunspergstrasse
8 Sandwirt
9 Elizabeth Pension
10 International
   Youth Hotel
14 Pension Bergland
17 Amadeus
19 Zum Jungen Fuchs
20 Goldene Krone
21 Institut St Sebastian
29 Naturfreundehaus
37 Zur Goldenen Ente
52 Hinterbrühl
53 Jugendgästehaus

PLACES TO EAT
2 Eurospar Supermarket
   & Restaurant
13 Restaurant
   Wegscheidstuben
23 Mozarteum Mensa
24 Vegy Vollwertimbiss
30 Eduscho
31 Sternbräu
33 Zum Eulenspiegel
35 Café Tomaselli
36 Café Konditorei Fürst
39 K+K Restaurant
   am Waagplatz
43 Toskana Mensa
48 Weisses Kreuz
49 St Paul's Stub'n

OTHER
1 ÖKISTA
   (Travel Agency)
3 Railway Station
   Post Office
4 Hauptbahnhof
5 Bundesbus Station
7 Avis & Hertz
11 Augustiner
   Bräustübl
12 Schloss Mirabell
   & Gardens
15 Salzburger
   Weissbierbrauerei
16 Billa Supermarket
18 St Sebastian
   Church; Mausoleum
   of Wolf Dietrich
22 Schnaitl Musik
   Pub
25 Mozart Residence
26 Haus der Natur
27 Cybercafé

28 Mönchsberg Lift
32 British Airways
34 Mozart's
   Birthplace
38 Shamrock Irish Pub
40 Main Tourist Office;
   American Express
41 Collegiate Church
42 The Rupertinum;
   Bistro Bio Terra
44 Residenz Gallery
   & State Rooms
45 Cathedral

46 Main Post Office
47 St Peter's Abbey
   & Catacombs
50 Stieglkeller
51 Hohensalzburg
   Fortress

EXCURSIONS

euro currency converter DM1 = €.51

the north at Autobahnstation Kasern is open from June to September.

Tourist offices and hotels sell the Salzburg Card, which provides free museum entry, free public transport and a bevy of reductions. It costs AS200/290/380 for 24/48/72 hours. Salzburg Plus is a pre-paid card including meals and accommodation starting at AS1560 – chances are you'll do just fine without it.

Money Banks are open from 8 am to noon and from 2 to 4.30 pm Monday to Friday. Currency exchange at the train station counters is available daily to at least 8.30 pm.

Post & Communications The post office at the Hauptbahnhof is open from 6 am to 11 pm daily, including for money exchange. The main post office, in the town centre, at Residenzplatz 9, is open from 7 am to 7 pm Monday to Friday, and from 8 to 10 am Saturday. The *Poste Restante* address is Bahnhofspostamt, Bahnhofplatz 5020.

The Cybercafé (☎ 84 26 16/22), Gstättengasse 27, is open from 2 pm to 10 pm and charges AS40 per half-hour in the surf.

Internet Resources Salzburg's Web site, with an English version and a free on-line accommodation booking function, is at www.salzburginfo.or.at.

Travel Agencies American Express (☎ 808 00) is next to the main tourist office at Mozartplatz 5. It is open 9 am to 5.30 pm Monday to Friday, and Saturday till noon. ÖKISTA (☎ 45 87 33), at Fanny-von-Lehnerstrasse 1, near the train station, keeps the same hours.

Medical & Emergency Services The Landeskrankenhaus hospital, St Johanns-Spital (☎ 44 820), is at Müllner Hauptstrasse 48, just north of the Mönchsberg.

Dial ☎ 141 for an ambulance.

Things to See & Do
Walking Tour The old town is a baroque masterpiece set amid the Kapuzinerberg and Mönchsberg mountains, both of which have a good network of footpaths. Take time to wander around the many plazas, courtyards, fountains and churches.

Start at the vast **Dom** (cathedral) on Domplatz, which has three bronze doors marked Hope, Faith, and Charity. Head west along Franziskanergasse and turn left into a courtyard for **St Peter's Abbey**, dating from 847 AD. The graveyard contains catacombs, which can be perused from 10.30 am till 5 pm in summer, and till 3.30 pm in winter (AS12/8). The western end of Franziskanergasse opens out into Max Reinhardt Platz, where you'll see the back of Fischer von Erlach's **Collegiate Church** on Universitätsplatz. This is considered an outstanding example of baroque architecture, although the cherubs and clouds above the altar border on parody.

Festung Hohensalzberg The fortress is Salzburg's centrepiece. It's a 15 minute wheeze up the hill to the castle, or you can take the Festungsbahn (a venicular railway, AS24 up, AS34 return) from Festungsgasse 4. Note the many turnip reliefs – this was the symbol of Archbishop Leonhard von Keutschach who funnelled a lot of money into expansion of the fortress. It's worth the extra AS40 for a guided tour of the torture chambers, state rooms, tower and two museums (give the third one, a corny exhibit of marionettes, a wide berth).

Museums In the Haus der Natur (☎ 84 26 53) at Museumplatz 5, you could easily spend hours wandering around the enlightening displays. Besides the usual flora, fauna and mineral exhibits there are sections on physics and astronomy (pity about the lack of signs in English). The 4th floor is a gory highlight with stomach-churning displays of deformed animals. It's open from 9 am to 5 pm daily (AS55/30).

In the **Residenz** (☎ 80 42 26 90), Residenzplatz 1, you can visit the baroque state rooms of the archbishop's palace (AS70, by guided tour only) and the gallery which houses a collection of 16th and 17th century Dutch and Flemish masterpieces (AS50).

The **Rupertinum** (☎ 80 42 23 36), Wiener-Philharmoniker-Gasse 9, has 20th century art and temporary exhibitions (AS40/20).

Mozart's **Geburtshaus** (birthplace), at Getreidegasse 9, and his **Wohnhaus** (residence) at Makartplatz 8, are popular but their displays overlap to a great extent. Entry costs AS70 and AS65 respectively, or AS110/85 for a combined ticket. They both contain musical instruments, sheet music and other memorabilia of the irreverent genius (see boxed text 'Amadeus, Amadeus'). The Wohnhaus is the better of the two and also houses the Mozart Sound and Film Museum (free).

Schloss Mirabell This palace was built by the worldly prince-archbishop Wolf Dietrich for his mistress in 1606. Its charming gardens featured in *The Sound of Music* and are a great place to while away the hours. 'Musical Spring' and other concerts are held in the palace. If it happens to be open, take a peek inside at the marble staircase, which is draped with baroque sculptures. The cost depends on the concert.

Mausoleum of Wolf Dietrich Hidden away in the graveyard of the 16th century St Sebastian Church on Linzer Gasse, this restored mausoleum has some wonderful epitaphs. In a piece of unparalleled arrogance, the archbishop commands readers to 'piously commemorate the founder of this chapel' (ie himself) and his close relations or expect 'God Almighty to be an avenging judge'. Mozart's father and widow are also buried in the graveyard.

Organised Tours

One-hour walking tours of the old town leave from the main tourist office (AS80). Other tours of Salzburg mostly depart from Mirabellplatz, including the heavily promoted *Sound of Music* tour.

Locals are bemused by its popularity with Anglo-Saxon audiences (the film was a flop in Austria). Tours last three to four hours, cost around AS350, take in major city sights featured in the movie and include a visit to the Salzkammergut region. If you take it lightly it can be brilliant fun:

Amadeus, Amadeus

Wolfgang Amadeus Mozart was only 35 years old when he died in 1791, yet he composed some 626 pieces, including 24 operas, 49 symphonies, over 40 concertos, 26 string quartets, seven string quintets and numerous sonatas for piano and violin. Haydn proclaimed him the 'greatest composer' of all-time, and Schubert effused that the 'magic of Mozart's music lights the darkness of our lives'.

Mozart was born in Salzburg and learned how to play the harpsichord at age three. Two years later, his musician father, Leopold, gave a small violin to the child prodigy who, without the benefit of lessons, played well enough, a few days later, to join a professional quartet. Leopold was quick to exploit his son's astounding talent, taking Wolfgang and his sister Nannerl (four years older and also exceptionally gifted) on a successful European concert tour.

At 14, Mozart was appointed director of the archbishop of Salzburg's orchestra. In 1781 he settled in Vienna, where he enjoyed his most productive years. He was also something of a ladies' man: at age 24 he boasted, 'If I had married everyone I jested with, I would have well over 200 wives'. A year later he married Constanze Weber (despite his obvious affections for her opera-singer sister, Aloysia).

In Vienna, Mozart also suffered his worst bouts of compulsive gambling – losing large sums in billiards, ninepins and cards. He also lived too hard and fast for his own good, ate poorly and attended all-night parties probably like those depicted in the Oscar-winning film *Amadeus* (1985). Upon his death, his body was dispatched to a ditch in St Mark's Cemetery in Vienna after a pauper's funeral.

---

euro currency converter DM1 = €.51

it's hard to forget manic Julie Andrews impersonators flouncing in the fields, screeching 'the hills are alive' in voices to wake the dead. On the other hand, if you've got an earnest group the tour can be tedious. (See the Jugendgästehaus under Places to Stay for the cheapest tour.)

Special Events
The Salzburg International Festival takes place from late July to the end of August, and includes music ranging from Mozart (of course!) to contemporary. Several events take place each day in different locations, with prices varying from AS50 to more than AS4000, with reductions for those under 26. The cheapest prices are for standing-room tickets, which can usually be pre-booked. Most things sell out months in advance. For information (starting in October) write to: Kartenbüro der Salzburger Festspiele, Postfach 140, A-5010 Salzburg. Try checking the ticket office closer to the event for cancellations (☎ 84 45 579, fax 80 45 760, email info@salzburgfestival.at), Herbert-von-Karajan-Platz 11. Opening hours during the festival are 9.30 am to 5 pm daily. Other important festivals are at Easter and Whit Sunday.

Places to Stay – Budget
Ask for the tourist office's hotel map which gives prices for hotels, pensions, six hostels and six camping grounds. Accommodation is at a premium during festivals. The tourist office can book private rooms (from AS250), but you can also ask for its list of rooms in the Kasern area, a cheaper area just north of the city limits.

Camping Camping Kasern (☎/fax 45 05 76, Carl-Zuckmayer-Strasse 4) just north of the A1 Nord exit, costs AS60 per adult and AS35 each for a car and tent (open April through October). From the main train station, take bus Nos 1, 2, 5, 6, 51 or 55 in the direction 'Centrum' and alight at the third stop (Mirabellplatz). Then cross the road to the corner of Paris-Lodron Strasse and take bus No 15 in the direction Kasern-Bergheim, alighting at the Jägerwirt stop.

Camping Gnigl (☎ 64 30 60, Parscher Strasse 4), east of Kapuzinerberg costs marginally less (open mid-May to mid-September). Take a bus to Mirabellplatz (see Camping Kasern), switch to bus No 29 and alight at the fifth stop (Minnesheimstrasse). Walk east two minutes on Minnesheimstrasse and take a left onto Parscher Strasse – the camp site is on your immediate right.

Hostels Party animals should head to the sociable International Youth Hotel, or Yo-Ho (☎ 87 96 49, fax 87 88 10, Paracelsusstrasse 9). There's a bar with loud music and cheap beer, and the staff are mostly young, native English-speakers. It's popular, and reservations are accepted no earlier than one day before. Beds per person are AS140 (eight-bed dorm), AS160 (four-bed dorm, own key) and AS180 (double room, own key). There's a 1 am curfew and it's open all day. Showers cost AS10, lockers AS10 and sheets (if required) AS20. Breakfasts are AS30 to AS55, dinners AS60 to AS75. The hotel also organises outings and shows The Sound of Music film daily.

The HI Jugendgästehaus (☎ 84 26 70-0, fax 84 11 01, Josef-Preis-Allee 18), is large, modern and busy, and probably the most comfortable hostel. Eight-bed dorms are AS164, four-bed rooms AS214 and doubles are AS264; all prices are per person and include an AS10 surcharge on the first night's stay. Telephone reservations are accepted or turn up at 11 am to be sure of a bed (reception may be shut otherwise). Bikes are rented for just AS95 per day. The daily Sound of Music tours are the cheapest in town – AS300, leaving at 8.45 am and 1.30 pm daily.

The HI Jugendherberge (☎ 87 50 30, fax 88 34 77, Haunspergstrasse 27) near the train station is open July and August and costs AS170. Institut St Sebastian (☎ 87 13 86/80, fax 87 13 85), through the big stone portal at Linzer Gasse 4, has a roof terrace and guest kitchens to boot. Dorm beds cost AS180 plus AS30 for sheets; singles/doubles are AS390/680 with shower/WC or AS330/580 without. Earplugs are useful for the early-morning church bells.

The *Naturfreundehaus (☎ 84 17 29, Mönchsberg 19)*, also called Gasthaus Bürgwehr, is clearly visible high on the hill, between the fortress and Café Winkler. Take the footpath up from near Max-Reinhardt-Platz, or the Mönchsberg lift (AS16 up, AS27 return) from Anton-Neumayr-Platz. It offers dorm beds for AS120 (showers AS10) and marvellous views. It has a restaurant (see Places to Eat) but rooms are only available from May through September.

Last but not least there are two HI hostels in the south: *Jugendherberge Aigen (☎ 62 32 48, fax 62 79 80, Aignerstrasse 34)* and *Eduard-Heinrich-Haus (☎ 62 59 76, Eduard-Heinrich-Strasse 2)*. Beds in both cost AS160.

Hotels & Pensions All prices quoted below are for high season.

Sandwirt (☎/fax 87 43 51, Lastenstrasse 6a), is near the rail line but the rooms are reasonably large and quiet. Singles/doubles are from AS300/480, using hall shower; there are doubles with private facilities for AS580.

Elizabeth Pension (☎/fax 87 16 64, Vogelweiderstrasse 52), charges AS300/520 for nicely renovated singles/doubles (AS350/560 with private shower cubicle in room). It's near the Breitenfelderstrasse stop for bus No 15, which heads to the centre every 15 minutes. Singles aren't available in July or August.

Zum Junger Fuchs (☎ 87 54 96, Linzer Gasse 54) has singles/doubles/triples for AS280/380/480, without breakfast. The rooms are better than the cramped halls would suggest.

Hinterbrühl (☎ 84 67 98, Schanzlgasse 12), is affordable for an old town location, with singles/doubles for AS470/620, using hall shower. Breakfast costs AS50. Reception in the downstairs restaurant is open from 8 am to nearly midnight.

Places to Stay – Mid-Range

Goldene Krone (☎ 87 23 00, Linzer Gasse 48), has singles/doubles with private shower/WC for AS570/900; some of the rooms have church-like groined ceilings.

Amadeus (☎ 87 14 01, fax 876 16 63/7, Linzer Gasse 43–45) just down the road charges AS680/1000 for singles/doubles with private facilities and TV.

The *Pension Bergland (☎ 87 23 18/0, fax 87 23 18/8, email pkuhn@sol.at, Rupertgasse 15)* has comparable quarters for AS560/920.

Out in the old town, try *Zur Goldenen Ente (☎ 84 56 22, fax 84 56 22/9, Goldgasse 10)* for something snazzier. All rooms have private bath/shower and TV, for prices from AS740/1050. The atmospheric restaurant (closed weekends) offers quality meals.

Places to Eat – Budget

There's a fruit and vegetable market at Mirabellplatz on Thursday morning. On Universitätsplatz and Kapitelplatz there are market stalls and fast-food stands. A *Billa* supermarket is on Schallmooser Hauptstrasse.

The large *Eurospar* supermarket by the Hauptbahnhof has a self-service restaurant; meals are around AS60, or half-price after 6 pm (open till 7 pm, 7.30 pm on Friday, 5 pm on Saturday, closed Sunday). The *Eduscho*, Getreidegasse 34, is a great spot for a coffee (AS8); you'll have to stand.

The best budget deals are in the university *mensas*. Lunches are served from 11.30 am to 2 pm on weekdays; set meals cost from AS40 for ISIC-card holders and from AS45 for others. The *Mozarteum Mensa* is between the Aicher Passage and Mirabellgarten. There are several mensas on the left bank, including the *Toskana (Sigmund Haffner Gasse 11)*.

One of the few vegetarian places in town is *Vegy Vollwertimbiss (☎ 87 57 46, Schwarzstrasse 21)*. This shop and restaurant has a salad buffet from AS35 and lunch menus from AS90. It's open from 10.30 am to 6 pm Monday to Friday. The *Bistro Bio Terra (☎ 84 94 14, Wiener-Philharmoniker-Gasse 9)* in the Rupertinum, is a worthy rival with pastas from AS66, health-food shakes for AS57 and a good *Eiscafé* (ice-coffee) for AS68.

The *Restaurant Wegscheidstuben (☎ 87 46 18, Lasserstrasse 1)* has a big menu, with pastas from AS75, juicy steaks from AS190 and pork dishes from AS115. It's an

EXCURSIONS

EXCURSIONS

archetypical Austrian place, frequented by locals, and it's open from 8 am to midnight, Tuesday to Saturday, and Sunday lunchtimes.

It's almost as if they're trying to keep *St Paul's Stub'n* (☎ *84 22 54, Herrengasse 16)* a secret from tourists. It's upstairs in the yellow house and completely anonymous from the outside. Pasta and tasty pizzas (from AS75) are served upstairs at the long wooden tables until late. It's open from 6 pm to 12.30 am daily.

Weisses Kreuz (☎ *84 56 41, Bierjodlgasse 6)*, does Balkan and some Viennese dishes; three-course menus start at just AS135. One highlight is the Serbian stuffed cabbage roulade (AS79). It's closed Tuesdays, except in summer.

The *Naturfreundehaus* up on Mönchsberg has stunning views and the food is good value, too, although you may have to send up a flare to attract a waiter (see also Places to Stay).

Coffee houses are a well-established tradition in Salzburg. *Café Tomaselli* (☎ *84 44 88, Alter Markt 9)* and *Café Konditorei Fürst* (☎ *84 37 59, Brodgasse 13)* face each other in an ideal spot overlooking Alter Markt. Both have newspapers, lots of cakes and outside tables.

Places to Eat – Mid-Range

Sternbräu (☎ *84 21 40, Griesgasse 23/Getreidegasse 34)* through the courtyard, has a labyrinth of dining rooms and a nice garden. It serves good Austrian food and fish specials from AS80 to AS240. It's open 9 am to midnight daily. Outside there's a self-service summer buffet and pizzeria.

K&K Restaurant am Waagplatz (☎ *84 21 56, Waagplatz 2)*, offers light dishes from AS85 and good medium-priced meals (eg roast suckling pig with fried potatoes for AS165). You can also splurge for a four-course menu at AS520.

Zum Eulenspiegel (☎ *84 31 80, Hagenauerplatz 2)* is, admittedly, a shade touristy, but the food is consistently good and the interior very homey. Mains range from AS158 to AS278, light meals cost AS80 to AS100, and the fish soup provencale is a must at AS89.

Beer Halls & Pubs

The atmospheric *Augustiner Bräustübl* (☎ *43 12 46, Augustinergasse 4)* proves that monks can make beer as well as anybody. The quaffing clerics have been supplying the lubrication for this huge beer hall for years. Beer is served in litre (AS56) or half-litre (AS28) mugs. Buy meat, bread and salad goods in the deli shops in the foyer (some are pricey); you can eat inside or in the large, shady beer garden. It's open from 3 pm (2.30 pm weekends) to 11 pm daily.

Stieglkeller (☎ *84 26 81, Festungsgasse 10)*, is another big beer hall (open May to September only). Ignore the leaflets for its hokey *Sound of Music* live show and head for the three-tiered garden section overlooking town. Food ranges from AS90 to AS180, and there's cheaper self-service beer upstairs. Hours are 10 am to 10 pm daily.

Try *Salzburger Weissbierbrauerei* (☎ *87 22 46/40)*, on the corner of Rupertsgasse and Virgilgasse, for wheat beer made on the premises (AS40 for half-litres of pale or dark). Snacks and light meals are also served. It's open from 10 am to midnight daily.

The *Schnaitl Musik Pub* (☎ *87 86 78, Bergstrasse 5)* has pool, videos and mostly local clientele. Most Fridays (not in summer) there's live rock or pop music; cover charge varies from nil to AS100. It opens from 7.30 pm (6.30 pm in winter) till 1 am daily.

The *Shamrock Irish Pub* (☎ *84 16 10, Rudolfskai 12)*, has live music nightly from 9 pm – folk, blues, soul, country, you name it (no cover charge). It's open from 3 pm (Sundays from 2 pm) until at least 2 am, daily.

Shopping

Few people leave Salzburg without sampling some Mozart confectionery. The chocolate-covered combinations of nougat and marzipan cost around AS5 apiece (cheaper in supermarkets). The 'original' *Mozartkugeln* at *Café Konditorei Fürst,* on Brodgasse, cost AS10 each, but they're worth it. Getreidegasse is the main shopping street for just about everything – eg clothing, food, souvenirs, Mozart balls.

Getting There & Away

Air The airport (☎ 858 02 51) handles regular scheduled flights to Amsterdam, Brussels, Frankfurt, London, Paris and Zürich. British Airways (☎ 84 21 08) has an office in the old town, at Griesgasse 29. For the airport counters of Austrian Airlines or Swissair, dial ☎ 85 44 11.

Train There are trains every 30 to 60 minutes to Munich (AS285, 1½ hours); Saturday and Sunday you're better off buying a *Wochenendkarte* (weekend ticket) for a regional RE train (AS245, two to 2½ hours). Fast trains leave for Vienna via Linz every hour (AS410). The express service to Klagenfurt (AS330) goes via Villach. The quickest way to Innsbruck is by the corridor train through Germany via Kufstein; trains depart at least every two hours (AS365). Call ☎ 17 17 or see the Austrian Railway's Web site at www.oebb.at (in German) for timetable and fare details.

Bus Bundesbuses depart from Südtiroler Platz (where there's a timetable board) across from the main train station, or call ☎ 46 60 for information. There are at least three departures a day to Kitzbühel (AS152, 2¼ hours with a change at Lofer). Buses also leave for the Salzkammergut region between 6.30 am and 8 pm daily, with destinations including Bad Ischl (AS120) and Mondsee (AS68). Bus links farther afield (eg Munich, Vienna or Prague) are very messy and involve changes between regional networks.

Busabout stops at the International Youth Hotel and also at Camping Kasern (see Places to Stay for addresses). Salzburg is on Busabout's clockwise 'red' loop that starts and ends in Amsterdam (via Berlin, Prague, Vienna, Budapest and Munich, among other stops). See the Getting There & Away chapter for details of Busabout passes.

Car & Motorcycle Three autobahns converge on Salzburg and form a loop round the city: the A1 from Linz, Vienna and the east, the A8/E52 from Munich and the west, and the A10/E55 from Villach and the south. Remember that you'll need to buy a pass (called a *Vignette*) if you use the Austrian autobahns. The weekly pass costs AS70 and can be bought at border posts, petrol stations or at motorway rest-stops. You'll be liable for a fine without one.

Car rental agencies in Salzburg include Avis (☎ 87 72 78), at Ferdinand Porsche Strasse 7, and Hertz (☎ 85 20 86), same address just around the corner.

Getting Around

To/From the Airport Salzburg airport is 4km west of the city centre. Bus No 77 goes there from the main train station.

Bus Bus drivers sell single bus tickets for AS25. Other tickets must be bought from Tabak shops, tourist offices or vending machines at most bus stops. For the city centre, day passes cost AS40, weekly passes AS110 and single tickets AS10. Children aged six to 15 years travel for half-price, while kids under age six go for free.

Car & Motorcycle Driving in the city centre is hard work. Parking places are very limited and much of the old town is pedestrian-access only. The largest car park near the centre is the Altstadt Garage (AS25 per hour) under the Mönchsberg. On streets with ticket machines (blue zones) a three-hour maximum applies during normal business hours (AS42, or AS7 for 30 minutes).

Other Transport Taxis cost AS35 (AS45 at night), plus about AS13 per kilometre in the centre or AS24 outside the city. To book a taxi ring ☎ 87 44 00.

Rent-a-Bike (☎ 88 87 31 63) at the train station is open 24 hours and charges AS80/100 for touring bikes for a half-day/full-day if you've got a valid train ticket (AS120/150 without). The Jugendgästehaus (see hostels under Places to Stay, earlier in this section) charges guests just AS60/90 for bicycles for the same periods.

Rates for pony-and-trap (Fiaker) for up to four passengers are around AS400 for 25 minutes and AS780 for 50 minutes (you can sometimes bargain the drivers down).

EXCURSIONS

NUREMBERG

☎ 0911 • pop 500,000

The dozen disastrous years of National Socialism haunt Nuremberg more than most other German cities, and for obvious reasons. During the 1930s the city was the main site for Nazi party rallies, and it was here that the infamous Nuremberg Laws revoking Jewish citizenship were enacted in 1935. After WWII the War Crimes Tribunal, now better known as the Nuremberg Trials, was held here.

But there are other aspects of Bavaria's second-largest city that, for the tourist, are worthy of inspection. For centuries it was

the unofficial capital of the (Germanic) Holy Roman Empire and preferred residence of German kings, who routinely convened their Diet, or parliament, here. Nuremberg was also the empire's 'Treasure Chest' from 1424 to 1800, acting guardian to the crown jewels and many of the priceless artworks on display today. And don't forget that Nuremberg's Christmas Market is Germany's most spectacular.

Orientation

Most main sights are within the Altstadt, which is ringed by reconstructed city walls

and a dry moat. The shallow Pegnitz River flows right through the centre of the city.

The Hauptbahnhof is just outside the city walls at the south-east corner of the Altstadt. The main artery, the mostly pedestrianised Königstrasse, takes you north from the Hauptbahnhof through Hauptmarkt and Rathausplatz and into Burgstrasse, which heads steeply uphill and brings you to the Kaiserburg.

The biggest attraction outside the Altstadt is the Reichsparteitagsgelände (also called Luitpoldhain), the Nazi rally ground southeast of the centre.

Information

Tourist Offices There are tourist offices in the Hauptbahnhof's main hall (☎ 233 61 31/32, fax 23 36 16 11, email tourismus@nuernberg.btl.de) and at Hauptmarkt 18 (☎ 233 61 35, fax 233 61 66). The former is open year-round from 9 am to 7 pm Monday to Saturday; the latter opens the same days until 6 pm. From October to April and during Christkindlesmarkt, both offices also see visitors on Sunday, 10 am to 1 pm and 2 to 4 pm.

The ADAC has a service hotline at ☎ 01805-10 11 12. The city lost & found service (☎ 26 10 70) is at Rothenburger Strasse 10, at the east end of the Hauptbahnhof.

Money There's a Reisebank in the Hauptbahnhof. Banks in the Altstadt include Commerzbank at Königstrasse 21 and a Hypovereinsbank at Königstrasse 3. American Express (☎ 23 23 97) has an office at Adlerstrasse 2 just off Königstrasse.

Post & Communications The main post office is at Bahnhofplatz 1 by the station. Nuremberg has several Internet cafes, including Cyberthek (☎ 446 68 93) at Pillenreuther Strasse 34 and Maximum (23 23 84) at Färberstrasse 11.

Internet Resources Nuremberg has a comprehensive Web site (also in English) at www.nuernberg.de.

Travel Agencies Atlas Reisen (☎ 20 67 50), Breite Gasse 72, offers the usual good discounts. Celtic Travel (☎ 45 09 74 20), Bulmannstrasse 26, specialises in travel to

NUREMBERG (NÜRNBERG)

PLACES TO STAY		
1	Jugendgästehaus	
9	Agneshof	
33	Pension Altstadt	
34	Hotel Avenue	
50	Pension Sonne	
53	Probst-Garni Hotel	
56	Am Jakobsmarkt	
57	Gasthof zum Schwänlein	
59	Meridien Grand Hotel Nürnberg	
62	Maritim Hotel	
63	InterCity Hotel	

PLACES TO EAT	
4	Burgwächter Restaurant
13	Enchilada
16	Alte Küch'n
18	Bratwursthäusle
23	Kettensteg
24	Café am Trödelmarkt
26	Naturkostladen Lotus
28	Heilig Geist Spital
40	Wok Man

42	Stefansbäck
49	Kaufhof; Markthalle
52	Doneria
55	Historische Bratwurstküche

OTHER	
2	Kaiserburg
3	Pilatushaus
5	Historischer Kunstbunker
6	Der Hase (The Hare)
7	Altstadthof Brewery
8	Albrecht Dürer Haus
10	Dürer Statue; Felsengänge
11	Fembohaus; Stadtmuseum
12	Meisengeige
14	Altes Rathaus
15	St Sebalduskirche
17	Spielzeugmuseum (Toy Museum)
19	Neues Rathaus
20	Tourist Office
21	Pfarrkirche Unsere Liebe Frau
22	Schöner Brunnen
25	Weinstadel

27	Café Lucas
29	O'Shea's
30	Hypovereinsbank
31	Mach 1
32	American Express
35	Treibhaus
36	Naussauer Haus
37	Tugendbrunnen
38	Lorenzkirche
39	Commerzbank
41	Atlas Reisen
43	Peter-Henlein-Brunnen
44	Hugendubel
45	Ehekarussell Brunnen
46	Maximum Internet Café
47	Buchhandlung Edelmann
48	Police Station
51	Amerika Haus; Dai Cinema
54	German National Museum
58	Handwerkerhof
60	Main Post Office
61	Tourist Office
64	Städtische Bühnen
65	Schauspielhaus/Kammerspiel

Ireland and Scotland. Plärrer Reisen (☎ 92 97 60), with an office at Gosterhofer Hauptstrasse 27, also has a last-minute ticket desk at the airport.

Bookshops & Libraries Hugendubel (☎ 236 20), Ludwigplatz 1, has a huge branch with lots of English-language books and a good selection of Lonely Planet titles. The Buchhandlung Edelmann (☎ 99 20 60), Kornmarkt 8, has a German travel section upstairs and some English-language novels downstairs. The research library at the German National Museum (see later in this section) has 50,000 volumes and 1500 periodicals.

Cultural Centres The Amerika Haus (☎ 20 33 27), Gleissbühlstrasse 13, near the Hauptbahnhof, runs an impressive range of cultural and artistic programs each month. There's an English-language discussion group and a resource library.

Laundry Schnell & Sauber has three coin laundries, all outside the Altstadt, that open from 6 am to midnight: at Sulzbacher Strasse 86 (tram No 8 to Deichslerstrasse) in the north-east; at Allersberger Strasse 89 (tram Nos 4, 7 and 9 to Schweiggerstrasse) in the south-east; and at Schwabacher Strasse 86 (U2, to St Leonhard) in the south-west. A load costs DM7, while drying is DM1 per 12 minutes.

Medical Services In a medical emergency, call the Bayerisches Rotes Kreuz (Bavarian Red Cross, ☎ 940 32 60). The closest city hospital, the Klinikum Nord (☎ 39 80) is at Professor-Ernst-Nathan-Strasse 1. Walk-in cases can also visit Dr Erler Unfallklinik (☎ 272 80) at Konthunazgarten 4–18.

Altstadt Walking Tour

This circuit, which goes north to the castle and loops counter-clockwise back to the market square, covers the main sights of the historic city centre over a leisurely two-hour walk. With stops, it can take the best part of two days; in this case, you may cleanly split the tour into north and south of the River Pegnitz.

Hauptmarkt The bustling Hauptmarkt has daily **markets** and is also the site of the famous Christkindlesmarkt (see Special Events later in this section). At the square's eastern end is the ornate Gothic **Pfarrkirche Unsere Liebe Frau** (1350–58) or simply the Frauenkirche; the figures beneath the clock, seven electoral princes, march clockwise three times around Charles IV, to chimed accompaniment every day at noon.

Near the tourist information office stands the 19m **Schöner Brunnen** (Beautiful Fountain), a stunning golden vision of 40 electors, prophets, Jewish and Christian heroes and other allegorical figures, rising from the square like a Gothic spire. It's a replica of the late-14th century original. On the market side hangs a seamless **golden ring**, polished bright by millions of hands; a local superstition has it that if you turn it three times, your wish will come true.

Altes Rathaus & Sebalduskirche Just north of Hauptmarkt is the Altes Rathaus (1616–22), a hulking pile with lovely Renaissance-style interiors. It houses the *Lochgefängnisse* (medieval dungeons, ☎ 231 26 90) which might easily put you off lunch. You must join a tour (DM4/2); from April to mid October and during the Christkindlesmarkt, they run daily every 30 minutes from 10 am to 4.30 pm.

Opposite the Altes Rathaus is the 13th century **St Sebalduskirche**, Nuremberg's oldest church that is replete with religious sculptures and symbols. Note the ornate carvings over the Bridal Doorway to the north, showing the Wise and Foolish Virgins. Inside, the highlight is the bronze **shrine of St Sebald**, a Gothic and Renaissance masterpiece which took its maker, Peter Vischer the Elder, and his two sons more than 11 years to complete.

Felsengänge Continue north along Rathausplatz, turn left into Halbwachsengässchen and you'll encounter the **Albrecht Dürer statue** in the square that bears his name. Directly underneath are the chilly **Felsengänge** (☎ 22 70 66), a four-story underground network burrowed into the sandstone in the 14th century to house a brewery and beer cellar. During WWII it served as an air-raid shelter. Take a jacket for the tours, daily at 11 am and 1, 3 and 5 pm (DM7/5, groups must number at least three).

Just north-east of here is the **Fembohaus** (☎ 231 25 95), Burgstrasse 15 (*not* Bergstrasse), a 16th century merchant house with amazing stucco and wood panelling which is home to the **Stadtmuseum** (entry DM4/2). This was due to reopen in 2000 after renovations.

Kaiserburg At the northern end of Bergstrasse, with a capped tower looming like a silent sentry, stands the **Kaiserburg** castle, which served for centuries as the 'treasure chest' of the Holy Roman Empire. The complex gives stunning views of the city and consists of three parts: the Kaiserburg and Stadtburg (the emperor's palace and city fortress) as well as the Burggrafenburg, which was largely destroyed by fire in 1420. Between its surviving towers was built the Kaiserstallung (Royal Stables), which today is the HI hostel.

The complex is roomier than the exterior lets on, embracing the Kaiser's living quarters, a Romanesque chapel, the Imperial and Knights' Halls, the **Sinwellturm** (tower, 113 steps), and an amazingly deep well (48m – they lower a platter of candles so you can see the depth) which still yields drinking water today. You can view everything for DM9/8, or just the well and tower for DM3/2.

Tiergärtnerplatz to Ludwigsplatz The western side of the castle touches **Tiergärtnerplatz**, with the **Albrecht Dürer Haus** (☎ 231 25 68), where Dürer, Germany's Renaissance draughtsman, lived from 1509 to 1528. The house, which features a large number of Dürer artefacts (entry DM5/3), was recently reopened with a new collection of the master's graphic works.

Opposite, in front of the **Pilatushaus** – marked by an armoured St George atop the beast – is Jürgen Goetz's 1984 bronze sculpture **Der Hase – Hommage á Dürer** (The Hare – A Tribute to Dürer). This nod to the *Junger Feldhase* of 1502 shows the dire results of tampering with nature (not that the tourists clambering over it seem to notice).

Nearby is the **Historischer Kunstbunker** (☎ 22 70 66), Obere Schmiedgasse 52, the shelter that housed the city's art treasures during the bombing raids of WWII. You can visit on tours (DM5) on Thursday, Saturday and Sunday at 3 pm from April to December (the rest of the year, Saturday and Sunday only).

A few blocks south of the Dürer house, after winding around the back of Sebalder Platz, you'll hit the **Spielzeugmuseum** (Toy Museum, ☎ 231 31 64) at Karlstrasse 13–15, exhibiting playthings from through the ages. It's open from 10 am to 5 pm Tuesday to Sunday and to 9 pm on Wednesday (DM5/2.50).

From the Toy Museum carry on south, take the first right on Weintraubengasse and the first left into the alley which leads to the impressive, half-timbered **Weinstadel**, an old wine depot festooned with geraniums in summer.

Cross the covered wooden **Henkersteg**, a two-part bridge spanning a tiny island which is the site of the old **Trödelmarkt** (flea market), and rest your heels in the lovely cafe of the same name (see Places to Eat later in this section).

Ludwigsplatz to Lorenzplatz South of the Henkersteg, continue along Hutergasse and turn south-west into Ludwigsplatz. At its south end, before the fortified **Weisser Turm** (White Tower), stands the amazing **Ehekarussell Brunnen**, a large metallic fountain with six interpretations of marriage (some of them quite harrowing) based on a verse by Hans Sachs, the medieval cobbler-poet. To the north-east on Hefnerplatz, you'll see another modern fountain, the **Peter-Henlein-Brunnen** dedicated to the 16th century tinkerer credited with making the first pocket watch.

Continue east on Karolinenstrasse to reach the city's oldest house, **Nassauer Haus**, which occupies a rebuilt 13th century tower at No 2.

Lorenzkirche Just east of Nassauer Haus, the **Lorenzplatz** is dominated by the massive

EXCURSIONS

Lorenzkirche (Church of St Lawrence), of which only the towers survived WWII. The highlight is its 15th century tabernacle with delicate carved strands winding up to the vaulted ceiling. Also remarkable are the stained glass windows (including a rosetta window 9m in diameter) and artworks such as Veit Stoss' *Engelsgruss* (Annunciation, 1517), a massive wooden carving suspended above the high altar.

On the north side of the church stands the **Tugendbrunnen**, a fountain with seven Virtues proudly spouting water from their breasts, in the shadow of a figure of Justice. Continuing north up Königstrasse will return you to Hauptmarkt, the start of the walking tour.

German National Museum

The Germanisches Nationalmuseum (☎ 133 10), Kartäusergasse 1, is one of the most important general museums of German culture, spanning the ancient to the early 20th century. It features works by German painters and sculptors, an archaeological collection, arms and armour, musical and scientific instruments and toys. It's open from 10 am to 5 pm Tuesday to Sunday, and to 9 pm on Wednesday. Admission costs DM6/3 (except Wednesday evening, when it's free). Free **guided tours** in English take place the first and third Sunday of each month at 2 pm, but you still pay regular admission.

In Kartäusergasse at the museum's entrance is the **Way of Human Rights**, a symbolic row of 29 white concrete pillars (and one oak tree) bearing the 30 articles of the Universal Declaration of Human Rights. Each pillar is inscribed in German and, in succession, the language of a people whose rights have been violated. While the intentions were noble, the result is a bit antiseptic.

Handwerkerhof

The Handwerkerhof, a re-creation of a crafts quarter of old Nuremberg, is a walled tourist trap by the Königstor. Open from March to December, it's about as quaint as a hammer on your thumbnail but if you're cashed up you'll find some decent merchandise (eg leather goods). The Bratwurstglöcklein im Handwerkerhof (see Places to Eat) is also good, with friendly service and good sausages, but the other restaurants are a little cheesy – accordion versions of *In the Mood* and violinists assaulting your table. The yard closes at 10 pm.

Reichsparteitagsgelände

Nuremberg's role during the Third Reich is emblazoned in minds around the world: the B&W images of ecstatic Nazi supporters thronging the city's flag-lined streets as goose-stepping troops salute their *Führer*.

The rallies were part of an orchestrated propaganda campaign that began as early as 1927 to garner support for the party. In 1933, Hitler decided that a purpose-built venue would be a better backdrop than the Altstadt, so the party planned an outsized complex in the Dutzendteichpark to the south-east (see boxed text 'Monument to Madness'). Nazi leaders hoped to bridge a metaphorical link between Nuremberg's illustrious past as **Reichstagstadt** (the parliamentary seat of the Holy Roman Empire) and the Third Reich's new rally centre (Reichsparteitag).

A chilling multi-media presentation, *Fascination and Terror*, can be seen in the current exhibit (☎ 231 56 66) in the rear of the Zeppelin Tribune. It's open from 10 am to 6 pm, Tuesday to Sunday, mid-May to October. The exhibit is free, but the presentation costs DM2/1.

Take the S2 to Frankenstadion (every 20 minutes); tram No 9 from the Hauptbahnhof to the Luitpoldhain-Volkspark; or tram No 4 or bus No 55 or 65 to Dutzendteich.

Court of Justice

The Justizgebäude (☎ 321 26 79), west of the Altstadt at Fürtherstrasse 110, is the state courthouse in which the war crimes trials were held after WWII. It's not normally open to visitors, though you can see the outside. Take the U1 towards Fürth. The trials, which were held in Room 600, were set in Nuremberg by the Allies for symbolic and practical reasons. The very laws passed by the Nazis to justify the arrest and later extermination of Jews were called the *Nürnberger Gesetze* (Nuremberg Laws),

Monument to Madness

The eerie Nazi-era grounds at 'Luitpoldhain' (Luitpold Grove) were originally laid out for a more constructive purpose – the Bavarian Jubilee Exhibition of 1906 – long before Hitler pressed them into party service. The 1930s blueprints foresaw the **Zeppelinwiese**, a military parade ground; the never-completed **Deutsches Stadion**, which was to seat 400,000; and the **Luitpoldarena**, designed for mass SS and SA parades. The **Kongresshalle**, the half-built pile which still stands today, was meant to outdo Rome's Colosseum in both scale and style, and is a fitting monument to Nazi megalomania.

Discussion about a meaningful use of the Luitpoldhain has been going on since 1945; nowadays the **Zeppelintribune** complex hosts sporting events (including the Noriscar races in June) and occasional rock concerts, while the Kongresshalle acts as a warehouse for a large mail-order firm. The latest proposal is to install a **documentation centre**, including an archive and museum, on the north side of the Kongresshalle by early 2001.

EXCURSIONS

passed in 1935. In addition, the building was one of few such complexes to survive the war intact.

The trials began shortly after the war and concluded on 1 October 1946, resulting in the conviction of 22 Nazi leaders and 150 underlings, and the execution of dozens. Among those condemned early on were Joachim von Ribbentrop, Alfred Rosenberg, Wilhelm Frick and Julius Streicher, the notoriously sadistic Franconian party leader and publisher of the anti-Semitic weekly *Der Stürmer*. Hermann Göring, the Reich's portly field marshal, cheated the hangman by taking a cyanide capsule in his cell.

Organised Tours
The tourist office operates walking tours that meet at the Hauptmarkt tourist office. There are daily two-hour tours in German (DM8, under 14's free) at 10 am and 2.30 pm (Wednesday only at 2.30 pm, no tours on major holidays). English-language walking tours (DM12/under 14's free, 2½ hours) run daily from May to October at 2 pm (and as an added bonus, include a visit to the castle that's not on the German tour).

History For All (☎ 33 27 35) conducts two-hour tours of the Nazi rally area at Luitpoldhain at 2 pm Saturday and Sunday from April to November (DM8/6). Meet at Luitpoldhain, the last stop of tram No 9.

The Nürnberger Altstadtrundfahrten (☎ 421 91 9) is a tourist train that loops

through the Altstadt for half-hour guided tours in German. The cost is DM7/6; they run from 10 am daily and start at Hauptmarkt.

Special Events
From the Friday before Advent to Christmas Eve, the Hauptmarkt is taken over by the famous **Christkindlesmarkt**. During the market, scores of stalls are set up selling mulled wine, spirits, roast sausages and various trinkets. Not to be missed are **Lebkuchen**, the big ginger-and-spice cookies normally eaten at Yuletide (although you can buy them here year-round).

Nuremberg celebrates its 950th birthday in the summer of 2000 – check with the tourist office for program details. The climax will be in mid-July, when the city stages a three-day anniversary blow-out, although special events are scattered over the whole year.

Places to Stay – Budget
Book rooms at the tourist information office for DM5 per room. Accommodation gets tight during the Christkindlesmarkt and the toy fair (a closed event) in late January to early February; that said, cheap rooms can be found at other times, especially if you book ahead.

Camping *Campingplatz im Volkspark Dutzendteich (☎ 81 11 22, Hans-Kalb-Strasse 56)* is near the lakes in the Volkspark, south-east of the city centre (U1 from the

euro currency converter DM1 = €.51

Hauptbahnhof takes you to Messezentrum, which is fairly close). It costs DM8 per person plus DM10 per site, and is open from early May to late September.

Hostels The excellent *Jugendgästehaus* (☎ 230 93 60, fax 23 09 36 11, Burg 2) is in the Kaiserstallung, next to the castle. Dorm beds, including sheets and breakfast, cost DM29 (juniors only). The cheapest option for those aged over 26 is the *Jugend-Hotel Nürnberg* (☎ 521 60 92, fax 521 69 54, Rathsbergstrasse 300), north of the city. Take the U2 to Herrnhütte, then bus No 21 north four stops. Dorm beds start at DM26, and there are singles/doubles from DM39/64; prices exclude breakfast which costs an extra DM7.50.

Pensions & Hotels The most reasonable pension in the city centre is the friendly *Probst Garni Hotel* (☎ 20 34 33, fax 205 93 36, Luitpoldstrasse 9), on the 3rd floor in a creaky building. The simple rooms are minuscule but so are the prices, DM55/70, or DM70/110 with toilet and shower (including breakfast).

Another good deal is *Pension Altstadt* (☎ 22 61 02, fax 22 18 06, Hintere Ledergasse 4), with bathless singles/doubles from DM50/90. Near the station is *Gasthof Zum Schwänlein* (☎ 22 51 62, fax 241 90 08, Hintere Sterngasse 11), which has simple singles/doubles from DM35/70.

The *Pension Sonne* (☎ 22 71 66, Königstrasse 45) is one of the city's prize budget places, with bathless singles/doubles for DM56/92.

The simple and friendly *Pension Vater Jahn* (☎/fax 44 45 07, Jahnstrasse 13), south-west of the Bahnhof, has rooms from DM43/75. *Haus Vosteen* (☎ 53 33 25, Lindenaststrasse 12), just north-east of the Altstadt, charges from DM38/80 for unpresumptuous rooms.

Places to Stay – Mid-Range

Just south of the Pegnitz River, the *Hotel Avenue* (☎ 24 40 00, fax 24 36 00, Josephsplatz 10) has modern, comfortable rooms with very good facilities for the price (from DM135/195).

Entering the *Agneshof* (☎ 21 44 40, fax 21 44 41 44, Agnesgasse 10), near the castle, is a pleasure; the staff are polite and the rooms and facilities worth the DM155/188.

The *Am Jakobsmarkt* (☎ 200 70, fax 200 72 00, Schottengasse 5), in a tiny courtyard near the south-west Spittlertor in the centre, has modern rooms with excellent amenities for DM148/194.

The *InterCity Hotel* (☎ 247 80, fax 247 89 99, Eilgutstrasse 8) at the Hauptbahnhof, offers no surprises from the chain's usual standard, with rooms from DM190/245.

Nicer is the *Holiday Inn Crowne Plaza* (☎ 402 90, fax 40 40 67, Valznerweiherstrasse 200) south-east of the centre, with rooms from DM185 for both singles and doubles.

Places to Stay – Top End

Probably the most luxurious top-end hotel is right in the centre – the *Le Meridien Grand Hotel Nürnberg* (☎ 232 20, fax 232 24 44, Bahnhofstrasse 1–3) opposite the Hauptbahnhof. It features tonnes of amenities, great service and a good location. Singles/doubles cost from DM224/320.

Its competitor *Maritim Hotel* (☎ 236 30, fax 236 38 36, Frauentorgraben 11), offers about the same level of luxury, plus an indoor swimming pool. Singles/doubles cost DM253/304. You can also book rooms via email reservierung.nur@maritim.de.

Places to Eat

Snacks & Fast Food At *Alte Küch'n* (☎ 20 38 26, Albrecht-Dürer-Strasse 3), the house speciality is *Backers*, a kind of savoury cake of grated potato served with apple sauce or bacon, accompanied by sauerkraut (from DM8.50). The *Markthalle* in the basement of the Kaufhof department store on Königstrasse, is a good deal, with Turkish meals for less than DM10. You'll also find here a baker, a butcher and a wine bar.

Wok Man (☎ 20 43 11, Breite Gasse 48), is a good fast-food Chinese place with beef fried noodles for DM4, mixed vegetables and beef with noodles for DM6.50 and big meals for DM10 (closes at 8 pm). Nearby,

Church near Füssen

Fountain of Flora & Nymphs, Linderhof Castle

The fairy-tale castle, Schloss Neuschwanstein

Mozart's grave, Salzburg

The 'Eagle's Nest', Hitler's retreat at Kehlstein

Night falls on Salzburg

Dachau Concentration Camp

Stefansbäck (Breite Gasse 70), has generous sandwiches from DM3.

The *Naturkostladen Lotus (☎ 25 36 78 96)*, on Untere Kreuzgasse, is a health-food shop with veggie pizzas for DM3.50 and good hot meals for DM7.50 to DM8.50. The fresh bread and cheese counter is worth a look for picnic supplies.

Königstrasse is the ticket for conventional fast food, including *McDonald's* at No 71, *Burger King* at No 72, and the *Doneria* at No 69 serving turkey doners for DM4.

Restaurants & Bistros A tip for money-conscious diners is *Sabberlodd (☎ 33 55 52, Wiesentalstrasse 21)* just north-west of the Altstadt in the backstreets of St Johannis (tram No 6). It offers generous plates of ravioli and mixed salads for around DM10, along with inexpensive house wines and draught beers.

Probably the loveliest place to sit on a sunny day is the *Café am Trödelmarkt (☎ 20 88 77)*, on an island overlooking the covered Henkersteg bridge and the Weinstadel. They do continental breakfasts from DM7, and filled baguettes and salads for DM11 to DM17.

The *Burgwächter Restaurant (☎ 22 21 26, Am Ölberg 10)* in the shadow of the castle, is a great place to sit for drinks or a steak; main courses average DM14, and they have a beer garden with wonderful views of the city.

A classic Nuremberg restaurant is the *Heilig Geist Spital (☎ 22 17 61, Spitalgasse 16)*, with a large dining hall spanning the river. There's an extensive wine list and Franconian specialities from DM17.

The best open-air option is the leafy *Kettensteg (☎ 22 10 81, Maxplatz 35)*, with a prime view of the Pegnitz, away from the crowds. It has traditional Franconian fare averaging DM16 and a pretty interior.

Enchilada (☎ 244 84 98, Obstmarkt 5), is a trendy Mexican place behind the market. Decent taco platters, combination burritos and nachos all cost between DM10 and DM17.

Nuremberg Sausage There's heated competition between Regensburg and Nuremberg over whose sausages are the best. Judge for yourself: the *Bratwursthäusle (☎ 276 95, Rathausplatz 2)*, cooks them over a flaming grill; DM9.50 for six, DM11.90 for eight (closed Sunday). Typically served with potato salad, sauerkraut or horseradish, the little links taste even better with a local Patrizier or Tucher brew. We found the *Bratwurstglöcklein im Handwerkerhof (☎ 22 76 25)* to be just as good and just as expensive – see Handwerkerhof earlier in this section.

Locals prefer the *Historische Bratwurstküche (☎ 205 92 88, Zirkel-schmiedegasse 26)*, in the south-west part of the Altstadt, in a renovated 15th century inn. It's cheaper and much more 'genuine'.

Entertainment

Listings The excellent *Plärrer* (DM4) is available throughout the city and is heavy enough to kill someone with. It's also the best source of gay and lesbian places and events. The tourist office publishes *Das Aktuelle Monats Magazin*, which also has cultural events listings.

Pubs & Bars A popular student bar is the *Treibhaus (☎ 22 30 41)*, on Karl-Grillenberger-Strasse. They also serve cheap, filling food.

O'Sheas's (☎ 23 28 95, Wespennest 6–8), on the Schütt island in the middle of town, has cavernous vaulted rooms, Guinness and Kilkenny on tap, and Irish dishes such as cottage pie and trimmings (DM13.60).

Café Lucas (☎ 22 78 45, Kaiserstrasse 22), draws the designer set for cocktails; there's a nifty outside section with a platform that overlooks the river. In the north-east of the Altstadt, the *Meisengeige (☎ 20 82 83, Am Laufer Schlagturm 3)*, is a comfortable hole-in-the-wall bar which is attached to a tiny cinema.

The *Altstadthof Brewery (☎ 22 27 17, Bergstrasse 19)*, near the castle, is touristy but has a pleasant old-style pub.

Discos *Mach 1 (☎ 20 30 30, Kaiserstrasse 1–9)*, right in the centre of town, is a cool basement club with house, hip-hop, 70s & 80s and soul music parties.

EXCURSIONS

Planet Dance (☎ *68 67 67, Kilianstrasse 108)*, north of the centre near Freudenpark, is an enormous hall with neo-folk, romantic, pop, industrial-strength rock and a friendly crowd. *Hirsch* (☎ *42 94 14, Vogelweiherstrasse 66)*, is a great live alternative music scene. Take the U1 to Frankenstrasse in Gibitzen Hof Garden, to the south,

Forum (☎ *408 97 44, Regensburger-strasse 334)*, hosts regular big-name concerts and has occasional gay parties; take the S2 to Frankenstadion.

Theatre & Classical Music The Schauspiel Nürnburg performs a huge range of theatre, including drama, comedy and young people's performances, at the *Schauspielhaus* and the *Kammerspiel*, while classical music and opera can be seen at the *Städtische Bühnen*. All venues are on Richard-Wagner-Platz; for tickets, call ☎ 231 35 14.

Cinemas The *Roxy* (☎ *488 40, Julius Loss-mannstrasse 116)*, shows English-language first-run films. The *DAI Cinema* (☎ *230 69 0)* at the Amerika Haus (see Cultural Centres earlier in this section) regularly screens first-run and classic Anglo-Saxon films.

Getting There & Away
Air Nuremberg airport (☎ 350 60), 7km from the centre, is served by regional and international carriers including Lufthansa (☎ 26 61 15), Air Berlin (☎ 36 47 43), KLM (☎ 52 20 96) and Air France (☎ 529 85 22).

Train Hourly trains run to/from Munich (DM61, two hours). Trains run hourly to/from Frankfurt (DM69, 2¼ hours) and Stuttgart (DM54, 2¼ hours). There are connections several times daily to Berlin (DM144, 5¾ hours), and several daily trains travel to Vienna and to Prague (six hours each).

Bus BEX BerLinien buses leave for Berlin daily at 12.10 pm and arrive from Berlin at 2.30 pm daily. The SuperSpar/standard cost for a one-way ticket is DM62/112; for a return ticket it's DM108/136. For Munich, the SuperSpar/standard tickets cost DM/76/129 for singles or DM139/149 for returns to Nuremberg.

Car & Motorcycle Several autobahns converge on Nuremberg, but only the north-south A73 joins B4, the ring road. Coming from Munich, you take the A9 autobahn north till you reach the turn off marked No 37 for the A73, which leads north-west to the ring road.

Ride Services There's an ADM Mitfahrbüro (☎ 194 40) at Strauchstrasse 1.

Getting Around
To/From Airport Bus No 20 is an express shuttle (DM12) running every 20 minutes between the airport and the Hauptbahnhof from 5.30 am to nearly midnight. A taxi to/from the airport will cost DM20 to DM25. A U-Bahn connection to the airport is expected to open in 2000.

Public Transport Walking's the ticket in the city centre. Tickets on the VGN bus, tram and U-Bahn/S-Bahn networks cost DM2.50/3.30 per short/long ride in the centre. A day pass costs DM6.60/DM10.50 for one/two persons.

Taxi Flag fall is DM4.80, and the tarif is DM2.20 per kilometre. You can also take a BahnTaxi (DM12 per couple) from the northern end of the Hauptbahnhof between 5 pm and 1 am; order it on the train or at the DB Reisezentrum in the Hauptbahnhof.

Bicycle The Allgemeiner Deutscher Fahrrad Club (ADFC), with an office (☎ 39 61 32) at Rohledererstrasse 13, organises group rides throughout the year. The Fahrradkiste (☎ 287 90 64), Knauerstrasse 9, has kids' bikes for DM9, trekking and mountain bikes for DM15, and tandems for DM30, all prices are per day.

Ride on a Rainbow (☎ 39 73 37), Adam-Kraft-Strasse 55, rents foldable/mountain/trekking bikes for DM10/14/18 per day.

The city tourist office sells the ADFC's *Fahrrad Stadtplan*.

Language

Pronunciation

English speakers sometimes hold onto their vowels too long when speaking German, which causes comprehension problems. Nevertheless, there are long vowels, like *pope*, and short ones, like *pop*. Another common mistake is a tendency to pronounce all vowels as if they have umlauts (**ä**, **ö** and **ü**). It's worth practising the difference, as they often change the tense and meaning of a word. In most other respects German pronunciation is fairly straightforward. There are no silent letters, and many foreign words (eg *Band*, for 'rock band') are pronounced roughly the same as in English.

Vowels

a	short, as the 'u' in 'cut', or long, as in 'father'
au	as the 'ow' in 'vow'
ä	short, as in 'hat', or long, as in 'hare'
äu	as the 'oy' in 'boy'
e	short, as in 'bet', or long, as in 'obey'
ei	as the 'ai' in 'aisle'
eu	as the 'oy' in 'boy'
i	short, as in 'inn', or long, as in 'marine'
ie	as in 'siege'
o	short, as in 'pot', or long, as in 'note'
ö	as the 'er' in 'fern'
u	as in 'pull'
ü	similar to the 'u' in 'pull' but with stretched lips

Consonants

Most consonants and their combinations are roughly similar to English ones, with a few exceptions. At the end of a word, consonants **b**, **d** and **g** sound a little more like 'p', 't' and 'k' respectively. There are no silent consonants.

ch	throaty, as in Scottish *loch*
j	as the 'y' in 'yet'
ng	always one sound, as in 'strong'
qu	as 'kv'

r	trilled or guttural
s	as in 'see' or as the 'z' in 'zoo'
sch	as the 'sh' in 'shore'
st	usually pronounced 'sht'
sp	usually pronounced 'shp'
v	more like an English 'f'
w	as an English 'v'
z	as the 'ts' in 'tsar'

Grammar

German grammar can be a nightmare for English speakers. Nouns come in three genders: masculine, feminine and neutral. The corresponding forms of the definite article ('the' in English) are *der*, *die* and *das*, with the basic plural form, *die*. Nouns and articles will alter according to the case (nominative, accusative, dative and genitive). Note that German nouns always begin with a capital.

Many German verbs have a prefix that is often detached from the stem and placed at the end of the sentence. For example, *fahren* means 'to go' (by mechanical means), *abfahren* means 'to depart'; a simple sentence with the prefixed verb *abfahren* becomes: *Um wieviel Uhr fährt der Zug ab?* (What time does the train leave?).

You should be aware that German uses polite and informal forms for 'you' (*Sie* and *Du* respectively). When addressing people you don't know well you should always use the polite form (though younger people will be less inclined to expect it). In this language guide we use the polite form unless indicated by 'inf' (for 'informal') in brackets.

The following words and phrases should help you through the most common travel situations. Those with the desire to delve further into the language should get a copy of Lonely Planet's *German phrasebook*.

Greetings & Civilities

Hello.	*Hallo* or *Grüss Gott.*
Good morning.	*Guten Morgen.*
Good day.	*Guten Tag.*
Good evening.	*Guten Abend.*

Goodbye.	*Auf Wiedersehen.*
Bye.	*Tschüss.*
Yes.	*Ja.*
No.	*Nein.*
Where?	*Wo?*
Why?	*Warum?*
How?	*Wie?*
Maybe.	*Vielleicht.*
Please.	*Bitte.*
Thank you (very much).	*Danke (schön).*
You're welcome.	*Bitte or Bitte sehr.*
Excuse me.	*Entschuldigung.*
I'm sorry/Forgive me.	*Entschuldigen Sie, bitte.*
I'm sorry. (to express sympathy)	*Das tut mir leid.*

Signs

Eingang/Einfahrt	Entrance
Ausgang/Ausfahrt	Exit
Auf/Offen/ Geöffnet	Open
Zu/Geschlossen	Closed
Rauchen Verboten	No Smoking
Polizei	Police
WC/Toiletten	Toilets
Damen	Women
Herren	Men
Bahnhof	Train Station
Hauptbahnhof	Main Train Station
Notausgang	Emergency Exit

Language Difficulties

I understand.	*Ich verstehe.*
I don't understand.	*Ich verstehe nicht.*
Do you speak English?	*Sprechen Sie Englisch?/Sprichst du Englisch?* (inf)
Does anyone here speak English?	*Spricht hier jemand Englisch?*
What does ... mean?	*Was bedeutet ...?*
Please write it down.	*Bitte schreiben Sie es auf.*

Paperwork

first name	*Vorname*
surname	*Familienname*
nationality	*Staatsangehörigkeit*
date of birth	*Geburtsdatum*
place of birth	*Geburtsort*
sex (gender)	*Geschlecht*
passport	*Reisepass*
identification	*Ausweis*
visa	*Visum*

Small Talk

What's your name?	*Wie heissen Sie?/Wie heisst du?* (inf)
My name is ...	*Ich heisse ...*
How are you?	*Wie geht es Ihnen?/Wie geht's dir?* (inf)
I'm fine, thanks.	*Es geht mir gut, danke.*
Where are you from?	*Woher kommen Sie/ kommst du?* (inf)
I'm from ...	*Ich komme aus ...*

Getting Around

I want to go to ...	*Ich möchte nach ... fahren.*

What time does the ... leave/arrive?	*Um wieviel Uhr fährt ... ab/kommt ... an?*
boat	*das Boot*
bus	*der Bus*
train	*der Zug*
tram	*die Strassenbahn*

Where is the ...?	*Wo ist ...?*
bus stop	*die Bushaltestelle*
metro station	*die U-Bahnstation*
train station	*der Bahnhof*
main train station	*der Hauptbahnhof*
airport	*der Flughafen*
tram stop	*die Strassenbahn- haltestelle*

the next	*der/die/das nächste*
the last	*der/die/das letzte*
ticket office	*Fahrkartenschalter*
one-way ticket	*einfache Fahrkarte*
return ticket	*Rückfahrkarte*
1st/2nd class	*erste/zweite Klasse*
timetable	*Fahrplan*
platform number	*Gleisnummer*
luggage locker	*Gepäckschliessfach*

I'd like to hire ...	*Ich möchte ... mieten.*
a bicycle	*ein Fahrrad*
a motorcycle	*ein Motorrad*
a car	*ein Auto*

Directions

Where is ...?	*Wo ist ...?*
How do I get to ...?	*Wie erreicht man ...?*
Is it far from here?	*Ist es weit von hier?*
Can you show me (on the map)?	*Könnten Sie mir (auf der Karte) zeigen?*

street	*die Strasse*
suburb	*der Vorort*
town	*die Stadt*
behind	*hinter*
in front of	*vor*
opposite	*gegenüber*
straight ahead	*geradeaus*
(to the) left	*(nach) links*
(to the) right	*(nach) rechts*
at the traffic lights	*an der Ampel*
at the next corner	*an der nächsten Ecke*
north	*Nord*
south	*Süd*
east	*Ost*
west	*West*

Around Town

I'm looking for ...	*Ich suche ...*
a bank	*eine Bank/ Sparkasse*
the church	*die Kirche*
the city centre	*das Stadtzentrum*
the ... embassy	*die ... Botschaft*
my hotel	*mein Hotel*
the market	*den Markt*
the museum	*das Museum*
the post office	*das Postamt*
a public toilet	*eine öffentliche Toilette*
a hospital	*ein Krankenhaus*
the police	*die Polizei*
the tourist office	*das Fremden verkehrsbüro*

I want to change ...	*Ich möchte ... wechseln.*
some money	*Geld*
travellers cheques	*Reiseschecks*

| What time does ... open/close? | *Um wieviel Uhr macht ... auf/zu?* |
| I'd like to make a phone call. | *Ich möchte telefonieren.* |

bridge	*die Brücke*
castle/palace	*die Burg/das Schloss*
cathedral	*der Dom*
forest	*der Wald*
island	*die Insel*
lake	*der See*
monastery/convent	*das Kloster*
river	*der Fluss*
tower	*der Turm*

Accommodation

I'm looking for ...	*Ich suche...*
a hotel	*ein Hotel*
a guesthouse	*eine Pension*
a youth hostel	*eine Jugendherberge*
a campground	*einen Campingplatz*

Where is a cheap hotel?	*Wo findet man ein preiswertes Hotel?*
Please write the address.	*Könnten Sie bitte die Adresse aufschreiben?*
Do you have a room available?	*Haben Sie ein Zimmer frei?*
How much is it per night/person?	*Wieviel kostet es pro Nacht/Person?*
May I see it?	*Darf ich es sehen?*
Where is the bathroom?	*Wo ist das Badezimmer?*
It's very noisy/ dirty/expensive.	*Es ist sehr laut/ dreckig/teuer.*

I'd like to book a ...	*Ich möchte ... reservieren.*
bed	*ein Bett*
cheap room	*ein preiswertes Zimmer*
single room	*ein Einzelzimmer*
double room	*ein Doppelzimmer*
room with two beds	*ein Zimmer mit zwei Betten*
room with shower and toilet	*ein Zimmer mit Dusche und WC*
dormitory bed	*ein Bett im Schlafsaal*

| for one night | *für eine Nacht* |
| for two nights | *für zwei Nächte* |

| I'm/We're leaving now. | *Ich reise/Wir reisen jetzt ab.* |

Shopping

I'd like to buy ...	*Ich möchte ... kaufen*
How much is that?	*Wieviel kostet das?*
Do you accept credit cards?	*Nehmen Sie Kreditkarten?*

bookshop	*Buchladen*
chemist/pharmacy	*Apotheke* (medicine) *Drogerie* (toiletries)
department store	*Kaufhaus*
laundry	*Wäscherei*

more	*mehr*
less	*weniger*
bigger	*grösser*
smaller	*kleiner*

Health

I need a doctor.	*Ich brauche einen Ärzt.*
Where is a hospital?	*Wo ist ein Krankenhaus?*
I'm ill.	*Ich bin krank.*
It hurts here.	*Es tut hier weh.*
I'm pregnant.	*Ich bin schwanger.*

I'm ...	*Ich bin ...*
diabetic	*Diabetiker*
epileptic	*Epileptiker*
asthmatic	*Asthmatike*

I'm allergic to antibiotics/ penicillin.	*Ich bin allergisch auf Antibiotika/ Penizillin.*

antiseptic	*Antiseptikum*
aspirin	*Aspirin*
condoms	*Kondome*
contraceptive	*Verhütungsmittel*
diarrhoea	*Durchfall*
medicine	*Medikament*
the pill	*die Pille*
sunblock cream	*Sonnencreme*
tampons	*Tampons*

Times, Dates & Numbers

What time is it?	*Wie spät ist es?*
It's (10) o'clock	*Es ist (zehn) Uhr.*
It's half past nine.	*Es ist halb zehn.*
in the morning	*morgens/vormittags*
in the afternoon	*nachmittags*
in the evening	*abends*
at night	*nachts*

When?	*wann?*
today	*heute*
tomorrow	*morgen*
yesterday	*gestern*

Monday	*Montag*
Tuesday	*Dienstag*
Wednesday	*Mittwoch*
Thursday	*Donnerstag*
Friday	*Freitag*
Saturday	*Samstag/Sonnabend*
Sunday	*Sonntag*

January	*Januar*
February	*Februar*
March	*März*
April	*April*
May	*Mai*
June	*Juni*
July	*Juli*
August	*August*
September	*September*
October	*Oktober*
November	*November*
December	*Dezember*

1	*eins*
2	*zwei /zwo*
3	*drei*
4	*vier*
5	*fünf*
6	*sechs*
7	*sieben*
8	*acht*
9	*neun*

10	*zehn*
11	*elf*
12	*zwölf*
13	*dreizehn*
14	*vierzehn*
15	*fünfzehn*
16	*sechzehn*
17	*siebzehn*
18	*achtzehn*
19	*neunzehn*
20	*zwanzig*
21	*einundzwanzig*
22	*zweiundzwanzig*
30	*dreissig*
40	*vierzig*
50	*fünfzig*
60	*sechzig*
70	*siebzig*
80	*achtzig*
90	*neunzig*
100	*einhundert*
1000	*eintausend*
10,000	*zehntausend*

one million   *eine Million*

FOOD

breakfast	*Frühstück*
lunch	*Mittagessen*
dinner	*Abendessen*
menu	*Speisekarte*
restaurant	*Gaststätte/Restaurant*
pub/bar	*Kneipe*
supermarket	*Supermarkt*
snack bar	*Imbiss*

I'm a vegetarian.   *Ich bin Vegetarier(in).*
I'd like something   *Ich möchte etwas zu*
   to drink, please.   *trinken, bitte.*
It was very tasty.   *Es hat mir sehr*
   geschmeckt.
The bill, please?   *Die Rechnung, bitte.*
Please keep the   *Das stimmt so.* (lit:
   change.   'that's OK as is')

Menu Decoder

Eating at a restaurant in a foreign country can easily be bewildering. Fortunately, throughout Germany, you'll usually find menus posted outside the entrance, giving

you all the time you need to decide whether something speaks to your tastes. We've put together a short list of useful vocabulary terms to help you steer what you hunger for onto your plate.

Soups (*Suppen*)

Brühe – bouillon
Erbsensuppe – pea soup
Frühlingssuppe or *Gemüsesuppe* – vegetable soup
Hühnersuppe – chicken soup
Linsensuppe – lentil soup
Tomatensuppe – tomato soup

Meat (*Fleisch*)

Brathuhn – roast chicken
Bratwurst – fried pork sausage
Eisbein – pickled pork knuckles
Ente – duck
Fasan – pheasant
Frikadelle – flat meatball
Hackfleisch – chopped or minced meat
Hackbraten – meatloaf
Kaninchen or *Hase* – rabbit
Hirsch – male deer
Huhn or *Hähnchen* – chicken
Kalbfleisch – veal
Lammfleisch – lamb
Putenbrust – turkey breast
Reh – venison
Rindfleisch – beef
Rippenspeer – spare ribs
Sauerbraten – marinated and roasted beef
Schinken – ham
Schnitzel – pounded meat, usually pork, breaded and fried
Schweinefleisch – pork
Truthahn – turkey
Wild – game
Wildschwein – wild boar

Seafood (*Meeresfrüchte*)

Aal – eel
Austern – oysters
Barsch – perch
Forelle – trout
Dorsch – cod
Fisch – fish

Hummer – lobster
Karpfen – carp
Krabben – shrimp
Lachs – salmon
Matjes – marinated herring
Miesmuscheln or *Muscheln* – mussels
Scholle – plaice
Seezunge – sole
Thunfish – tuna

Vegetables *(Gemüse)*
Blumenkohl – cauliflower
Brokkoli – broccoli
Bohnen – beans
Erbsen – peas
Gurke – cucumber
Kartoffel – potato
Kohl – cabbage; can be *rot* (red), *weiss* (white) or *grün* (green)
Möhre – carrot
Paprika – bell/sweet pepper
Pilze – mushrooms
Rosenkohl – brussels sprouts
Spargel – asparagus
Tomate – tomato
Zwiebel – onion

Fruit *(Obst)*
Ananas – pineapple
Apfel – apple
Apfelsine or *Orange* – orange
Aprikose – apricot
Banane – banana
Birne – pear
Erdbeere – strawberry
Kirschen – cherries

Pampelmuse – grapefruit
Pfirsich – peach
Pflaume – plum
Weintrauben – grapes
Zitrone – lemon

Some Common Dishes
Auflauf – casserole
Eier, Rühreier – eggs, scrambled eggs
Eintopf – stew
Königsberger Klopse – meatballs in caper sauce
Kohlroulade – cabbage leaves stuffed with minced meat
Rollmops – pickled herring
Salat – salad

Cooking Methods
Frittiert – deep-fried
Gebacken – baked
Gebraten – pan-fried
Gefüllt – stuffed
Gegrillt – grilled
Gekocht – boiled
Geräuchert – smoked
Geschmort – braised
Paniert – breaded

Drinks *(Getränke)*
Bier – bier
Kaffee – coffee
Milch – milk
Mineralwasser – fizzy bottled mineral water
Saft – juice
Tee – tea
Wein – wine

Glossary

(pl) indicates plural

Abfahrt – departure (trains)
Abtei – abbey
ADAC – Allgemeiner Deutscher Automobil Club (German Automobile Association)
Allee – avenue
Altstadt – old town
Ankunft – arrival (trains)
Antiquariat – antiquarian bookshop
Apotheke – pharmacy
Arbeitsamt – employment office
Arbeitserlaubnis – work permit
Ärztlicher Notdienst – emergency medical service
Aufenthaltserlaubnis – residency permit
Auflauf, Aufläufe (pl) – casserole
Ausgang, Ausfahrt – exit
Aussiedler – German settlers who have returned from abroad (usually refers to post-WWII expulsions), sometimes called Spätaussiedler.
Autobahn – motorway
Autonom – left-wing anarchist
AvD – Automobilclub von Deutschland (Automobile Club of Germany)

Bad – spa, bath
Bahnhof – train station
Bahnsteig – train station platform
Bau – building
Bedienung – service
Berg – mountain
Besenwirtschaft – seasonal wine restaurant indicated by a broom above the doorway
Bezirk – district
Bibliothek – library
Bierkeller – cellar pub
Bierstube – traditional beer pub
Bildungsroman – literally 'novel of education'; literary work in which the personal development of a single individual is central
Bratkartoffeln – fried or roasted potatoes
BRD – Bundesrepublik Deutschland or, in English, FRG (Federal Republic of Germany). The name for Germany today; orginally applied to the former West Germany.
Brücke – bridge
Brunnen – fountain or well
Bundesland – federal state
Bundesrat – upper house of German Parliament
Bundestag – lower house of German Parliament
Bundesverfassungsgericht – Federal Constitutional Court
Burg – castle
Busbahnhof – bus station

CDU – Christian Democratic Union
Christkindlmarkt – Christmas market; *see also* Weihnachtsmarkt
CSU – Christian Social Union; Bavarian offshoot of CDU

DB – Deutsche Bahn (German national railway)
DDR – Deutsche Demokratische Republik or, in English, GDR (German Democratic Republic). The name for the former East Germany. *See also* BRD.
Denkmal – memorial
Deutsche Reich – German Empire. Refers to the period from 1871 to 1918.
DJH – Deutsches Jugendherbergswerk (German youth hostels association)
Dirndl – traditional women's dress (Bavaria only)
Dom – cathedral
Dorf – village
DZT – Deutsche Zentrale für Tourismus (German National Tourist Office)

Eingang – entrance
Eintritt – admission
Einwanderungsland – country of immigrants
Eiscafé – ice-cream parlour

Fahrplan – timetable
Fahrrad – bicycle

Fasching – pre-Lenten carnival (in Southern Germany)

FDP – Free Democrats

Ferienwohnung, Ferienwohnungen (pl) – holiday flat or apartment

Fest – festival

Flammekuche – Franco-German dish consisting of a thin layer of pastry topped with cream, onion, bacon and, sometimes, cheese or mushrooms, and cooked in a wood-fired oven. Found on menus in the Palatinate and the Black Forest.

Fleets – canals in Hamburg

Flohmarkt – flea market

Flughafen – airport

Föhn – an intense autumn wind in the Agerman Alps and Alpine Foothills

Forstweg – forestry track

Franks – Germanic people influential in Europe between the 3rd and 8th centuries

Friedhof – cemetary

Freikorps – WWI volunteers

Fremdenverkehrsamt – tourist office

Fremdenzimmer – tourist room

FRG – Federal Republic of Germany; see also BRD

Frühstück – breakfast

Garten – garden

Gasse – lane or alley

Gastarbeiter – literally 'guest worker'; labourer from Turkey, Yugoslavia, Italy or Greece after WWII to help rebuild Germany

Gästehaus, Gasthaus – guesthouse

Gaststätte – informal restaurant

GDR – German Democratic Republic (the former East Germany); see also BRD, DDR

Gedenkstätte – memorial site

Gemütlichkeit – literally 'cosiness'

Gepäckaufbewahrung – left-luggage office

Gesamtkunstwerk – literally 'total artwork', integrates painting, sculpture and architecture

Gestapo – Nazi secret police

Glockenspiel – literally 'bell play'; carillon, usually on a cathedral, sounded by mechanised figures often in the form of religious or historical characters

Gründerzeit – literally 'foundation time'; the period of industrial expansion in Germany following the founding of the German Empire in 1871

Hafen – harbour, port

halbtrocken – semi-dry (wine)

Hauptbahnhof – main train station

Heide – heath

Das Heilige Römische Reich – the Holy Roman Empire, which lasted from the 8th century to 1806. The German lands compromised the bulk of the Empire's territory.

Herzog – duke

Heu Hotels – literally 'hay hotels'; cheap forms of accommodation usually set in farmhouses and similar to bunk barns in the UK

Hitlerjugend – Hitler Youth organisation

Hochdeutsch – literally 'High German'; standard spoken and written German developed from a regional Saxon dialect

Hochkultur – literally 'high culture'; meaning 'advanced civilisation'

Hof, Höfe (pl) – courtyard

Höhle – cave

Hotel Garni – a hotel without a restaurant where you are only served breakfast

Imbiss – stand-up food stall; also see Schnellimbiss

Insel – island

Jugendgästehaus – youth guesthouse of a higher standard than a youth hostel

Jugendherberge – youth hostel

Jugendstil – Art Nouveau

Junker – originally a young, noble landowner of the Middle Ages; later used to refer to reactionary Prussian landowners

Kabarett – cabaret

Kaffee und Kuchen – literally 'coffee and cake'; traditional afternoon coffee break in Germany

Kaiser – emperor; derived from 'Caesar'

Kanal – canal

Kantine – cafeteria, canteen

Kapelle – chapel

Karneval – pre-Lenten festivities (along the Rhine)

Karte – ticket

Kartenvorverkauf – ticket booking office

Kino – cinema
Kirche – church
Kloster – monastery, convent
Kneipe – bar
Kommunales Kino – alternative or studio cinema
Konditorei – cake shop
König – king
Konsulat – consulate
Konzentrationslager (KZ) – concentration camp
Kreuzgang – monastery
Kristallnacht – literally 'night of broken glass'; attack on Jewish synagogues, cemeteries and businesses by Nazis and their supporters on the night of 9 November 1938 that marked the beginning of full-scale persecution of Jews in Germany. Also known as *Reichspogromnacht*.
Kunst – art
Kunstlieder – early German 'artistic songs'
Kurfürst – prince elector
Kurhaus – literally 'spa house', but usually a spa town's central building, used for social gatherings and events and often housing the town's casino
Kurort – spa resort
Kurtaxe – resort tax
Kurverwaltung – spa administration
Kurzentrum – spa centre

Land, Länder (pl) – state
Landtag – state parliament
Lederhose – traditional leather trousers with attached braces
Lesbe, Lesben (pl) – lesbian (n)
lesbisch – lesbian (adj)
lieblich – sweet (wine)
Lied – song

Maare – crater lakes in the Eifel Upland area west of the Rhine
Markgraf – margrave; German nobleman ranking above a count
Markgrafschaft – the holding of a Markgraf
Markt – market
Marktplatz (often abbreviated to Markt) – marketplace or square
Mass – one-litre tankard or stein of beer
Meer – sea

Mehrwertsteuer (MwST) – value-added tax
Meistersinger – literally 'master singer'; highest level in the medieval troubadour guilds
Mensa – university cafeteria
Milchcafé – milk coffee, *café au lait*
Mitfahrzentrale – ride-sharing agency
Mitwohnzentrale – an accommodation-finding service (usually long-term)
Münster – minster or large church, cathedral
Münzwäscherei – coin-operated laundrette

Norden – north
Notdienst – emergency service

Ossis – literally 'Easties'; nickname for East Germans
Ostalgie – a romanticised yearning back to the GDR era, derived from 'nostalgia'
Osten – east
Ostler – old term for an Ossi
Ostpolitik – former West German chancellor Willy Brandt's foreign policy of 'peaceful co-existence' with the GDR

Palast – palace, residential quarters of a castle
Pannenhilfe – roadside breakdown assistance
Paradies – architectural term for a church vestibule or ante-room
Parkhaus – car park
Parkschein – parking voucher
Parkscheinautomat – vending machine selling parking vouchers
Passage – shopping arcade
Pfand – deposit for bottles and sometimes glasses (in beer gardens)
Pfarrkirche – parish church
Plattdeutsch – literally 'Low German'; German dialect spoken in parts of north-west Germany
Platz – square
Postamt – post office
Postlagernd – poste restante
Priele – tideways on the Wattenmeer on the North Sea coast

Radwandern – bicycle touring
Rathaus – town hall

Ratskeller – town hall restaurant
Reich – empire
Reichspogromnacht – *see* Kristallnacht
Reisezentrum – travel centre in train or bus stations
Reiterhof – riding stable or centre
Ruhetag – literally 'rest day'; closing day at a shop or restaurant
Rundgang – tour, route

Saal, Säle (pl) – hall, room
Sammlung – collection
Säule – column, pillar
Schatzkammer – treasury
Schiff – ship
Schiffahrt – literally 'boat way'; shipping, navigation
Schloss – palace, castle
Schnaps – schnapps
Schnellimbiss – stand-up food stall
Schwul, Schwule (pl) – gay
See – lake
Sekt – sparkling wine
Selbstbedienung (SB) – self-service (restaurants, laundrettes etc)
Skonto – discount
Soziale Marktwirtschaft – literally 'social market economy'; German form of mixed economy with built-in social protection for employees
Spätaussiedler – see Aussiedler
Speisekarte – menu
Sportverein – sport association
SS – Schutzstaffel; organisation within the Nazi party that supplied Hitler's bodyguards, as well as concentration-camp guards and the Waffen-SS troops in WWII
Stadt – city or town
Stadtbad, Stadtbäder (pl) – public pool
Stadtwald – city or town forest
Stasi – GDR secret police (from Ministerium für Staatssicherheit, or Ministry of State Security)
Stau – traffic jam
Staudamm, Staumauer – dam
Stausee – reservoir
Stehcafé – stand-up cafe
Strasse (often abbreviated to Str) – street
Strausswirtschaft – seasonal wine pub indicated by wreath above the doorway, also known as a Besenwirtschaft

Streifenkart – public transport strip ticket of 10
Süden – south
Szene – scene (ie where the action is)

Tageskarte – daily menu or day ticket on public transport
Tal – valley
Teich – pond
Thirty Years' War – pivotal war in Central Europe (1618–48) that began as a German conflict between Catholics and Protestants
Tor – gate
Trampen – hitchhiking
Treuhandanstalt – trust established to sell off GDR assets after the Wende
trocken – dry (wine)
Trödel – junk
Turm – tower

Übergang – transit or transfer point
Ufer – bank

verboten – forbidden
Verkehr – traffic
Viertel – quarter, district
Volkslieder – folk song

Wald – forest
Waldfrüchte – wild berries
Wäscherei – laundry
Wattenmeer – tidal flats on North Sea coast
Wechselstube – currency exchange office
Weg – way, path
Weihnachtsmarkt – Christmas market; see also Christkindlmarkt
Weingut – wine-growing estate
Weinkeller – wine cellar
Weinprobe – wine tasting
Weinstube – traditional wine bar
Wende – 'change' of 1989, ie the fall of communism that led to the collapse of the GDR and German reunification
Weser Renaissance – an ornamental architectural style found around the Weser River
Wessis – literally 'Westies'; nickname for West Germans
Westen – west
Westler – old term for a Wessi

Wies – meadow
Wirtschaftswunder – Germany's post-WWII 'economic miracle'
Wurst – sausage

Zahnradbahn – cog-wheel railway
Zeitung – newspaper

Zimmer Frei – room available (accommodation)
Zimmervermittlung – room-finding service; *see also* Mitwohnzentrale
ZOB – Zentraler Omnibusbahnhof (central bus station)
Zuschlag – Surcharge

LONELY PLANET

Phrasebooks

Lonely Planet phrasebooks are packed with essential words and phrases to help travellers communicate with the locals. With colour tabs for quick reference, an extensive vocabulary and use of script, these handy pocket-sized language guides cover day-to-day travel situations.

- handy pocket-sized books
- easy to understand Pronunciation chapter
- clear & comprehensive Grammar chapter
- romanisation alongside script to allow ease of pronunciation
- script throughout so users can point to phrases for every situation
- full of cultural information and tips for the traveller

'... vital for a real DIY spirit and attitude in language learning'
— *Backpacker*

'the phrasebooks have good cultural backgrounders and offer solid advice for challenging situations in remote locations'
— *San Francisco Examiner*

Arabic (Egyptian) • Arabic (Moroccan) • Australian *(Australian English, Aboriginal and Torres Strait languages)* • Baltic States *(Estonian, Latvian, Lithuanian)* • Bengali • Brazilian • British • Burmese • Cantonese • Central Asia (Uyghur, Uzbek, Kyrghiz, Kazak, Pashto, Tadjik • Central Europe *(Czech, French, German, Hungarian, Italian, Slovak)* • Eastern Europe *(Bulgarian, Czech, Hungarian, Polish, Romanian, Slovak)* • Ethiopian (Amharic) • Fijian • French • German • Greek • Hebrew • Hill Tribes • Hindi & Urdu • Indonesian • Italian • Japanese • Korean • Lao • Latin American Spanish • Malay • Mandarin • Mediterranean Europe *(Albanian, Croatian, Greek, Italian, Macedonian, Maltese, Serbian, Slovene)* • Mongolian • Nepali • Pidgin • Pilipino (Tagalog) • Quechua • Russian • Scandinavian Europe *(Danish, Finnish, Icelandic, Norwegian, Swedish)* • South-East Asia *(Burmese, Indonesian, Khmer, Lao, Malay, Tagalog Pilipino, Thai, Vietnamese)* • South Pacific Languages • Spanish (Castilian) *(also includes Catalan, Galician and Basque)* • Sri Lanka • Swahili • Thai • Tibetan • Turkish • Ukrainian • USA *(US English, Vernacular, Native American languages, Hawaiian)* • Vietnamese • Western Europe *(Basque, Catalan, Dutch, French, German, Greek, Irish, Italian, Portuguese, Scottish Gaelic, Spanish (Castilian), Welsh)*

Lonely Planet Journeys

Journeys is a unique collection of travel writing – published by the company that understands travel better than anyone else. It is a series for anyone who has ever experienced – or dreamed of – the magical moment when they encountered a strange culture or saw a place for the first time. They are tales to read while you're planning a trip, while you're on the road or while you're in an armchair in front of a fire.

These outstanding titles explore our planet through the eyes of a diverse group of international writers. JOURNEYS books catch the spirit of a place, illuminate a culture, recount a crazy adventure or introduce a fascinating way of life. They always entertain, and always enrich the experience of travel.

MALI BLUES
Traveling to an African Beat
Lieve Joris (translated by Sam Garrett)
Drought, rebel uprisings, ethnic conflict: these are the predominant images of West Africa. But as Lieve Joris travels in Senegal, Mauritania and Mali, she meets survivors, fascinating individuals charting new ways of living between tradition and modernity. With her remarkable gift for drawing out people's stories, Joris brilliantly captures the rhythms of a world that refuses to give in.

THE GATES OF DAMASCUS
Lieve Joris (translated by Sam Garrett)
This best-selling book is a beautifully drawn portrait of day-to-day life in modern Syria. Through her intimate contact with local people, Lieve Joris draws us into the fascinating world that lies behind the gates of Damascus. Hala's husband is a political prisoner, jailed for his opposition to the Assad regime; through the author's friendship with Hala we see how Syrian politics impacts on the lives of ordinary people.

THE OLIVE GROVE
Travels in Greece
Katherine Kizilos
Katherine Kizilos travels to fabled islands, troubled border zones and her family's village deep in the mountains. She vividly evokes breathtaking landscapes, generous people and passionate politics, capturing the complexities of a country she loves.

'beautifully captures the real tensions of Greece' – *Sunday Times*

KINGDOM OF THE FILM STARS
Journey into Jordan
Annie Caulfield
Kingdom of the Film Stars is a travel book and a love story. With honesty and humour, Annie Caulfield writes of travelling in Jordan and falling in love with a Bedouin with film-star looks.

She offers fascinating insights into the country – from the tent life of traditional women to the hustle of downtown Amman – and unpicks tight-woven western myths about the Arab world.

LONELY PLANET

Lonely Planet Travel Atlases

Lonely Planet has long been famous for the number and quality of its guidebook maps. Now we've gone one step further and produced a handy companion series: Lonely Planet travel atlases – maps of a country produced in book form.

Unlike other maps, which look good but lead travellers astray, our travel atlases have been researched on the road by Lonely Planet's experienced team of writers. All details are carefully checked to ensure the atlas corresponds with the equivalent Lonely Planet guidebook.

- full-colour throughout
- maps researched and checked by Lonely Planet authors
- place names correspond with Lonely Planet guidebooks
- no confusing spelling differences
- legend and travelling information in English, French, German, Japanese and Spanish
- size: 230 x 160 mm

Available now: Chile & Easter Island ● Egypt ● India & Bangladesh ● Israel & the Palestinian Territories ● Jordan, Syria & Lebanon ● Kenya ● Laos ● Portugal ● South Africa, Lesotho & Swaziland ● Thailand ● Turkey ● Vietnam ● Zimbabwe, Botswana & Namibia

Lonely Planet TV Series & Videos

Lonely Planet travel guides have been brought to life on television screens around the world. Like our guides, the programs are based on the joy of independent travel and look honestly at some of the most exciting, picturesque and frustrating places in the world. Each show is presented by one of three travellers from Australia, England or the USA and combines an innovative mixture of video, Super-8 film, atmospheric soundscapes and original music.

Videos of each episode – containing additional footage not shown on television – are available from good book and video shops, but the availability of individual videos varies with regional screening schedules.

Video destinations include: Alaska ● American Rockies ● Argentina ● Australia – The South-East ● Baja California & the Copper Canyon ● Brazil ● Central Asia ● Chile & Easter Island ● Corsica, Sicily & Sardinia – The Mediterranean Islands ● East Africa (Tanzania & Zanzibar) ● Cuba ● Ecuador & the Galapagos Islands ● Ethiopia ● Greenland & Iceland ● Hungary & Romania ● Indonesia ● Israel & the Sinai Desert ● Jamaica ● Japan ● La Ruta Maya ● London ● The Middle East (Syria, Jordan & Lebanon ● Morocco ● New York City ● Northern Spain ● North India ● Outback Australia ● Pacific Islands (Fiji, Solomon Islands & Vanuatu) ● Pakistan ● Peru ● The Philippines ● South Africa & Lesotho ● South India ● South West China ● South West USA ● Trekking in Uganda & Congo ● Turkey ● Vietnam ● West Africa ● Zimbabwe, Botswana & Namibia

The Lonely Planet TV series is produced by: Pilot Productions
The Old Studio
18 Middle Row
London W10 5AT, UK

Lonely Planet Online

Whether you've just begun planning your next trip, or you're chasing down specific info on currency regulations or visa requirements, check out Lonely Planet Online for up-to-the-minute travel information.

As well as miniguides to more than 250 destinations, you'll find maps, photos, travel news, health and visa updates, travel advisories and discussion of the ecological and political issues you need to be aware of as you travel. You'll also find timely upgrades to popular guidebooks that you can print out and stick in the back of your book.

There's an online travellers' forum (The Thorn Tree) where you can share your experience of life on the road, meet travel companions and ask other travellers for their recommendations and advice.

There's also a complete and up-to-date list of all Lonely Planet travel products including travel guides, diving and snorkeling guides, phrasebooks, atlases, travel literature and videos, and a simple online ordering facility if you can't find the book you want elsewhere.

Lonely Planet Diving & Snorkeling Guides

Beautifully illustrated with full-colour photos throughout, Lonely Planet's Pisces books explore the world's best diving and snorkeling areas and prepare divers for what to expect when they get there, both topside and underwater.

Dive sites are described in detail with specifics on depths, visibility, level of difficulty, special conditions, underwater photography tips and common and unusual marine life present. You'll also find practical logistical information and coverage on topside activities and attractions, sections on diving health and safety, plus listings for diving services, live-aboards, dive resorts and tourist offices.

LONELY PLANET

Guides by Region

Lonely Planet is known worldwide for publishing practical, reliable and no-nonsense travel information in our guides and on our Web site. The Lonely Planet list covers just about every accessible part of the world. Currently there are thirteen series: travel guides, shoestring guides, walking guides, city guides, phrasebooks, audio packs, city maps, travel atlases, diving & snorkeling guides, restaurant guides, first-time travel guides, healthy travel and travel literature.

AFRICA Africa on a shoestring ● Africa – the South ● Arabic (Egyptian) phrasebook ● Arabic (Moroccan) phrasebook ● Cairo ● Cape Town ● Cape Town city map● Central Africa ● East Africa ● Egypt ● Egypt travel atlas ● Ethiopian (Amharic) phrasebook ● The Gambia & Senegal ● Healthy Travel Africa ● Kenya ● Kenya travel atlas ● Malawi, Mozambique & Zambia ● Morocco ● North Africa ● South Africa, Lesotho & Swaziland ● South Africa, Lesotho & Swaziland travel atlas ● Swahili phrasebook ● Tanzania, Zanzibar & Pemba ● Trekking in East Africa ● Tunisia ● West Africa ● Zimbabwe, Botswana & Namibia ● Zimbabwe, Botswana & Namibia travel atlas
Travel Literature: The Rainbird: A Central African Journey ● Songs to an African Sunset: A Zimbabwean Story ● Mali Blues: Traveling to an African Beat

AUSTRALIA & THE PACIFIC Auckland ● Australia ● Australian phrasebook ● Bushwalking in Australia ● Bushwalking in Papua New Guinea ● Fiji ● Fijian phrasebook ● Healthy Travel Australia, NZ and the Pacific ● Islands of Australia's Great Barrier Reef ● Melbourne ● Melbourne city map ● Micronesia ● New Caledonia ● New South Wales & the ACT ● New Zealand ● Northern Territory ● Outback Australia ● Out To Eat – Melbourne ● Out to Eat – Sydney ● Papua New Guinea ● Pidgin phrasebook ● Queensland ● Rarotonga & the Cook Islands ● Samoa ● Solomon Islands ● South Australia ● South Pacific Languages phrasebook ● Sydney ● Sydney city map ● Sydney Condensed ● Tahiti & French Polynesia ● Tasmania ● Tonga ● Tramping in New Zealand ● Vanuatu ● Victoria ● Western Australia
Travel Literature: Islands in the Clouds ● Kiwi Tracks: A New Zealand Journey ● Sean & David's Long Drive

CENTRAL AMERICA & THE CARIBBEAN Bahamas, Turks & Caicos ● Bermuda ● Central America on a shoestring ● Costa Rica ● Cuba ● Dominican Republic & Haiti ● Eastern Caribbean ● Guatemala, Belize & Yucatán: La Ruta Maya ● Jamaica ● Mexico ● Mexico City ● Panama ● Puerto Rico
Travel Literature: Green Dreams: Travels in Central America

EUROPE Amsterdam ● Amsterdam city map ● Andalucía ● Austria ● Baltic States phrasebook ● Barcelona ● Berlin ● Berlin city map ● Britain ● British phrasebook ● Brussels, Bruges & Antwerp ● Budapest city map ● Canary Islands ● Central Europe ● Central Europe phrasebook ● Corsica ● Croatia ● Czech & Slovak Republics ● Denmark ● Dublin ● Eastern Europe ● Eastern Europe phrasebook ● Edinburgh ● Estonia, Latvia & Lithuania ● Europe on a shoestring ● Finland ● France ● French phrasebook ● Germany ● German phrasebook ● Greece ● Greek Islands ● Greek phrasebook ● Hungary ● Iceland, Greenland & the Faroe Islands ● Ireland ● Italian phrasebook ● Italy ● Krakow ● Lisbon ● London ● London city map ● London Condensed ● Mediterranean Europe ● Mediterranean Europe phrasebook ● Norway ● Paris ● Paris city map ● Poland ● Portugal ● Portugal travel atlas ● Prague ● Prague city map ● Provence & the Côte d'Azur ● Romania & Moldova ● Rome ● Russia, Ukraine & Belarus ● Russian phrasebook ● Scandinavian & Baltic Europe ● Scandinavian Europe phrasebook ● Scotland ● Slovenia ● Spain ● Spanish phrasebook ● St Petersburg ● Switzerland ● Trekking in Spain ● Ukrainian phrasebook ● Vienna ● Walking in Britain ● Walking in Ireland ● Walking in Italy ● Walking in Spain ● Walking in Switzerland ● Western Europe ● Western Europe phrasebook
Travel Literature: The Olive Grove: Travels in Greece

INDIAN SUBCONTINENT Bangladesh ● Bengali phrasebook ● Bhutan ● Delhi ● Goa ● Hindi & Urdu phrasebook ● India ● India & Bangladesh travel atlas ● Indian Himalaya ● Karakoram Highway ● Kerala ● Mumbai (Bombay) ● Nepal ● Nepali phrasebook ● Pakistan ● Rajasthan ● Read This First: Asia & India ● South India ● Sri Lanka ● Sri Lanka phrasebook ● Trekking in the Indian Himalaya ● Trekking in the Karakoram & Hindukush ● Trekking in the Nepal Himalaya
Travel Literature: In Rajasthan ● Shopping for Buddhas

LONELY PLANET

Mail Order

L onely Planet products are distributed worldwide. They are also available by mail order from Lonely Planet, so if you have difficulty finding a title please write to us. North and South American residents should write to 150 Linden St, Oakland, CA 94607, USA; European and African residents should write to 10a Spring Place, London NW5 3BH, UK; and residents of other countries to PO Box 617, Hawthorn, Victoria 3122, Australia.

ISLANDS OF THE INDIAN OCEAN Madagascar & Comoros ● Maldives ● Mauritius, Réunion & Seychelles

MIDDLE EAST & CENTRAL ASIA Arab Gulf States ● Central Asia ● Central Asia phrasebook ● Hebrew phrasebook ● Iran ● Israel & the Palestinian Territories ● Israel & the Palestinian Territories travel atlas ● Istanbul ● Istanbul to Cairo ● Jerusalem ● Jordan & Syria ● Jordan, Syria & Lebanon travel atlas ● Lebanon ● Middle East on a shoestring ● Syria ● Turkey ● Turkey travel atlas ● Turkish phrasebook ● Yemen
Travel Literature: The Gates of Damascus ● Kingdom of the Film Stars: Journey into Jordan

NORTH AMERICA Alaska ● Backpacking in Alaska ● Baja California ● California & Nevada ● Canada ● Chicago ● Chicago city map ● Deep South ● Florida ● Hawaii ● Honolulu ● Las Vegas ● Los Angeles ● Miami ● New England ● New Orleans ● New York City ● New York city map ● New York, New Jersey & Pennsylvania ● Pacific Northwest USA ● Puerto Rico ● Rocky Mountain ● San Francisco ● San Francisco city map ● Seattle ● Southwest USA ● Texas ● USA ● USA phrasebook ● Vancouver ● Washington, DC & the Capital Region ● Washington DC city map
Travel Literature: Drive Thru America

NORTH-EAST ASIA Beijing ● Cantonese phrasebook ● China ● Hong Kong ● Hong Kong city map ● Hong Kong, Macau & Guangzhou ● Japan ● Japanese phrasebook ● Japanese audio pack ● Korea ● Korean phrasebook ● Kyoto ● Mandarin phrasebook ● Mongolia ● Mongolian phrasebook ● North-East Asia on a shoestring ● Seoul ● South-West China ● Taiwan ● Tibet ● Tibetan phrasebook ● Tokyo
Travel Literature: Lost Japan

SOUTH AMERICA Argentina, Uruguay & Paraguay ● Bolivia ● Brazil ● Brazilian phrasebook ● Buenos Aires ● Chile & Easter Island ● Chile & Easter Island travel atlas ● Colombia ● Ecuador & the Galapagos Islands ● Healthy Travel Central & South America ● Latin American Spanish phrasebook ● Peru ● Quechua phrasebook ● Rio de Janeiro ● Rio de Janeiro city map ● South America on a shoestring ● Trekking in the Patagonian Andes ● Venezuela
Travel Literature: Full Circle: A South American Journey

SOUTH-EAST ASIA Bali & Lombok ● Bangkok ● Bangkok city map ● Burmese phrasebook ● Cambodia ● Hanoi ● Healthy Travel Asia & India ● Hill Tribes phrasebook ● Ho Chi Minh City ● Indonesia ● Indonesia's Eastern Islands ● Indonesian phrasebook ● Indonesian audio pack ● Jakarta ● Java ● Laos ● Lao phrasebook ● Laos travel atlas ● Malay phrasebook ● Malaysia, Singapore & Brunei ● Myanmar (Burma) ● Philippines ● Pilipino (Tagalog) phrasebook ● Singapore ● South-East Asia on a shoestring ● South-East Asia phrasebook ● Thailand ● Thailand's Islands & Beaches ● Thailand travel atlas ● Thai phrasebook ● Thai audio pack ● Vietnam ● Vietnamese phrasebook ● Vietnam travel atlas

ALSO AVAILABLE: Antarctica ● The Arctic ● Brief Encounters: Stories of Love, Sex & Travel ● Chasing Rickshaws ● Lonely Planet Unpacked ● Not the Only Planet: Travel Stories from Science Fiction ● Sacred India ● Travel with Children ● Traveller's Tales

FREE Lonely Planet Newsletters

W e love hearing from you and think you'd like to hear from us.

Planet Talk

Our FREE quarterly printed newsletter is full of tips from travellers and anecdotes from Lonely Planet guidebook authors. Every issue is packed with up-to-date travel news and advice, and includes:

- a postcard from Lonely Planet co-founder Tony Wheeler
- a swag of mail from travellers
- a look at life on the road through the eyes of a Lonely Planet author
- topical health advice
- prizes for the best travel yarn
- news about forthcoming Lonely Planet events
- a complete list of Lonely Planet books and other titles

To join our mailing list, residents of the UK, Europe and Africa can email us at go@lonelyplanet.co.uk; residents of North and South America can email us at info@lonelyplanet.com; the rest of the world can email us at talk2us@lonelyplanet.com.au, or contact any Lonely Planet office.

Comet

O ur FREE monthly email newsletter brings you all the latest travel news, features, interviews, competitions, destination ideas, travellers' tips & tales, Q&As, raging debates and related links. Find out what's new on the Lonely Planet Web site and which books are about to hit the shelves.

Subscribe from your desktop: www.lonelyplanet.com/comet

Index

Text

Bold indicates maps.

Bold indicates maps.

Boxed Text

Schnellbahn-Netzplan

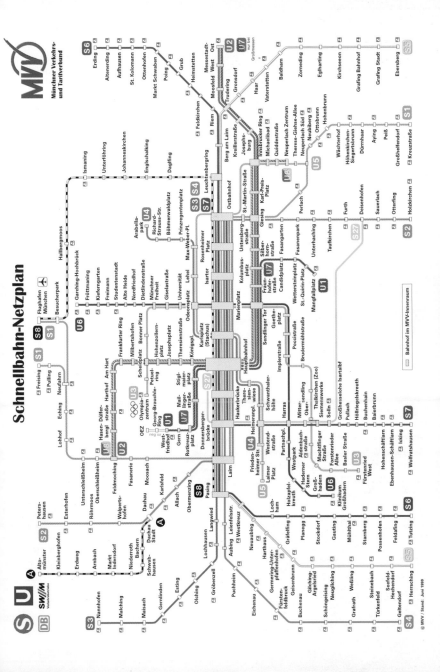

Münchner Verkehrs- und Tarifverbund

© MVV / Stand: Juni 1999

MAP 2

MAP 3

MAP 5

Karlsfeld

Tunnel   Otto - Warburg - Str

Allacher

ANGE

BIRKENRIED

ALLACH

LUDWIGSFELD

FASANERIENORD

SIEDLUNG
AM LERCHENAUER
SEE

KOLONIE
EGGARTEN

Moosach

Allach

Dachauer

Strasse

Olymp
park

LANGWIED

LOCHHAUSEN

Von - Kahr-   Strasse

Menzingerstrasse

Georg - Brauchle - Ring

MOOSACH

Westfriedhof

BORSTEI

Olymp
stadion

NEULANGWIED

Obermenzing

Baldurstrasse

AUBING

Langwied   strasse

Verdi   Strasse

NEULUSTHEIM

Schlopark

GERN

Bergson-

Aubing

Leienfelsstrasse

Aubinger   Strasse

Papinger St.

Pasing

NYMPHENBURG

Nymphenburg

Arnulf

Rotkreuz
platz

Dietrichstrasse

NEUHAUSE

Malling

Nymphenburge

strasse

Neuaubing

Westkreuz

Landsberger   Strasse

Laim

Arnultstrasse

Weinberger - strasse

Agnes-   Bernauer-

Landsberger   Strasse

Donnersberger-
brücke

Planegger Strasse

Blumenauer

Strasse

Zschokkestrasse

Laimer
Platz

Friedenheimer
Strasse

Strasse

Westend
strasse

Strasse

WOHNCENTER
WEST

Westend
strasse

Helmpertsa
platz

WESTEND
SCHWANTHALE
HOHE

Messe
geland

LOCHHAM

Wittelsbacher

Forstenrieder

LAIM

Wieland

Theresie
wiese

Pocc
strass

Lochham

KLEINHADERN

Strasse

Westpark (Ost)

Ammersee   Strasse   Westpark (Ost)

Harras

Gräfelfing

Ammersee

Strasse

Waldwiesen

Hadener
Stern

Hugauer-
kreuth

Westpark (West)

UNTERSENDLING

Partnach-
platz

GRÄFELFING

NEUHADERN

Grosshadern

Würmtalstrasse

Forster

Waltriedhof   strasse

MITTERSENDLING

Brudermü
strasse

Planegger Strasse

Klinikum
Grosshadern

Heckenstaller

strasse

Bruder

Planegg

PLANEGG

Waldfriedhof

Sdpark

Olympiastrasse

Hogwörther   Strasse

Mitte
sendling

Thal
kirche

KREUZHOF

Boschetsrieder   Strasse

Obersend-
ling

Planegger   Strasse

Forst

FÜRSTENRIED-
OST

Machtlfinger
Strasse

Aidenba-
chstrasse

OBERSENDLING

Kasten

Allee

Forstenrieder
Alle

FÜRSTENRIED-
WEST

Forstenrieder

Fürstenried
West

Basler
Straße

Siemens-
werke

MARIA

NEURIED   Strasse

Olympiastrasse

Gautinger   Strasse

MAXHOF

FORSTENRIED

HINTERBRUH

PRINZ-
LUDWIGS-
HÖHE

NEU-
FORSTENRIED

STADT
SOLLN

SOLLN

Solln

MAP 5

Forstenrieder   Park

UNTERDILL

MAP 2

MAP 4

MAP 7A

MAP 7

MAP 6

FELDMOCH-
INGER

HARTOP

LERCHENAU

KIEFERN
GARTEN

FROTTMANINGER
HEIDE

GROSSLAPPEN

KLEINLAPPEN

KULTURHEIM

Harthof

AM HART

Kiefern-
garten

Am Hart

KALTHERBERG

FREIMANN

Freimann

Feringasee

Gr. Fübach
Brumbach

UNTERFÖHRING

Milbertshofen

MILBERTSHOFEN

Frankfurter
Ring

Studenten-
stadt

STUDENTENSTADT

JOHANNESKIRCHEN

RIESENFELD

Milbertshofen

Alte-
Heide

Nordfriedhof

Hirschau

ST EMMERAM

Johanneskirchen

Olympia-
zentrum

GEORGENSCHWAIGE

Petuelring

Nordfried-
hof

Johanneskirchner Strasse

Johanneskirchen

Olympiasee

Scheidplatz

Luitpold-
park

OBERFÖHRING

OBERFÖHRING

ENGLSCHALKING

Olympiaberg

Bonner
Platz

Dietlinden-
strasse

BIEDERSTEIN

FIDELIOPK

COSIMAPARK

Englschal-
king

Rheinstrasse

HIRSCHAU

HERZOG-
PARK

PRIEL

DAGLFING

SCHWABING

Münchener
Freiheit

KLEIN
HESSELOHE

Arabella
park

Englschalkinger Strasse

Daglfing

DENNING

Gisela-
strasse

Englischer
Garten

Richard-
Strauss-
Strasse

ARABELLPARK

Riem

RIEM

Theresien-
strasse

Universität

BOGEN-
HAUSEN

Böhmerwald-
platz

Bürgerpark

PARKSTADT

Königs-
platz

Odeons-
platz

Prinzregenten-
platz

BOGENHAUSEN

ZAMDORF

Riemer Strasse

Karlsplatz

Max II
Platz

Prinzregentenstrasse

Truderinger

Töginger Strasse

Töginger Strasse

Sendlinger

Isartor

STEINHAUSER

Berg Am
Laim

AM MOOSFELD

Theresien
wiese

HAIDHAUSEN

Leuchten-
bergring

Truderinger

Trudering

KIRCHTRUDERING

Goethe-
platz

Fraunhofer-
strasse

Rosenheimer
Platz

Ostbahn-
hof

BAUMLKIRCHEN

BERG AM LAIM

JOSEPHSBURG

STRASSTRUDERING

Süd-
bahn-
hof

Kolumbus-
platz

St Martin-
strasse

Karl-Preis
Platz

Innsbrucker
Ring

Michaelibad

MICHAELIBURG

Wasserburger Landstrasse

TRUDERING

NEUTRUDERING

Silberhorn-
strasse

Werinher Strasse

Ostpark

GARTENSTADT
TRUDERING

THALKIRCHEN

SIEBENBRUNN

Untersberg-
strasse

Giesing

RAMERS DORF

Quidde
strasse

TRUDERINGER
GRENZKOLONIE

GIESING

STADEL

Stadelheimer

Neuperlach
Zentrum

NEUPERLACH

Tierpark
Hellabrunn

HEIM

NEUHARLACHING

Ständlerstrasse

Therese-
Giehse-
Allee

EINSIEDEL

HARLACHING

PERLACH

Perlach

Neuperlach
Süd

Fasangarten

INTERBIBER

WALDPERLACH

MENTERSCHWAIGE

Fasanpark

FASANENPARK

FASANGARTEN

NEUBIBERG

Neubiberg

Perlacher   Forst

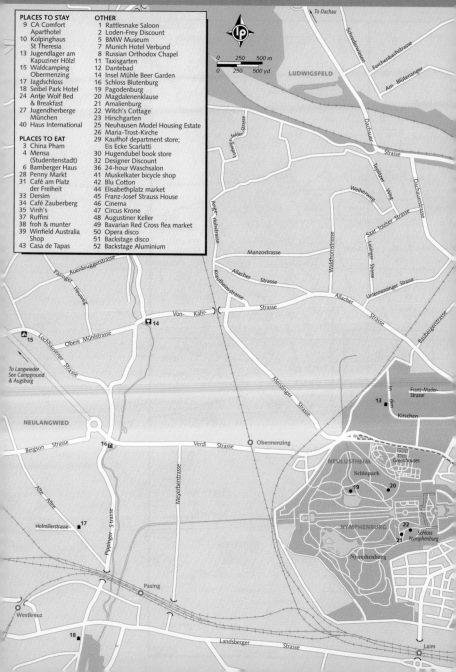

MAP 3

PLACES TO STAY
9 CA Comfort Aparthotel
10 Kolpinghaus St Theresia
13 Jugendlager am Kapuziner Hölzl
15 Waldcamping Obermenzing
18 Jagdschloss
18 Seibel Park Hotel
24 Antje Wolf Bed & Breakfast
27 Jugendherberge München
40 Haus International

PLACES TO EAT
3 China Pham
4 Mensa (Studentenstadt)
6 Bamberger Haus
28 Penny Markt
31 Café am Platz der Freiheit
33 Dersim
34 Café Zauberberg
35 Vinh's
37 Ruffini
38 froh & munter
39 Winfield Australia Shop
43 Casa de Tapas

OTHER
1 Rattlesnake Saloon
2 Loden-Frey Discount
5 BMW Museum
7 Munich Hotel Verbund
8 Russian Orthodox Chapel
11 Taxisgarten
12 Dantebad
14 Insel Mühle Beer Garden
16 Schloss Blutenburg
19 Pagodenburg
20 Magdalenenklause
21 Amalienburg
22 Witch's Cottage
23 Hirschgarten
25 Neuhausen Model Housing Estate
26 Maria-Trost-Kirche
29 Kaufhof department store; Eis Ecke Scarlatti
30 Hugendubel book store
32 Designer Discount
36 24-hour Waschsalon
41 Muskelkater bicycle shop
42 Blu Cotton
44 Elisabethplatz market
45 Franz-Josef Strauss House
46 Cinema
47 Circus Krone
48 Augustiner Keller
49 Bavarian Red Cross flea market
50 Opera disco
51 Backstage disco
52 Backstage Aluminium

To Dachau

LUDWIGSFELD

NEULANGWIED

NEULUSTHEIM

NYMPHENBURG

Nymphenburg

Schloss Nymphenburg

Obermenzing

Pasing

Westkreuz

Laim

To Langwieder See Campground & Augsburg

MAP 3

MAP 4

FROTTMANINGER HEIDE

Kiefen-garten U

SCHWABING

0   250 m

Destouchesstrasse

Herzog- Strasse

Münchener Freiheit

Kaiserstrasse

Hohenzollernstrasse

Franz- Joseph- Strasse

PLACES TO STAY
7 Holiday Inn Crowne Plaza
15 Gästehaus am Englischen Garten
26 Am Kaiserplatz
44 München Park Hilton

PLACES TO EAT
9 Tantris
16 Don Quixote
18 El Cortijo
19 Bobolovsky's
27 Simera
29 Egger
36 Reiter Imbiss
36 Gaststätte Leopold
37 Eis Boulevard
38 Café Roxy
40 Café Monopteros
41 Café Reitschule

OTHER
1 Hallhuber factory outlet
2 Leder Wirkes
3 Aumeister beer garden
4 Sankt Emmerams Mühle Beer Garden
5 Rare antiques market
6 Who's Perfect
8 Zannantonio
10 Jacques Weindepot
11 Shenanigans pub
12 Erlöserkirche
13 Hirschau beer garden
14 Seehaus beer garden
17 Church of St. Sylvester
20 Munich Laughing & Shooting Company
21 Paddy's/Hopfendolde bar
22 Rag Republic
23 Skyline disco
24 Munich's First Diner
25 Galerie Helmut Leger
28 Kunst-Oase
31 Lardy's
32 Lehmkuhl bookshop
33 Günther Murphy's Irish Tavern
34 Werneck-Schlösschen
35 Seidlvilla gallery
39 Shamrock pub
42 Chinesischer Turm (Chinese Tower)
43 Monopteros
45 St. Georgkirche
46 Bavarian National Museum
47 Schack Gallery
48 Hypo-Bank tower
49 Cosimabad

Taunusstrasse

Frankfurter   Ring

Freimann

FREIMANN

Domagk- strasse

Studenten-stadt

Föhringer   Ring

STUDENTENSTADT

0   250   500 m
0   250   500 yd

Neusser Strasse

Alte Heide U

Schenkendorfstrasse

Nordfriedhof

Hirschau

SANKT EMMERAM

Leopoldstrasse

Parzivalstrasse

Bonner Platz U

Rheinstrasse

BIEDERSTEIN

Dietlinden-strasse

Isar mit

Johanneskirchner Strasse

OBERFÖHRING

FIDELIOPK

See Enlargement

SCHWABING

Herzog- Strasse

Hohenzollernstrasse

Franz- Joseph- Strasse

Münchener Freiheit

Dietlinden- Strasse

Klein-hesseloher See

KLEIN-HESSELOHE

HIRSCHAU

HERZOG-PARK

Prinzregenten-strasse

Flamm- Strasse

Lohengrin- strasse

Waitnried- allee

Cosimastrasse

PRIEL

COSIMAPARK

MAP 7

Englischer Garten

Universität U

Oberföhringer   Strasse

Effnerstrasse

Odinstrasse

Arabellapark

Englischalkinger   Strasse

ARABELLPARK

John- Kennedy- Br

Ifflandstrasse

Max- Joseph- Brücke

Maurer- kirche

Bülowstrasse

Richard-Strauss-Strasse

Denninger

Strasse

Burgerpark

PARKSTADT

MAP 7A

Wildenmayer- Strasse

Mohlstrasse

Holbeinstrasse

Böhmerwald-platz

BOGENHAUSEN

The triumphal Siegestor

Kunstplattform: chess it out!

Schloss Nymphenburg: the Royal family's summer residence

Hypo-Bank: monster or marvel?   Maximilineum: seat of the Bavarian Parliament

MAP 5

Weinberger- Strasse

Gotthard Strasse

Agnes-

Laimer
Platz

LAIM

15

Aindorferstrasse

LOCHHAM

To
Lindau

KLEINHADERN

Ammersee Strasse

Senftenauer-

Willibald-

Blumenauer- Strasse

Planegger Strasse

Haderun Strasse

Waldwiesen Strasse

Großhaderner Strasse

GRÄFELFING

Haderner
Stern

Guardini-

NEUHADERN

Holzapfel-
kreuth

Strasse

Grosshadern

Würmtal- Strasse

Lochhamer Strasse

Marchioninistrasse

Einsteinstrasse

Klinikum
Grosshadern

GROSSHADERN

Furstenrieder Strasse

Waldfriedhof

Münchener Strasse

KREUZHOF

0   250   500 m
0   250   500 yd

Tischlerstrasse

Kasten- Allee

Forst

FÜRSTENRIED-
OST

Forstenrieder
Allee

FÜRSTENRIED-
WEST

Forstenrieder Strasse

Fürstenried
West

Basler
Strasse

Drygalski Allee

FORSTENRIED

MAXHOF

NEU-
FORSTENRIED

strasse

Olympia

Herterich strasse

STADT
SOLLN

To Füssen,
Oberammergau

MAP 5

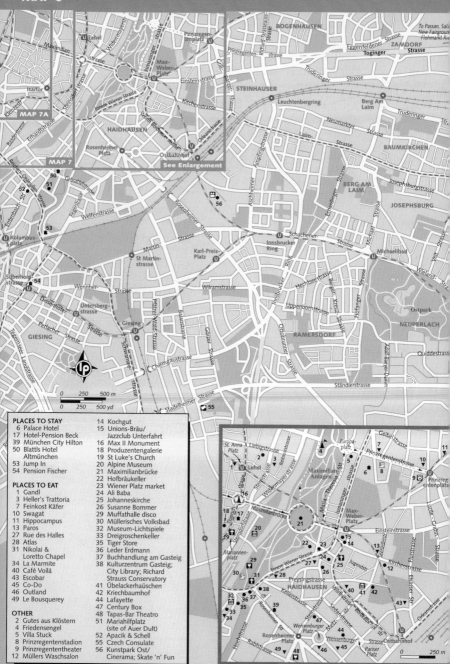

MAP 6

PLACES TO STAY
6 Palace Hotel
17 Hotel-Pension Beck
39 München City Hilton
50 Blattls Hotel Altmünchen
53 Jump In
54 Pension Fischer

PLACES TO EAT
1 Gandl
3 Heller's Trattoria
7 Feinkost Käfer
10 Swagat
13 Hippocampus
13 Paros
27 Rue des Halles
28 Atlas
31 Nikolai & Loretto Chapel
34 La Marmite
40 Café Voilà
45 Escobar
46 Co-Do
47 Outland
49 Le Bousquerey

OTHER
2 Gutes aus Klöstern
4 Friedensengel
5 Villa Stuck
8 Prinzregentenstadion
9 Prinzregententheater
12 Müllers Waschsalon

14 Kochgut
15 Unions-Bräu/ Jazzclub Unterfahrt
16 Max II Monument
18 Produzentengalerie
19 St Luke's Church
20 Alpine Museum
21 Maximiliansbrücke
22 Hofbräukeller
23 Wiener Platz market
24 Ali Baba
25 Johanneskirche
26 Susanne Bommer
29 Muffathalle disco
30 Müllerisches Volksbad
32 Museum-Lichtspiele
33 Dreigroschenkeller
35 Tiger Store
36 Leder Erdmann
37 Buchhandlung am Gasteig
38 Kulturzentrum Gasteig; City Library; Richard Strauss Conservatory
41 Übelackerhäuschen
42 Kriechbaumhof
44 Lafayette
47 Century Box
48 Tapas-Bar Theatro
51 Mariahilfplatz (site of Auer Dult)
52 Apacik & Schell
55 Czech Consulate
56 Kunstpark Ost/ Cinerama; Skate 'n' Fun

MAP 7

AP 7A

Giselastr 1

Josephs-platz

Joseph-Adalbertstrasse
Alter Nördlicher Friedhof
Schellingstrasse

Nordend strasse

Leopoldstrasse

Siegestor

33

32

31

Ludwig-Maximilians-Universität

Universität

Geschwister-Scholl-Platz

Theresienstrasse

Technische Universität

Gabelsbergerstrasse

Königs-platz

Propyläen

Brienner Strasse

Karolinen-platz

Karlstrasse

Alter Botanischer Garten

Elisenstrasse

Hauptbahnhof

Maximilians-platz

Karlsplatz

Promenade-platz

Neuhauser

Strasse

Herzogspitalstrasse

Marienplatz

Viktualien-markt

Max-Joseph-Platz

Hofgarten

Odeons-platz

Residenz

Maximilianstrasse

Theatinerstrasse

Maximilianstrasse

Isartor

Frauenstrasse

Sendlinger Tor

Gärtnerplatz

ISAR-VORSTADT

Glockenbach

Südfriedhof

Goetheplatz

Grossmarkthalle

Fraunhofer-strasse

Isar

MAP 7

Lederhosen Atelier Mahla

DAVID PEEVERS

PLACES TO STAY

21 Astron Hotel Deutsche Kaiser
23 4 You München
24 Alfa Hotel
25 Regent
26 Amba Hotel
27 REMA Hotel-Esplanade
33 Hotel Excelsior
40 Jugendhotel Marienherberge
41 Euro Youth Hotel
42 Hotel Helvetia
45 Hotel Eder
51 Hotel Königshof
65 Hotel Bayerischer Hof; Night Club
86 Kempinski Vier Jahreszeiten München
89 Opera Garni
93 Rafael
122 Hotel Arosa
129 Hotel Atlanta
141 Hotel Monaco
143 Hotel Cristal
146 Hotel Mirabell
148 Pension Marie-Luise
149 Pension Alpina
150 Andi (Comfort) Hotel
151 CVJM-YMCA
159 Hotel-Pension Utzelmann
160 Hotel Kraft
169 Hotel Blauer Bock
176 Hotel-Pension am Markt
180 Hotel Schlicker
193 Hotel Advokat
204 Deutsche Eiche

PLACES TO EAT

4 Cafe Tombosi
9 Dukatz im Literaturhaus
11 Hunsinger Pacific/Fortuna Musikbar
39 Pizzeria Ca doro's
48 Vinzenzmurr
49 Müller Bakery; Nordsee; Grillpfanne
54 McDonald's
69 Andechser Am Dom
70 Münchner Suppenküche
74 Welser Küche
90 Haxenbauer
92 Planet Hollywood
94 Shoya
95 Zerwirkgewölbe
96 Alois Dallmayr
109 Metropolitan
111 Café Glockenspiel
123 Hundskugel
124 Prinz Myschkin
128 Vinzenzmurr
131 Höflinger; Wiener's Buffet
133 Ziegler
142 Gute Stube
144 Kebab Antep
145 Sultan
147 Gap
153 Kandil Restaurant
156 Café Osteria La Vecchia Masseria
161 Mensa
162 Jinny's Thai Food
163 Trattoria La Fiorentini
164 Café am Beethovenplatz
173 Löwenbräu Stadt Kempten
175 Bratwurstherzl; Zum Alten Markt
179 Weisses Bräuhaus
187 Buxs

188 New World Cafe
194 Königsquelle
195 Ganga
197 Joe Peña's

GALLERIES & MUSEUMS

2 Kunstverein Gallery
3 Theatre Museum
6 Egyptian Art Museum
62 Hunting & Fishing Museum
63 Galerie für angewandte Kunst (Künstlerhaus am Lenbachplatz)
71 Kunsthalle der Hypo-Kulturstiftung
78 Residenz; Residenzmuseum; Egyptian Art Museum
100 Toy Museum
170 Stadtmuseum; Filmmuseum
181 Centre for Unusual Museums
183 Valentin Museum
189 Jewish Museum
198 Galerie Karin Sachs
199 Galerie Dany Keller
201 Galerie Klewan

OTHER

1 Diana Temple
5 Hofgartentor
7 Theatinerkirche St Kajetan
8 Culta Fashion
10 Delta Airlines/El Al Offices
12 Soul City; Nachtcafé
13 Wittelsbach Fountain
14 Börse (Stock Exchange)
15 Bernheimer House
16 Neptune Fountain
17 Park Café/Disco
18 Magistrate's Court
19 Japan Air Lines
20 Walk-In Medical Centre
22 ADM-Mitfahrzentrale; City Mitwohnzentrale
28 Police Station
29 Radius Bicycle Hire
30 Sussman Bookshop
31 Tourist Office
32 Hertie Department Store
34 Bahnhof-Apotheke
35 EurAide
36 ABR Travel Agency
37 Main Post Office; Postbank
38 Times Online Bistro
43 Hypovereinsbank
44 Sabene Airlines
46 German Alpine Club
47 Tengelmann
50 Kaufhof
52 Karlstor
53 Hugendubel Bookshop
55 Obletter Spielwaren Toys
56 Tretter
57 Karstadt am Karlstor
58 Bürgersaal
59 Augustiner-Grossgaststatte
60 Richard Strauss Fountain
61 Michaelskirche
64 American Express
66 Loden-Frey
67 Frauenkirche
68 Hirmer
72 Hugendubel Bookstore
73 Feldherrnhalle
75 Eduard Meier Shoes

76 Bogner
77 Lion Statues
79 Brunnenhof
80 Residenz Theater
81 Former Central Post Office
82 Wallach
83 Nationaltheater
84 Münzhof (Former Mint)
85 Cada
87 Kammerspiele Theatre
88 Far Out Disco
91 Hofbräuhaus
97 Jodlwirt
98 Ludwig Beck Department Store
99 Altes Rathaus
101 Deutsche Bank
102 Fischbrunnen
103 Tourist Office
104 Glockenspiel Tower
105 Rathaus Tower Entry
106 Neues Rathaus
107 Mariensäule (St Mary's Column)
108 Hugendubel
110 Hypovereinsbank
112 Sport Schuster
113 Umweltladen (environmental shop)
114 Central Tourist Office
115 Spanisches Fruchthaus
116 Kaufhof Department Store
117 Hallhuber
118 World of Music (WOM)
119 Karstadt am Dom
120 Internet Café
121 Damenstiftskirche
125 Sport Scheck
126 Asamkirche
127 Linkshänderladen
130 Sendlinger Tor
132 Asamhof; Cipriani
134 Glashaus
135 Bottles
136 Goethe Institut
137 NY NY
138 Iwan
139 Atelier Cinema
140 Deutsches Theater
152 ADFC (Bicycle Club)
154 Foto Reparatur
155 Schuh Seibel
157 Sauter Photographic
158 ADAC
165 The Stud
166 Sport Kopf
167 Ochsengarten
168 Münchner Marionettentheater
171 Geobuch Bookshop
172 Alter Peter
174 Maypole on Viktualienmarkt
177 Heiliggeistkirche
178 Sparkasse Bank
182 I-Düpferl
184 Braunauer Hof
185 Die Zahnbürste
186 Master's Home
190 British Council
191 Café Vogler
192 Billiard Café
196 CD-Börse
200 Bei Carla
202 Schnell & Sauber Laundry
203 Interview
205 Old Mrs Henderson

MAP 8 EXCURSIONS

MAP LEGEND

CITY ROUTES

Freeway .... Freeway	‗‗‗‗ .... Unsealed Road
Highway ...... Primary Road	——→ ... One Way Street
Road ... Secondary Road	.... Pedestrian Street
Street .... Street	⊓⊓⊓⊓⊓ ..... Stepped Street
Lane .... Lane	)══ .... Tunnel
.... On/Off Ramp	══ .... Footbridge

HYDROGRAPHY

.... River, Creek	⌒⌒ .... Dry Lake; Salt Lake
.... Canal	⊙ .... Spring; Rapids
.... Lake	.... Waterfalls

REGIONAL ROUTES

══ ... Tollway, Freeway	
══ .... Primary Road	
‗‗‗ ... Secondary Road	
.... Minor Road	

BOUNDARIES

▬▪▬ .... International	
▪▬▪▬ .... State	
▬ ▬ .... Disputed	
▬▬ ...... Fortified Wall	

TRANSPORT ROUTES & STATIONS

├──○─ .... Train	─ ─ ─ ☐ .... Ferry
├──Ⓢ─ .... S-Bahn	─ ─ ─ .... Walking Trail
═══Ⓤ═ .... U-Bahn	· · · · · .... Walking Tour
├─ ┼ ─┤ . Underground Train	.... Path
▬▪▬▪ .... Tramway	▬▬▬ ... Pier or Jetty

AREA FEATURES

.... Building	.... Market
❀ ... Park, Gardens	..... Sports Ground
⋏ .... Beach	.... Campus
.... Cemetery	.... Plaza

POPULATION SYMBOLS

○ **CAPITAL** .... National Capital	● **CITY** .... City	◉ Village .... Village
◎ **CAPITAL** .... State Capital	● **Town** .... Town	.... Urban Area

MAP SYMBOLS

▪ .... Place to Stay	▼ .... Place to Eat	● .... Point of Interest

✈ .... Airport	⌂ Embassy, Consulate	🏛 .... Museum	🅿 ..... Swimming Pool
⊡ . Archaeological Site	⚓ .... Fountain	🅿 .... Parking	⊡ .... Synagogue
⊖ .... Bank	◉ .... Golf Course	✚ ...... Police Station	☎ .... Telephone
☐ .... Bus Terminal	⊕ .... Hospital	✉ .... Post Office	☐ .... Theatre
🏰 .... Castle, Chateau	⊡ ...... Internet Cafe	⊡ .... Pub or Bar	▪ .... Tomb
✝ ☗ . Cathedral, Church	⚲ .... Monument	⊗ ... Shopping Centre	⊙ . Tourist Information
☐ .... Cinema	☾ .... Mosque	🏛 ...... Stately Home	⌂ .... Zoo

Note: not all symbols displayed above appear in this book

LONELY PLANET OFFICES

Australia
PO Box 617, Hawthorn, Victoria 3122
☎ 03 9819 1877 fax 03 9819 6459
email: talk2us@lonelyplanet.com.au

USA
150 Linden St, Oakland, CA 94607
☎ 510 893 8555 TOLL FREE: 800 275 8555
fax 510 893 8572
email: info@lonelyplanet.com

UK
10a Spring Place, London NW5 3BH
☎ 020 7428 4800 fax 020 7428 4828
email: go@lonelyplanet.co.uk

France
1 rue du Dahomey, 75011 Paris
☎ 01 55 25 33 00 fax 01 55 25 33 01
email: bip@lonelyplanet.fr
www.lonelyplanet.fr

World Wide Web: www.lonelyplanet.com *or* AOL keyword: lp